MW00478838

DISPARITIES

DISPARITIES

Slavoj Žižek

Bloomsbury Academic
An imprint of Bloomsbury Publishing Plc

B L O O M S B U R Y

LONDON • OXFORD • NEW YORK • NEW DELHI • SYDNEY

Bloomsbury Academic

An imprint of Bloomsbury Publishing Plc

50 Bedford Square	1385 Broadway
London	New York
WC1B 3DP	NY 10018
UK	USA

www.bloomsbury.com

BLOOMSBURY and the Diana logo are trademarks of Bloomsbury Publishing Plc

First published 2016

British Library Cataloguing-in-Publication Data
A catalogue record for this book is available from the British Library.

ISBN:	HB:	9781474272704
	ePDF:	9781474272711
	ePub:	9781474272728

Library of Congress Cataloging-in-Publication Data
A catalog record for this book is available from the Library of Congress.

Typeset by Fakenham Prepress Solutions, Fakenham, Norfolk NR21 8NN
Printed and bound in India

For Kostja and Tim, with all our disparities!

CONTENTS

INTRODUCTION: IS HEGEL DEAD – OR ARE WE DEAD (IN THE EYES OF HEGEL)?

When the Kraken wakes

I believe there has been no dangerous vacillation or crisis of German culture this century that has not been rendered more dangerous by the enormous and still continuing influence of this philosophy, the Hegelian.

The premise of the present book is a simple one: yes, Nietzsche is right (in this statement from 'The Use and Abuse of History'[1]), although not in the scathing sense intended by him. Hegel's thought effectively is a kind of philosophical giant squid, a dangerous and monstrous creature whose long conceptual tentacles enable it to exert influence, often from invisible depths. The popular metaphor for the subterranean subversive work is that of a mole.[2] The story begins with Shakespeare's Hamlet, who congratulates the ghost of his father for continuing to speak from under the stage: 'Well said, old mole!' (*Hamlet*, act 1, scene 5). Hegel refers to this scene in the Conclusion of his *Lectures on the History of Philosophy* in order to characterize the subterranean work – not of a ghost, but of the World Spirit in laying ground for a new epoch:

> Spirit often seems to have forgotten and lost itself, but inwardly opposed to itself, it is inwardly working ever forward (as when Hamlet says of the ghost of his father, 'Well said, old mole! canst work i' the ground so fast?') until grown strong in itself it bursts asunder the crust of earth which divided it from the sun, its Notion, so that the earth crumbles away.[3]

In *The Eighteenth Brumaire of Louis Bonaparte*, Marx takes over the mole metaphor: when a European revolution finally explodes, 'Europe will leap from its seat and exult: Well burrowed, old mole!'[4] This story of repetitions reaches its self-sublation (*Selbst-Aufhebung*) in Michael Hardt and Toni Negri's *Empire* where they propagate the formula: 'Marx's Mole is Dead!'[5] The reasons are obvious: the Mole comes all too close to implying some substantial Reason which, through its cunning, secretly pulls the strings of history. Sometimes, Hegel makes this point in an even more direct and vulgar way, as in his letter to Niethammer from 1816:

> I adhere to the view that the world spirit has given the age marching orders. These orders are being obeyed. The world spirit, this essential, proceeds irresistibly like a closely drawn armored phalanx advancing with imperceptible movement, much as the sun through thick and thin. Innumerable light troops flank it on all sides, throwing themselves into the balance for or against its progress, though most of them are entirely ignorant of what is at stake and merely take head blows as from an invisible hand.[6]

It is difficult to imagine a notion more obviously out of sync with contemporary sensibility. What seems to offer itself as a no less obvious replacement for 'mole' is, of course, 'rhizome', a complex network of interconnections without a central controlling agency. However, in my Stalinist mind, the fact that Deleuze borrowed this term from Jung[7] is not a mere insignificant accident – it points towards a deeper link (no wonder that, in his early text on Sacher-Masoch [1961], Deleuze extensively relies on Jung in his critique of Freud).[8] For this reason, I am tempted to propose, as a replacement for the unfortunate mole, the much more disturbingly disgusting image of *Kraken*, a gigantic squid.[9]

The element in which a Kraken thrives is water, and it is by no means an accident that Thales of Miletus, usually counted as 'the first philosopher', a representative of so-called Ionian materialists, posited as the substance of everything, as the first principle out of which everything emerges, water.[10] In his commentary, Aristotle noted the surprising nature of this choice: from a traditional mythic standpoint, the foundation of everything, the primordial substance, is (Mother) Earth, while water comes second as the disrupting/moving/corroding element. In the further development of pre-Socratic thought, this first substitution (water instead of earth) opens up the way for further replacements (fire instead of water, etc.). So if we posit as the primordial element water instead of earth, the change is not symmetrical within the space of the same opposition earth/water:

the structure of the whole space changes, a foreign element wins over the stability of home, a fluid process wins over the stability of a firm substance. What this means, in more abstract terms, is that, although both earth and water may appear to be elements of a preconceptual mythic space, water as the primordial principle *already functions as a concept*, in contrast to earth as a mytho-poetic entity. Or, as Hegel put it, water as the primordial principle is no longer the material water but an ideal entity. The shift from mole to Kraken is primarily the change in the element in which entity dwells – from earth to water.

The mythic Kraken, this ultimate figure of an abject, a gigantic creature sleeping for an eternity at the bottom of the ocean and set to awaken from his slumber in an apocalyptic age, was celebrated by Alfred Tennyson in his poem from 1830: 'There hath he lain for ages, and will lie / Battening upon huge sea worms in his sleep, / Until the latter fire shall heat the deep; / Then once by man and angels to be seen, / In roaring he shall rise and on the surface die.' Are our times – more precisely, the times of capitalist modernity – not such an epoch of the awakened Kraken? Is Kraken not a perfect image of the global Capital, all-powerful and stupid, cunning and blind, whose tentacles regulate our lives?

A report from the trenches of dialectical materialism

Insofar as Hegel's dialectics is, at its most basic, a theory of modernity, a theory of the break between tradition and modernity, the properly dialectic moment of a historical process is precisely the moment when the Kraken awakens and disrupts the smooth surface, the moment when Kraken's disruptive power of negativity is felt in all its destructive impact. What are explosions of unexpected economic crises, of 'irrational' social violence, if not the echoes of the whips of Kraken's tentacles? Even today, there is no thinker more capable of discerning these echoes than Hegel.

Nietzsche's dismissal of Hegel is just the extreme case of a stance which was most clearly expressed by the title of Benedetto Croce's book on Hegel: *What Is Alive and What Is Dead in Hegel?* If Hegel is not proclaimed dead outright, he is treated as a kind of living dead who continues to haunt us only because he forgot that he is already dead. Perhaps, however, the time has come to do what Adorno suggested half a century ago, namely, to turn this question around and to ask: what if, from an authentic Hegelian standpoint, it is we who are dead, not Hegel? In one of the Marx brothers' movies, Groucho tests the pulse of a patient, holding his fingers on the patient's wrist and comparing the rhythm with the flow of the seconds as indicated on his hand watch, and exclaims: 'Either my watch stopped working or you are dead!' The present book endeavours to provide a kind of Hegelian diagnostic of our present moment; in order to achieve this, it takes as its starting point the concept of *disparity*, and it deploys figures of disparity in the sense of *figurae veneris* in erotics: different positions or figurations of disparity.

Disparity is a concept that designates what, in a more descriptive language, we may call the disruptive effects of the awakened Kraken. The present book follows these disruptive effects of Kraken's tentacles in three main domains: ontological, aesthetic, and theologico-political. At the ontological level, disparity is at its most radical ontological difference, so the first part of the book deals with the persistence of ontological difference in our capitalist-technological world which is getting more and more one-dimensional. At the aesthetic level, the disparate element is the repelling X targeted by a series of partially overlapping notions: ugly, disgusting, abject, and so on. The theological name for disparity is, of course, god as the radical otherness with regard to the order of being, while in politics it is the millenarian prospect of a radical new beginning based upon the erasure of the past, and it is easy to imagine the explosive potential of combining the two.

The triadic structure of the book thus repeats the classic triad of Truth, Beauty and the Good, focusing on the disruptive power of the Kraken in each of the three. Part I tackles the topic of ontological difference in the age of science: first, after outlining different aspects of the notion of disparity, it deploys the antinomies of universalized scientific reason (in a dialogue with Wark, Morton, Johnston and Chiesa); then, it deals with two philosophical reactions to the predominance of scientific reason, the attempt of the 'object-oriented ontology' to re-enchant the world (Bryant), and the transcendental attempt to demonstrate how scientific investigation has to rely on a discursive normativity of mutual recognition which cannot itself be grounded scientifically (Pippin, Brandom). Part II analyses the role of ugliness and disgust in modern subjectivity: first, it reconstructs the Hegelian path towards modern nonfigurative art (Pippin); then, it deploys the versions of abject, from creepiness to disgust (Kristeva, Kotsko); finally, it outlines the contours of 'subjective destitution' in art (Shakespeare, Beckett). Part III confronts the ongoing theologico-political mess: first, by articulating the shifts in the triangle of authority, costume and friendship from Schiller's plays to the contemporary world (Zupančič); then, by entering into the intricacies of divine in-existence (Dupuy); and, finally, by deploying the passage from traumatized subject to subject itself as trauma (Schuster, Malabou). A short conclusion draws some political implications of the notion of disparity.

In each of these three domains, a brutal battle is going on, a struggle against the different forms of obfuscating disparity. This struggle is philosophy – or, as Louis Althusser put it decades ago, condensing the teachings of the classics into a single concise formula: philosophy is, in the last instance, class struggle in the field of theory: 'Marxist-Leninist philosophy, or dialectical materialism, represents the proletarian class struggle *in theory*.'[11] This is what is really new in Lenin's *Materialism and Empirio-Criticism*, in spite of this work's serious theoretical mistakes: a new practice of philosophy based on the axiomatic certainty that philosophy is a form of (class) struggle. And Althusser had no illusions about the brutality of this struggle: 'In the battle that is philosophy all the techniques of war, including looting and camouflage, are permissible.'[12] G. K. Chesterton wrote: 'There is no such thing as fighting on the winning side; one fights to find out which is the winning side.'[13] This paradox holds perfectly for the philosophical warfare in which one does not simply fight to defend a predefined position: one rather fights in order to discern which this position is.

This is why, when a philosopher deals with another philosopher, his or her stance is not that of dialogue but of division, of drawing the line that separates truth from falsity, from Plato whose focus is the line that divides truth from mere opinion up to Lenin obsessed with the line that separates materialism from idealism. As Alain Badiou said, a true Idea is one that divides. The present book is an exercise in this art of delimitation: its aim is to specify the contours of the dialectical-materialist notion of disparity by way of drawing a line that separates it from other deceptively similar forms of thought, from Julia Kristeva's abjection to Robert Pippin's and Robert Brandom's version of self-consciousness, from object-oriented ontology to the topic of posthumanity, from the god of negative theology to millenarian politics. The method of such a procedure is not learned in advance, it emerges retroactively – one should remember here Pascal Quignard's definition of method: 'Method is the road after we traversed it.'[14] Method is not learned in advance: it emerges retroactively.

PART ONE

THE DISPARITY OF TRUTH: SUBJECT, OBJECT AND THE REST

1 FROM HUMAN TO POSTHUMAN ... AND BACK TO INHUMAN: THE PERSISTENCE OF ONTOLOGICAL DIFFERENCE

The word 'disparity' occurs three times in a key passage from the Foreword to Hegel's *Phenomenology of Spirit* where he provides the most concise explanation of what it means to conceive Substance also as Subject:

> The disparity which exists in consciousness between the 'I' and the substance which is its object is the distinction between them, the *negative* in general. This can be regarded as the *defect* of both, though it is their soul, or that which moves them. That is why some of the ancients conceived the *void* as the principle of motion, for they rightly saw the moving principle as the *negative*, though they did not as yet grasp that the negative is the self. Now, although this negative appears at first as a disparity between the 'I' and its object, it is just as much the disparity of the substance with itself. Thus what seems to happen outside of it, to be an activity directed against it, is really its own doing, and Substance shows itself to be essentially Subject.[1]

Crucial is the final reversal: the disparity between subject and substance is simultaneously the disparity of the substance with itself – or, to put it in Lacan's terms, disparity means that the lack of the subject is simultaneously the lack in the Other: subjectivity emerges when substance cannot achieve full identity with itself, when substance is in itself 'barred', traversed by an immanent impossibility or antagonism. In short, the subject's epistemological ignorance, its failure to fully grasp the opposed substantial content, simultaneously indicates a limitation/failure/lack of the substantial content itself. Therein also resides the key dimension of the theological revolution of Christianity: the alienation of man from god has to be projected/transferred back into god itself, as the alienation of god from itself (therein resides the speculative content of the notion of divine *kenosis*) – this is the Christian version of Hegel's insight into how the disparity of subject and substance implies the disparity of substance with regard to itself. This is why the unity of man and god is enacted in Christianity in a way which fundamentally differs from the way of pagan religions where man has to strive to overcome his fall from god through the effort to purify his being from material filth and elevate himself to rejoin god. In Christianity, on the contrary, god falls from itself, he becomes a finite mortal human abandoned by god (in the figure of Christ and his lament on the cross 'Father, why have you forsaken me?'), and man can only achieve unity with god by identifying with *this* god, god abandoned by itself.

Aspects of disparity

Disparity should be added to the series of notions which offer themselves as the ultimate Master Signifiers of dialectical materialism (negativity, parallax, etc.).[2] The reason that it is a newcomer in this series is that we search for it in vain in Hegel: 'disparity' is one of the proposed English translations of *Ungleichkeit* (inequality), the term used by Hegel in the quoted passage (and at many other places) – and here, exceptionally, the translation works better than the original. (Why? Here is the list of connotations of 'parity' negated by 'dis-': correspondence, consistency, equivalence, unity, similarity, likeness, uniformity, parallelism, congruity.) At its most elementary, disparity points towards a Whole whose parts do not fit together, so that the Whole appears as an artificial composite, its organic unity forever ruined. Imagine a living body which appears natural, but then we notice that one of the limbs is metallic, that one of its eyes is made of glass, that the teeth in its mouth are part of artificial prosthesis, and so forth. The totality which unites the terms is a false totality, a wrong

Wholeness: a combination of elements which, when they are stitched together, pretend to form on organic Whole, while a close analysis easily demonstrates that there is a kind of classificatory confusion or short-circuit in putting them together. The terms do not really belong together: what is obfuscated is that there is fundamentally only one element and its gap (the void of what this element is lacking, its symmetrical counterpart), and the second element is a heterogeneous intruder filling the gap. Say, there is no higher encompassing unity between theology and modern science, so that it would be possible to say (as neo-Thomists like to do) that science is dealing with finite material reality, while theology provides the wider frame of the infinite Absolute which grounds finite reality. When Pope John Paul II received Stephen Hawking, he allegedly told him: 'We are well in agreement, mister astrophysicist: what happens after the Big Bang is your domain; what happens before is ours.' Even if this exchange did not really take place, it seems to make the right point – *se non e vero, e ben'trovato* – but does it really? Is it not rather a case of wrong Wholeness? When the pope claimed that science deals with what occurred after the Big Bang and theology with what went on before, he presupposes a common space between the two within which theology deals with one side and science with the other; this, however, is exactly what doesn't work, such synthesis is a fake, the void of what went on before the Big Bang cannot be filled in by theology, it is a void *immanent to scientific space* which only science can deal with and propose solutions (which quantum cosmology is effectively doing: there are already alternate theories of the universe claiming that the Big Bang is not the absolute beginning since our universe follows the endless rhythm of collapses and births ['Big Bangs']). In other words, in the two cases, we are simply not talking about the same Big Bang.

Lacan's thesis is that sexual difference is in exactly the same way a false unity of the opposite: man and woman are not the two halves of an organic Whole, or two opposed principles or forces whose eternal struggle makes our universe alive. Man and woman are not located on the same ontological level, they are not two species of the same genus. The primordial couple is rather that of woman and void (or death: *das Mädchen und der Tod*), and the man comes second, it fills in this void, thus introducing imbalance into the universe. So when Mao wrote 'Women hold up half of heaven', this should in no way be read to imply that the other half of heaven is held up by men. It rather means that the other half is empty – and, as such, a source of disorder. So we should read this claim of Mao's together with his famous statement: 'There is great chaos under heaven – the situation is excellent.'

Recall the old Jewish story of Jacob who fell in love with Rachel and wanted to marry her; his father, however, wanted him to marry Leah,

Rachel's elder sister. In order that Jacob might not be tricked by the father or by Leah, Rachel taught him to recognize her at night in bed. Before the sexual event, Rachel felt guilty towards her sister, and told her what the signs were. Leah asked Rachel what would happen if he recognized her voice. So the decision was that Rachel would lie under the bed, and while Jacob is making love to Leah, Rachel would make the sounds, so he wouldn't recognize that he's having sex with the wrong sister ... Here we have an unexpected version of Lacan's *il n'y a pas de rapport sexuel*: it is not enough to get a man and a woman doing it in a bed, a voice which emanates from someone hidden beneath the bed is needed for it to somehow function. Something formally similar happens in a memorable passage towards the end of Chapter 1 of Marcel Proust's *The Guermantes Way*, a novel which is part of his *In Search of Lost Time*:[3] using the phone for the first time, Marcel (the narrator of the novel) talks to his grandmother; the voice he hears is subtracted from the 'natural' totality of the body to which it belongs, out of which it emerges as an autonomous partial object, an organ which can magically survive without the body whose organ it is – it is as if it stands 'alone beside me, seen, without the mask of her face'. So what happens to the body when it is separated from its voice, when the voice is subtracted from the wholeness of the person? For a brief moment, we see 'a world robbed of fantasy, of the affective frame and sense, a world out of joint'.[4] Grandmother appears to Marcel outside the fantasmatic horizon of meaning, outside the rich texture of her warm, charming person – all of a sudden, he sees her 'red-faced, heavy and common, sick, lost in thought, following the lines of a book with eyes that seemed hardly sane, a dejected old woman whom I did not know'. Again, it is only by breaking up the organic unity of grandmother, by subtracting her voice from her body, that we arrive at what she 'truly is'.[5]

In Lacanian terms, Proust enacts in this scene what Lacan calls *separation* between an object (grandmother, in this case) and 'what is in it more than itself', the *objet petit a* as the decentred core of its being. So what if we understand separation (in Lacan's precise meaning) along the lines of the separation of milk: milk is thrown into a separator, a centrifugal device that separates milk into cream and skimmed milk? In a homologous way, the analyst-separator enables the analyst to 'separate' cream (object *a*) from ordinary reality which, after it is 'skimmed', becomes visible in all its grey misery.

The properly philosophical lesson of these ridiculous peripeties is crucial: the organic ('immediate', as Hegel would have put it) unity of a phenomenon is by definition a trap, an illusion which masks underlying antagonisms, and the only way to arrive at the truth is to brutally cut into parts this unity in order to render visible its artificial and composed character. This holds from the personal level (in order for Marcel to perceive the truth about his grandmother, he has to take apart and ruin his experience of the unity of her personality, to divide it into an autonomous obscene voice and the disgusting bodily remainder) up to the social level (the organic unity of a social body has to be ruined by the class division). At the conceptual level, this means that truth is on the side of abstraction, reduction, subtraction, and not on the side of organic totality. The re-established unity, the 'synthesis' of unilateral abstractions, remains at the level of abstractions and cannot but appear as a monstrous montage, a nonorganic Whole which looks like the face of Frankenstein's monster. One of the standard reproaches to Hegel is that the auto-movement of notions in a dialectical process is an artificial movement of abstractions and not an actual organic movement – to this, one should reply with a yes, with the addition that therein, precisely, resides Hegel's point.[6]

The ontological axiom of disparity is that such a disparate structure is universal, constitutive of (what we experience as) reality: reality which we experience is never 'all'; in order to generate the illusion of 'all' it has to be supplemented by a disparate artificial element which fills in its gap or hole, as in a movie set composed of 'real' elements (trees, tables, walls), but with a painted background which creates the illusion that we are in a 'real' external world. The first philosopher who clearly saw this was Kant: the reality we experience is non-all, inconsistent, we cannot totalize it without getting caught in antinomies, so that the only way to experience reality as a consistent Whole is to supplement it with transcendental Ideas.

This lesson holds even at the most intimate level of personal experience. When a subject is confronted with an extremely intense event (brutal torture, absolute disgust, over-intense *jouissance*), it cannot accept it as part of its ordinary reality, so it experiences a loss of reality. This is why *jouissance* concerns the very fundamentals of what one is tempted to call the psychoanalytic ontology. Psychoanalysis chances upon the fundamental ontological question, 'Why is there something instead of nothing?' apropos of the experience of the 'loss of reality' (*Realitätsverlust*), when some traumatic, excessively intense encounter affects the subject's ability to assume the full ontological weight of his world-experience. From the very outset of his teaching, Lacan emphasized the inherent and irreducible *traumatic* status of existence: 'By definition, there is something so improbable about all existence that one is in effect perpetually questioning oneself about its reality.'[7] Later, after the crucial turn of his teaching, he links existence ('as such', one is tempted to add) to *jouissance* as that which is properly traumatic, that is, whose existence can never be fully assumed, and which is thus forever perceived as spectral, pre-ontological. The link to Kant is again crucial here: in order to experience something as part of our reality, it has to fit the frame that determines the coordinates of our reality; Kant's name for this frame is the transcendental scheme, and the psycho-analytic name is fantasy. This is why, from the strict Freudian standpoint, fantasy is on the side of reality, it sustains the subject's 'sense of reality': when the fantasmatic frame disintegrates, the subject undergoes a 'loss of reality' and starts to perceive reality as an 'irreal' nightmarish universe with no firm ontological foundation; this nightmarish universe – the Lacanian Real – is not 'pure fantasy' but, on the contrary, *that which remains of reality after reality is deprived of its support in fantasy*. Or, as Chesterton put it with breathtaking precision:

> It is a poor idea of fantasy which takes it to be a world apart from reality, a world clearly showing its unreality. Fantasy is precisely what reality can be confused with. It is through fantasy that our conviction of the worth of reality is established; to forgo our fantasies would be to forgo our touch with the world.[8]

In other words, what we experience as reality is always truncated, filtered; some dimension is excluded from it and can appear only as fiction, as 'not a part of our reality'. Let us say that I am forced to witness a scene of extreme torture – there is no way for me to perceive it as a part of my reality, I have to tell myself something like 'this cannot be real, I must be dreaming ...' So although, from the 'objective' standpoint, the scene of torture is part of the same real world in which I live my daily life, I have to 'fictionalize' it in order to endure it. From my military service, I remember how, just a couple of days in, I accepted this weird and stupid world as my reality, but the price I've paid for it was that my previous civil life appeared to me as a kind of dreamscape, not part of my reality. And after I finished my service and returned home, what surprised me was how fast the reverse operation was done: after a few days, the army life appeared to me as a vague spectral universe which somehow didn't really happen (although I was haunted by scenes from it for decades). And the same disparity is at work in every procedure of classification: when we subdivide a genus into its species, the subdivision is never full and all-inclusive, and there is always one subspecies or element which functions like a filler, that is, which presents itself as just one among the species but is effectively a stand-in for what eludes the very principle of this classification (like Borges's famous classification of dogs which includes as its species 'all dogs who have no place in this classification'). Such an affirmation of exception to a universal notion cannot but appear anti-Hegelian, Kierkegaardian even: is Hegel's point not precisely that every existence can be subsumed under universal essence through a notional mediation? But what if we conceive it as the elementary figure of what Hegel called 'concrete universality'? Concrete universality is not the organic articulation of a universality into its species or parts or organs; we approach concrete universality only when the universality in question encounters among its species or moments itself in its oppositional determination, in an exceptional moment which denies the universal dimension and is as such its direct embodiment. Within a hierarchical society, such an element of exception are those at the bottom, like the 'Untouchables' in India. In contrast to Gandhi, Dr Ambedkar

> underlined the futility of merely abolishing Untouchability: this evil being the product of a social hierarchy of a particular kind, it was the entire caste system that had to be eradicated: 'There will be out castes [Untouchables] as long as there are castes.' ... Gandhi responded that, on the contrary, here it was a question of the foundation of Hinduism, a civilization which, in its original form, in fact ignored hierarchy.[9]

Although Gandhi and Ambedkar respected each other and often collaborated in the struggle for the dignity of the Untouchables, their difference is here insurmountable: it is the difference between the 'organic' solution (solving the problem by way of returning to the purity of the original non-corrupted system) and the truly radical solution (identifying the problem as the 'symptom' of the entire system, the symptom which can only be resolved by way of abolishing the entire system. Ambedkar saw clearly how the structure of four castes does not unite four elements which belong to the same order: while the first three castes (priests, warrior kings, merchant producers) form a consistent All, an organic triad, the Untouchables are like Marx's 'Asiatic mode of production', the 'part of no part', the inconsistent element which holds within the system the place of what the system as such excludes – and as such, the Untouchables stand for universality. Effectively, there are no castes without outcasts; as long as there are castes, there will be an excessive excremental zero-value element which, while formally part of the system, has no proper place within it. Gandhi obfuscates this paradox, as if a harmonious structure integrating all its elements is possible. The paradox of the Untouchables is that they are doubly marked by the excremental logic: they not only deal with impure excrements, their own formal status within the social body is that of an excrement. This is why the properly dialectical paradox is that, if one is to break out of the caste system, it is not enough to reverse the status and elevate the Untouchables into the 'children of god'; the first step should rather be exactly the opposite one: to *universalize* the excremental status to the whole of humanity.

These paradoxes are crucial if we want to understand properly the key Hegelian notion of concrete universality. One way to explain concrete universality is to imagine a plurality of similar phenomena or objects, say, a plurality of human beings: how do we, through comparing them, arrive at the universal notion which encompasses them all? Which features do we abstract from the wealth of their empirical properties? It is not enough to say that we focus on features shared by all entities, and *only* by these entities; the question remains which features are more 'essential'. But how do we judge this? Why is, say, speech more 'essential' than wearing a dress? The answer is: the 'essential' feature is the one which 'mediates' all others, functioning as their immanent presupposition (wearing a dress presupposes collaboration among humans coordinated by speech). The two standard candidates for such 'concrete universality' are labour and speech (man as a tool-making animal, man as a speaking animal), followed by other candidates (religion or at least some sense for the sacred and ritual, etc.). We can play here the endless games of which comes first: did language emerge out of the need for cooperation, or does labour presuppose speech to become a specifically human labour? Much more important is the fact that mediation does not equal empirical genesis: the universal mediating role does not belong to the element which was the empirical starting point of the evolution of the phenomenon in question. For example, money, which, with capitalism, becomes the pivotal moment of the social totality in the guise of capital, begins as a secondary instrument to facilitate exchange of commodities; it is only with capitalism that (as Marx put it in pure Hegelese) the result retroactively posits its own presuppositions, i.e. that a secondary moment becomes the pivotal point which regulates entire social reproduction. Furthermore, one should also not underestimate the usefulness of idiosyncratic definitions which elevate a trivial marginal feature into a pivotal point (in the style of 'man is the animal which is bothered by what to do with its excrements', 'man is the animal which clips its nails', etc.). Such definitions, although in themselves obviously ridiculous, nonetheless make us aware of unexpected connections: they allow us to take note of a crucial but usually ignored characteristic of some 'essential' feature. Say, the fact that humans are bothered by their excrements, that they try to get rid of them, render them invisible, make them disappear, says a lot about the exclusions and prohibitions on which the symbolic universe is based; to quote Kristeva, behind every symbolic universe there is an abject lurking.

In the standard view which privileges speech or labour, sexuality, although no less universal (or even more universal: there are sexually active humans who never worked), is not considered something specific to humans. Of course the way human beings make love is specifically human, it involves perversions, rituals of seduction, economic interests and power plays, but all these phenomena are the result of how the natural substance of sexuality is transformed by culture – the agent of transformation is here not sexuality itself but social and cultural processes. However, psychoanalysis radically differs from this view: Freud focuses on sexuality because, for him, the most elementary break with animal life, the passage to a meta-physical dimension, happens here, in the emergence of a sexual passion detached from the biological needs of animal coupling. This is why Christianity is opposed to sexuality, accepting it as a necessary evil only if it serves its natural purpose of procreation – not because in sexuality our lower nature explodes, but precisely because sexuality competes with pure spirituality as the primordial meta-physical activity. The Freudian hypothesis is that the passage from animal instincts (of mating) to sexuality proper (to drives) is the primordial step from physical realm of biological (animal) life to meta-physics, to eternity and immortality, to a level which is heterogeneous with regard to the biological cycle of generation and corruption. (This is why the Catholic argument that sex without procreation, whose aim is not procreation, is animal, is wrong: the exact opposite is true, sex spiritualizes itself only when it abstracts from its natural end and becomes an end-in-itself.) Plato was already aware of this when he wrote about Eros, erotic attachment to a beautiful body, as the first step on the way towards the supreme Good; perspicuous Christians (like Simone Weil) discerned in sexual longing a striving for the Absolute. Human sexuality is characterized by the impossibility of reaching its goal, and this constitutive impossibility eternalizes it, as is the case in the myths about great lovers whose love persists beyond life and death. Christianity conceives this properly meta-physical excess of sexuality as a disturbance to be erased, so it is paradoxically Christianity itself (especially Catholicism) which wants to get rid of its competitor by way of reducing sexuality to its animal function of procreation: Christianity wants to 'normalize' sexuality, spiritualizing it from without, imposing on it the external envelope of spirituality (sex must be done with love and respect for the partner, in a cultivated way, etc.), and thereby obliterating its immanent spiritual dimension: the dimension of unconditional passion. In this precise sense, for Freud, sexuality is the 'concrete Universal' of humankind.

Two more specifications have to be added here. The Hegelian concrete universality is not just a blind lifeless abstraction, a feature shared by all its moments, what Hegel calls a universal-in-itself; it is a universal-for-itself, a universal which appears as such, in contradistinction to its particular elements. Let's take the case of a modern individual: it is universal-for-itself since it experiences itself as universal, not tied down to the particular context of its contingent situation. A teacher or a bus driver is not just a particular case of a human being, he experiences himself as a (universal) human being who accidentally ended up as a teacher or a bus driver.

Last but not least, the 'concrete universality' of a certain phenomenon or field is not so much some universal feature shared by all its elements but rather a gap, antagonism or obstacle which holds this field together. In classic Marxism, social antagonism (class struggle) is not just a negative factor, that which permanently destabilizes social edifice, it is simultaneously that which overdetermines and in this sense 'holds together' this edifice (all social institutions are ultimately different ways to deal with class struggle). Let's take the state as a social institution. It is not only that the state is the general institution for regulating social life and its reproduction, and that, in a class society, this institution is biased, privileging one class and oppressing the other. One should drop the very idea that a 'true' state would be a neutral instrument serving all its citizens, and that, in a class society, the ruling class appropriates and (mis)uses this instrument. The neutrality of the state is as such an ideological mystification since the state emerges only in class societies, with the function to enable social reproduction in the conditions of class antagonism. In other words, the state is not an apparatus which gets twisted or biased in a class society, it is twisted and biased in its very nature or concept.

The same goes for justice (right). One should read the Spinozan equation of power and right against the background of Pascal's famous *pensée*:

Equality of possessions is no doubt right, but, as men could not make might obey right, they have made right obey might. As they could not fortify justice they have justified force, so that right and might live together and peace reigns, the sovereign good.[10]

Crucial in this passage is the underlying 'formalist' logic: the form of justice matters more than its content – the form of justice should be maintained even if it is, as to its content, the form of its opposite, of injustice. And, one might add, this discrepancy between form and content is not just the result of particular unfortunate circumstances, but constitutive of the very notion of justice: justice is 'in itself', in its very notion, the form of injustice, namely, a 'justified force'. Usually, when we are dealing with a fake trial in which the outcome is fixed in advance by political and power interests, we speak of a 'travesty of justice' – it pretends to be justice, while it is merely a display of raw power or corruption posing as justice. But what if justice is 'as such', in its very notion, a travesty? Is this not what Pascal implies when he concludes, in a resigned way, that if power cannot come to justice, then justice should come to power?

Against the univocity of being

The conclusion that imposes itself from these paradoxes of universality is that we have to part ways here with the notion of the 'univocity of being', whose main proponent in our times was Deleuze. The assertion of the univocity of being can play a positive role in enabling us to dismiss all notions of ontological hierarchy, from the theological vision of the universe as a hierarchical Whole with God as the only full Being at the top, up to the vulgar Marxist hierarchy of social spheres (economic infrastructure as the only full reality, ideology as somehow 'less real', part of illusory superstructure). Along the same lines, one could interpret Dziga Vertov's (Eisenstein's great opponent) *Man with a Movie Camera* as an exemplary case of cinematic communism: the affirmation of life in its multiplicity, enacted through a kind of cinematic parataxis, a setting side-by-side of a series of daily activities – washing one's hair, wrapping packages, playing piano, connecting phone wires, dancing ballet – which reverberate in each other at a purely formal level, through the echoing of visual and other patterns. What makes this cinematic practice communist is the underlying assertion of the radical 'univocity of being': all the displayed phenomena are equalized, all the usual hierarchies and oppositions among them, inclusive of the official communist opposition between the Old and the New, are magically suspended (recall that the alternate title of Eisenstein's *The General Line*, shot at the same time, was precisely *Old and New*). Communism is here presented not so much as the hard struggle for a goal (the new society to come), with all the pragmatic paradoxes this involves (the struggle for the new society of universal freedom should obey the harshest discipline, etc.), but as a fact, a present collective experience.

Univocity of being (directed against the Aristotelian ontology) found its greatest proponent in Spinoza, who draws the ultimate consequence from it: he radically suspended the 'deontological' dimension, that is, what we usually understand by the term 'ethical' (norms which prescribe to us how we should act when we have a choice) – and this in a book called *Ethics*, which is an achievement in itself. In his famous reading of the Fall, Spinoza claims that God had to utter the prohibition 'You should not eat the apple from the Tree of Knowledge!' because our capacity to know the true causal connection was limited. For those who know, one should say: 'Eating from the Tree of Knowledge is dangerous for your health.' Adam thus:

> took the revelation to be not an eternal and necessary truth, but a law – that is, an ordinance followed by gain or loss, not depending necessarily on the nature of the act performed, but solely on the will and absolute power of some potentate, so that the revelation in question was solely in relation to Adam, and *solely through his lack of knowledge* a law, and God was, as it were, a lawgiver and potentate. From the same cause, namely, from lack of knowledge, the Decalogue in relation to the Hebrews was a law.[11]

Two levels are opposed here, that of imagination/opinion and that of true knowledge. The level of imagination is anthropomorphic: we are dealing with a narrative about agents giving orders that we are free to obey or disobey; God himself is here the highest prince who dispenses mercy. The true knowledge, on the contrary, delivers the nonanthropomorphic causal nexus of impersonal truths. One is tempted to say that Spinoza here out-Jews Jews themselves: he extends iconoclasm to man himself – not only 'do not paint god in man's image', but 'do not paint man himself in man's image'. In other words, Spinoza here moves a step beyond the standard warning not to project onto nature human notions like goal, mercy, good and evil, and so on – we should not use them to conceive man himself. The key words in the quoted passage are '*solely through his lack of knowledge*' – the whole 'anthropomorphic' domain of law, injunction, moral command, and so forth is based on our ignorance. What Spinoza thus rejects is the necessity of what Lacan calls the Master Signifier, the reflexive signifier that fills in the very lack of the signifier. Spinoza's own supreme example of 'God' is here crucial: when conceived as a mighty person, god merely embodies our ignorance of true causality. One should recall here notions like 'flogiston' or Marx's 'Asiatic mode of production' or, as a matter of fact, today's popular 'postindustrial society' – notions which, while they appear to designate a positive content, merely signal our ignorance. Spinoza's unheard-of endeavour is to think ethics itself outside the 'anthropomorphic' moral categories of intentions, commandments, and the like – what he proposes is *stricto sensu* an *ontological ethics*, an ethics deprived of the deontological dimension, an ethics of 'is' without 'ought'. In clear contrast to Spinoza, Lacan (in *Encore*) emphasizes the 'deontic' dimension of being itself: to say that something 'is' always implies that it 'has to be'; here is his comment on Aristotle's *to ti ēn einai*, 'what would indeed have happened if it had quite simply come to be':

What was to be. And it seems that here there is conserved the pedicle that allows us to situate from where this discourse of being is produced. It is quite simply that of *being at someone's heel, being under someone's orders*. What was going to be if you had heard what I am ordering you. Every dimension of being is produced from something which is along the line, in the current of the discourse of the master who, uttering the signifier, expects from it what is one of the effects of the bond, assuredly, not to be neglected, which results from the fact that the signifier commands. The signifier is first of all and from its dimension imperative.[12]

At its most radical, disparity does not refer just to the gap between parts or spheres of reality, it has to be brought to self-relating and include the disparity of a thing with regard to itself – or, to put it another way, the disparity between part of a thing and nothing. A is not just not-B, it is also and primarily not fully A, and B emerges to fill in this gap. It is at this level that we should locate ontological difference: reality is partial, incomplete, inconsistent, and the Supreme Being is the illusion imagined in order to fill in (obfuscate) this lack, this void that makes reality non-all. In short, *ontological difference* – the difference between non-all reality and the void that thwarts it – is obfuscated by the difference between the 'highest' or 'true' being (god, actual life) and its secondary shadows.

Posthuman, transhuman, inhuman

From the Heideggerian standpoint, today's global scientific-technological civilization poses a threat to ontological difference – what Heidegger calls a 'danger' immanent in our way of life. The popular expression of this threat is a more or less commonly accepted premonition that today, we (humanity) are approaching a radical mutation, the entry into a 'posthuman' mode of being. This mutation is sometimes described as a threat to the very essence of being human, while sometimes it is celebrated as the passage into a new Singularity (collective mind, a new cyborg entity, or another version of the Nietzschean Overman). Furthermore, this mutation is both theoretical and practical, felt by all of us – who can measure the implications and consequences of biogenetics, of new prosthetic implants which will merge with our biological body, of new ways to control and regulate not only our bodily functions but also our mental processes?

Two opposed tendencies coexist within this orientation towards 'overcoming human', posthumanism and transhumanism, which vaguely refer to the duality of culture and science. 'Posthumanists' (Donna Haraway and others) are cultural theorists who note how today's social and techno-logical progress more and more undermines our human exclusivity: the lesson of ecology is that we are ultimately one of the animal species on our Earth, that animality is part of our innermost nature, that there is no clear ontological gap that separates us from the animal kingdom, while contemporary science and technology make more and more visible the extent to which our innermost identity has to rely on technological devices and crutches – we are what we are through technological mediation. So while, for posthumanists, 'humans' are a weird species of animal cyborgs, 'transhumanists' (Ray Kurzweil and others) refer to recent scientific and technologial innovations (AI, digitalization) which point towards the emergence of a Singularity, a new type of collective intelligence.

This transhumanist orientation stands for the fourth stage in the devel-opment of antihumanism: neither theocentric antihumanism (on account of which US religious fundamentalists use the term 'humanism' as synon-ymous with secular culture) nor the French 'theoretical antihumanism' which accompanied the structuralist revolution in the 1960s (Althusser, Foucault, Lacan), but also not the 'deep-ecological' antihumanist reduction of humanity to just one of the animal species on Earth, the species which derailed the balance of life on Earth through its *hubris* and is now facing the justified revenge of the Mother Earth. However, even this fourth stage is not without history. In the first decade of the Soviet Union, the so-called bio-cosmism enjoyed extraordinary popularity: a strange combination of vulgar materialism and Gnostic spirituality which formed occult shadow-ideology, the obscene secret teaching, of the Soviet Marxism.

It is as if today, 'bio-cosmism' is re-emerging in a new wave of 'posthuman' thought. The spectacular development of biogenetics with its scientific practices (cloning, direct DNA interventions, etc.) is gradually dissolving frontiers between humans and animals on the one side as well as between humans and machines on the other, giving rise to the idea that we are on the threshold of a new form of Intelligence, a 'more-than-human' Singularity in which mind will no longer be submitted to bodily constraints, inclusive of sexual reproduction. Out of this prospect a weird shame emerged: the shame about our biological limitations, our mortality, the ridiculous way we reproduce ourselves – what Gunther Anders called the 'Promethean shame',[13] ultimately simply the shame that 'we were born and not manufactured'. Nietzsche's idea that we are the 'last men' laying the ground for our own extinction and the arrival of a new Overman is thereby given a scientific-technological twist. However, we should not reduce this 'posthuman' stance with the paradigmatically modern belief in the possibility of the total technological domination over nature – what we are witnessing today is an exemplary dialectical reversal: the slogan of today's 'posthuman' sciences is no longer domination but surprise (contingent, nonplanned) emergence. Jean-Pierre Dupuy detected a weird reversal of the traditional Cartesian anthropocentric arrogance which grounded human technology, the reversal clearly discernible in today's robotics, genetics, nanotechnology, artificial life and AI researches:

> how are we to explain that science became such a 'risky' activity that, according to some top scientists, it poses today the principal threat to the survival of humanity? Some philosophers reply to this question by saying that Descartes's dream – 'to become master and possessor of nature' – has turned wrong, and that we should urgently return to the 'mastery of mastery'. They have understood nothing. They don't see that the technology profiling itself at our horizon through 'convergence' of all disciplines aims precisely at nonmastery. The engineer of tomorrow will not be a sorcerer's apprentice because of his negligence or ignorance, but by choice. He will 'give' himself complex structures or organizations and he will try to learn what they are capable of by way of exploring their functional properties – an ascending, bottom-up approach. He will be an explorer and experimenter at least as much as an executor. The measure of his success will be more the extent to which his own creations will surprise him than the conformity of his realization to the list of preestablished tasks.[14]

The motor of this self-sublation (*Selbst-Aufhebung*) of man is the ongoing scientific progress in evolutionary biology, neurology and cognitivist brain sciences which holds the promise of the total scientific self-objectivization of humanity: evolutionary theory can explain how humanity gradually emerged out of animal life, and, in this sense, it can also account for itself (for the rise of cognitive mechanisms which allowed humanity to develop the scientific approach to reality). The question nonetheless persists: does this operation of closing the loop (accounting for oneself) really succeed? Here one should be absolutely clear: these accounts are, in spite of their imperfections, in a certain sense simply and rather obviously *true*, so one should abandon all obscurantist or spiritualist reference to some mysterious dimension that eludes science. Should we then simply endorse this prospect? In philosophy, the predominant form of resistance to the full scientific self-objectivization of humanity which nonetheless admits science's achievements is the neo-Kantian transcendental state philosophy (whose exemplary case today is Habermas): our self-perception as free and responsible agents is not just a necessary illusion, but the transcendental a priori of every scientific knowledge. For Habermas:

> the attempt to study first-person subjective experience from the third-person, objectifying viewpoint, involves the theorist in a performative contradiction, since objectification presupposes participation in an intersubjectively instituted system of linguistic practices whose normative valence conditions the scientist's cognitive activity.[15]

Habermas characterizes this intersubjective domain of rational validity as the dimension of 'objective mind' which cannot be understood in terms of the phenomenological profiles of the community of conscious selves comprised in it: it is the intrinsically intersubjective status of the normative realm that precludes any attempt to account for its operation or genesis in terms of entities or processes simpler than the system itself. (Lacan's term for this 'objective mind' irreducible to the Real of raw reality as well as to the Imaginary of our self-experience is, of course, the big Other.) Neither the phenomenological (imaginary) nor neurobiological (real) profiling of participants can be cited as a constituting condition for this socially 'objective mind'.

In the same Habermasian mode, Robert Pippin claims that, even if some day scientists succeed in total naturalization of humanity, explaining how self-consciousness emerged out of natural evolution, this has no consequences for philosophy:

> Of course, it is possible and important that some day researchers will discover why animals with human brains can do these things and animals without human brains cannot, and some combination of astrophysics and evolutionary theory will be able to explain why humans have ended up with the brains they have. But these are not philosophical problems and they do not generate any philosophical problems.[16]

What Pippin performs here is, of course, the basic transcendental turn: the point is not that self-consciousness is too complex a phenomenon to be accounted for in scientific terms but that, in this case, all psycho-neuronal analysis is simply irrelevant since it moves at a totally different level from pure self-consciousness, which is not a psychological fact but an a priori that sustains all our activity inclusive of neurological research. Here we reach a certain limit: how do we relativize the truth-domain of science? Is the transcendental approach enough, or does this approach have to be sustained by a limitation at the level of content? In somewhat simplified terms: is it enough to state that positive science cannot account for its own possibility, that it has to presuppose the free argumentative procedure which characterizes science? Or should we supplement this transcendental point with some proof of the empirical limitations of scientific explanations ('no brain science can really explain how human mind functions')?

One has to concede that some scientific experiments lead to results which cannot simply be dismissed as irrelevant. A recent experiment conducted by Karolinska Institutet in Sweden demonstrated that the experience of being inside one's own body is not as self-evident as one might think: neuroscientists 'created an out-of-body illusion in participants placed inside a brain scanner. They then used the illusion to perceptually "teleport" the participants to different locations in a room and show that the perceived location of the bodily self can be decoded from activity patterns in specific brain regions.' The sense of 'owning one's body' is therefore not to be taken for granted: it is 'an enormously complex task that requires continuous integration of information from our different senses in order to maintain an accurate sense of where the body is located with respect to the external world.'[17]

The signification of such experiments is double. First, they provide a clear argument against the spiritualist reading of the out-of-body experience as a proof that our soul is not irreducibly located in our body since it can freely float outside it: if one can generate the out-of-body experience through technological manipulation of our body, then our 'inner' self-experience is strictly immanent to our body. Second, they also render problematic at least the notion, crucial to the philosophy of finitude, that we are irreducibly 'embedded', that our self-experience as constrained to the standpoint of our (mortal) body is the ultimate horizon of our entire experience: the experiment indicates that our self-experience as 'embodied' is the result of complex neuronal processes which can also go wrong.

A more nuanced approach is thus needed which leaves behind Habermas's and Pippin's transcendental-idealist position. Wilfrid Sellars gives the duality of (materialist) content and (transcendental) form a decidedly materialist twist. Accepting the gap between methodology (priority of transcendental horizon) and ontology (full naturalization), that is, recognizing that direct naturalization is strictly pre-Hegelian, Sellars, in an unambiguously materialist way, upholds the *priority* of the scientific image by famously insisting that 'in the dimension of describing and explaining the world, science is the measure of all things, of what is, that it is, and of what is not, that it is not' ... Yet the manifest image remains indispensable as the originary medium for the normative. To the extent that this normative framework does not survive, Sellars warned, 'man himself would not survive' ... Science cannot lead us to abandon our manifest self-conception as rationally responsible agents, since to do so would be to abandon the source of the imperative to revise. It is our manifest self-understanding as persons that furnishes us, qua community of rational agents, with the ultimate horizon of rational purposiveness with regard to which we are motivated to try to understand the world. Shorn of this horizon, all cognitive activity, and with it science's investigation of reality, would become pointless.[18]

Along these lines, Ray Brassier defines materialism with the Marxist-sounding notion of the 'determination-in-the-last-instance', which should be opposed to the similar notion of overdetermination: 'determination-in-the-last-instance is the causality which renders it universally possible for any object X to determine its own "real" cognition, but only in the last instance.'[19] Overdetermination is transcendental, that is to say, the point of transcendentalism is that a subject cannot ever fully 'objectivize' itself, i.e. reduce itself to a part of 'objective reality' in front of him, since such reality is always-already transcendentally constituted by subjectivity: no matter to what extent I succeed in accounting for myself as a phenomenon within the 'great chain of being', as the result determined by a network of natural (or supernatural) reasons, this causal image is always-already overdetermined by the transcendental horizon which structures my approach to reality. To this transcendental overdetermination, Brassier opposes the naturalist determination in the last instance: a serious materialist has to presume that every subjective horizon within which reality appears, every subjective constitution or mediation of reality, has to be ultimately determined by its place within objective reality, i.e. it has to be conceived as part of the all-encompassing natural process.[20]

The big question thus continues to haunt us: what – if anything – resists total scientific self-objectivization? Although, in contrast to scientific self-objectivization, ooo (object-oriented ontology) aims at re-enchanting reality, it shares with the scientific view the notion that the ontological-transcendental horizon can be reduced to one among many ontic relations between objects-things. Bryant is therefore right in naming his view 'onticology' as opposed to ontology. Our problem is, on the contrary:

how are we to be materialists without regressing to an ontic view? The answer deployed in the present book is that the dimension that resists self-objectivization is not human self-experience but the 'inhuman' core of what German Idealism calls negativity, what Freud called death drive, and even what Heidegger referred to as 'ontological difference': a gap or abyss which forever precludes the exclusively ontic view of humans as just another object among objects.[21] This dimension is beyond any transcendental horizon, it aims at reaching the In-itself; however, the In-itself is not 'out there', we do not reach it after we subtract from reality our subjective additions; the In-itself is 'here', in the very subjective excess to what appears to us as objective reality.

To discern this excess, one should distinguish between posthumanism and the thought of postsubjectivity: one can well imagine a humanism based on the rejection of Cartesian subjectivity (along the lines of 'real humans engaged in an actual life-process, not the dead abstraction of *cogito*'), as well as an antihumanist subjectivity (subject as a monstrous excess that unsettles the limits of the human lifeworld). The predominant version nonetheless involves the rejection of both terms: humanism and/ or the thought of Subject are both falsely universal, the form of universal human Subject that they sustain relies on a hidden norm (privileging Western white males) and thus excludes others who do not fit its implicit unitary model (women, other races, etc.).

Our wager is here to accentuate the gap that separates subject from humans and to assert the antihuman subject: the 'empty' Cartesian subject ($) is not an abstraction from the fullness of actual life but a primordial empty form which, afterwards, gets filled with the 'human' stuff (the 'wealth of a person'). This 'empty' subject cannot be opposed to a reject, it *is* a reject, it is what remains after we subtract all 'human' content. It is as a reject that this subject is universal: in every structure of subject-positions, universality is embodied in its 'part of no-part', in the element for which there is no proper place in the structure, the element which is forever out of joint. We thus have two opposed forms of universality: the normative universality of a model, a particular form in which an ideological universality reaches its full actual existence (Western white male as a model of humanism, as a being which is 'fully human'), and the universality which is embodied in the reject of the structure (a subject is universal precisely insofar as it is excluded from all particular social positions so that all that remains is the empty form of universality).

Kant, who was the first to introduce the split between subject (the void of pure negativity) and person (the particular wealth of emotional etc. 'pathological' content), was therefore the first philosophical antihumanist.

Humanism is premodern, pre-Cartesian, reducing man to the high point of creation, instead of conceiving of him as a subject which stands outside creation. (In a sense, modern science also already is 'posthuman' since its universe is irreducible to our everyday human reality: as Richard Feynman put it decades ago, nobody can really 'understand' quantum physics since 'understanding' means translating into the terms of our spontaneous commonsense notion of reality – the quantum universe is and remains forever foreign to our lifeworld, 'counterintuitive' [the gap that separates modern science from our everyday notion of reality opens up already with Galileo].)

The idea that the growth of Artificial Intelligence poses a threat to our human identity is one of the popular topics of our public debates. The true danger is supposed to reside well beyond the prospect that, with intelligent robots progressively replacing us, unemployment will explode (and, incidentally, would such a prospect not be a blessing in a rationally organized economy?): what if AI machines become self-conscious (in some transhuman sense unknown to us) and unite their awareness in a living entity much above our human abilities, playing with us, using us as its toys or simply ignoring us, even annihilating us? How will we relate to such a higher Intelligence? Will we be able to enter a meaningful relationship with it at all? Will our eventual encounter with it be a destructive trauma (the end of humanity), an exhilarating self-transcendence (we will merge with this Intelligence, blissfully swimming in it), or something entirely different?

However, as philosophers, when we hear that modern science and technology pose a threat to our human identity, the first thing we should do is to raise the elementary philosophical question: which notion of 'human', of the specific human dimension, guides us; which notion are we presupposing in advance as an implicit measure of being-human when we formulate such threats? For Heidegger, for example, traditional metaphysical humanism itself misses the essence of being-human, which is why humanist protests against the reign of technology are ultimately futile. And we should learn from Heidegger's insistence on the topic of finitude and failure: the very core of being-human is marked by a structure of immanent limitation, of not being 'fully' what one is, of one's identity being constitutively thwarted. The paradox is that if we take this limit or obstacle away and imagine a 'full' human being deprived of its perverse spin, we lose humanity itself. In other words, this very immanent limitation, the failure to be what one is, is constitutive of being-human. This is why humans always fantasize of a state in which they would finally be 'fully human' – to be fully human equals being over-human. The catch is that this very failure to be fully human triggers what we refer to as 'cultural creativity', that is, it pushes us towards continuing self-transcendence. In other words, in posthuman perspective, emancipation of humanity turns into emancipation from humanity, from the limitations of a mere being-human. There is a deeper Hegelian necessity in this reversal: being-human implies in its very notion an incompleteness, a gap separating a human being from being 'fully' human, so that (in the same way, for Hegel, a perfect state is no longer a state but a religious community) a perfect human being is no longer human. Far from being just a theoretical problem, this ambiguity already affects our daily lives – as Franco Berardi put it succinctly, 'the next game will be about neuro-plasticity':

> Mapping the activity of the brain is going to be the main task of science in the next decades, while wiring the activity of the collective brain will be the main task of technology.[22]

Berardi is also right to emphasize the traumatic impact of such 'wiring':

> Not only the psychic dimension of the unconscious is disturbed, but the fabric of the neural system itself is subjected to trauma, overload, disconnection. The adaptation of the brain to the new environment involves enormous suffering, a tempest of violence and madness.[23]

While agreeing with Berardi's diagnostic, one should nonetheless reject his tendency to understand the ongoing 'wiring the activity of the collective brain' in the terms of the struggle between self-organization of sensitive singularities and neuro-totalitarianism ('autonomous organization of cognitive workers, or the matrix of bio-financial capitalism'[24]). Such a focus on the antagonism courts the danger of all too quickly attributing all 'bad' aspects of this 'wiring', the suffering and disorientation that it unleashes, to its capitalist-totalitarian co-optation, while extolling its 'liberating' potentials unleashed when the 'wiring' is controlled by the self-organization of cognitive workers. What gets lost in such an approach is the immensely violent and traumatic impact of 'wiring' our mental activity: it is a process which literally undermines the very core of what it means to be a human being.

Hyperobjects in the age of Anthropocene

It is crucial to bear in mind that the exploding neuroplasticity is just one aspect of a global process whose obverse is the rise of so-called 'anthropocene'. Ecology is today one of the major ideological battlefields, with a whole series of strategies to obfuscate the true dimensions of the ecological threat: (1) simple ignorance: it's a marginal phenomenon, not worthy of our preoccupation, life (of capital) goes on, nature will take care of itself; (2) science and technology can save us; (3) leave the solution to the market (higher taxation of the polluters, etc.); (4) superego pressure on personal responsibility instead of large systemic measures: each of us should do what he/she can – recycle, consume less, etc.; (5) maybe the worst of them all is the advocating of a return to natural balance, to a more modest, traditional life by means of which we renounce human hubris and become again respectful children of our Mother Nature – this whole paradigm of Mother Nature derailed by our hubris is wrong.[25] Why?

The core of ecological crisis is a phenomenon noted already by Marx, the so-called metabolic rift caused by expanding capitalist productivity: 'Labor pounds and wheedles rocks and soil, plants and animals, extracting the molecular flows out of which our shared life is made and remade. But those molecular flows do not return from whence they came' (xiii). When such a rift caused by human industry begins to pose a threat to the very reproduction of life on the Earth, so that humanity literally becomes a geological factor, we enter a new era of the Anthropocene: 'The Anthropocene is a series of metabolic rifts, where one molecule after another is extracted by labor and technique to make things for humans, but the waste products don't return so that the cycle can renew itself' (xiv). McKenzie Wark designates the agency of this growing rift with the ironic term, the 'Carbon Liberation Front': 'The Carbon Liberation Front seeks out all of past life that took the form of fossilized carbon, unearths it and burns it to release its energy. The Anthropocene runs on carbon' (xv). There is a paradox in the very heart of this notion of the Anthropocene: humanity became aware of its self-limitation as a species precisely when it became so strong that it influenced the balance of the entire life on earth. It was able to dream of being a Subject until its influence on nature (earth) was marginal, that is, against the background of stable nature.

Notions like 'rift' and perturbed 'cycle' seem to rely on their opposite, a vision of a 'normal' state of things where the cycle is closed and the balance re-established, as if the Anthropocene (where human activity introduces imbalance and opens up the metabolic rift) should be overcome by reinstalling human species into a balanced natural order. Wark's key achievement is to reject thoroughly this path: there never was such a balance, nature in itself is already unbalanced, the idea of Nature as a big Mother is just another image of the divine big Other. Although, for Wark, I am one of the big bad guys, since I embody 'all the old vices' (17) of contemplative materialism detached from praxis, I agree with his basic approach of dismissing Nature as the last figure of the big Other:

> the God who still hid in the worldview of an ecology that was self-correcting, self-balancing and self-healing – is dead ... The human is no longer that figure in the foreground which pursues its self-interest against the background of a wholistic, organicist cycle that the human might perturb but with which it can remain in balance and harmony, in the end, by simply *withdrawing* from certain excesses. (xii)

Consequently, after the death of the God-Father, the masculine Reason, we should also endorse the death of the Goddess-Nature: 'To dispense with the invisible hand, and with homeostatic ecology as a basic metaphor, is to live once again after God is dead' (209). It is not only that we never encounter nature in-itself, i.e. that the nature we encounter is always-already caught in the antagonistic interaction with collective human labour – the gap that separates our (human) power of totalizing mediation (through labour) from nature in its intractability (nature as that which resists our grasp) is irreducible. Nature is not an abstract in-itself but primarily what we encounter in our labour as a resisting counterforce. However, we have to take a further step here: the fiction of a stable nature disturbed by human interventions is wrong even as an inaccessible ideal which we may approach if we withdraw as much as possible from our activity – nature is already in itself disturbed, out of joint: 'We still tend to think that if we *stop* certain actions, an ecology will right itself and return to homeostasis. But perhaps that is not the case ... What if there is only an unstable nature?' (200).

The rift between labour and the intractable nature should be supplemented not only by a rift within nature itself which makes it forever unstable, but also by a rift which splits from within humanity itself. This rift which explodes in modernity is the 'divorce between the sensation of the world and the idea of it' (105). We should not read this rift in the traditional humanist-Marxist sense of the 'alienation' of the 'higher' theoretical activity from the living collective practice: the living practical experience of reality cannot be elevated into the ultimate resort – therein resides the lesson of modern science and technology. The 'inhuman' realm (exemplarily the field of quantum oscillations) is beneath our direct experience, accessible only through scientific theories: this queer world of particle physics 'is so far below the threshold of human perception that we struggle for language to describe it' (165) – what we do not have is not so much an appropriate language (we can construct that easily enough) but much more an appropriate sensation-experience of this queer world as a part of our reality. The same holds for the Carbon Liberation Front: our knowledge about CLF 'is a knowledge that can only be created via a techno-scientific apparatus so extensive that it is now an entire planetary infrastructure' (180). Here also, as Wagner would have put it, *die Wunde schliesst der Speer nur der sie schlug.*

Wark's final point of reference, the unsurpassable horizon, remains what he calls the 'shared life', and every autonomization of one of its moments amounts to a fetishizing alienation: 'Our species-being is lost from shared life when we make a fetish of a particular idea, a particular love, or a particular labor' (107). Here, however, we should raise a double question. First, is such an interruption of the flow of shared life, such a focusing on an idea, a beloved, a task, not precisely what Badiou calls Event? So far from dismissing such cuts as cases of alienation, should we not celebrate them as the highest expression of the power of negativity? Furthermore, does our access to the nonhuman molecular level of, say, the quantum universe not presuppose precisely such a cut from our shared daily life? We are dealing here with a properly Hegelian paradox: Hegel praises the 'molar' act of abstraction, the reduction of the complexity of a situation to the 'essential', to its key feature, as the infinite power of Understanding. The truly hard thing is not to bear in mind the complexity of a situation but to brutally simplify the situation: we see the essential form, not the details. The difficult thing is to see classes, not microgroups fighting each other; to see the subject, not the Humean flow of mental states. We are not talking here just of ideal forms or patterns but of the Real: the void of subjectivity is the Real which is obfuscated by the wealth of 'inner life'; class antagonism is the Real which is obfuscated by the multiplicity of social conflicts. (The possible counterargument here is: but can Hegel think a historical process in which a lower contingent meaningless fact is a key factor of the change in the molar sphere [like the fall of Rome owing to lead in their pottery]?)

We should thus move over the Deleuzian opposition between molecular and molar which ultimately reduces the molar level to a shadowy theatre of representations with regard to the molecular level of actual productivity and life-experience: true, the metabolic rift is operative and can only be established at a 'lower' molecular level, but this molecular level is so low that it is imperceptible not only to 'molar' big politics or social struggles but also to the most elementary life-experience and engagement. It can only be accessed through 'high' theory – in a kind of self-inverted twist, it is only through the highest that we get to the lowest.[26]

Science, of course, has its own 'molecular' material base, scientific measuring apparatuses. Although these apparatuses are made by humans and form part of our ordinary reality, they enable us gain access to weird domains which are *not* part of our experiential human reality, from quantum oscillations to genome:

> There is something inhuman about science. Its modes of perception, modeling and verifying are outside the parameters of the human sensorium, even though they are dependent on an apparatus that is itself the product of human labor. The objects of science are not dependent on human consciousness. And yet science happens in history, constrained by forms of social organization of a given type and of a given time. As such, existing social relations are a fetter upon science in its pursuit of the inhuman sensations of the nonhuman real. (208)

Along these lines, Karen Barad is right to point out the narrowness of Bohr's notion of apparatus: apparatuses have their own history, they are the product of social practices and as such they refract the larger world of forces and relations of production. Crucial here is the distinction between nonhuman and inhuman: nonhuman resides at the same level as human, it is part of the ordinary world in which humans confront nonhuman things and processes. Apparatuses are something different, they are neither human nor nonhuman but inhuman: 'The inhuman mediates the nonhuman to the human. This preserves the queer, *alien* quality of what can be produced by an apparatus – particle physics for example – without saying too much about the nonhuman in advance' (164). In short, while apparatuses are immanent to the human, a product of human productive and scientific engagement with reality, they are simultaneously inhuman in the sense that they enable us to discern the contours of a real which is not part of our reality. The truly weird element in the triad of humans, the reality they confront, and the apparatuses they use to penetrate reality is thus not the intractable external reality but apparatuses which mediate between the two extremes, humans and nonhuman reality. Apparatuses enable humans not only to get to know the real which is outside the scope of their experiential reality (like quantum waves); they also enable them to construct new 'unnatural' (inhuman) objects which cannot but appear to our experience as freaks of nature (gadgets, genetically modified organisms, cyborgs, etc.).[27] The power of human culture is not only to build an autonomous symbolic universe beyond what we experience as nature, but to produce new 'unnatural' natural objects which materialize human knowledge. We not only 'symbolize nature', we as it were denaturalize it from within.[28]

In order to properly understand these forthcoming transformations, we have to change the very 'spontaneous' conceptual apparatus by means of which we conceptualize our environs. Following this need, Timothy Morton[29] introduced the concept of *hyperobjects*: objects like global warming (and radioactive plutonium and even human language) that are so massively distributed in time and space as to transcend spatiotemporal specificity. As such, hyperobjects are characterized by a series of interconnected features which unsettle the basic coordinates of our ordinary reality. They are *viscous*: they adhere to any other object they touch, no matter how hard an object tries to resist – the more an object tries to resist a hyperobject, the more glued to the hyperobject it becomes. They are *nonlocal*: they are massively distributed in time and space to the extent that their totality cannot be realized in any particular local manifestation, and, as such, they become more substantial than the local manifestations they produce. They are *phased* (phasing is 'like non-locality, but with a rhythm section added', as Stephen Muecke put it in his review of Morton's book): they occupy a higher dimensional space than entities we can normally perceive. Thus, hyperobjects appear to come and go in three-dimensional space, but would appear differently to an observer with a higher multi-dimensional view. They are *interobjective*: they are formed by relations between more than one object, so that we can only perceive the imprint, or 'footprint', of a hyperobject upon other objects.

For example, global warming is a hyperobject that is formed by interactions between the sun, fossil fuels and carbon dioxide, among other objects; it is made apparent through emissions levels, temperature changes and ocean levels, making it seem as if it is a product of scientific models, rather than an object that predated its own measurement. It affects meteorological conditions, such as tornado formation: objects don't feel global warming as such, they experience tornadoes as they cause damage in specific places. Global warming is phased, which means that, within our experiential reality, it does not have a continuous existence: we see a tornado here, a drought there, a flood somewhere else, but to see global warming itself, we would need a different view, an insight into a different dimension. Hyperobjects only become visible during ecological crises, which means that they are as a rule experienced as a threat toward organic matter, what Morton calls a 'demonic inversion of the sacred substances of religion'. It is easy to see how such an invisible hyperobject which can affect our very survival acquires a spiritual quality – Morton even ironically entertains the idea that hyperobjects might be elevated into sacred objects of reverential care in the era to come. As such, hyperobjects are harbingers of what Franco Berardi aptly designated the state 'after the future': they force us 'to abandon the modern habit of redemptively imaging a better future, for now we have to hesitate in front of what hyperobjects are placing right in front of us: that we are not in charge of the future anymore, because it might well be without us.'[30]

Instead of conceiving ourselves as historical agents enacting progress, we have to accept that 'all around is darkness and impenetrable gloom', as Boris Godunov sings in his great monologue in Mussorgsky's opera; however, the paradox is that this terrifying prospect does not reduce human agents to helpless tiny particles in the world machinery. Reality is impenetrable not just because it transcends the constrained horizon of finite human being but also because we humans are unable to control and predict the effects on our own activity on our natural environs. Therein resides the paradox of anthropocene: humanity became aware of its self-limitation as a species precisely when it became so strong that it influenced the balance of the entire life on earth. It was able to dream of being a Subject until its influence on nature (earth) was marginal, that is, against the background of stable nature. The paradox is thus that the more the reproduction of nature is human mediated, the more humanity becomes a 'decentred' agent unable to regulate the process of its exchange with nonhuman nature. This is why it is not enough to insist on the nontransparency of objects, on how objects have a hidden core withdrawn from human reach: what is withdrawn is not just the hidden side of objects but above all the true dimension of the subject's activity. The true excess is not the excess of objectivity which eludes the subject's grasp but the excess of the subject itself, that is to say, what eludes the subject is the 'blind spot', the point at which it is itself inscribed into reality.

Is today's all-pervasive hyperobject not the market? Although we are all rationally aware that the market is kept alive by the ultracomplex activity of millions of participants, and that all that 'actually exists' are individuals and things caught into the market operations, we experience the market as an independent all-powerful entity, a behemoth which controls and regulates our activity. No wonder that with markets, ideological prosopopoeia reaches its heyday: today, in our cynical and rational times, we all become animists when we deal with markets, markets talk as living persons, they express their 'satisfaction' or 'worry' at political measures. And, to go even further, is the ultimate hyperobject not language itself? All these are cases of the so-called self-transcendence, a process analysed in detail by Jean-Pierre

Dupuy in his *The Mark of the Sacred*[31] and equivalent to what Lacan calls the 'big Other', what Hegel called 'externalization' (*Entäusserung*), and what Marx called 'alienation' (the term 'self-transcendence' was coined by Friedrich von Hayek): how, out of the interaction of individuals, can the appearance of an 'objective order' arrive which cannot be reduced to that interaction, but is experienced by the individuals involved as a substantial agency which determines their lives? It is all too easy to 'unmask' such a 'substance', to show, by means of a phenomenological genesis, how it gradually becomes 'reified' and sedimented; the problem is that the presupposition of such a spectral or virtual substance is in a way cosubstantial with being-human – those who are unable to relate to it as such, those who directly subjectivize it, are called psychotics.[32]

The task here is to leave behind the standard 'subjectivist' reading of Hegelian 'reconciliation' whose clearest instance is Lukács's *History and Class Consciousness*,[33] but which also underlies Marx's reference to Hegel. According to this reading, in reconciliation, the subject recognizes itself in the alienated substance (substantial content); that is, it recognizes in it the reified product of its own work, and thereby reappropriates it, transforms it into a transparent medium of its self-expression. The key feature here is that the subject, the agent of reappropriation, is in the singular (even if it is conceived as a collective subject); what thereby disappears is the dimension of what Lacan calls the 'big Other', the minimally 'objectivized' symbolic order, the minimal self-transcendence which alone sustains the dimension of intersubjectivity – intersubjectivity can never be dissolved into the direct interaction of individuals.

The key to the notion of alienation is a tension inscribed into its very core. First, there is alienation in the sense of 'reification': a content which is effectively the product of the subject's (collective) activity is falsely experienced as an autonomous entity which controls the subject, so that, in the act of liberation, the subject should reappropriate to itself its alienated substance, recognize in it its own product. Then, there is alienation in the sense of the individual subject alienated from its social substance, experiencing itself as a singularity which confronts an alien world. Therein resides the difference between capitalism and primitive 'organic' society: in the latter, the subject is fully immersed into its social substance, it lacks individual autonomy and freedom, but it is precisely for this reason that it is not alienated. In capitalism, the subject is freed from its substantial links, but this very freedom makes it alienated, an individual deprived of its concrete social substance. In *Grundrisse*, Marx tries to think both dimensions together: in a capitalist society, a subject is alienated in both senses; it is an abstract individual deprived of its social substance and for this reason confronting an alien world in which it doesn't recognize its own creation. Consequently, the point of the proletarian revolution is to enable the social subject to reappropriate to itself the alienated social substance, to recognize in it its own work. But is this idea of dis-alienation as the reappropriation of the alienated social substance as self-evident as it appears? What renders it problematic is the underlying notion of *self*-alienation: there is no Self which precedes alienation, the Self emerges only through its alienation, alienation is its constitutive feature (or, in Lacanese, subject is constitutively 'barred'). The only way to overcome alienation, the only 'dis-alienation' possible, is therefore to transfer the bar also on the substantial Other itself (from which subject is alienated) – in Lacanese, to accept that 'there is no big Other', that there is a lack in the Other itself, that the Other is inconsistent, traversed by antagonisms, structured around impossibilities.

This is why one should reject not only the (in)famously stupid 'dialectical-materialist' substitution of 'idea' with 'matter' as the absolute (so that dialectics becomes a set of dialectical 'laws' of matter's movement), but also Lukács's more refined 'materialist reversal of Hegel', his substitution of Hegel's 'idealist' subject-object (the absolute Idea) with the proletariat as the 'actual' historical subject-object. Lukács's 'reversal' also implies a formalist and non-Hegelian separation of the dialectical method from the material to which it is applied: Hegel was right to describe the process of the subject's alienation and reappropriation of the 'fetishized' or reified substantial content, he just did not see that what he described as the Idea's self-movement is actually a historical development which culminates in the emergence of the substanceless subjectivity of the proletariat and its reappropriation of the alienated substance through a revolutionary act. The reason we should reject this 'materialist reversal' is that it remains all too idealist: locating Hegel's idealism in the 'subject' of the process (the 'absolute Idea'), it fails to see the subjectivist 'idealism' inherent in the very matrix of the dialectical process (the self-alienated subject which reappropriates its 'reified' substantial content, positing itself as the absolute subject-object).

There are two ways to break out of this 'idealism': either one rejects Hegel's dialectics as such, dismissing the notion of the subjective 'mediation' of all substantial content as irreducibly 'idealist', proposing to replace it with a radically different matrix (Althusser: structural [over] determination; Deleuze: difference and repetition; Derrida: *différance*; Adorno: negative dialectics with its 'preponderance of the objective'); or else one rejects such a reading of Hegel (focused on the idea of 'reconciliation' as the subjective appropriation of the alienated substantial content) as 'idealist', as a misreading which remains blind to the true subversive core of Hegel's dialectic. This is our position: the Hegel of the absolute Subject swallowing up all objective content is a retroactive fantasy of his critics, starting with the later Schelling's turn to 'positive philosophy'. This 'positivity' is found also in the young Marx, in the guise of the Aristotelian reassertion of positive forces or potentials of Being preexisting logical or notional mediation. One should thus question the very image of Hegel-the-absolute-idealist presupposed by his critics – they attack the wrong Hegel, a straw man. What are they unable to think? The pure processuality of the subject which emerges as 'its own result'. This is why talk about the subject's *self*-alienation is deceptive, as if the subject somehow precedes its alienation – what this misses is the way the subject emerges through the 'self-alienation' of the substance, *not* of itself.

Biology or quantum physics?

Although we should not reduce philosophy to a methodological and epistemological reflection upon the status of scientific discoveries, scientific practice definitely is – as Alain Badiou put it – one of the 'generic procedures' to which philosophy is linked. It is the task of philosophy to reflect on the presuppositions and implications of the radical scientific breakthroughs, from relativity theory and quantum physics to evolutionary biology and brain sciences, from psychoanalysis to historical materialism. In this multiplicity of scientific references, every philosophy unavoidably privileges *one* science, so that one can almost say: tell me which science you privilege and I will tell you what kind of philosopher you are. One of the struggles among philosophers is thus also the struggle about which science deserves the priority to assume this paradigmatic role. Along these lines, Adrian Johnston repeatedly addresses a reproach to me: why do I choose quantum physics and not evolutionary biology, biogenetics and brain sciences as my main scientific reference? When I propose the quantum universe as universally relevant, as possessing a universal ontological scope, am I not guilty of a short circuit between a particular ontic domain deployed by quantum physics and universal ontology? Do I not use quantum physics as a formal matrix to account even for the paradoxes of human freedom? This counterargument sounds convincing: 'a reliance upon quantum physics for a thoroughly materialist account of free subjects is neither necessary (this is because of such life-scientific resources as emergentism, neuroplasticity, and epigenetics, all of which break with the deterministic and monistic naturalism...) nor even remotely feasible.'[34] And effectively, since subjectivity emerged as an emergent property of living beings, is it not logical that we should focus on this process of the self-overcoming of an organism in order to explain it? This is why Johnston claims that 'biology, rather than physics, is the key scientific territory for the struggles of today's theoretical materialists.'[35] Is this not the proper answer to the question raised long ago by Hegel, Hölderlin and Schelling in 'The Earliest System-Programme of German Idealism': 'The question is this: how must a world be constituted for a moral entity?' However, it is precisely with regard to this question that I insist on the priority of quantum physics, and this is also why I cannot follow Johnston's ontological stratification: inanimate nature functions and can be scientifically explained without absences, just by deterministic laws that regulate the mechanical interaction of positive objects; with life and then awareness, absences have to be taken into account. My counterargument here is that no emergentist miracle can get us from 'full' inanimate nature to life and awareness: inanimate nature cannot be the zero-level out of which higher ontological levels emerge, there must be some absentials at work already there, prior to inanimate materiality, to render possible the emergence of life out of matter and of awareness out of life. In other words, it is only this tension between the proto-reality of quantum vibrations, a reality of absences, and the positive reality which results from the collapse of quantum waves that allows for the self-overcoming of inanimate matter: quantum waves are the 'absentials' of even the most inanimate positive material reality. Was Hegel not on the trace of this 'absentials' in his interpretation of ancient Greek atomism: the void is not the empty space around the atoms but the void in the very heart of atoms, and it is this void that is the zero-level of subjectivity?

But are we justified in dismissing the relevance of evolutionary biology and brain sciences? Johnston himself refers to Terrence Deacon's *Incomplete Nature*, and, as the very title of the book indicates, Deacon directly evokes the ontological incompleteness of nature as the only way to account scientifically for the emergence of mind from matter: 'Mind didn't exactly emerge from matter, but from constraints on matter.'[36] Constraint means here an inner obstacle or limit which prevents some possibilities of being realized, some roads not to be taken, not accidentally but necessarily (even if it appears that it happens only by accident). Therein, in overlooking this positive, enabling, role of constraints, resides the failure of Luc Besson's 2014 film *Lucy*, a thriller which plays with the idea of what would have happened if a human being were to be able to use not only 10 per cent of our brain, as we usually do, but more, 20 per cent, 40 per cent, up to 100 per cent. (Incidentally, the movie is so full of stupid mistakes that it could have been made much better if Besson himself had used at least 10 per cent of his own brain while writing and directing it!) What sustains human inventiveness and spirituality is the very fact that we use only 10 per cent of our brain: the void of the unused possibilities sets in motion creative invention. It's vaguely like the statue of Venus of Milo: the very fact that her hands are missing triggers our mind into imagining different versions of how the complete statue would have been, while having a complete statue would necessarily generate a feeling of vulgar plenitude.

How, then, does this constraint function? Deacon's starting point is that one cannot relate the phenomena of 'a function, reference, purpose, or value' to physical matter since each of these phenomena 'is in some way incomplete': 'Longing, desire, passion, appetite, mourning, loss, aspiration – all are based on an analogous intrinsic incompleteness, an integral withoutness.' The reason these phenomena cannot be explained in physical terms or linked to physical processes is that there is something missing in them which Deacon labels an 'absential' or an 'absential feature', a neologism for what is missing from our understanding of the physical dimension of these phenomena.[37] Life, sentience and higher-order human mental processes cannot be explained in terms of computations and cybernetic processes, nor can biology be derived from, reduced to, or predicted from physics: 'Computations and cybernetic processes are insentient because they are not teleodynamic in their organization.'[38]

In a first approach, it may seem that all that Deacon is proposing is a new version of emergentism: with life, a new level of self-organization emerges characterized by autopoiesis and immanent teleology (orientation towards future goals); this self-organization has a dynamic structure which exerts a causal power of its own and cannot be accounted for in the terms of the mechanical laws regulating the interaction of inanimate particles – say, what an organ does can only be explained through the reference to the whole organism and its goals. With the emergence of human mind, a new form of causality emerges: the causality of abstract ideas where it appears as if we enter a domain of realism (in the medieval sense of the term, i.e. as opposed to nominalism) – Platonic universals not only exist but exert direct influence on material processes:

> Brains have elaborated this causal realism to an extreme, and minds capable of symbolic reference can literally bring even the most Platonic of conceptions of abstract form into the realm of causal particulars ... A concept like justice can determine the restriction of movement of diverse individuals deemed criminal because of only vaguely related behaviors

each has produced; and a concept like money can mediate the organization of the vastly complex flows of materials and energy, objects and people, from place to place within a continent. These abstract generals unquestionably have both specific and general physical consequences. So human mind can literally transform arbitrarily created abstract general features into causally efficacious specific physical events.[39]

In his comments on this passage from Deacon, Johnston is right to point out two implicit theoretical references at work here: the Marxist theory of commodity fetishism as well as the Freudian notion of the efficiency of fantasies (which determine people's actual behaviour). We effectively get here a gradual progress from nominalism to realism: inanimate nature is nominalist (individual objects acting on each other), while conscious beings function in a realist way, displaying the efficiency of abstract universals. But is this notion of absentials sufficient to account for the specific nature of the human mind? Deacon focuses on two aspects of absentials: absence in the sense of presence of a higher level invisible from the standpoint of a lower level, i.e. the surplus of self-organization over the present matter (when we divide an organism into its material parts, we look in vain among these parts for what makes the dynamic unity of the organism – in order to grasp this unity, we have to conceive the organism as a minimally ideal form that reproduces itself through the continuous transformation of its part); and absence in the sense of the immanent teleology of an organism, its orientation towards the future (an organism does things which can only be accounted for by a reference to its future states which are by definition absent from its presence, like doing something in order to achieve something else, coupling, building a nest, etc.). There is, however, another, much more radical sense of absentials which underlies Deacon' s parallel between absentials and the incorporation of zero into mathematics:

The difficulty we face when dealing with absences that matter has a striking historical parallel: the problems posed by the concept of zero ... One of the greatest advances in the history of mathematics was the discovery of zero. A symbol designating the lack of quantity was not merely important because of the convenience it offered for notating large quantities. It transformed the very concept of number and revolutionized the process of calculation. In many ways, the discovery of the usefulness of zero marks the dawn of modern mathematics. But as many historians have noted, zero was at times feared, banned, shunned, and worshiped during the millennia-long history that preceded its acceptance in the West. And despite the fact that it is a cornerstone of mathematics and a critical building block of modern science, it remains problematic, as every child studying the operation of division soon learns.[40]

What was so terrifying about zero as a number? Zero as a 'symbol designating the lack of quantity' puts the very absence (lack) of quantity at the same level as positive quantities, it treats the absence (lack) of a property as just another positive property. What we encounter here is the logic of differentiality rendered nicely by an old Yugoslav joke about a Montenegrin (people from Montenegro were stigmatized as lazy in the former Yugoslavia): why does a Montenegro guy, when going to sleep, put at the side of his bed two glasses, one full and one empty? Because he is too lazy to think in advance if he will be thirsty during the night ... The point of this joke is that the absence itself has to be positively registered: it is not enough to have one full glass of water, since, if the Montenegrin will not be thirsty, he will simply ignore it – this negative fact itself has to be taken note of by the empty glass, i.e. no-need-for water has to be materialized in the void of the empty glass. Differentiality thus cannot be reduced to the platitude that blue is not red, etc., but to a much more precise point: 'blue is not red' is not the same as 'blue is not yellow.' This point is clearly made in a well-known joke from socialist Poland: a customer enters a store and asks, 'You probably don't have butter, or do you?' The answer: 'Sorry, but we are the store which doesn't have toilet paper; the one across the street is the one which doesn't have butter!'

Ferdinand de Saussure was the first to formulate the notion of differentiality, pointing out that the identity of a signifier resides only in a series of differences (the features which distinguish it from other signifiers) – there is no positivity in a signifier, it 'is' only a series of what it is *not*. At this point, an obvious commonsense reproach arises which should be given all its weight: if all signifiers are just the combination of differences from other signifiers, why then does not the entire network of signifiers collapse into itself? How can such a system retain a minimum of stability? One should introduce here self-reflexivity into the signifying order: if the identity of a signifier is nothing but the series of its constitutive differences, then every signifying series has to be supplemented – 'sutured' – by a reflexive signifier which has no determinate meaning (signified), since it stands only for the presence of meaning as such (as opposed to its absence); in a further dialectical twist, one should add that the mode of appearance of this supplementary signifier which stands for meaning as such is non-sense (Gilles Deleuze developed this point in *The Logic of Sense*).

Another way to approach this exceptional signifier is to conceive it as the signifier of pure difference: not just the difference between positive terms, but difference as such. It is this signifier of difference that, in Lacan's famous definition, represents the subject for another signifier. That is to say, the ontological status of the subject is that of a zero, void, so its signifier can only be a signifier designating a lack – or, to paraphrase Hegel, subject is not a substance which withdraws/appears; subject is appearance (appearing-to-itself) which autonomizes itself and becomes an agent against its own substantiality. The subject's self-withdrawal or split is thus much more radical than the self-withdrawal of every object split between its appearance (in interaction with other objects) and its substantial content, its withdrawn In-itself: subject is not just split like every object between its phenomenal qualities (actualizations) and its inaccessible virtual In-itself; subject is divided between its appearance and the void in the core of its being, not between appearance and its hidden substantial ground. It is only against this background that one can understand in what sense subject effectively 'is' an object: since subject is the self-appearing of nothing, its 'objective correlate' can only be a weird object whose nature is to be the embodiment of nothing, an 'impossible' object, an object the entire being of which is an embodiment of its own impossibility, the object called by Lacan *objet a*. In order to conceive this status of *objet a*, we have to accomplish a move from lacking object to object which stands for the lack, which gives body to it – only this object 'is' subject.

In his wonderful book on Schubert's *Winterreise*, Ian Bostridge deploys the implications of the fact that, as we learn in the very first lines of the first song, the narrator comes to and leaves the house as a stranger. We never learn the reason why he leaves: was he thrown out by the prohibitive father of the family, was he rejected by the girl, did he escape out of fear of marriage promulgated by the girl's mother? This vagueness which creates anxiety is a positive feature in itself: it positively defines the narrator as a kind of empty place between parentheses, as a barred subject in the Lacanian sense of $. Subject is a kind of empty place between parentheses, and this emptiness is constitutive of the subject, it comes first, it is not the result of a process of abstraction or alienation: the barred/empty subject is not abstracted from the 'concrete' individual or person fully embedded in its lifeworld, this abstraction/withdrawal from all substantial content constitutes it. The 'fullness of a person', its 'inner wealth', is what Lacan calls the fantasmatic 'stuff of the I', imaginary formations which fill in the void that 'is' subject. Here also enters what Lacan calls *objet a*: *objet a* (as the stand-in for a lack) is the objectal correlate of the empty subject, that which causes anxiety. Back to *Winterreise*: *objet a* of the narrator is not the secret true reason why he had to leave the house, it is the very cause/agent of the narrator's 'emptying' into a stranger whose true motivations are obscure and impenetrable. As such, *objet a* is the object which would have been lost the moment we were to learn the 'true' particular cause of why the narrator left the house.

More precisely, there are two aspects of *objet a*, two modes of its functioning: *objet a* as the third intruding element which disturbs the harmony of a couple, the non-relationship (antagonism) embodied (the chimney sweep on the top of the couple of man and woman – officer and maid – in Kierkegaard's famous example of classification); and *objet a* as surplus-enjoyment embodied, as subject's prosthetic supplements which enhances enjoyment. How do the two relate? Does sex without partner, with a single subject and its prosthetic gadgets, still function against the background of antagonism, i.e. does the prosthetic supplement ultimately fill in the gap of the missing intersubjective partner, of the other with whom relationship is impossible, so that a subject with prosthesis is a fantasy of pure gadget-*jouissance*? Or does a subject with prosthesis effectively suspend intersubjectivity?

A prosthetic element ultimately supplements – fills in – the gap of sexual nonrelationship; however, since sexual nonrelationship is constitutive of human sexuality, the obverse also holds, there is no actual interpersonal sexual relation without a prosthetic supplement. This supplementary element is (exactly like Kierkegaard's chimney sweep) an obstacle to sexual relation which simultaneously renders it possible. What we should bear in mind here is that intersubjectivity is not primordial: we don't have first pure intersubjectivity which then gets distorted and the need arises for prosthetic supplements. Intersubjectivity, the symbolic space of mutual exchange and recognition, is not a 'natural' state for a human being, it is something that emerges through a long and painful process: prior to other subjects, every subject's first partner is the Other qua (maternal) Real Thing.

How is such an entity which functions as the appearance of nothing to itself possible? The answer is clear: such a nonsubstantial entity has to be purely relational, with no positive support of its own. What happens in the passage from substance to subject is thus a kind of reflective reversal: we pass from the secret core of an object inaccessible to other objects to *inaccessibility as such* – $ is nothing but its own inaccessibility, its own failure to be substance. Therein resides Lacan's achievement: the standard psychoanalytic theory conceives the Unconscious as a psychic substance of subjectivity (the notorious hidden part of the iceberg) – all the depth of desires, fantasies, traumas, etc. – while Lacan *desubstantializes the*

Unconscious (for him, the Cartesian *cogito* is the Freudian subject), thereby bringing psychoanalysis to the level of modern subjectivity. (It is here that we should bear in mind the difference between the Freudian Unconscious and the 'unconscious' neurological brain processes: the latter do form the subject's natural 'substance', i.e. subject only exists insofar as it is sustained by its biological substance; however, this substance is not subject.)

The basic operation – or, rather, the modus operandi – of the subject is the tearing apart of every substantial unity; it is no wonder that Hegel celebrates Understanding, precisely in its aspect of analysing, tearing the unity of a thing or process apart, as 'the most astonishing and greatest of all powers, or rather the absolute power' – as such, it is, surprisingly (for those who stick to the common view of dialectics), characterized in exactly the same terms as Spirit which is, with regard to the opposition between Understanding and Reason, clearly on the side of Reason: 'Spirit is, in its simple truth, consciousness, and forces its moments apart.' Everything turns on how we are to understand this identity-and-difference between Understanding and Reason: it is not that reason adds something to the separating power of Understanding, re-establishing (at some 'higher level') the organic unity of what Understanding has torn apart, supplementing analysis with synthesis; Reason is, in a way, not more but *less* than Understanding, it is – to put it in Hegel's well-known terms of the opposition between what one wants to say and what one actually says – what Understanding, in its activity, *really does*, in contrast to what it wants-means to do. Reason is therefore not another facility supplementing Understanding's 'one-sidedness': the very idea that there is something (the core of the substantial content of the analysed thing) which eludes Understanding, a transrational Beyond out of its reach, is the fundamental illusion of Understanding. In other words, all we have to do to get from Understanding to Reason is to *subtract* from Understanding its constitutive illusion – Understanding is not too abstract/violent, it is, on the contrary, as Hegel put it apropos of Kant, *too soft towards things*, afraid to locate its violent movement of tearing things apart into things themselves. In a way, it is epistemology versus ontology: the illusion of Understanding is that its own analytic power – the power to make 'an accident as such … that what is bound and held by something else and actual only by being connected with it … obtain an existence all its own, gain freedom and independence on its own account' – is only an 'abstraction', something external to 'true reality' which persists out there intact in its inaccessible fullness. In other words, it is the standard critical view of Understanding and its power of abstraction (that it is just an impotent intellectual exercise missing the wealth of reality) which contains the core illusion of Understanding. To put it in yet another way, the mistake of Understanding is to perceive its own negative activity (of separating, tearing things apart) only in its negative aspect, ignoring its 'positive' (productive) aspect – Reason is Understanding itself in its productive aspect.

The act of abstraction, of tearing apart, can also be understood as the act of self-imposed blindness, of refusing to 'see it all'. What Hegel calls 'negativity' can also be put in the terms of insight and blindness, as the 'positive' power of 'blindness', of ignoring parts of reality. How does a notion emerge out of the confused network of impressions we have of an object? Through the power of 'abstraction', of blinding oneself to most of the features of the object, reducing the object to its constitutive key features. The greatest power of our mind is not to see more, but to see *less* in a correct way, to reduce reality to its notional determinations – only such 'blindness' generates the insight into what things effectively are. This tension between insight and blindness accounts for the fact that Hegel uses the term *Begriff* (notion) in two main opposed meanings: 'notion' as the very core, the essence, of the thing, and 'notion' as 'mere notion' in contrast to 'the thing itself'; and one should bear in mind that the same goes for his use of the term 'subject': the subject as elevated above the objective, as the principle of life and mediation of objects, and the subject as designating something 'merely subjective', a subjectively distorted impression in contrast to the way things out there really are. It is all too simple to oppose these two aspects as the 'lower' one, pertaining to the abstract approach of Understanding (the reduction of the subject to the 'merely subjective'), and the 'higher' one, involving the truly speculative notion of the Subject as the mediating principle of Life of reality; the point is, rather, that the 'lower' aspect is the key constituent of the 'higher' one. One overcomes the 'merely subjective' by, precisely, fully endorsing it – recall again the passage from the Preface to *Phenomenology* where Hegel celebrates the disjunctive power of 'abstract' Understanding: Hegel does not overcome the abstract character of Understanding by substantially changing it (synthesis instead of abstraction, etc.), but by perceiving in new light this same power of abstraction: what first appears as the weakness of Understanding (its inability to grasp reality in all its living complexity, its tearing apart of the living texture of reality) is its greatest power.

What this means is that abstraction is not just subjective, the outcome of our simplifying and partial analysis of the thing: it is to be located in the very heart of the thing itself. For example, Marx deployed how abstraction rules the reality of capitalism: when he describes capital's mad self-enhancing circulation, which reaches its apogee in today's meta-reflexive speculations on futures, it is far too simplistic to claim that the spectre of this self-engendering monster pursuing its interests with no regard for human or environmental concerns is an ideological abstraction, and that, behind this abstraction, there are real people and natural objects on whose productive capacities and resources capital's circulation is based and on which it feeds like a gigantic parasite. The problem is that this 'abstraction' is not only characteristic of our (the financial speculator's) misperception of social reality, but that it is 'real' in the precise sense of determining the structure of material social processes themselves: the fate of whole swathes of the population and sometimes of whole countries can be decided by the 'solipsistic' speculative dance of Capital, which pursues its goal of profitability with blessed indifference to how its movements will affect social reality. Therein lies the fundamental systemic violence of capitalism, much more uncanny than the direct precapitalist socio-ideological violence: it is no longer attributable to concrete individuals and their 'evil' intentions, but is purely 'objective', systemic, anonymous.

This brings us to the properly dialectical notion of abstraction: what makes Hegel's 'concrete universality' infinite is that *it includes 'abstractions' in concrete reality itself, as their immanent constituents.* That is to say, which is, for Hegel, the elementary move of philosophy with regard to abstraction? To abandon the commonsense empiricist notion of abstraction as a step away from the wealth of concrete empirical reality with its irreducible multiplicity of features: life is green, concepts are grey, they dissect, mortify, concrete reality. (This commonsense notion even has its pseudodialectical version, according to which such 'abstraction' is a feature of mere Understanding, while 'dialectics' recuperates the wealth of reality.) Philosophical thought proper begins when we become aware of how *such a process of 'abstraction' is inherent to reality itself*: the tension between empirical reality and its 'abstract' notional determinations is immanent to reality, it is a feature of 'things themselves.' Therein resides the anti-nominalist accent of philosophical thinking – say, the basic insight of Marx's 'critique of political economy' is that the abstraction of the value of a commodity is its 'objective' constituent.

This is how we should distinguish the 'true infinity' from the 'spurious (or bad) infinity': the bad infinity is the asymptotic process of discovering newer and newer layers of reality – reality is posited here as the In-itself which can never be fully grasped, only gradually approached, i.e. all we can do is to discern particular 'abstract' features of the transcendent/inaccessible wealth and fullness of the 'real thing'. The movement of 'true infinity' is exactly the opposite one: one includes the process of 'abstraction' into the 'thing itself'. This brings us, unexpectedly, to the question: what is a dialectical self-deployment of a notion? Imagine, as a starting point, our being caught in a complex and confused empirical situation which we try to understand, we try to bring some order into it. Since we never start from the zero-point of pure pre-notional experience, we begin with the double movement of directly applying to this situation the abstract-universal notions at our disposal, and of analysing the situation, comparing its elements among themselves and with our previous experiences, generalizing, formulating empirical universals. Sooner or later, we became aware of inconsistencies in the notional schemes we use to understand the situation: something which should have been a subordinates species seems to encompass and dominate the entire field; different classifications and categorizations clash, without us being able to decide which one is more 'true'; and so forth. In our spontaneous mind-frame, we dismiss such inconsistencies as signs of the deficiency of our understanding: reality is much too rich and complex for our abstract categories, we will never be able to deploy a notional network able to capture its entire wealth … Then, however, if we have a refined theoretical sense, we sooner or later notice something strange and unexpected: it is not possible to clearly distinguish the inconsistencies of our notion of an object from the inconsistencies which are immanent to this object itself. The 'thing itself' is inconsistent, full of tensions, struggling between its different determinations, and the deployment of these tensions, this struggle, is what makes it 'alive'. Take a particular state: when it malfunctions, it is as if its particular (specific) features are in tension with the universal Idea of the State; or take the Cartesian *cogito*: the difference between me as a particular person embedded in a particular lifeworld and myself as abstract Subject is part of my very particular identity, since to act as abstract Subject is a feature that characterizes individuals in modern Western society.

This, finally, brings us back to our starting point, to quantum physics: why quantum physics as the basic scientific reference, why not the triumphant triad of evolutionary biology, biogenetics and brain sciences? If we interpret the 'absential' nature of the symbolic order that characterizes the functioning of the human mind in this precise sense (differentiality, the mark of a lack as such, the positive ontological role of abstraction), can we really account for the emergence of the human subjectivity out of biological organisms via a reference to the above-mentioned triad? Is it not that something stronger is needed, a more paradoxical structure of reality, if we are to account for the possibility of the emergence of the symbolic order in it? And here quantum physics enters: what makes it so 'spooky' is not its radical heterogeneity with regard to our common sense, but rather its uncanny resemblance to what we consider specifically human – here, effectively, one is tempted to say that quantum physics 'deconstructs' the standard binary opposition of nature and culture. Let us go quickly through the list of these features:[41]

- Within the symbolic order, possibility as such possesses an actuality of its own, that is, it produces real effects: say, father's authority is fundamentally virtual, a threat of violence. In a similar way, in the quantum universe, the actual trajectory of a particle can only be explained if one takes into account all of its possible trajectories within its wave function. In both cases, the actualization doesn't simply abolish the previous panoply of possibilities: what might have happened continues to echo in what actually happens as its virtual background.

- Both in the symbolic universe and in the quantum universe, we encounter what Lacan calls 'knowledge in the real': if, in the famous double-slit experiment, we observe an electron's trajectory in order to discover through which of the two slits it will pass, the electron will behave as a particle; if we do not observe it, it will display the properties of a wave – as if the electron somehow knew whether it is being observed or not. Is such behaviour not limited to the symbolic universe in which our 'taking ourselves to be X' makes us act like X?

- When quantum physicists try to explain the collapse of the wave function, they resort again and again to the metaphor of language: this collapse occurs when a quantum event 'leaves a trace' in the observation apparatus, when it is 'registered' in some way. We obtain here a relationship of externality – an event becomes fully itself, it realizes itself, only when its external surroundings 'take note' of it – which echoes the process of symbolic realization in which an event fully actualizes itself only through its symbolic registration, inscription into a symbolic network, which is external to it.

- Furthermore, there is a temporal dimension to this externality of registration: a minimum of time always elapses between a quantum event and its registration, and this minimal delay opens up the space for a kind of ontological cheating with virtual particles (an electron can create a proton and thereby violate the principle of constant energy, on condition that it reabsorbs it quickly enough, i.e. before its environs 'take note' of the discrepancy. This delay also opens up the way for temporal retroactivity: the present registration decides what must have happened – for example, if, in the double-slit experiment, an electron is now observed, it will not only (now) behave as a particle, its past will also retroactively become ('will have been') that of a particle, in a homology with the symbolic universe in which a present radical intervention (the rise of a new Master Signifier) can retroactively rewrite the (meaning of the) entire past (to quote Borges, with the emergence of Kafka, Poe and Dostoyevsky are no longer what they have been – i.e. from the standpoint of Kafka, we can see in Poe and Dostoyevsky dimensions which previously were not there).

So what is the lesson of the fact that these four interconnected features – the actuality of the possible, knowledge in the real, the delay of (symbolic) registration, retroactivity – occur both at the quantum level and in the symbolic universe? It is simply that we should reject the straight evolutionary model of how higher levels of reality emerge out of lower levels (life out of inanimate matter, mind out of life) in which the basic level is that of inanimate matter with no absentials and just direct mechanical causality, and where out of this basic level then absentials gradually play a greater and greater role. Lack and absences must be here from the very beginning, already at the zero level, which means that physical external determinist reality cannot be the zero level. How to break this deadlock without regressing into spiritualism? Quantum physics provides here an answer: it is the gap between material reality and quantum proto-reality which makes possible the gradual self-overcoming of material reality.

One of the names for ontological disparity in quantum physics is *decoherence*. For decades, it was fashionable to take a scientific notion like Big Bang or Black Hole and apply it metaphorically more or less to whatever one wants. What one should do here is, on the contrary, to look at the precise ontological duality at work in decoherence, a duality totally foreign to classical metaphysical dualities (the sphere of Ideas in contrast to the 'lower' sphere of material objects, the sphere of actual life experience in contrast to the illusions it generates, etc.). Decoherence refers to the so-called collapse of the quantum field of oscillations, to the passage from quantum universe defined by the superposition of states (a superposition which forms a coherent multiplicity) to classic 'realist' universe composed of self-identical objects. In this passage, a radical simplification occurs: the coherent mulplicity of superposed states 'decoheres', one option is cut off from the continuum of others and posited as a single reality.

Was Schelling not the first to outline a homologous structure in his couple of preontological proto-reality and the (transcendentally constituted) reality? Schelling's true breakthrough, his distinction, first introduced in his essay on human freedom from 1807, between (logical) Existence and the impenetrable Ground of Existence, the Real of prelogical drives: this proto-ontological domain of drives is not simply 'nature', but the spectral domain of the not yet fully constituted reality. Schelling's opposition of the proto-ontological Real of drives (the Ground of being) and the ontologically fully constituted Being itself thus radically displaces the standard philosophical couples of Nature and Spirit, the Real and the Idea, Existence and Essence, and so forth. The real Ground of Existence is impenetrable, dense, inert, yet at the same time spectral, 'irreal', ontologically not fully constituted, while Existence is ideal, yet at the same time, in contrast to the Ground, fully 'real', fully existing.

The paradox (for the metaphysical tradition) is here that our ordinary stable reality emerges as the result of the subtractive act (decoherence) out of the fluid quantum oscillations. In our standard metaphysical (and commonsense) tradition, the primal reality is firm actual objects which are then surrounded by the aura of virtual waves that emanate from them. With regard to the distinction between subjective and objective, actual real things exist 'objectively', while virtual oscillations arise from their subjective (mis)perception. What 'objectively' exists in the quantum universe is, on the contrary, only wave oscillations, and it is the subject's interventions which transforms them into a single objective reality. In other words, what causes the decoherence of these oscillations, what constitutes objective reality, is the subjective gesture of a simplifying decision (measurement).

What this presupposes is a minimal gap between things in their immediate brute proto-reality and the registration of this reality in some medium (of the big Other): the second is in a delay with regard to the first. The agency which registers the collapse of the wave function is not in any sense 'creating' the observed reality, it is registering an outcome which remains fully contingent. Furthermore, the whole point of quantum physics is that many things go on before registration: in this shadowy space, 'normal' laws of nature are continuously suspended – how? Imagine that you have to take a flight on day x to pick up a fortune the next day, but do not have the money to buy the ticket; but then you discover that the accounting system of the airline is such that if you wire the ticket payment within twenty-four hours of arrival at your destination, no one will ever know it was not paid prior to departure. In a homologous way,

> the energy a particle has can wildly fluctuate so long as this fluctuation is over a short enough time scale. So, just as the accounting system of the airline 'allows' you to 'borrow' the money for a plane ticket provided

you pay it back quickly enough, quantum mechanics allows a particle to 'borrow' energy so long it can relinquish it within a time frame determined by Heisenberg's uncertainty principle ... But quantum mechanics forces us to take the analogy one important step further. Imagine someone who is a compulsive borrower and goes from friend to friend asking for money ... Borrow and return, borrow and return – over and over again with unflagging intensity he takes in money only to give it back in short order ... A similar frantic shifting back and forth of energy and momentum is occurring perpetually in the universe of microscopic distance and time intervals.[42]

This is how, even in an empty region of space, a particle emerges out of Nothing, 'borrowing' its energy from the future and paying for it (with its annihilation) *before the system notices this borrowing*. The whole network can function like this, in a rhythm of borrowing and annihilation, one borrowing from the other, displacing the debt onto the other, postponing the payment of the debt – it is really like the subparticle domain playing Wall Street games with the futures. What this presupposes is a minimal gap between things in their immediate brute reality and the registration of this reality in some medium (of the big Other): one can cheat insofar as the second is in a delay with regard to the first. The theological implications of this gap between the virtual proto-reality and the fully constituted one are of special interest. Insofar as 'god' is the agent who creates things by way of observing them, the quantum indeterminacy compels us to posit a god who is *omnipotent, but not omniscient*: 'If God collapses the wave functions of large things to reality by His observation, quantum experiments indicate that He is not observing the small.'[43] The ontological cheating with virtual particles (an electron can create a proton and thereby violate the principle of constant energy, on condition that it reabsorbs it before its environs 'take note' of the discrepancy) is a way to cheat god himself, the ultimate agency of taking note of everything that goes on: god himself doesn't control the quantum processes, therein resides the atheist lesson of quantum physics. Einstein was right with his famous claim 'God doesn't cheat' – what he forgot to add is that god himself can be cheated. Insofar as the materialist thesis is that 'God is unconscious' (God doesn't know), quantum physics effectively is materialist: there are microprocesses (quantum oscillations) which are not registered by the God-system. And insofar as God is one of the names of the big Other, we can see in what sense one cannot simply get rid of god (big Other) and develop an ontology without big Other: god is an illusion, but a necessary one.

The theory of decoherence is an attempt to explain the collapse of a wave function, that is, the passage from the netherworld of quantum oscillations to our ordinary reality, in an immanent way. The role of external observer in the theory of decoherence is therefore ambiguous, and therein resides its strength. Its basic claim is that decoherence (collapse of the wave oscillations) occurs only at the 'higher' macroscopic level, being registered by an observer – at the quantum level, nothing changes, coherence remains. This, however, in no way implies that we have to presuppose an external observer in whose eyes (in whose registering mechanism) decoherence occurs. One is almost tempted to claim that theorists of decoherence apply a new version of the old dialectical-materialist law of the passage of quantity into a new quality: when quantum interaction reaches a certain quantity, wave function collapses since the object in a way begins to 'observe itself.' Therein resides the strength of decoherence theory: it endeavours to articulate the purely immanent way a quantum process engenders the mechanism of its 'observation' (registration). Does it succeed? It is up to the science itself to provide an answer.

2 OBJECTS, OBJECTS ... AND THE SUBJECT

Re-enchanting nature? No, thanks!

The core of object-oriented ontology (ooo) developed by Levi Bryant[1] can be summed up by the formula: from subject back to substance. And, insofar as subject is correlative with modernity (recall Lacan's thesis about the Cartesian subject as the subject of modern science), we can also say that ooo follows the premise rendered by the title of Bruno Latour's famous book *We Were Never Modern*: it endeavours to bring back the premodern enchantment of the world. The Lacanian answer to this should be a paraphrase of his correction of the formula 'god is dead' (god was always-already dead, he just didn't know it): we were always-already modern (we just didn't know it). The main target of ooo is thus not transcendental philosophy with its subject/object dualism but modern science with its vision of 'grey' reality reduced to mathematical formalization: ooo tries to supplement modern science with a premodern ontology which describes the 'inner life' of things.

Bryant (who, before his engagement in ooo, was a Lacanian psychoanalyst) resorts to Lacan's 'formulas of sexuation' to articulate the basic difference between traditional (or modern) metaphysics and ooo: metaphysics follows the masculine side of universality grounded in a transcendent exception (god or subject who grounds or constitutes objective reality), while ooo follows the feminine side of non-all without exception (there is no transcendent exception, reality is composed of objects who are all on the same ontological level, and there is no way to totalize this multiverse of objects since they are withdrawn from each other, with no overreaching object to totalize them).[2] This is why, when Bryant speaks about 'the difference between ontologies of presence and transcendence and ontologies of immanence and withdrawal' (269), he groups the four concepts in an unexpected way: instead of pairing immanence with presence and transcendence with withdrawal (which would be much closer to our spontaneous intuition: is presence not by definition immanent, is transcendence not withdrawn from our reach?), he pairs presence with transcendence (the transcendent ground of being is fully self-present) and immanence with withdrawal (there is no transcendent ground, all there is is the immanent multiverse of objects withdrawn from each other).

In his deployment of the ontology of immanence/withdrawal, Bryant begins by asserting the primacy of ontology over epistemology, and rejecting the modern subjectivist notion according to which, before we proceed to analyse the structure of reality, we should critically reflect upon our cognitive apparatus (how is our cognition possible in the first place? what is its scope and limitation?). Following Roy Bhaskar, Bryant turns around the transcendental question: how does reality have to be structured so that our cognition of reality is possible? The answer is provided by the basic premise of ooo: 'It is necessary to staunchly defend the autonomy of objects or substances, refusing any reduction of objects to their relations, whether these relations be relations to humans or other objects' (26). This is why there is no place for subject in Bryant's edifice: subject is precisely a nonsubstantial entity fully reducible to its relations to other entities.

From the Hegelian-Lacanian standpoint, the tension between the epistemological and the ontological dimensions is resolved in a totally different way: the object is inaccessible, any attempt to seize it ends up in antinomies, and so forth; we reach the object in itself not by somehow seeing through these epistemological distortions but by transposing episte-mological obstacles into the thing itself. Quentin Meillassoux does exactly the same with regard to the experience of facticity and/or absolute contin-gency: he transposes what appears to transcendental partisans of finitude as the limitation of our knowledge (the insight that we can be totally wrong about our knowledge, that reality in itself can be totally different from our notion of it) into the most basic positive ontological property of reality itself – the absolute '*is simply the capacity-to-be-other as such, as theorized by the agnostic*. The absolute is the *possible transition*, devoid of reason, of my state towards any other state whatsoever.'[3] But this possibility is no longer a "possibility of ignorance", *viz.*, a possibility that is merely the result of my inability to know ... rather, it is the *knowledge* of the very real possi-bility'[4] in the heart of the In-itself:

> We must show why thought, far from experiencing its intrinsic *limits* through facticity, experiences rather its *knowledge* of the absolute

through facticity. We must grasp in fact not the inaccessibility of the absolute but the unveiling of the in-itself and the eternal property of what is, as opposed to the perennial deficiency in the thought of what is.[5]

In this way, 'facticity will be revealed to be a knowledge of the absolute *because we are going to put back into the thing itself what we mistakenly mistook to be an incapacity in thought*. In other words, instead of construing the absence of reason inherent in everything as a limit that thought encounters in its search for the ultimate reason, we must understand that this absence of reason *is*, and can *only* be the *ultimate* property of the entity'.[6] The paradox of this quasi-magical reversal of epistemological obstacle into ontological premise is that 'it is through facticity, and through facticity alone, that we are able to make our way towards the absolute': the radical contingency of reality, this 'open possibility, this "everything is equally possible", is an absolute that cannot be de-absolutized without being thought as absolute once more'.[7]

Here, one should also establish a link with the great conflict about how to interpret indeterminacy in quantum physics: for the 'orthodox' quantum physicists, this epistemological indeterminacy is simultaneously ontological, a property of 'reality' itself which is 'in itself' indeterminate; while for those, from Einstein onwards, who persist in classical 'realism-of-necessity', the epistemological indeterminacy can only mean that quantum physics doesn't offer a complete description of reality, that is, that there are some hidden variables it doesn't take into account. To put it in a somewhat problematic and exaggerated way, the Einsteinian critics try to re-Kantianize quantum physics, excluding from its grasp reality in-itself.

Meillassoux is well aware that quantum physics, with its uncertainty principle and the assertion of the role the observer plays in the collapse of the wave function, seems to undermine the notion of objective reality independent of any observer and thus give an unexpected boost to Kantian transcendentalism; however, as he points out, their similarity is deceptive, it obfuscates a fundamental difference: 'Certainly, the presence of an observer may eventually affect the effectuation of a physical law, as is the case for some of the laws of quantum physics – but the very fact that an observer can influence the law is itself a property of the law which is not supposed to depend upon the existence of an observer'.[8] In short, while in Kant's transcendentalism the 'observer'-subject constitutes what he observes, in quantum physics the observer's active role itself is reinscribed into physical reality.

Bryant may appear to have performed this same move: does he not assert repeatedly that the withdrawal of the object from the subject (i.e. the knowing or perceiving object) is simultaneously self-withdrawal, the self-splitting of the object, the withdrawal of the object with regard to itself? 'Withdrawal is not an accidental feature of objects arising from *our* lack of direct access to them, but is a constitutive feature of all objects regardless of whether they relate to other objects' (32). Bryant here draws a parallel between this universal ontological structure of the 'divided object' and the Lacanian divided/barred subject, concluding that 'all objects are akin to Lacanian divided subjects, $':

> no object ever actualizes the subterranean volcanic core with which its virtual proper being is haunted. This virtual domain is like a reserve or excess that never comes to presence. It is not simply that objects are, in themselves, fully actual and only withdrawn for other objects relating to them, but rather that objects are withdrawn in themselves. (281–2)

Bryant thus proposes a kind of universalized transcendental structure: each object (1) perceives other objects not the way they are in themselves but as interpreted through its own frame, and (2) this frame as such is also inaccessible, so that the object doesn't see what it doesn't see (i.e. what it doesn't see is akin to Rumsfeld's 'unknown unknowns'). This pan-transcendentalism justifies him in applying the Kantian term 'transcendental illusion' to capture the way objects relate to one another:

> The transcendental illusion thus generated by the manner in which objects relate to one another is one in which the states 'experienced' by a system are treated as other objects *themselves*, rather than system-specific entities generated by the organization of the object itself. In other words, the object treats the world it 'experiences' as reality *simpliciter*, rather than as system-states produced by its own organization. (160)

Bryant applies this notion of the impenetrability of objects to the Lacanian topic of the impenetrability of the Other's desire, to the enigma of *Che vuoi?*, what does the Other want from me, beneath all that he says to me:

> Desire, it could be said, embodies our non-knowledge with respect to the Other's desire. Embodied in all intersubjective relations is the sense that despite the fact that we are being addressed by the Other, we nonetheless do not know *why* the Other is addressing us. Put differently, we do not know the desire that animates the Other's relation to us. In

this regard, the desire of the Other closely mirrors the phenomenon of operational closure with respect to systems. The Other perturbs us in a variety of ways, but we are unable to determine what intentions lie behind the Other's interaction with us. (187)[9]

In a further radicalization, Bryant includes in this series god himself (if he exists):

> *every* entity, up to and including God if God exists, is like a Lacanian divided or barred subject, $, such that, regardless of whether or not it is related to another entity, each entity is withdrawn with respect to itself. Put differently, no entity is fully self-present to itself, but rather every entity necessarily contains blind spots or is opaque to itself. Withdrawal here is the very structure of entities, not an accidental relation of how one entity relates to another entity. (265)

Such a notion of god who is opaque to himself was elaborated already by Schelling who wrote about the impenetrable ground of god, that which is in god more than god himself. However, ooo does not pursue the next step of Schelling's ratiocination: how does *logos* arise out of this pluriverse in which 'objects have no direct access to one another and … each object translates other objects with which it enters into non-relational relations' (27)?

A detour: Ideology in pluriverse

Bryant's vision of a pluriverse without any totalizing agent which would be fully self-present is not limited to abstract ontological considerations: he derives from it a series of pertinent political insights. One of the interesting implications of the notion of 'democracy of objects', of our reality as the multiverse of actants, is to render problematic the standard notion of 'demystifying critique':

> An activist political theory that places all its apples in the basket of content is doomed to frustration insofar as it will continuously wonder why its critiques of ideology fail to produce their desired or intended social change. Moreover, in an age where we are faced with the looming threat of monumental climate change, it is irresponsible to draw our distinctions in such a way as to exclude nonhuman actors. (24)

Bryant provides here a convincing and pertinent example of ecology in our capitalist societies: why do all ideologico-critical calls fail to mobilize people, why is the large majority not ready to engage in serious action? If we take into account just the ideological discursive mechanisms, this failure becomes inexplicable and we have to invoke some deep processes of 'ideological mystification'. But if we widen our focus and include other actants, other processes in social reality that influence our decisions, like biased media reports, economic pressures on workers (threat of losing employment), material limitations, and so forth, the absence of engagement becomes much more understandable. Recall Jane Bennett's description of how actants interact at a polluted trash site: how not only humans but also the rotting trash, worms, insects, abandoned machines, chemical poisons, and so on each play their (never purely passive) role.[10] There is an authentic theoretical and ethico-political insight in such an approach.

There is another twist which enables the ruling ideology to survive: its proper genius is discernible in how ideology's obscene underside works. We are dealing here with what we may call the logic of inherent transgression: the affected subject, the subject addressed by an ideological edifice, does not take ideological injunctions seriously, he mocks them, dismisses them cynically, but this very 'resistance' is in advance taken into account and serves the reproduction of the ideological edifice. Suffice it to mention two cases from communist regimes. Political jokes were definitely a kind of 'resistance' to the ruling ideology, but a 'resistance' which generated obscene enjoyment that made accommodation much easier. Similarly, communist education failed miserably; instead of producing subjects dedicated to the building of socialism, it produced cynics who distrusted politics and were prone to withdraw into private life – and who were as such ideal subjects of the communist regime.

This example of the ambiguous role of political jokes makes it clear that the fake 'resistance' is not only on the side of the individuals but also and especially on the side of institutions of power themselves (perhaps one should conceive a bureaucratic apparatus also as a machine to produce enjoyment). How? Let us begin with the topic of fetishism. Eric Santner has described how, in a post-traditional capitalist society, the king's two bodies (his ordinary mortal body and his sublime body which materializes the state itself) are transposed onto the commodity's two bodies (its material properties which account for its use-value and its 'other sublime body' which materializes its abstract exchange-value).[11] He follows here indications by Marx who, in his *Capital*, draws a parallel between the commodity fetishism and the fetishism in interpersonal relationships (in a traditional society, the auratic properties of a king or another master-figure appears as his direct properties, although they are effectively only the effect of how other people relate to him). In both cases, the ideal pole (the king's symbolic title, the exchange-value) has to materialize itself in a body whose materiality is ethereal, spectral, like the bodies of ghosts and vampires – no spirit without spirits, as Schelling put it two centuries ago. Is this redoubling of a body, this emergence of a spectral body which supplements the ordinary material body, necessary, or can we arrive at the ideal dimension, can we make it effective, without the supplement of a spectral materiality?

But perhaps this is the wrong way to pose the question. That is to say, what a true dialectical materialist has to insist on, against vulgar materialism, is that ordinary material objects are not the starting point out of which, through a process of idealization, the spectral of another sublime body is generated; on the contrary, to arrive at ordinary material reality, something – an excess – has to be subtracted from the Real, and this Real is neither ordinary reality nor the sublime spectral reality. In the same way, the sacred is not simply generated out of the ordinary secular reality: in order for the ordinary secular reality to emerge, something has to be subtracted from it, and this subtracted excess then returns in the guise of the sacred.

Along these lines, Santner gives a new twist to Marx's labour theory of value: at its most basic, it is not about abstract value around which the prices of objects oscillate, but about glamour and glory, about the ritual value of objects. (Years ago, Lacan already reproached Marx for not taking into account, above use and exchange value, also ritual value.) The 'value' that human labour produces above the use value of its products is all that makes a product more than a mere object of utility: its glamour, its aesthetic value, its sacred value, its entire symbolic weight. In this sense, the 'value theory of labour' means that the symbolic value of an object is also not a direct property of this object but is generated by our treatment of this object.

Accordingly, the labour that produces ritual value is what is in labour more than the goal-directed activity – this labour itself is a ritualized activity which generates an enjoyment of its own. Let's take an extreme example: state bureaucracy. Franz Kafka's genius was to eroticize bureaucracy, *the* nonerotic entity if there ever was one. In Chile, when a citizen wants to identify himself to the authorities,

> the clerk on duty demands that the poor petitioner produce proof that he was born, that he isn't a criminal, that he paid his taxes, that he registered to vote, and that he's still alive, because even if he throws a tantrum to prove that he hasn't died, he is obliged to present a

'certificate of survival'. The problem has reached such proportions that the government itself has created an office to combat bureaucracy. Citizens may now complain of being shabbily treated and may file charges against incompetent officials ... on a form requiring a seal and three copies, of course.[12]

This is state bureaucracy at its most crazy. Are we aware that this is our only true contact with the divine in our secular times? What can be more 'divine' than the traumatic encounter with the bureaucracy at its craziest – when, say, a bureaucrat tells us that, legally, we don't exist? It is in such encounters that we get the glimpse of another order beyond the mere terrestrial everyday reality. Like God, bureaucracy is simultaneously all-powerful and impenetrable, capricious, omnipresent and invisible. Kafka was well aware of this deep link between bureaucracy and the divine: it is as if, in his work, Hegel's thesis on the State as the terrestrial existence of God is 'buggered', given a properly obscene twist. It is *only* in this sense that Kafka's works stage a search for the divine in our deserted secular world – more precisely, they not only search for the divine, they *find* it in state bureaucracy.

There are two memorable scenes in Terry Gilliam's *Brazil* which perfectly stage the crazy excess of bureaucratic *jouissance* perpetuating itself in its auto-circulation. After the hero's plumbing breaks down and he leaves a message to the official repair service for urgent help, Robert De Niro enters his apartment, a mythical-mysterious criminal whose subversive activity is that he listens on the emergency calls and then immediately goes to the customer, repairing his plumbing for free, bypassing the inefficient state repair service's paperwork. Indeed, in a bureaucracy caught in his vicious cycle of *jouissance*, the ultimate crime is to simply and directly do the job one is supposed to do – if a state repair service actually does its job, this is (at the level of its unconscious libidinal economy) considered an unfortunate by-product, since the bulk of its energy goes into inventing complicated administrative procedures that enable it to invent ever new obstacles and thus postpone indefinitely the work. In a second scene, we meet – in the corridors of a vast government agency – a group of people permanently running around, a leader (big shot bureaucrat) followed by a bunch of lower administrators who shout at him all the time, asking him for a specific opinion or decision, and he nervously spurts out fast, 'efficient' replies ('This is to be done by tomorrow latest!' 'Check that report!' 'No, cancel that appointment!'...). The appearance of a nervous hyperactivity is, of course, a staged performance which masks a self-indulgent nonsensical spectacle of imitating, of playing 'efficient administration'. Why do they walk around all the time? The leader, whom they follow, is obviously not on the way from one to another meeting – the meaningless fast walk around the corridors is all he does. The hero stumbles from time to time across this group, and the Kafkaesque answer is, of course, that this entire performance is here to attract his gaze, staged for his eyes only. They pretend to be busy, not to be bothered by the hero, but all their activity is here to provoke the hero into addressing a demand to the group's leader, who then snaps back nervously 'Can't you see how busy I am!' or, occasionally, does the reverse, greets the hero as if he was waiting for him for a long time, mysteriously expecting his plea.

What this example of bureaucracy makes clear is that the very ultimate failure of bureaucratic machinery is what sustains it, what makes it efficient, since this failure opens up the space for the surplus-enjoyment. At the utilitarian level, a bureaucratic apparatus works to regulate things and resolve problems: courts distribute justice, police investigates crimes, and so on. There is, however, always a surplus over this pragmatic function, a bureaucratic machine always gets caught in the vicious cycle of reproducing its own movement, creating problems in order to be able to work on them, and this circularity generates surplus-enjoyment. From the purely utilitarian standpoint, getting caught in this circular movement has to appear as a failure to do the job properly and efficiently, but it is this very failure which generates the excess of enjoyment. A true bureaucrat is busy all the time, achieving nothing, frantically turning in circles and ignoring calls to just do some simple thing that would really help people.

One can also make the same point in the terms of investiture: the proper work of bureaucracy is, among other things, to allocate individuals to job positions, to make them occupy posts for which they are effectively qualified; however, the very failure of such allocations, the fact that people feel out of place at their posts, that they have troubles with their investiture, is what opens up the space for the obscene surplus-enjoyment. If I occupy the post of a judge, the surplus-enjoyment I get from it is that I screw things up precisely while I follow the rules closely, i.e. through my very ultra-efficiency and excessive engagement.

It is at this level that we should also locate the phenomenon of *misinterpellation* elaborated by James Martel.[13] Misinterpellation works in two directions: a subject recognizes him/herself in an interpellation that wasn't even effectively enunciated but just imagined by him/her, like the fundamentalist who recognizes himself in a call of god (however, one can argue that this case is universal – does the interpellated subject generally not imagine the big Other [god, country, etc.] which addresses him/her?); and a subject recognizes him/herself in an interpellation which didn't target him, as in the well-known anecdote about how Che Guevara became minister of economy (at an inner circle meeting immediately after the victory of the revolution, Fidel asked 'Is there an economist here among you?' and Che quickly replied 'Yes!' confusing 'economist' with 'communist'). A more pertinent example here is the interpellation of individuals into subjects of human rights: when black slaves in Haiti recognized themselves as the subjects of human rights declared by the French Revolution, they of course in some sense 'missed the point' – the fact that, although universal in their form ('all men'), human rights effectively privileged white men of property; however, this very 'misreading' had explosive emancipatory consequences. This is what Hegel's Cunning of Reason is about: human rights were 'really meant' to be accepted only by white men of property, but their universal form was their truth. It was thus the first interpellation which was wrong, but the true interpellation could only actualize itself through the false one, as its secondary misreading.

This inefficiency, of course, sometimes reaches its limit and can no longer be contained through the incorporation of inherent transgressions into the system. We can effectively imagine ideology as an autopoietic system which encounters a problem when external perturbations become so strong that they can no longer be interpreted within its framework – say, the situation in Russia in early 1917 was such that it was no longer possible for the ruling ideology to integrate (or to account for in its terms) the 'external' (nondiscursive) perturbations (the costs of a war which was more and more perceived as meaningless; the dissatisfaction of peasants without land). The Bolsheviks imposed a totally different ideological frame which succeeded in integrating and accounting for these prediscursive perturbations. Hitler succeeded in a similar way in early 1930s, imposing a new ideological framework which accounted for nonideological perturbations that affected Germany at that time (economic crisis, moral disintegration, etc.). The lesson of these examples is that, although one should include into analysis external (transideological) perturbations, the crucial factor is how these perturbations will be accounted for (symbolized) by an ideological edifice. In the struggle in Germany, Hitler won over the alternate communist reading of the crisis; his victory was, of course, also a product of extra-ideological factors (the brute state force was mostly supporting him, he had much greater access to financial resources, etc.), but the crucial moment was achieving ideological hegemony.

On a subject which is not an object

Why does ooo ignore the key role of this 'totalizing' symbolic gesture, of what Lacan called 'quilting point'? For Bryant, each autopoietic system is self-enclosed in the sense that it selectively interprets external perturbations, so that the In-itself remains its inaccessible blind spot; however, in the case of subject, this structure is different, the blind spot is not simply the mark of the inaccessibility of the transcendent In-itself, but the inscription of the perceiving subject itself into reality – the hole in reality is not simply the excess of the In-itself. But is this not also the claim of ooo? Does ooo not emphasize that an organism is doubly limited: objects that affect it are inaccessible in their transcendent core, plus the very interpretative frame which constrains the approach to objects is inaccessible as such – it's not only that there are aspects of objects that I don't see, I also don't see what I don't see, that is, I am unaware of the very limit that separates what I can see from what I cannot see:

> Because information is premised on a prior distinction that allows events in the environment to take on information value, it follows that systems, in their relation to other objects, always contain *blind spots*. What we get here is a sort of object-specific transcendental illusion produced as a result of its closure. As Luhmann remarks in *Ecological Communication*, 'one could say that a system can see only what it can see. It cannot see what it cannot. Moreover, it cannot see that it cannot see this. For the system this is something concealed "behind" the horizon that, for it, has no "behind"'. If systems can only see what they can see, cannot see what they cannot see, and cannot see that they cannot see this, then this is because any relation to the world is premised on system-specific distinctions that arise from the system itself. As a consequence of this, Luhmann elsewhere remarks that, '[t]he conclusion to be drawn from this is that the connection with the reality of the external world is established by the blind spot of the cognitive operation. Reality is what one does not perceive when one perceives it. (160)

The last sentence effectively sounds like a variation on Lacan's motif of the Real as impossible – however, it is precisely this apparent proximity which enables us to draw a sharp line of distinction. In ooo, the distinction is between an object's virtual inner essence (what Harman calls its 'volcanic core') and its qualities actualized in the object's relations to other objects. Let us imagine a brand new electric shaving machine which by mistake falls into a manhole and is left there to disintegrate slowly – its potential to shave would remain a purely virtual property of the object in itself, never actualized in a relation to other objects. One can, of course, argue that such examples are weak: the property to shave did depend on the machine's relations with other objects since it was produced for that purpose. But the main point is that this division is still a division between something and something – between the relational appearing and the inaccessible 'volcanic core' of an object – so in what sense can it be said that it implies the self-withdrawal of the object, not just the withdrawal of its virtual core for other objects which interact with it? In some (very imprecise) sense, it can be said that the object's inner virtual 'volcanic core' is withdrawn from the surface of its relations to other objects, but this inner core is still fully there, not withdrawn from itself in any sense. Such self-withdrawal is only compatible with the self-division of the Freudian subject if we conceive of this latter division as the division between the surface of the conscious subject's self-awareness (what we call 'Self') and the substantial 'depth' of the subject's unconscious traumas, desires, and so forth. If there is a self-withdrawal, there has to be a Self from which its own substance is withdrawn – and one cannot in any meaningful sense call the actual relations of an object to other objects this object's Self.

How, then, are we to read the passage from Luhmann quoted by Bryant: 'the connection with the reality of the external world is established by the blind spot of the cognitive operation. Reality is what one does not perceive when one perceives it'? It can be read in the standard ooo way: reality in-itself is the inaccessible virtual core of objects, and it is in this sense the blind spot of our seeing, what we don't see in what we see. Or we can read it in a more complex Lacanian way and discern in it an additional reflexive twist: the Real is not the In-itself of objects beyond our perceptive reach, it resides *in the very 'subjective excess' which distorts our access to reality.*

The main trap to be avoided apropos of the Lacanian Real is to 'Kantianize' it, i.e. to read the Lacanian distinction between the Real and reality as a new version of Kant's distinction between the noumenal Thing-in-itself and the phenomenal reality. When, in his seminar on the *Ethics of Psychoanalysis*, Lacan dwells on the subtle difference between *Ding* and *Sache* in German,[14] he resists the obvious solution that *Ding* is a brutal raw Real outside of or preceding the Symbolic, while *Sache* is already a thing symbolized, the matter that is to be debated (this is why we talk of *die Sache des Denkens*, a 'matter of thought', not of *das Ding des Denkens*). While conceding that *die Sache* is a symbolically mediated thing, 'the work of all and everyone', not the thing-in-itself, independent of us, but the 'thing itself', what we are all struggling with, he adds that *das Ding* is (in one of its original meanings, at least) even more 'social' than *die Sache*: it names the assembly itself, the gathering of those set to debate *die Sache* – in Iceland, for example, Parliament is called *Allthing* ('the gathering of all'), in remembrance of the ancient yearly gatherings of the representatives of all groups in order to debate and make key decisions about their communal life. So we should not oppose *Ding* and *Sache* as real and symbolic, or *Ding* and *objet a* as the Real which is totally external and prior to the Symbolic (to human community) versus what remains once the symbolic universe is here (*objet a* as the remainder of the process of the symbolization of the Real), as the Real which is externally internal to the Symbolic. Consequently, we should also not oppose *das Ding* and inner-worldly things of external reality ('real things out there') as the Real radically external to the Symbolic, radically outside the scope and grasp of our unconscious desires and fantasies, and the Real which is already symbolized, structured and perceived through a network of symbolic determinations, as well as libidinally invested. For Lacan, the Real qua *das Ding* is not only definitely not the same as reality-in-itself, things out there independently of us, with no relation to us; *das Ding* is, on the contrary, a weird thing whose status is thoroughly libidinal – it is a purely fantasmatic notion of the absolute-incestuous object that would fully satisfy our desire or that would bring full *jouissance*. (This is why Lacan says that the ultimate *Ding* is mother.) In other words, *das Ding* as radically external to the Symbolic is simultaneously radically internal to it, it is a spectre of absolute Otherness generated by the distance from the Real introduced by the Symbolic. The only things 'out there' independently of us are particular material things (if we can construct how they are independently of us); *das Ding* as the absolute point of reference behind and beneath these things is precisely what the subject adds to things, its fantasmatic projection/construction.

Hegel distinguishes between reality and actuality (*Wirklichkeit*): reality is contingent external reality, not fully rational, while actuality is a reality which actualizes a notion, a reality in which the inner necessity of Reason transpires. Say, a barbaric state in which lawless violence reigns is part of reality, but it is not actual, it does not actualize the Idea of a state (it is in this sense that, for Hegel, actual is rational and vice versa). From the Lacanian standpoint, we should introduce here another difference, the one between actuality and the Real, not reality: actuality is a reality which actualizes a notional possibility, reality at the level of its Notion, while the Real is (1) virtual: it is not part of reality but a kind of inexistent point of reference with no place in reality which, in its absence, structures reality. Let us take an attractor in mathematics: all positive lines or points in its sphere of attraction only approach it in an endless fashion, never reaching its form – the existence of this form is purely virtual, being nothing more than the shape towards which lines and points tend. However, precisely as such, the virtual is the Real of this field: the immovable focal point around which all elements circulate. (2) An obstacle to the actualization of the potentials of an entity, an X which prevents this actualization. Say, the Real is that which prevents a man from being fully a man, it is the class struggle which prevents a society from becoming a harmonious Whole, it is the sexual antagonism which prevents sexual difference from becoming a duality of masculine and feminine principles. (3) Finally, it is a contingent meaningless fact not grounded in any preceding notional possibility, like the explosion 'out of nowhere' of passionate love. These paradoxical properties which cannot but appear incompatible originate in the fact that the Lacanian Real is the 'impossible' point of the coincidence of opposites: the Real is the In-itself external to (symbolized) reality, but it is simultaneously the obstacle that makes the In-itself inaccessible; it is the excess of content over form (recall Plato's question if pieces of our reality like dust and excrements also are what they are through participating in their Idea) AND the excess of form over content (a pure form which cannot be actualized in any content).

So, again, why does ooo ignore this reflexive twist? According to the flat ontology proposed by Bryant, all objects are situated on the same plane, possessing the same reality; however, language and a process in material reality are not at the same level, there is no point of direct contact between the two – while language 'mirrors' the entire reality, it is constrained by its own horizon, by what is visible from within this horizon, so that when we are inside, we don't see this limitation, we don't see the outside. But does this not hold for every object, does not every object perceive (relate to) its environs in a selective way, from within a constraining frame? So where resides the misunderstanding of ooo's critique of Lacan, of Lacan's alleged unjustified privileging of the symbolic as the ultimate generator and horizon of our experience of reality?

To put it succinctly, ooo reads the privilege of the symbolic asserted by Lacan as a form of transcendental exception: everything in language comes from contingent empirical sources – everything except the form of language itself. There are good reasons to read Lacan in this way. Lacan fully assumes the fact that every language is embedded in a particular lifeworld and is as such traversed by its traces: language is not a neutral transcendental frame of reality, it is fully penetrated or distorted by contingent historical forces, antagonisms, desires, which forever twist and pervert its purity. (Lacan's name for language distorted/twisted/traversed by the pathology of historical contingency is *lalangue*, 'llanguage'.) Recall

Walter Benjamin's essay 'On Language in General and Human Language in Particular', in which the point is not that human language is a species of some universal language 'as such' which also comprises other species: there is no actually existing language other than human language – but, in order to comprehend this 'particular' language, one *has* to introduce a minimal difference, conceiving it with regard to the gap which separates it from language 'as such'. The particular language is thus the 'really existing language', language as the series of actually uttered statements, in contrast to the formal linguistic structure. This Benjaminian lesson is missed by Habermas, who does precisely what one should *not* do – he posits the ideal 'language in general' (pragmatic universals) *directly* as the norm of the actually existing language. Along the lines of Benjamin's title, we should describe the basic constellation of the social law as that of the 'Law in general and its obscene superego underside in particular'. The 'Part' as such is thus the 'sinful' unredeemed and unredeemable aspect of the Universal – in concrete political terms, every politics that grounds itself in a reference to some substantial (ethnic, religious, sexual, lifestyle, etc.) particularity is by definition reactionary.

This, however, is not all – and we should give to this 'not all' all the weight of the Lacanian *pas-tout*. The fact that not-all of language is traversed by social antagonisms, scarred by traces of social pathology, does not mean that there is an exception, an aspect of language (in this case, its form) which cannot be reduced to social reality and its antagonisms since it provides the a priori frame through which we relate to reality. It is precisely because there is nothing which escapes social mediation that not-all of language is socially mediated: *what escapes social mediation is not something exempted from it but the metatranscendental social mediation of the very linguistic frame through which we perceive and relate to reality.* When we conceive language as a mirror which is always-already distorted/traversed by the pathology of social antagonisms, we ignore *the way this mirror is itself included into reality as a mode of its distortion.* Language is not only traversed by antagonisms/traumas – the supreme trauma is that of language itself, of how language brutally destabilizes the real. The same goes for the individual's relation to language: we usually take a subject's speech with all its inconsistencies as an expression of his/her inner turmoil, ambiguous emotions, and so on; this holds even for a literary work of art: the task of psychoanalytic reading is supposed to be to unearth the inner psychic turmoil which found its coded expression in the work of art. Something is missing in such a classic account: speech does not only register or express a traumatic psychic life; the entry into speech is in itself a traumatic fact ('symbolic castration'). What this means is that we should include in the list of traumas that speech tries to cope with the traumatic impact of speech itself. The relationship between psychic turmoil and its expression in speech should thus also be turned around: speech does not simply express or articulate psychic turmoil; at a certain key point, psychic turmoil itself is a reaction to the trauma of dwelling in the 'torture-house of language'.

It is in this sense that not-all of language is traversed by social antagonisms: language is not only a medium exposed to social (and sexual and …) antagonisms, one has to include the way language itself is antagonistic in its very form; this supplement makes the totality not-all, inconsistent. Or, to put it another way: one cannot include language into reality since what appears to us as reality is already transcendentally constituted through a horizon of meaning sustained by language. We have to introduce here the distinction between the transcendentally constituted phenomenal reality and the Real: the way to be a consequent materialist is not to directly include subject into reality, as an object among objects, but to bring out the Real of the subject, the way the emergence of subjectivity functions as a cut in the Real.

Resistance, stasis, repetition

How to do this? The key is provided by the properly speculative ambiguity of *resistance* deployed by Rebecca Comay: to resist means to revolt against the established order, to open it up, to demand change (as in the French *Résistance* against the German occupation or the Leftist celebration of 'sites of resistance'), but it can also designate the conservative attitude of resisting change and progress, the power of inertia (as with the conservative Catholics who resist abortion and gay marriages). This ambiguity is at work in the very heart of the Freudian notion of resistance (*Widerstand*): resistance is not only the force that opposes the progress of the analytic treatment (unconscious desires resist their public disclosure, symptoms keep back their meaning), it can also stand for that which resists the oppressive socio-ethical order and strives for liberation (a classical case: through a hysterical symptom, a subject expresses its resistance to the normative structure that prohibits it from indulging in obscene sexual desires). The point is, of course, that one cannot resolve this ambiguity by way of imposing a distinction between the two meanings of the term – the ambiguity is immanent, the two meanings are connected. Resistance to the analytic treatment is not just an obstacle, it simultaneously opens up the way to access the Unconscious. Every analysis is thus ultimately an analysis of resistances: when the patient resists in any way to some suggestion of the analyst, this indicates that a sensitive point was disturbed. Or, as Lacan put it succinctly, repression and the return of the repressed are the two sides of the same phenomenon.

Such a coincidence of the opposites is brought to its self-reference in the notion of *stasis*: stasis designates stability, immobility, opposition to change, but simultaneously change, the disturbance of established order of things, by excessive fixation, sticking out. Imagine a habitual flow of things, the circle of life, of generation and destruction – and then something weird happens, not something new but just a kind of fixation. Instead of continuous circulation which guarantees global stability, the fixation on a particular element (an idiosyncratic object of passion) derails the stability of the whole process. Drive is the Freudian name for such a fixation: a repetitive stuckness which interrupts the regular flow of things. Maybe this is also how we should read Benjamin's *Dialektik im Stillstand*: not as a cancellation of the dialectical movement, but as a stasis which undermines the fragile balance of the totality in question. Is such a *Dialektik im Stillstand* not needed in today's global-capitalist society whose monotonous dynamics can only be interrupted by some kind of obstinate stasis?

And this brings us back to Hegel: is his example of such a 'stuckness' not Judaism? Instead of changing in accordance with the spirit of time, instead of participating in historical progress, Jews stubbornly remained stuck at a particular state of religious development, ridiculously clinging to their arbitrary rituals and rules, and rejecting freedom that comes with Christianity. But are things as simple as that? Is Hegel just playing the old anti-Semitic card? Is the Jewish 'stuckness' not for Hegel a condition of the Christian event? And is the Christian event not the case of an even more extreme stuckness – of the fixation to a singular person as a living god?

Another aspect of this ambiguity of stasis is the parallel between the two extremes that characterize psychoanalytic interpretation as well as dialectical analysis. Dialectical thinking oscillates between the two extremes of mechanical application of triadic formulas (there is no surprise, the result is clear in advance) and of chaotic improvisation (the process becomes confused, it is not clear in what way Hegel will improvise the way out of a deadlock). The Freudian interpretation also oscillates between the two extremes of the mechanical imposition of the standard Freudian clichés (Oedipus complex, etc.) which makes it clear in advance how the interpretation will proceed, and the 'infinite analysis', the endless process of discovering ever new unconscious links; the interpretation is thus simultaneously always-already finished (we know in advance its final point) and forever caught in the infinite maze of arbitrary links:

you can't terminate: either you never get there or you've always already gotten there, and in any case the very fantasy of the 'there' will prove to have been the ultimate impediment to reaching it. This brings us to the central paradox of psychoanalysis, which also happens to be the essential paradox of the dialectic and part of its ongoing provocation. On the one hand, resistance is the fundamental obstacle to analysis. With their incessant digressions, diversions, and prevarications, the resistances to analysis are always on the verge of derailing it forever. On the other hand, without resistance, without delay, there would be nothing but 'wild analysis' – which is to say there would be no analysis at all, only the shadow cast by the all-knowing authority of the analyst or even by analysis itself qua personified subject-supposed-to-know. Any truth that presents itself immediately, without impediment, is itself an impediment – an empty abstraction, a fetish of pure meaning marooned from history, a blind bit of theory thrust upon the analysand with no means of mobilizing it. Meaning must be postponed in order to be articulated: judgment must be deferred; every decision about truth, value, or signification must be suspended.[15]

In psychoanalysis as well as in a dialectical process, the rule is thus that there is no 'normal' progress, no proper measure between the two extremes of precipitation towards a premature conclusion and endless wandering in a maze. Impediment, inertia, blind repetitions, meaningless fixations, and so forth are simultaneously superfluous and necessary. One of the eternal reproaches to Hegel is that, in his thought, every antagonism is always automatically radicalized and thereby resolved – but what if things simply remain stuck, caught in inertia? The reply is that, far from being an embarrassing failure of the dialectical process, this happens all the time in it – from the very beginning of Hegel's logic. That is to say, how do we get ('pass') from Being to Nothing? Being gets stuck unto itself, no passage occurs to plurality of entities, and this very stuckness of pure Being makes it a figure of nothing. The same goes for phrenology (the development stuck in a dead bone), revolutionary Terror (the process caught in a self-destructive vortex), etc. In short, the solution is not to oscillate between the two extremes but to isolate the point of the coincidence of the opposites: the point at which a sudden radical closure is the only way to keep the horizon truly open against false evolutionary openness (this is what Hegel aims at in his Absolute Knowing), as well as the point at which the sudden closure emerges as the 'truth' of the endless openness itself. This brings us back to the 'peculiar speculative compulsion to repeat'[16] which plays a key role in the constitution of a speculative judgement. What makes a judgement a speculative one is not directly its objective properties but the way a subject reads it: one tries to pass through it as we usually do it, just smoothly following its meaning, but then we get stuck, things do not hold together, the text resists our comprehension, so we have to return to the beginning and read the sentence again, in a different way. There is no direct way to read correctly such a judgement since *la vérité surgit de la méprise*, the true meaning emerges only through our – the reader's – reaction to the first reading. Therein resides the paradox of a speculative judgement: the most subtle meaning can only emerge through interruption, inhibition, through our experience of 'something not working':

> interruption is what generates repetition, it is its cause, it causes a return to the sentence itself. This is also why Hegel speaks [in his 1817 Heidelberg lectures on logic] of 'experience', for experience is clearly linked to interruption, to resistance, so to speak. Experience is always experience of something not working, of something that inhibits the usual flow of things, and hence of resistance ... The speculative sentence resists. It resists common ways of thought and this resistance is its first crucial characteristic ... Resistance is necessary and impossible at the same time (and recall this is the defining characteristic of what Lacan calls the Real).

In what, more closely, does this failure consist? At its most basic, it concerns the relationship between subject and predicate of the speculative judgement. Let us take Hegel's 'infinite judgement' *Der Geist ist ein Knochen* (Spirit is a bone) from the subchapter on phrenology in his *Phenomenology* – how should we read it is a speculative judgement? The first, immediate, reading reduces it to the most vulgar version of materialist reductionism: what is our most noble part, our spiritual essence, is conditioned by the shape of our skull – of a bone which is the most mechanical and 'dead' part of our body. (Today's more popular version of such reductionist 'infinite judgement' is 'The Spirit is a genome'.)[17] Such a claim stops the flow, it gets us into a deadlock, it doesn't make any sense – isn't there a radical opposition, contradiction even, between Spirit (the most subtle dynamics of meaning) and a bone (the immobile piece of dead matter)? What the reader has to realize in the second reading is that *this contradiction, this unbearable tension, is the subject, the disparity or negativity that forms the core of a subject*. The subject emerges as the point of resistance to its objectivization. It is in this sense that the very basic idealist proposition 'Subject is an object' should be read as a speculative judgement: its truth is not that Subject is a kind of absolute Substance which grounds/

constitutes every objectivity, but that 'subject' is the very clash/disparity between subject and object made sensible by their identification – or, more precisely, what exists are only objects, and 'subject' is nothing but the extreme non-coincidence of the object with itself. So what do we gain by formulating the proposition in this twisted way instead of directly saying 'subject is not an object'? If we say it directly, we posit subject as another substantial entity apart from 'ordinary' objects – what gets lost is the fact that 'subject' is nothing but the non-coincidence of an object with itself. This is how one should understand Hegel's claim that, in a speculative judgement,

> the general nature of the judgment or proposition, which involves the distinction of Subject and Predicate, is destroyed by the speculative proposition, and the proposition of identity which the former becomes contains the counter-thrust [recoil: *Gegenstoß*] against that subject-predicate relationship.[18]

This paradox of absolute recoil – the recoil which retroactively creates what it recoils from – accounts for the key ingredient of Freud's theory, the 'labour theory of the unconscious',[19] which should be conceived in parallel with the 'labour theory of value': the unconscious 'value' of a dream is exclusively the product of 'dream-work', not of the dream-thoughts on which dream-work exercises its transformative activity, in the same way that the value of a commodity is the product of the work spent on it. The paradox here is that it is the very cyphering/obfuscation of the dream-thought, its translation into the dream texture, that engenders the properly unconscious content of a dream. Freud emphasizes that the true secret of the dream is not its content (the 'dream-thoughts'), but the form itself:

> The latent dream-thoughts are the material which the dream-work transforms into the manifest dream … The only essential thing about dreams is the dream-work that has influenced the thought-material … Analytic observation shows further that the dream-work never restricts itself to translating these thoughts into the archaic or regressive mode of expression that is familiar to you. In addition, it regularly takes possession of something else, which is not part of the latent thoughts of the previous day, but which is the true motive force for the construction of the dream. This indispensable addition is the equally unconscious wish for the fulfillment of which the content of the dream is given its new form. A dream may thus be any sort of thing in so far as you are only taking into account the thoughts it represents – a warning, an

intention, a preparation, and so on; but it is always also the fulfillment of an unconscious wish and, if you are considering it as a product of the dream-work, it is only that. A dream is therefore never simply an intention, or a warning, but always an intention, etc., translated into the archaic mode of thought by the help of an unconscious wish and transformed to fulfill that wish. The one characteristic, the wish-fulfillment, is the invariable one; the other may vary. It may for its part once more be a wish, in which case the dream will, with the help of an unconscious wish, represent as fulfilled a latent wish of the previous day.[20]

The key insight is, of course, the 'triangulation' of latent dream-thought, manifest dream-content, and the unconscious wish, which limits the scope of – or, rather, directly undermines – the hermeneutic model of the interpretation of dreams (the path from the manifest dream-content to its hidden meaning, the latent dream-thought), which travels in the opposite direction to the path of the formation of a dream (the transposition of the latent dream-thought into the manifest dream-content by the dream-work). The paradox is that this dream-work is not merely a process of masking the dream's 'true message': the dream's true core, its unconscious wish, inscribes itself only through this process of masking, so that the moment we retranslate the dream-content back into the dream-thought expressed in it, we lose the 'true motive force' of the dream – in short, it is the process of masking itself which inscribes into the dream its true secret. One should therefore reverse the standard notion of penetrating deeper and deeper into the core of the dream: it is not that we first move from the manifest dream-content to the first-level secret, the latent dream-thought, and then, taking a step further, go even deeper, to the dream's unconscious core, the unconscious wish. The 'deeper' wish is located in the very gap between the latent dream-thought and the manifest dream-content. It is only this 'labour theory of the unconscious' that enables us to read correctly Freud's comparison of the dream-work with the capitalist production process. In order to explain the distinction between the (conscious) wish encoded in a dream and the dream's unconscious desire, Freud compares the wish to the contractor (manager, entrepreneur) and the unconscious desire to the capital that finances (covers the libidinal expenses of) the translation of this wish into a dream:

> To speak figuratively, it is quite possible that a day thought plays the part of the contractor (*entrepreneur*) in the dream. But it is known that no matter what idea the contractor may have in mind, and how desirous he may be of putting it into operation, he can do nothing without capital;

he must depend upon a capitalist to defray the necessary expenses, and this capitalist, who supplies the psychic expenditure for the dream is invariably and indisputably *a wish from the unconscious*, no matter what the nature of the waking thought may be.[21]

In a superficial reading, it may appear that the work proper (dream-work) is just a mediator between the conscious wish and the unconscious capital: the contractor (conscious wish) borrows from the unconscious the capital to finance its translation into the dream-language. Here, however, we have to take into account Freud's insistence on how the unconscious desire 'infects' the dream only through the dream-work: the exclusive source of the unconscious desire is the work of encoding/masking of the dream-thoughts, it does not have a substantial being outside this work.

Speculative judgement

The paradox of 'absolute recoil' thus provides the formal structure of a subject: (the X that will have been) a subject endeavours to represent itself in a signifier, the representation fails, and the subject *is* this failure (of its own representation). To put it another way, a subject endeavours to subjectivize/symbolize (integrate into its universe of meaning) a certain reality, but there is always some remainder that resists subjectivization/symbolization, and the subject is strictly correlative to this nonsymbolized remainder (called by Lacan *objet petit a*). Subject is thus again the outcome of the failure of subjectivization. And a similar paradox holds for language: subject is a distortion of language, what prevents language from neutrally mirroring reality, what disturbs the symmetry of a symbolic edifice and inscribes into it a pathological partiality. (The subject's inscription occurs in S_1, the Master Signifier which represents the subject for other signifiers. This is why, according to Lacan, the discourse of science which endeavours to be 'objective' relies on the foreclosure of the subject.) However, if we subtract this subjective distortion of language we lose language itself: language exists only as distorted, curtailed, thwarted by its own impossibility.

From here, we can get an approximate idea on how a speculative judgement works: thinking 'awaits a predicate, which is assigned to a subject, but in the predicate it encounters the substance of the predicate. Thereby the subject is no longer what it assumed it is and the same goes as much for the predicate as well as for their relation.' Back to 'Spirit is a bone': after the beginning ('Spirit is …') the reader awaits a predicate that will be assigned to Spirit and will thereby determine it; but the predicate is so overwhelming and weird that it seems to annihilate the subject. 'Bone' (which stands here for inert materiality) doesn't function as a predicate but becomes a substance of its own which leaves no place for subject – or, to quote Hegel:

> Starting from the Subject as though this were a permanent ground, it finds that, since the Predicate is really the Substance, the Subject has passed over into the Predicate, and, by this very fact, has been sublated; and, since in this way what seems to be the Predicate has become the whole and the independent mass, thinking cannot roam at will, but is impeded by this weight.[22]

So how do we get out of this deadlock? How does 'the subject reappear in the predicate'? Here is Ruda's concise formulation: the reader 'is thrown back into the subject, which changed its nature, namely it lost the very stable substance picture-thinking attributed to it, and it is precisely this loss of substance (i.e. an empty subject) that reappears in the predicate'. In short, the subject reappears in the guise of utter 'contradiction', negativity – which means that the reader has to leave behind the notion of Spirit as a 'stable substance' and recognize the subject as that which 'bounces back' from the material substance (bone) as its void, its negative core. The Spirit with which we began was a full and stable spiritual Substance; the Spirit that re-emerges is the pure 'spirit of contradiction', the evanescent point of self-relating negativity, the void in/of Substance.

Speculative judgement thus involves the experience of a loss – but with a twist. From a properly dialectical perspective, what is lost in the experience of a loss (the loss of something substantial) is ultimately *loss itself*, its true self-relating nature: the object that we experience as lost fills in the gap of the loss. There is thus a kind of temporal reversal at work in the experience of a loss: it appears as if what is lost precedes the loss, while effectively the loss comes first and every object that is experienced as lost is a retroactive formation which fills in the gap opened up by the loss. In other words, what is obfuscated in the experience of a loss is that a loss is always the loss of a loss: to arrive at the most radical dimension of loss, we should lose the lost object itself.

The struggle for black emancipation in the United States is a perfect example of such a loss, especially Malcolm X's change of position in 1964, a singular ethico-political achievement. While in prison, the young Malcolm joined the Nation of Islam, and, after his parole in 1952, he engaged in its struggle, advocating black supremacy and the separation of white and black Americans – for him, 'integration' was a fake attempt of the black to become like the white. However, in 1964, he rejected the Nation of Islam and, while continuing to emphasize black self-determination and self-defence, he distanced himself from every form of racism, advocating emancipatory universality; as a consequence of this 'betrayal', he was killed by three Nation of Islam members in February 1965. When Malcolm adopted 'X' as his family name, thereby signalling that the slave traders who brought the enslaved Africans from their homeland brutally deprived them of their family and ethnic roots, of their entire cultural lifeworld, the point of this gesture was not to mobilize the blacks to fight for the return to some primordial African roots, but precisely to seize the opening provided by X, an unknown new (lack of) identity engendered by the very process of slavery which made the African roots forever lost. The idea is that this X which deprives the blacks of their particular tradition offers a unique chance to redefine (reinvent) themselves, to freely form a new identity much more universal than white people's professed universality. Although Malcolm X found this new identity in the universalism of Islam, he was killed by Muslim fundamentalists.

Therein resides the hard choice to be made: yes, blacks are marginalized, exploited, humiliated, mocked, also feared, at the level of everyday practices; yes, they experience daily the hypocrisy of liberal freedoms and human rights; but in the same movement they experience the promise of true freedom with regard to which the existing freedom is false – it is *this* freedom that fundamentalists escape. The true loss is thus not the loss of authentic African roots, but the loss of this loss itself: when a black African is enslaved and torn out of his roots, he in a way not only loses these roots but retroactively realizes that he never really fully had these roots: what he, after this loss, experiences as his roots is a retroactive fantasy, a projection filling in the void. And the same holds for human rights: yes, one can convincingly demonstrate the particular content that gives the specific ideological spin to the notion of human rights; yes, universal human rights are effectively the rights of white male property owners to exchange freely on the market, exploit workers and women, as well as exert political domination. However, this is only half of the story: when we experience the gap between the false universality of human rights and the particular injustices this universal form justifies, this gap should not push us to renounce human rights and freedoms as a fake, but to begin to struggle for their content. Is the entire struggle for human rights not also the struggle for this content? First, women (beginning with Mary Wollstonecraft) demanded the same rights, then the slaves in Haiti did it in the first successful black uprising (for which they are punished even today), and so forth.

The basic form of an ideological process is thus not that of the gradual corruption of an authentic beginning but, on the contrary, the gradual becoming-true of a fake beginning. This is why the 'hypocrisy' argument has a very limited scope: after we establish that the Western freedom-and-equality is a fake which covers up the reality of exploitation and domination, the right way to proceed is not to reject freedom-and-equality as such, to dismiss it as a mere hypocritical mask of domination, but to struggle for what freedom-and-equality means, to fill it with a new content. If we just dismiss the universal form, we end up in Stalinist communism which, after denouncing Western freedoms as false, 'merely formal', abolished freedom as such, or in the weird stance of Jacques Verges who, after his bitter experience of how democratic France treated the Algerians, ended up defending neo-Nazis and Pol Pot. Hegel articulated this paradox clearly apropos of self-consciousness (the thinking subject) as formally evil:

> Abstractly, being evil means singularizing myself in a way that cuts me off from the universal (which is the rational, the laws, the determinations of spirit). But along with this separation there arises being-for-self and for the first time the universally spiritual, laws – what ought to be. So it is not the case that [rational] consideration has an external relationship to evil: it is itself what is evil.[23]

Does the Bible not say exactly the same thing? The serpent promises Adam and Eve that, by eating the fruit of the tree of knowledge, *they* will become like God; and *after the two do it*, God says: 'Behold, Adam has become like one of us' (Gen. 3.22). Hegel's comment is: 'So the serpent did not lie, for God confirms what it said.' Then he goes on to reject the claim that what God says is meant with irony: 'Cognition is the principle of spirituality, and this ... is also the principle by which the injury of the separation is healed. It is in this principle of cognition that the principle of "divinity" is also posited.'[24] Subjective knowledge is not just the possibility to choose evil or good, 'it is the consideration or the cognition that *makes* people evil, so that consideration and cognition [themselves] are what is evil, and that [therefore] such cognition is what ought not to exist [because it] is the *source* of evil'.[25] This is how one should understand Hegel's dictum from his *Phenomenology* that Evil is the gaze itself which perceives Evil everywhere around it: the gaze which sees Evil excludes itself from the social Whole it criticizes, and this exclusion is the formal characteristic of Evil. And Hegel's point is that the Good emerges as a possibility and a duty only through this primordial or constitutive choice of Evil: we experience the Good when, after choosing Evil, we become aware of the utter inadequacy of our situation. Here, also, the Fall itself creates the notion of the state from which it is a fall.

We should thus reject the Gnostic view according to which Evil pertains to matter as such; from the Gnostic standpoint, the Fall is, at its most basic, the 'transition from the insubstantial to the substance', as Thomas Mann put it in the well-known passage from *The Magic Mountain*:

And life? Life itself? Was it perhaps only an infection, a sickening of matter? Was that which one might call the original procreation of matter only a disease, a growth produced by morbid stimulation of the immaterial? The first step toward evil, toward desire and death, was taken precisely then, when there took place that first increase in the density of the spiritual, that pathologically luxuriant morbid growth, produced by the irritant of some unknown infiltration; this, in part pleasurable, in part a motion of self-defense, was the primeval stage of matter, the transition from the insubstantial to the substance. This was the Fall.[26]

One should be more precise here: matter as such is not evil, it is just stupid – a meaningless, mute persistence out there in space; life as such is also not evil, although it is more and more (the more it progresses towards higher forms of self-organization) a cycle of brutal struggle, suffering, and pain. Evil arises when Spirit withdraws itself from matter, from its positive inertia, and posits itself for-itself, as a self-relating negativity, in the singularity of self-awareness (as pure self-consciousness, I am just a *cogito*, the empty form of self-relating at a distance from all positive content). Evil is purely spiritual: in nature, being condenses itself into the dense inertia of matter; Spirit comes to exist by way of condensing itself into the punctuality of a Self at a distance from nature, and is as such the very opposite of the 'transition from the insubstantial to the substance' – it is the emergence of the insubstantial Void in the midst of substantial nature.

And this, finally, brings us back to our starting point: the relationship between subject and substance. Subject is not a substance which withdraws/appears; subject is appearance (appearing-to-itself) which autonomizes itself and becomes an agent against its own substantiality. The subject's self-withdrawal or split is thus much more radical than the self-withdrawal of every object split between its appearance (in interaction with other objects) and its substantial content, its withdrawn In-itself: subject is not just split like every object between its phenomenal qualities (actualizations) and its inaccessible virtual In-itself; subject is divided between its appearance and the void in the core of its being, not between appearance and its hidden substantial ground. It is only against this background that one can understand in what sense subject effectively 'is' an object – this, then, is the Lacanian answer to the object-oriented ontology: yes, subject is also an object, but which object? The object that subject 'is' is what Lacan calls *objet a*, a strange object which is not only lacking, never fully here, always eluding the subject, but is in itself nothing but the embodiment of a lack. That is to say, since subject is the self-appearing of nothing, its 'objective correlate' can only be a weird object whose nature is to be the embodiment of nothing, an 'impossible' object, an object the entire being of which is an embodiment of its own impossibility, the object called by Lacan *objet a*, an object whose status is that of an anamorphosis: a part of the picture which, when we look at the picture in a direct frontal way, appears as a meaningless stain, but acquires the contours of a known object when we change our position and look at the picture from the side. Lacan's point is even more radical: the object-cause of desire is something that, when viewed frontally, is nothing at all, just a void – it acquires the contours of something only when viewed sideways. The most beautiful case of it in literature occurs when, in Shakespeare's *Richard II*, Bushy tries to comfort the Queen, worried about the unfortunate King on a military campaign:

> Each substance of a grief hath twenty shadows,
> Which shows like grief itself, but is not so;
> For sorrow's eye, glazed with blinding tears,
> Divides one thing entire to many objects;
> Like perspectives, which rightly gazed upon
> Show nothing but confusion, eyed awry
> Distinguish form: so your sweet majesty,
> Looking awry upon your lord's departure,
> Find shapes of grief, more than himself, to wail;
> Which, look'd on as it is, is nought but shadows
> Of what it is not.

This is *objet a*: an entity that has no substantial consistency, which is in itself 'nothing but confusion', and which acquires a definite shape only when looked upon from a standpoint distorted by the subject's desires and fears – as such, as a mere 'shadow of what it is not'. As such, *objet a* is the strange object which is nothing but the inscription of the subject itself into the field of objects, in the guise of a stain which acquires form only when part of this field is anamorphically distorted by the subject's desire. The extraordinarily modern definition of poetry from *A Midsummer Night's Dream*, act 5, scene 1, points in the same direction:

The lunatic, the lover and the poet
Are of imagination all compact:
One sees more devils than vast hell can hold,
That is, the madman: the lover, all as frantic,
Sees Helen's beauty in a brow of Egypt:
The poet's eye, in fine frenzy rolling,
Doth glance from heaven to earth, from earth to heaven;
And as imagination bodies forth
The forms of things unknown, the poet's pen
Turns them to shapes and gives to airy nothing
A local habitation and a name.

Indeed, as Mallarmé put it centuries later, poetry talks about '*ce seul objet dont le Néant s'honore*'. Shakespeare deploys here a triad: a madman sees devils everywhere (misperceives a bush as a bear); a lover sees sublime beauty in an ordinary face; a poet 'gives to airy nothing a local habitation and a name'. In all three cases we have the gap between ordinary reality and a transcendent ethereal dimension, but this gap is gradually reduced: the madman simply misperceives a real object as something else, not seeing it as what it is (a bush is perceived as a threatening bear); a lover maintains the reality of the beloved object, which is not cancelled, but merely 'transubstantiated' into the appearance of a sublime dimension (the beloved's ordinary face is perceived as it is, but it is *as such* elevated – I see beauty *in* it, as it is); with a poet, transcendence is reduced to zero, i.e. empirical reality is 'transubstantiated' (not into an expression/ materialization of some higher reality, but) into a materialization of *nothing*. A madman directly *sees* God, he mistakes a person for God (or Devil); a lover sees God (divine beauty) *in* a person; a poet only sees a person against the background of Nothingness.

How is such an entity which functions as the appearance of nothing to itself possible? The answer is clear: such a nonsubstantial entity has to be purely relational, with no positive support of its own. What happens in the passage from substance to subject is thus a kind of reflective reversal: we pass from the secret core of an object inaccessible to other objects to *inaccessibility as such* – $ is nothing but its own inaccessibility, its own failure to be substance. Therein resides Lacan's achievement: the standard psychoanalytic theory conceives the Unconscious as a psychic substance of subjectivity (the notorious hidden part of the iceberg) – all the depth of desires, fantasies, traumas, etc. – while Lacan *de-substantializes the Unconscious* (for him, the Cartesian *cogito* is the Freudian subject), thereby bringing psychoanalysis to the level of modern subjectivity. (It is here that we should bear in mind the difference between the Freudian Unconscious and the 'unconscious' neurological brain processes: the latter do form the subject's natural 'substance', i.e. subject only exists insofar as it is sustained by its biological substance; however, this substance is not subject.)

Subject is not somehow more actant than objects, a mega-actant actively positing all the world of fundamentally passive objects, so that against this hubris one should assert the active role of all objects. Subject is at its most fundamental a certain gesture of passivization, of not-doing, of withdrawal, of passive experience. Subject is '*ce qui du réel pâtit du signifiant*' (Lacan), its activity is a reaction to this basic feature. So it is not that ooo does take into account subjectivity, merely reducing it to a property or quality of one among other objects: what ooo describes as subject simply does not meet the criteria of subject – *there is no place for subject in ooo*.

Subject does not stand for active intervention, it is not an agent that shapes, exploits, dominates objects. All the varieties of the calls to intervene, to engage, to change things already presuppose a withdrawal, as if I am somehow at a distance from reality, which is why I have to be solicited to reach out and engage in it; and this presupposed distance *is* the subject at its purest – the zero-level stance of a subject is Bartleby's *I would prefer not to*. Along these lines, Aaron Schuster argues that 'the profound desire of the id is to sleep, and it's the superego that constantly harasses and presses for frenetic activity': 'psychic life is not a spontaneous *energeia* but is sustained by a normative pressure. Living is a duty, the most basic imperative of all imperatives, implied and transmitted in the chain of signifiers whose nature is imperative.'[27] In short, it is not 'natural' for a human being to go on living: living is a habit that has to be learned, the continuation of life can only take place under the annoying pressure of the superego. Subject is like the lethargic woman in David Lynch's films: she has to be awakened from her immobile inertia through brutal shocks from the outside. Death drive is here no longer another name for immortality, the compulsion-to-repeat which insists beyond life and death, but quite literally the subject's spontaneous tendency towards permanent immobility.

The standard thesis of the so-called philosophy of practice is that we are always-already, constitutively, immersed into a life-form, that our thought is always-already 'practical', rooted in social practice, that even the most contemplative thought arises out of some deadlock of our life-form – and yet we are continuously solicited to engage. Here we encounter a reversal of the standard paradox of the prohibition of the impossible: the injunction to do what is already in itself necessary and unavoidable. The presupposition of this paradox is that there is a distance, an exemption, in the very heart of engaged being-in-the-world; Rowan Williams called this exemption the basic dislocation, out-of-jointness, of our existence.

Here we encounter the mistake of Althusser and others who reduce subject to the imaginary illusion of self-recognition – the idea is that 'subject' is an effect of imaginary mis-recognition, of a short circuit which gives rise to the illusory self-experience as a free autonomous agent, obfuscating the complex presubjective (neuronal or discursive) processes which generate this illusion. The task of the theory of subjectivity is then to describe these processes, as well as to outline how one can break out of the imaginary circle of subjectivity and confront the presubjective process of subjectivization. The Hegelian (and Lacanian) counterargument here is that 'subjectivization' (the formation of the subjective space of meaning) effectively is grounded in a closure of the circle of self-recognition, that is, in an imaginary obfuscation of a traumatic Real, of the wound of antagonism; however, this 'wound', this trauma, this cut in/of the real, is *the subject itself at its zero-level*, so that, to paraphrase the famous line from Wagner's *Parsifal, the subject is itself the wound it tries to heal* (note that Hegel says the same about spirit). This 'absolute contradiction', this radical coincidence of the opposites – the 'wound of nature', the loss of 'organic unity', *and* simultaneously the very activity to heal this wound by way of constructing a universe of meaning; the production of sense with a traumatic core of nonsense; the point of absolute singularity (of the 'I' excluding all substantial content) in which universality comes to itself, is 'posited' as such – is what defines and constitutes subjectivity. One of Hegel's names for this abyss of subjectivity that he takes from the mystic tradition is the 'night of the world', the withdrawal of the Self from the world of entities into the void that 'is' the core of the Self, and it is crucial to notice how in this gesture of self-withdrawal (in clinical terms, the disintegration of all 'world', of all universe of meaning), extreme closure and extreme openness, extreme passivity and extreme activity, overlap. In the 'night of the world', extreme self-withdrawal, cutting of the links with reality around us, overlaps with our extreme openness to reality: we drop all symbolic screens which filter our access to reality, all protective shields, and we risk a kind of total exposure to the disgust of the Real. As to its content, it is a position of radical passivity (of a Kantian transcendental subject suspending its constitution of reality), but as to its form, it is a position of radical activity, of violently tearing oneself out of the immersion into reality: I am utterly passive, but my passive position is grounded in my withdrawal from reality, in a gesture of extreme negativity.

It is in this sense that the 'democracy of objects' in which subjects are conceived as one among the objects-actants obfuscates the Real of subjects, the cut that *is* the Real. And the crucial point to be noted here is that every direct access to 'subjectless objects' which ignores or bypasses this cut or wound that 'is' the subject already has to rely on transcendental constitution: what it describes as a pluriverse of actants is formed by a certain transcendental vision of reality. In other words, the problem with subjectless objects is not that they are too objective, neglecting the role of subject, but that what they describe as a subjectless world of objects is too subjective, already within an unproblematized transcendental horizon. We do not reach the In-itself by way of tearing away subjective appearances and trying to isolate 'objective reality' as it is 'out there', independently of the subject; the In-itself inscribes itself precisely into the subjective excess, gap, inconsistency that opens up a hole in reality. This gap is missed both by ooo and by transcendentalism in all its contemporary versions, from Heidegger to Habermas: although the two are big opponents, they both retain the transcendental horizon (the historical disclosure of being in Heidegger, the a priori of symbolic communication in Habermas) as the ultimate horizon of our thinking.

The subject's epigenesis

The question raised by Malabou in her *Avant demain* is: how are we to think together the transcendental a priori and genesis? Is the transcendental a priori simply the atemporal frame that conditions every (temporal, empirical) genesis, or does it have a genesis of its own? Can we think the genesis of the transcendental a priori itself without losing the very dimension of the transcendental? At this most sensitive point of his theoretical edifice, Kant resorts to the term 'epigenesis' (not 'genesis') which designates the phenotypic actualization of a underlying genotypic model – say, the coming-alive of a genetic code in an actual individual, or, for Kant, the actualization of the transcendental frame in concrete sensible experience of reality. Malabou draws here the parallel with the distinction between the hypocentre and the epicentre of an earthquake: its epicentre is the point at which the subterranean hypocentre touches the surface, actualizes itself, appears at the surface. In a homologous way, epigenesis is the occasion, the encounter of contingent objects in experience, which actualizes the transcendental network. But does this mean that epigenesis is just a secondary phenomenon, the process of the empirical deployment of a pre-given code or formula? Biology emphasizes that the contingent circumstances of the actualization of a genetic code make it not only selective, activating just some of its ingredients, but can also change this code itself, making it adopt some of the contingent variations. Malabou here goes a step further and emphasizes that epigenesis cannot be reduced to a blind interaction of genetic code and environment: it is a selective active process, like the performer's reading of a musical score or the interpretative reading of a literary text – in short, it is a hermeneutic activity in which 'sense touches the biological necessity.' This aspect is as a rule ignored by biogenetic science, which is why it misses the proper dimension of subjectivity. If we follow consequently this line of reasoning, we have to problematize the very notion of the transcendental a priori as a fixed formal frame which precedes its actualization. That is to say, if we conceive the transcendental a priori as a kind of genetic code of our mind which precedes our mind's activity in its dealing with external reality, then we fetishize it into a kind of inaccessible In-itself given to us only through partial (selective, twisted) readings. But the transcendental a priori is not only always interpreted, historicized, never given 'as such'; 'transcendental' is the very grid or frame of our interpretation, of our – the subject's – partial, biased reading of reality.

Subject emerges in/from epigenesis, it is the point/agent of the epigenetic interpretation/actualization of its given nature: through epigenetic activity, the subject appropriates itself – receives, actualizes, relates to – its capacity of self-determination, its spontaneity. True, there is the hypocentre of self-determination, its inborn inaccessible background, but this In-itself has to appear in (self-)experience, and this experience is always-already partial, interpretation, historical. And, again, the crucial point is that this In-itself is not yet transcendental, there is no a priori transcendental frame which is then interpretatively appropriated – 'transcendental' is always at a distance from the In-itself, it is the very frame or screen of this distance. In other words, it is this very inaccessibility of the true noumenal Self that enables subjectivization, i.e. that opens up the space of interpretative freedom, of the subject's autonomous self-invention – 'transcendental' is Kant's name for this withdrawal of the noumenal origin of subjectivity. The gap that separates the Origin from its subjective appropriation is not only epistemological but also ontological, it is the space of freedom, the restriction which pushes the subject towards autonomous self-invention.[28] The point is thus to conceive the very limitation of subjectivity as the ultimate resort of its free autonomous creativity.

What, then, is this new dimension that emerges in the gap itself? It is that of the transcendental I itself, of its 'spontaneity': the third space between phenomena and noumenon itself, the subject's freedom/spontaneity, which – although, of course, it is not the property of a phenomenal entity, so that it cannot be dismissed as a false appearance which conceals the noumenal fact that we are totally caught in an inaccessible necessity – is also not simply noumenal? In a mysterious subchapter of his *Critique of Practical Reason* entitled 'Of the Wise Adaptation of Man's Cognitive Faculties to His Practical Vocation' (5:146–8), Kant endeavours to answer the question of what would happen to us if we were to gain access to the noumenal domain, to the *Ding an sich*: the direct access to the noumenal domain would deprive us of the very 'spontaneity' which forms the kernel of transcendental freedom; it would turn us into lifeless automata, or, to put it in today's terms, into 'thinking machines'. The implication of this passage is much more radical and paradoxical than it may appear. If we discard its inconsistency (how could fear and lifeless gesticulation coexist?), the conclusion it imposes is that, at the level of phenomena as well as at the noumenal level, we – humans – are a 'mere mechanism' with no autonomy and freedom: as phenomena, we are not free, we are a part of nature, a 'mere mechanism', totally submitted to causal links, a part of the nexus of causes and effects, and as noumena, we are again not free, but reduced to a 'mere mechanism'. (Is what Kant describes as a person which directly knows the noumenal domain not strictly homologous to the utilitarian subject whose acts are fully determined by the calculus of pleasures and pains?) *Our freedom persists only in a space in between the phenomenal and the noumenal.* It is therefore not that Kant simply limited causality to the phenomenal domain in order to be able to assert that, at the noumenal level, we are free autonomous agents: we are only free insofar as our horizon is that of the phenomenal, insofar as the noumenal domain remains inaccessible to us. Kant's own formulations are here misleading, since he often identifies the transcendental subject with the noumenal I whose phenomenal appearance is the empirical 'person', thus shrinking from his radical insight into how the transcendental subject is a pure formal-structural function beyond the opposition of the noumenal and the phenomenal.[29]

3 SELF-CONSCIOUSNESS, WHICH SELF-CONSCIOUSNESS? AGAINST THE RENORMALIZATION OF HEGEL

In defence of Hegel's madness

In *Un Coup de Dés*, Mallarmé mentions a wing 'in advance fallen back from a failure to take flight' – maybe, this circular move captures best the underlying insight of what Hegel called Absolute Knowing: not a circle of taking a flight and then falling back, but the paradox of falling back which precedes the attempt to take off. This paradox is what Hegel (also) calls 'absolute recoil' (*Gegenstoß*): the counter-action (here: falling down) precedes the action whose failure it enacts, so that the action emerges retroactively as a spectre present only in the traces of its failure. It is against the background of this paradox that we should also read the notion of 'recurvature' which concludes the circular movement of a Concept's self-deployment: 'The determinateness, as determinate Concept, is *bent back into itself* [*zurückgebogen*] out of externality; it is the Concept's own immanent *character*.'[1] So we should not read this 'recurvature' as a simple 'bending back into itself' of a concept from its self-externalization: if we do, we miss the fact that there is no substantial Concept which plays with itself the game of externalization and returning to itself. The 'return to itself' literally constitutes that to which it returns; that is, there is no Concept prior to its return to itself, this priority is a retroactive illusion.

And, insofar as the Hegelian dialectical process can be characterized as the process of sublation, one should bear in mind here a subtle distinction between sublation (*Aufhebung*) and self-sublation (*Selbst-Aufhebung*):[2] simple sublation can still be conceived as a work of an external agent who, through its perlaboration of an immediate thing, 'sublates' it in the three senses of the German term mobilized by Hegel (say, when I make a table out of raw wood, I annihilate the piece of wood I am working on, but I also maintain it in a new form and elevate it to a higher level, that of a human product that serves a specific cultural need). But what is missing here is the reflexive turn by means of which, when I 'sublate' immediate natural objects, I simultaneously 'self-sublate' myself into a skilled worker. Self-sublation is therefore a profoundly materialist concept: it describes how the Infinite does not designate a separate domain distinct from the Finite – the Infinite is nothing but the self-sublation of the Finite, it emerges only through its return-to-itself from the Finite.

Furthermore, insofar as the immanent self-deployment of a Concept is often characterized by Hegel as a process in which things become what they always-already are, we should also note here the complex temporal structure of the dialectical process noted by Aldouri[3] who, in his articulation of the 'distinction between the temporality of the 'always-already' of the actual, as the context in which spirit is moving, and the 'not-yet' actualization of the actual at the different moments of articulation' added 'a third mode of temporality that renders philosophically intelligible the two', a mode that signals the radical opening of the dialectical process and that could be recaptured as its 'not-yet always-already'. This opening is thus not simply the opening towards the future but a much more radical opening towards the past – the moment it is not yet decided not what will become out of the things but what they always-already were.

It is this speculative core of Hegel's thinking that makes him a notoriously 'difficult' writer: many of his statements run against our common sense and cannot but appear as crazy speculation. In his detailed reading of Hegel's *Phenomenology of Spirit*,[4] Robert Brandom attempts to systematically 'renormalize' Hegel, i.e. to demonstrate how Hegel's most extravagant formulations, when properly (re)interpreted, make sense in our common space of meaning. I highly appreciate Brandom's attempt – it is a model of clear argumentative reasoning which consistently pursues the basic insight on which it relies. However, I want to argue against such 'domestication' of Hegel and defend Hegel's 'madness': Hegel's statements *have* to shock us, and this excess cannot be explained away through interpretation, since the truth they deliver hinges on that.

The immediacy of mediation

What Brandom leaves behind in his 'renormalization' of Hegel is primarily the dimension of self-relating. Let's take two basic Hegelian concepts: determinate negation and mediation (*Vermittlung*). Brandom interprets them as the series of exclusions and inclusions that constitute the identity of every object. 'Determinate negation' means that if the chair I am sitting on is made of plastic then it is not made of metal or wood; if it is white then it is not brown or grey or any other colour; and so forth. 'Mediation' encapsulates the intricate relation to other objects and processes which made this chair what it is: the plastic it is made of presupposes industrial production based on scientific knowledge as well as the culture in which it was made; and so forth. There is nothing specifically 'dialectical' in this, just a commonsense realist universe:

> Properties stand to one another in relations of modally robust *exclusion*. An object's possessing one property *precludes* it from exhibiting some others, in the sense that it is *impossible* to exhibit the incompatible properties simultaneously. Nothing can be at once both a bivalve and a vertebrate. This *ex*clusion structure induces a corresponding *in*clusion structure: if Coda *were* a dog, then Coda *would be* a mammal, for everything incompatible with being a mammal is incompatible with being a dog. It is these counterfactual-supporting exclusions and inclusions that are codified in laws of nature.

The dialectics of inclusion and exclusion is here reduced to the interplay of included and excluded properties of a thing: this One-thing is grey, wooden, manmade, with three legs, etc., so it is not red, metallic, manufactured, four-legged, etc. What is missing is exclusion brought to self-reference: the One (an entity) excludes also its own properties in the sense that it 'is' none of them but achieves its self-identity by way of what Hegel calls negative self-relationship. This is also why Brandom (like Pippin apropos of positing and external reflection) remains caught in the infinite game of mediation and immediacy, thereby missing the key passage from determinate negation to negative determination (what structural linguistics calls differentiality): it is not only that what a thing is, its properties, is determined by what it is not, by the properties it excluded, it is also that the very absence of property can count as a property. With regard to the couple of mediation and immediacy, this means that it is not enough to assert the mediated nature of every immediacy – we have to add the immediacy of mediation itself, as Hegel does, for example, apropos of the pure Self: 'The 'I', or becoming in general, this mediation, on account of its simple nature, is just immediacy in the process of becoming, and is the immediate itself.'[5] Brandom deploys the mutual dependence of mediation and immediacy (difference and identity): every identity is mediated, it is sustained by a network of differences from what this object is not, from all other objects; but since he ignores the immediacy of mediation itself, he concludes that mediation cannot count as the ultimate foundation for the simple reason that each of these other objects also possesses its own specific determinate identity, and if

> their determinate identities (what distinguishes them one from another) are taken likewise to consist in their relations to others similarly conceived, then the whole scheme is threatened by incoherence. The strategy amounts to seeing each individual as 'borrowing' its moment of diversity from (depending for the intelligibility of its determinate difference from others upon) that of other, different, individuals, which stand in diverse determinate relations to the first.

In short, the totality of interrelated phenomena cannot be grounded exclusively in differentiality since, in this case, it 'hangs in the air': if every thing, including all others, is grounded differentially, then there is ultimately no identity from which things are differentiated … This, incidentally, is an old reproach to Hegel fomulated already by Schelling (who dismissed Hegel's thought as a 'negative philosophy' in need of an immediate positive Ground) and recently reformulated by Dieter Henrich. Lacan's answer to this reproach is that the symbolic order precisely is such a differential structure which 'hangs in the air', and, furthermore, than this 'hanging in the air', this lack of roots in any substantial positive reality, is what subjectivizes the symbolic structure.

In order to elaborate the idea of a subjectivized structure, we need to radicalize the notion of differentiality, bringing it to self-referentiality. The crucial consequence of differential identity is that the very absence of a feature can itself count as a feature, as a positive fact – if every presence arises only against the background of potential absence, then we can also talk about the presence of absence as such. For example, something not happening can also be a positive event – recall the famous dialogue from 'Silver Blaze' between Scotland Yard detective Gregory and Sherlock Holmes about the 'curious incident of the dog in the night-time':

> 'Is there any other point to which you would wish to draw my attention?'
> 'To the curious incident of the dog in the night-time.'
> 'The dog did nothing in the night-time.'
> 'That was the curious incident.'

This positive existence of the absence itself, the fact that the absence of a feature is itself a positive feature which defines the thing in question, is what characterizes a differential order, and, in this precise sense, differentiality is the core feature of dialectics proper. Consequently, Jameson was right to emphasize, against the standard Hegelian-Marxist rejection of structuralism as 'undialectical', that the role of the structuralist explosion in the 1960s was 'to signal a reawakening or a rediscovery of the dialectic'.[6] This is also why, in a nice jab at cultural studies' fashionable rejection of 'binary logic', Jameson calls for 'a generalized celebration of the binary opposition' which, brought to self-referentiality, is the very matrix of structural relationality or differentiality. Furthermore, insofar as Hegel is *the* dialectician and his *Phenomenology of Spirit* is the unsurpassed model of dialectical analysis, Jameson is fully justified in drawing his nonintuitive conclusion: 'it is certain that the *Phenomenology* is a profoundly structuralist work *avant la lettre*.'[7] (The link between this differentialist approach and Hegelian dialectics was clearly perceived by Roman Jakobson.)

But if absence itself can function as presence or as a positive fact – if, for example, women's lack of a penis is in itself a 'curious incident' – then presence (man's possession of a penis) can also arise only against the background of its (possible) absence. But how, precisely? Here we need to introduce self-reflexivity into the signifying order: if the identity of a signifier is nothing but the series of its constitutive differences, then every signifying series has to be supplemented – 'sutured' – by a reflexive signifier which has no determinate meaning (signified), since it stands only for the presence of meaning as such (as opposed to its absence). The first to fully articulate the necessity of such a signifier was Lévi-Strauss, in his famous interpretation of '*mana*'; his achievement was to demystify mana, reducing its irrational connotation of a mythic or magical power to a precise symbolic function. Lévi-Strauss's starting point is that language as a bearer of meaning by definition arises at once, covering the entire horizon: 'Whatever may have been the moment and the circumstances of its appearance in the ascent of animal life, language can only have arisen all at once. Things cannot have begun to signify gradually.'[8] This sudden emergence, however, introduces an imbalance between the two orders of the signifier and the signified: since the signifying network is finite, it cannot adequately cover the endless field of the signified in its entirety. In this way,

> a fundamental situation perseveres which arises out of the human condition: namely, that man has from the start had at his disposition a signifier-totality which he is at a loss to know how to allocate to a signified, given as such, but no less unknown for being given. There is always a non-equivalence or 'inadequation' between the two, a non-fit and overspill which divine understanding alone can soak up; this generates a signifier-surfeit relative to the signifieds to which it can be fitted. So, in man's effort to understand the world, he always disposes of a surplus of signification ... That distribution of a supplementary ration ... is absolutely necessary to insure that, in total, the available signifier and the mapped-out signified may remain in the relationship of complementarity which is the very condition of the exercise of symbolic thinking.[9]

Every signifying field thus has to be 'sutured' by a supplementary zero-signifier, 'a *zero symbolic value*, that is, a sign marking the necessity of a supplementary symbolic content over and above that which the signified already contains'.[10] This signifier is 'a symbol in its pure state': lacking any determinate meaning, it stands for the presence of meaning *as such* in contrast to its absence; in a further dialectical twist, the mode of appearance of this supplementary signifier which stands for meaning as such is non-sense (Deleuze developed this point in *The Logic of Sense*). Notions like mana thus 'represent nothing more or less than that *floating signifier* which is the disability of all finite thought'.[11]

The first thing to note here is Lévi-Strauss's commitment to scientific positivism: he grounds the necessity of 'mana' in the gap between the constraints of our language and infinite reality. Like the early Badiou and Althusser, he excludes science from the dialectics of lack that generates the need for a suturing element. For Lévi-Strauss, 'mana' stands for the 'poetic' excess which compensates for the constraints of our finite predicament, while the effort of science is precisely to suspend 'mana' and provide direct adequate knowledge. Following Althusser, one can claim that 'mana' is an elementary operator of ideology which reverses the lack of our knowledge into the imaginary experience of the ineffable surplus of Meaning. The next step towards 'suture' proper consists of three interconnected gestures: the *universalization* of 'mana' (the zero-signifier is not just a mark of ideology, but a feature of every signifying structure); its *subjectivization* (redefining 'mana' as the point of the inscription of the subject into the signifying chain); and its *temporalization* (a temporality which is not empirical but logical, inscribed into the very signifying structure). In other words, this zero-signifier is the immediacy of mediation at its purest: a signifier whose identity consists only in its difference, i.e. which gives body to difference as such. This is why it represents the subject for other signifiers: subject is, at its most elementary, difference as such.[12]

The stick in itself, for us, for itself

Brandom begins his reading of *Phenomenology* with an interpretation of the notion of experience (*Erfahrung*) in the short Preface; it is here that he performs his first great act of 'renormalization', trying to translate into common sense Hegel's paradoxical claim that when, in an experience, we compare our notion of a thing to this thing itself (which serves as the standard by means of which we measure the adequacy of our notion) and establish that our notion does not fit the thing, we not only have to change our notion of the thing (the way this thing is 'for us') – what has to change is also the very standard by means of which we measured the adequacy of our notion, the thing itself. Brandom evokes here the simple example of a straight stick which, half-submerged in water, appears to us as bent: when we pull the stick out of the water, we immediately see that the stick is really (in itself) straight – so in what sense does the experience here also change the thing itself? Wasn't the stick the same (straight) the whole time, we just changed our (erroneous) notion of it? Brandom agrees that 'the "new, true object" which "emerges to consciousness" is *not* the straight stick. (After all, *it* didn't change; it was straight all along.)' What changed was our notion (representation) of the stick-in-itself: we thought that the stick-in-itself is also bent (like our perception of it), but now we realize that the bent stick was only our wrong representation. This is the sense in which

> in the alteration of the knowledge the object itself becomes to consciousness something which has in fact been altered as well. What alters is the status of the bent-stick representing, what it is to

consciousness. It had enjoyed the status of being to consciousness what the stick is in itself. But now its status has changed to being *to* consciousness only what the stick was *for* consciousness: an appearance … The 'new, true object' is the bent-stick representation revealed *as* erroneous, as a *mis*representation of what is now *to* the subject the way things really are: a straight stick. This representing is 'true' not in the sense of representing how things really are, but in the sense that what is now to consciousness is what *it* really is: a mere appearance, a misrepresenting. That is why 'This new object contains the annihilation of the first; it is the experience constituted through that first object'.

Brandom resolves the paradox so that he introduces three levels of the object (stick, in this case): the way the stick is for us, our notion/perception of the stick (it appears bent); the way the stick-in-itself appears to us (i.e. the way we presume the stick is in itself); and the way the stick really is in itself, independently of us (straight). So what changes in our experience is not the stick-in-itself but just the second level, the way we perceived its In-itself: what we presumed to be the stick-in-itself now changes into a false appearance:

> the object that was taken to be in itself reveals itself, via incompatibilities, as in fact … only what it was for consciousness. That moment of independence of the object, Hegel argues, is essential for the possession by our concepts of determinate content. Incompatibility is significant only for and in this process.

This solution only works if we posit a strict difference between the order of ideas (that compose our knowledge) and the order of things (the way they are in themselves): in the process of knowledge, our ideas change, they gradually approach the way things are in themselves, while things in themselves remain the way they are, unaffected by the process of knowledge. This 'asymmetry between the order and connection of ideas and that of things' is formulated by Brandom in terms of the difference between material incompatibility and deontic incompatibility: the same object (stick) cannot be at the same time straight and bent, the two properties are incompatible; but we can in our mind entertain two incompatible ideas about an object, this is just deontically inappropriate: 'It is *impossible* for one object simultaneously to exhibit materially incompatible properties (or for two incompatible states of affairs to obtain), while it is only *inappropriate* for one subject simultaneously to endorse materially incompatible commitments.' The progress of knowledge is therefore 'the process in and through which more and more of how the world really is, what is actually materially incompatible with what in the objective alethic sense, becomes incorporated in material incompatibilities deontically acknowledged by subjects.' In short, our knowledge progresses when, upon discovering incompatibilities in our notion of an object, we discard the inappropriate aspects and in this way bring our notion of the object closer to its reality – contradiction can exist only in our knowledge, not in the thing itself, which is why we progress precisely by way of discarding contradictions:

> Here 'how things objectively are', or are 'in themselves' means 'always already are anyway', in the sense that how they are *in* themselves swings free of how they are *for* the subject. That sort of independence is presupposed by their functioning as a normative standard for assessment of appearances, a standard which what things are for the subject may or may not satisfy.

Or, to put it in the terms of the classic distinction between reference (that X we are talking about) and sense (what we are saying about it), the reference is constant, the external standard we are gradually approaching, while sense is constantly changing. Throughout history of humanity, people have talked about water, and while the sense of the term gets gradually richer (say, with modern science, we discover the chemical composition of water, H_2O), 'the reference is constant':

> It is what ties the whole process together into a unity, grouping a whole class of senses together as representings of the same represented way the world is, more or less explicit expressions of the same implicit content. The senses that (according to the reconstructed genealogy) elaborate, express, and culminate in that constant, unifying content, by contrast, are various and variable, differing in the extent to which and the ways in which they make that implicit content explicit. They are the moment of disparity of form of expressing of the identical content expressed. Up until the very end (the current, temporary culmination), the senses, the ways things are for consciousness, are never quite right, never fully adequate expressions of their content, still subject to error and failure when they are applied to novel particulars. But the way things are in themselves, reality, persists unchanged and unmoved by the flux of its appearances.

But does such a reading not run against Hegel's concise definition of speculative thinking: '*Speculative thinking* consists solely in the fact that thought holds fast contradiction, and in it, its own self'?[13] Does Brandom, who, like Kant, is not ready to 'hold fast' to contradictions in things themselves, thereby not display a 'tenderness for the things of this world', as Hegel put it in his famous comment on Kant's antinomies from his 'small' (*Encyclopaedia*) *Logic*:

> What is made explicit here is that it is the content itself, namely, the categories on their own account, that bring about the contradiction. This thought, that the contradiction which is posited by the determinations of the understanding in what is rational is essential and necessary, has to be considered one of the most important and profound advances of the philosophy of modern times. But Kant's solution is as trivial as the viewpoint is profound; it consists merely in a tenderness for the things of this world. The stain of contradiction ought not to be in the essence of what is in the world; it has to belong only to thinking reason, to the essence of the spirit. It is not considered at all objectionable that the world as it appears shows contradictions to the spirit that observes it; the way the world is for subjective spirit, for sensibility, and for the understanding, is the world as it appears. But when the essence of what is in the world is compared with the essence of spirit, it may surprise us to see how naively the humble affirmation has been advanced, and repeated, that what is inwardly contradictory is not the essence of the world, but belongs to reason, the thinking essence.[14]

To clarify this key passage, let us return to the unfortunate stick. When we are dealing with a straight stick which, when partially submerged in water, falsely appears as a bent stick, one can effectively conceive the process of knowledge as the process of gradually approaching the reality of the stick, the way it exists in itself, independently of our perception. However, one should introduce here the difference between objects which are what they are independently of our notion of them (like a straight stick) and objects which change when their for-itself (or for-us) changes:

> For such a being can change what it is *in* itself by changing what it is *for* itself. Call a creature 'essentially self-conscious' if what it is *for* itself, its self-conception, is an essential element of what it is *in* itself. How something that is essentially self-conscious *appears* to itself is part of what it *really* is.

Imagine a stick which remains straight in reality (in itself) only insofar as it appears as a bent stick – therein resides the role of ideology, of ideological illusion: an 'alienated' society can reproduce itself (in its actuality) only through its illusory/false self-appearance or self-perception – the moment it appears to itself the way it actually is, this actuality disintegrates. In a homologous way, psychoanalysis deals with entities which exist only insofar as they are not adequately self-conscious or 'for themselves': for Freud (at least in the early phase of his work), a symptom disappears after the subject (whose symptom it is) gains access to its meaning, that is, it persists only insofar as its meaning remains unknown. (In a closer analysis, we soon realize that things are more complex: are symptoms also not forms of 'objectified' self-consciousness, are they not formations in the guise of which I register the truth about myself that remains inaccessible to my consciousness?) One should distinguish here simple self-consciousness (being aware of something) from 'self-consciousness' as the act of symbolic registration: I can be aware of the meaning of a symptom of mine without really assuming this meaning – while I know what it means, I block the symbolic efficiency of this knowledge, i.e. this knowledge doesn't really affect my subjective position.

For Brandom, the In-itself is by definition noncontradictory, and the entire dynamics (movement) is on the cognitive/subjective side: one passes from one failed concept to another more adequate one which will also fail, etc., but this movement is not the movement in the thing itself … Does Brandom here not do the exact opposite of Hegel? When Hegel confronts an epistemological inconsistency or 'contradiction' which appears as an obstacle to our access to the object itself (if we have incompatible notions of an object, they cannot all be true), Hegel resolves this dilemma by way of transposing what appears as an epistemological obstacle into an ontological feature, a 'contradiction' in the thing itself. Brandom, on the contrary, resolves an ontological inconsistency by way of transposing it into epistemological illusion/inadequacy, so that reality is saved from contradiction.

Recall Adorno's classic analysis of the antagonistic character of the notion of society. In a first approach, the split between the two notions of society (Anglo-Saxon individualistic-nominalistic and the Durkheimian organicist notion of society as a totality which pre-exists individuals) seems irreducible, we seem to be dealing with a true Kantian antinomy which cannot be resolved via a higher 'dialectical synthesis' and which elevates society into an inaccessible Thing-in-itself; however, in a second approach, one should merely take note of how this radical antinomy which seems to preclude our access to the Thing *already is the thing itself* – the fundamental feature of today's society *is* the irreconcilable antagonism between totality and the individual.

Instead of rejecting the Hegelian false reconciliation, one should reject as illusory the very notion of dialectical reconciliation; that is, one should renounce the demand for a 'true' reconciliation. Hegel was fully aware that reconciliation does not alleviate real suffering and antagonisms – his formula of reconciliation from the foreword to his *Philosophy of Right* is that one should 'recognize the Rose in the Cross of the present', or, to put it in Marx's terms, in reconciliation, one does not change external reality to fit some Idea, one recognizes this Idea as the inner 'truth' of this miserable reality itself. The Marxist reproach that, instead of transforming reality, Hegel only proposes its new interpretation, thus in a way misses the point – it knocks on an open door, since, for Hegel, in order to pass from alienation to reconciliation, one has to change not reality but the way we perceive it and relate to it.

How does truth progress? For Hegel, we do not compare our notion of truth (for us) with the truth in-itself and, in this way, gradually approach the truth in-itself. Hegel is a thinker of radical immanence: in the process of experience, we compare a notion with itself, with its own actualization or exemplification. Hegel is here radically anti-Platonist: in the gap that separates a notion from its examples, the truth is on the side of examples, examples bring out immanent inconsistencies of a notion, so when examples do not fit a notion we should transform this notion itself.

One should problematize here Brandom's opposition of non-normative objective reality and the discursive normative universe: the whole point of Hegel's idealist reversal of the standard notion of truth as *adequatio ad rem* (the correspondence of our thoughts to things) into *adequatio* of a thing to its own concept (what for a/one – *was für ein* – house is this house? Is it really a house? Does it fit the notion of a house?) is that *a certain normative split characterizes reality itself*: real objects never fully fit their notion. Let us take Hegel's classic example, that of the state. No empirical state is a 'true state', fully adequate to its notion, and when we realize this, we have to change also this notion itself. For example, the medieval feudal Christian state was not a failure only when we measure it by the standards of the modern democratic state respecting human freedoms and rights, it was a failure in its own terms (it systematically failed to realize the ideal of a harmonious hierarchic social body), and the result of this failure was that we had to change this ideal notion itself. So what happens at the end of this process? Do we finally get the true notion of State with the concept of modern constitutional monarchy described by Hegel in his philosophy of right? No: the ultimate result is that the 'contradiction' (antagonism) is internal to the notion of State as such, so that a 'true' state is no longer a state. To get a community that would meet the basic criteria of a 'true state' (harmonious social body), we have to pass from State to Religion, to a religious community – and here antagonisms explode again … What we get at the end of the entire system is not a final rest but the circularity of the movement itself.

But, one might reply, the State is in itself a normative (deontic) entity, so what about simple objects like chairs or tables? Hegel's idealist wager is that even here there is a normative dimension at work in reality itself. That is to say, what is the point of Hegel's dialectical deduction of one form of life or reality to another – for example, how do we pass from plants to animal life in his philosophy of nature? What Hegel proposes is not just a classification of forms of life from lower ones to higher ones: each higher form of life is 'deduced' from the lower one as an attempt to resolve its inner inconsistency, so that there definitely is a movement of norm-motivated change in reality itself. If an object doesn't fit its notion, one has to change both, including the notion. There is more in an example of a notion than in a notion of which the example is an example, i.e. the gap between a notion and its example is internal to the notion itself. Here, the opposition between subjective deontic incompatibility and objective incompatibility breaks down: it is not that objective incompatibility means that this cannot happen in reality; reality *is* incompatibility embodied. Brandom is right when he locates dynamics in normative contradictions, but he is not ready to follow Hegel's idealism and locate the normative tension in things themselves. Here is his crucial formulation:

> We are to start with phenomena, with how things are *for* consciousness, with how they *seem* or *appear*, with the contents we grasp and express. The idea that there is some way things *really* are, *in* themselves, the concept of what is represent*ed*, what we are thinking and talking *about* by grasping and expressing those contents, is to be understood in terms of features of those contents themselves. The representational dimension of concept use is to be explained in terms of what it is to take or treat conceptual contents *as* representings, what it is for them to be representings *for* or *to* us. Reference is to be explained as an aspect of sense. The way in which the very idea of noumena is to be explicated and elaborated from features of the historical trajectory by which phenomena (conceptual contents) develop and are determined is the essence of Hegel's distinctive version of the semantics of sense and reference.

A certain ambiguity clings to these formulations: is the inconsistency of phenomena, of our approaches or notions, itself the Real, or is the Real, the thing-in-itself, a substantial entity outside the symbolic space, which we approach and (mis)interpret through conflicting notions? For Hegel as well as for Lacan, one touches the Real only in/through the 'contradictions' (failures, discrepancies) of our notions of the real, not in the sense that we correct our wrong commitments when we encounter contradiction, but more radically: this 'contradiction' is the Real itself. And, incidentally, this notion of the Real also enables us to reply to Meillassoux's claim that my (and 'perhaps' Badiou's) positions

> consist at bottom in making of materialism a 'misfired correlationism'. Ever since Derrida in particular, materialism seems to have taken the form of a 'sickened correlationism': it refuses both the return to a naïve pre-critical stage of thought *and* any investigation of what prevents the 'circle of the subject' from harmoniously closing in on itself. Whether it be the Freudian unconscious, Marxist ideology, Derridean dissemination, the undecidability of the event, the Lacanian Real considered as the impossible, etc., these are all supposed to detect the trace of an impossible coincidence of the subject with itself, and thus of an extra-correlational residue in which one could localize a 'materialist moment' of thought. But in fact, such misfires are only further correlations among others: it is always *for* a subject that there is an undecidable event or a failure of signification … When one clogs up the Subject, one does not go outside it: instead, one merely constructs a transcendental or speculative Wobbly Subject – a subject that is assured *a priori*, and according to a properly absolute Knowing, for which things always turn out badly in its world of representations.[15]

The point I try to make is subtly different. My aim, as well as Meillassoux's, is to break out of the transcendental circle and reach the In-itself. However, in contrast to Meillassoux, I thoroughly reject the standard 'realist' approach which tries to somehow distinguish in objects the way they merely appear to us and the way they are in themselves, independently of how they relate to us. (Meillassoux even rehabilitates here the distinction between primary and secondary qualities of an object: primary properties are those we can perceive with more than one sense [we can see and touch the form of a hard object] and therefore belong to the object as it is in itself, while secondary properties [taste, colour] are perceived only by one sense and therefore do not belong to the object as it is in itself.) This approach of trying to subtract from the object its appearance (what we, perceiving subjects, allegedly, added to it, the subjective excess) in order to arrive at or, rather, distil the object's In-itself, is to be rejected thoroughly. My point is that one should proceed in exactly the opposite way: subject is inscribed into the real, it touches the real, precisely at the point of the utmost 'subjective' excess, in what it adds to the object, in the way it distorts the object. Let's take the most traditional case imaginable: class struggle. There is no neutral 'impartial' approach to it, no metalanguage, every apprehension of class struggle is already 'distorted' by the subject's engagement in it, and this distortion, far from preventing our direct approach to the actuality of class struggle, *is* in itself the real of the class struggle – it is in this very failure to subtract its own partial perspective and reach the object that the Real inscribes itself, that the subject touches the Real. So it is not just that the subject always fails, etc.: *it is through this failure that the subject reaches the Real.*

So, to introduce some order in this proliferation of appearances, first, we begin with naive reality (things simply are what they appear to be); then, 'things are not what they seem', the gap between appearance and reality arises; then, we get it that the essence behind appearance is itself an appearance, the appearance of what lies beyond what we see (brought to extreme, this 'appearing of essence' functions as 'appearing to appear' – a situation in which a mask masks the fact that there is nothing beneath it: what we [mis]took for a mask is reality itself). At this point, it may appear that all there is is just appearances and their interplay; however, what cannot be reduced to a mere appearance is the very gap that separates a mere appearance from the appearance of essence. At its most radical, the Real is thus not an In-itself beyond illusory appearances but the very gap that separates different levels of appearances.

Action and responsibility

A tension homologous to that of the process of cognition also characterizes the course of human actions. Hegel's first definition of action sounds surprising: 'Action alters nothing and opposes nothing. It is the pure form of a transition from a state of not being seen to one of being seen, and the content which is brought out into the daylight and displayed is nothing else but what this action already is in itself.'[16] This aspect of Hegel's theory of action is crucial: there is no tension between the acting agent and the object the agent is acting upon, no 'forcing' of the object, no struggle with the material, no heroic effort to impose subjective form on the material, no radical Otherness in the material, no impenetrable X that resists the acting agent. The appearance of struggle and resistance of the material should be reinterpreted as the sign of the immanent contradiction of the action itself. Let us take the Stalinist forced collectivization of land in the late 1920s: the desperate stubborn resistance of individual farmers to this action expressed the inner 'contradiction' and weakness of the project of collectivization itself; the tragic consequences of the collectivization – millions of dead farmers in the Ukraine hunger, the loss of the majority of livestock, etc. – 'brought out into the daylight and displayed what this action already was in itself'. Therein resides what Lebrun called Hegel's 'immobilism': there is nothing new that emerges in a dialectical process, everything is already here, the transition is purely formal, things don't change but merely become what they always-already were ... So is Hegel a traditional metaphysician who reduces change (development, progress) to the circular movement of absolutely immanent self-deployment? It is here that Hegel's novelty arises: true, things only become what they always-already were, there is no change here, but there is a change at a much more radical level – not the change from what the things were to what they are now, but the change in what they always-already were. The mechanism is here the one of retroactivity: an expression of the past (determined by it) engenders what it expresses, that is, things become what they already were – what changes in a dialectical process is the eternal past itself. We are predetermined by fate, but we can change this fate itself.

To put it another way, Hegel's point is not that 'nothing really changes' in a change, that we only establish (make explicit) what things always-already were. His point is a much more precise one: in order for the things to 'really change', we must first accept that they have already changed. One here has to turn around the old evolutionist notion of change which first takes place 'in the underground', invisible as such, within the frame of the old form, and finally, when this old form can no longer contain the new content, it falls away and the new form imposes itself. (There is an ambiguity here in Marx: he often describes the tension between forces and relations of production in these evolutionary terms, but he also asserts the primacy of formal subsumption of the forces of production under capital over their material subsumption – first, old [artisanal] forces are subsumed under capital, and then, gradually, they are replaced by modern industrial forces.)

Every action is characterized by the tension between the explicit goal pursued by the agent and its unintended consequences. Brandom inter-prets Hegel here with reference to Davidson: when I press a bell button which is (unbeknown to me) connected to a bomb and thereby trigger a catastrophic explosion, 'I am responsible for it in the sense that it is "mine": I did it. But it is *imputed* to me only under the intentional descriptions:

the ones appearing in a specification of my purpose, the descriptions that specify the deed as something I had reason to do.' So although I am responsible for the explosion (since I triggered it), what can be imputed to me is only the act of pressing the bell button with the intention of ringing the bell.[17] The first thing to do here is to include unconscious motivations: I commit an act with a clear conscious intention, but its unintended consequence realizes my unconsciously desired goal? It is weird that, in his long and detailed analyses of responsibility without conscious intention, despite the fact that he repeatedly talks about Oedipus, Brandom never mentions Freud and psychoanalysis, although, for Freud, Oedipus's murder of his father and incest with his mother are exemplary cases of unconsciously motivated acts. Freud returns to the 'heroic' position: a subject is responsible also for the unintended consequences of his acts (slips of tongue, dreams, etc.) since they were motivated by unconscious desires. I bring you a glass of wine and I slip in front of you, spilling it on your shirt – thereby expressing my concealed hatred of you?

Even without considering unconscious motivations, we should also introduce here the difference between consequences which are nonintended in the sense of simple externality and consequences which, although not intended, proceed immanently from the process triggered by the agent. Let's return to the bell at the entrance to a house which is connected to a bomb – when I press it, the explosion ruins the building; but since I had no idea of this connection and just wanted to visit a friend in the house, I am in no way responsible for the catastrophic consequence. The case of Stalinism is fundamentally different: let's imagine an honest communist fully engaged in working for the Soviet state in the 1920s – even if his sincere intention is to bring about a new, just and free society, the actual outcome (Stalinist terror, gulags, etc.) is an immanent consequence of his activity, i.e. it was inscribed into the very immanent logic of Soviet communism. (Let us take an extreme case of the gap that separates *Handlung* from *Tat*: the Chinese Cultural Revolution. As a *Handlung*, it intended to revolutionize social relations in the direction of communism, while as a *Tat*, its unintended ultimate consequence for which Mao was 'objectively responsible' was the explosion of capitalism in China.)

True, Hegel writes apropos of action that 'the purpose and the end must by their very nature be *general*, and so abstract, while what is actually accomplished must by its very nature be *fully determinate*, that is, concrete'. But contingency does not only enter at the level of the circumstances of the actualization of an end: what if the contingent aspects of an action are the very inner intentions of its agents? It is in this sense that Hegel speaks about the 'spiritual animal kingdom', his term for the complex interaction of individuals in a market society: each individual participating in it is moved by egotist concerns (personal wealth, pleasures, power), but the Whole of it regulated by the 'invisible hand' of the market actualizes universal welfare and progress. The further point here is that individual motivations and universal goal are necessarily disparate: the common good can realize itself only if individuals follow their particular egotist ends – if they directly want to act for the common good, the result is as a rule catastrophic ... So it is not just that contingent individual goals reveal themselves to be means of the higher universal Goal, or, as Hegel put it, 'the immediate character of an action in its further content is reduced to a means. In so far as such an end is a finite one, it may in turn be reduced to a means to some further intention, and so on in an infinite progression.'[18] One should take a further step here: what appears from the individual's standpoint a mere means is the true goal of the entire movement. As Marx put it, individuals engage in social productivity and develop means of production in order to satisfy their private needs and desires; but, from the standpoint of totality, their private needs and desires are themselves mere means to achieve the true goal, the development of social productivity.

Recollection, forgiveness, reconciliation

Here enters the Hegelian narrative of forgiveness through recollection: once a course of action is accomplished and its consequences, intended and unintended, laid out, it becomes possible to tell the story of how the initial intention got transformed in the course of its execution. There is no higher Idea which regulates the interaction between the initial idea-goal and its transformations through corrections: retroactively, the original goal has to be changed to fit the process, and unilateral acts are 'forgiven' insofar as they can be shown to play a role in a wider process which actualizes a more fundamental goal.

Brandom's formula of reconciliation is the unity (mutual dependence) of creating and finding, of positing and presupposing. In a traditional universe, normative structures are presupposed as objective fact, while in modern alienation, they are reduced to expressions of subjective attitudes. The 'reconciliation' is achieved when both aspects are perceived in their interaction and mutual dependence: there is no normative substance in itself, normative structures exist only through the constant interaction of individuals engaged in them; however, the necessary result of this interaction is what Dupuy calls the 'self-transcendence' of a symbolic structure – to be operative, a normative system has to be perceived as autonomous and in this sense 'alienated'. A somewhat pathetic example: when a group of people fights for communism, they of course know that this Idea exists only through their engagement, but they nonetheless relate to it as to a transcendent entity which regulates their lives and for which they may even be ready to sacrifice their lives. One should note here that, for Hegel, alienation is precisely the view which conceives objective normative structures as mere expressions/products of subjective activity, as its 'reified' or 'alienated' effects. In other words, overcoming alienation is for Hegel not the act of dissolving the illusion of autonomy of normative structures but accepting this 'alienation' as necessary. Spiritual Substance is Hegel's name for the 'big Other', and insofar as the illusion of 'big Other' is necessary for the functioning of the symbolic order, one should reject as pseudomaterialist the thought that wants to dismiss this dimension. The big Other is effective, it exerts its efficiency in regulating real social processes, not in spite of its nonexistence but *because* it doesn't exist – only an inexistent virtual order can do the job.

As expected, Brandom devalues the entire 'hermeneutics of suspicion' (Marx–Nietzsche–Freud) as a version of the naturalist reduction of norms to causality, as the relativization of norms to the expression or effect of some non-normative actual process: for Marx, normative structures are part of ideological superstructure and as such conditioned by objective economic processes; for Freud, normative structures are conditioned by unconscious libidinal processes. In Hegel's terms, Freud thus (following Nietzsche) reduces 'noble' consciousness to its 'low' pathological motivations: moral altruism is sustained by envy and a spirit of revenge, etc. But does Freud really do this? Here is how Brandom describes the judge who practises a hermeneutics of suspicion: 'The judge exercises his own authority, attributing and holding the agent responsible for the action under a different kind of description, seeing it not as the acknowledgment of a norm but only the evincing of a desire or inclination.' Is the pychoanalyst (a psychoanalytic interpreter) such a judge? No, for a simple reason: psychoanalytic interpretation is not objective knowledge about what goes on in the patient – the proof of its truth is precisely and only in how the patient subjectively assumes it. In his (unpublished) Seminar XVIII on a 'discourse which would not be that of a semblance', Lacan provided a succinct definition of the truth of interpretation in psychoanalysis: 'Interpretation is not tested by a truth that would decide by yes or no, it unleashes truth as such. It is only true inasmuch as it is truly followed.' There is nothing 'theological' in this precise formulation, only the insight into the properly dialectical unity of theory and practice in (not only) psychoanalytic interpretation: the 'test' of the analyst's interpretation is in the truth effect it unleashes in the patient. This is how we should also (re)read Marx's Thesis XI: the 'test' of Marxist theory is the truth effect it unleashes in its addressee (the proletarians), in transforming them into emancipatory revolutionary subjects. The *locus communis* 'You have to see it to believe it!' should always be read together with its inversion: 'You have to believe [in] it to see it!' Although one may be tempted to oppose them as the dogmaticism of blind faith versus openness toward the unexpected, one should insist also on the truth of the second version: truth, as opposed to knowledge, is, like a Badiouian Event, something that only an engaged gaze, the gaze of a subject who 'believes in it', can see. Think of love: in love, only the lover sees in the object of love that X which causes love, so the structure of love is the same as that of the Badiouian Event which also exists only for those who recognize themselves in it: there is no Event for a nonengaged objective observer.

Incidentally, the same point can be made about traumatic experiences as the main figure of the external cause of a pathological development of a subject. In his analysis of 'Wolfsman', Freud isolated as the early traumatic event that marked his life the fact that, as a child of one-and-a-half years, he witnessed the parental *coitus a tergo* (sexual act in which the man penetrates the woman from behind). However, originally, when this scene took place, there was nothing traumatic in it: far from shattering the child, he just inscribed it into his memory as an event the sense of which was not clear at all to him. Only years later, when the child became obsessed with the question where children come from and started to develop infantile sexual theories, did he draw out this memory in order to use it as a traumatic scene embodying the mystery of sexuality. The scene was traumatized, elevated into a traumatic Real, only retroactively, in order to help the child to cope with the impasse of his symbolic universe (his inability to find answers to the enigma of sexuality). So, again, the external cause (the traumatic experience) does not exert its causal power directly, its efficiency is always mediated by a subjectivized symbolic space which cannot be reduced to objective facts.

In the domain of politics, the hermeneutics of suspicion reaches its climax in Stalinism. The passage from Leninism to Stalinism also concerns the relationship between intended goal and unintended consequences. The Leninist category of 'objective meaning' of your acts refers to the unintended but necessary consequences, as in 'you may have acted out of your best humanitarian intentions, but your acts objectively served the class enemy' – the Party is an agent which has direct and privileged access to this 'objective meaning'. Stalinism brings us back to a perverted version of the premodern 'heroic' attitude; that is, it again closes the gap between subjective intentions and objective consequences: objective consequences are projected back into the agent as his/her (secret) intentions, as in 'you pretended to act out of the best humanitarian intentions, but secretly you wanted to serve the class enemy'.

With regard to the relationship between noble consciousness (taking the other's statements in the spirit of trust, accepting the normative commitment they declare) and vicious consciousness (interpreting others' statements from the standpoint of irony), discerning beneath them 'pathological' motivations [egotism, utilitarian interest, search for pleasures] or reducing them to effects of objective mechanisms), Brandom pulls the standard transcendental trick: in order to be taken seriously, even the most suspicious interpretation of our acts, reducing them to lower motivations or objectively determined mechanism, already has to presuppose an attitude of trust, i.e. it has to presume that this interpretation itself is not just an expression of 'lower' motivations but a deployment of serious rational argumentation:

> we have always already implicitly committed ourselves to adopting the edelmütig stance, to identifying with the unity that action and consciousness involve, to understanding ourselves as genuinely binding ourselves by conceptual norms that we apply in acting intentionally and making judgments ... The determinate contentfulness of the thoughts and intentions even of the niederträchtig is in fact intelligible *only* from an edelmütig perspective.

Hegel and Brandom are here opposed in a way which is far from concerning just an accent: Brandom asserts the transcendental primacy of trust which is always-already presupposed by any reductionist-suspicious ironic attitude, while Hegel's entire effort goes into explaining why trust needs the detour of true irony and suspicion to assert itself – it cannot stand on its own. The consequences of this shift are radical: when Brandom claims that Absolute Knowing stands for 'a move from the relations between individuals and their conceptually articulated norms exhibiting the structure of *irony* to exhibiting the structure of *trust*', he thereby opens up the way to conceive Absolute Knowing as a promise of a future state of humanity in which modern alienation will be left behind and harmony will be re-established. In his periodization of history, after traditional societies in which norms are taken as a substantial In-itself, and modern alienated societies in which norms are reduced to expressions of subjective attitudes, there comes the projected postmodern 'final form of mutual recognition as reciprocal confession and forgiveness':[19] 'Unlike the earlier stories, this one outlines something that hasn't happened yet: a future development of Spirit, of which Hegel is the prophet: the making explicit of something already implicit, whose occurrence is to usher in the next phase in our history.'

So what, precisely, is supposed to happen in this postmodern third stage? Here is Brandom's formula: 'finding and making show up as two sides of one coin, two aspects of one process, whose two phases – experience and its recollection, lived forward and comprehended backward, the inhalation and exhalation that sustain the life of Spirit – are each both makings and findings.' The basic idea seems clear: traditional culture accepts norms (our normative substance) as substantially given, so they pre-exist us, we just have to find them; modern culture of alienation reduces them to an expression of our subjective attitudes, i.e. norms are something that we make, create; what is needed is a synthetic view which sees how our reality is 'at once the institution and the application of conceptual norms, both a making and a finding of conceptual contents': 'Spirit exists insofar as we *make* it exist by *taking* it to exist.' But does this last proposition not indicate a necessary illusion? If we make it exist by taking it to exist, does this not mean that we can only make it exist by way of pretending that it already exists? It is like the old Yugoslav joke about the conscript who pleaded insanity in order to avoid military service: his 'symptom' was to compulsively examine every paper at his reach and exclaim 'That's not it!'; when he is examined by the military psychiatrists, he does the same, so the psychiatrists finally give him a paper confirming that he is released from military service. The conscript reaches for it, examines it, and exclaims: 'That's it!' Here, also, the search for an object itself generates this object.

The core of the dialectic of doing and finding thus resides in a necessary retroactive illusion: in order to *do* it, you have to act *as if it is already done*. Say, to liberate yourself, you must take yourself to be already free. The decisive break thus happens before it actually takes place: it is a pure immaterial event which turns around the entire symbolic economy of the situation. Whenever a political revolution happens, the actual overthrow is as a rule preceded by a magical moment when everyone, including those in power, all of a sudden realizes that the game is over. In women's or black liberation, the oppressed first have to experience their subordination as unjust, which means they have to experience themselves as essentially free, only *then* they can start fighting for their freedom. (Back in the 1960s, Herbert Marcuse made this same point succinctly when he wrote that freedom is a condition of liberation.) To overthrow a tyrant, you must act as if the game is already over, as if his rule already hangs in the air. Is this not the message of Christianity? In contrast to the Jews who await the arrival of the Messiah, for Christians the Messiah *has already arrived* (in the figure of Christ): through Christ, we are already redeemed, and it is this certainty that »it already happened« which gives us the strength to engage in the long and painful struggle of our actual redemption.

Opposed to this notion of a break which happens before it actually happens is Hegel's notion of the subterranean 'weaving of the Spirit', where the gradual disintegration takes place within the old formal order and this old order falls apart when everything is already decided, just registering the change after the fact. Every revolution consists of two different aspects, factual revolution plus spiritual reform, that is, actual struggle for state power plus the virtual struggle for the transformation of customs, of the substance of everyday life – what Hegel called the 'silent weaving of the Spirit', which undermines the invisible foundations of power, so that the formal change is the final act of taking note of what already took place; like the cartoon figure suspended in the air which falls down only when it looks down and notices that it is suspended in the air, one has only to remind the dead form that it is dead, and it disintegrates. Hegel quotes the famous passage from Denis Diderot's *Nephew of Rameau* about the 'silent, ceaseless weaving of the Spirit in the simple inwardness of its substance':

> it infiltrates the noble parts through and through and soon has taken complete possession of all the vitals and members of the unconscious idol; then 'one fine morning it gives its comrade a shove with the elbow, and bang! crash! the idol lies on the floor'. On 'one fine morning' whose noon is bloodless if the infection has penetrated to every organ of spiritual life.[20]

(Furthermore, this ambiguity is strictly homologous to the ambiguity of Hegel's dialectic of infinite goal where the illusion is that the game is already over, that everything already happened, that the goal is already achieved – but the illusion is also that the goal is not yet achieved, that our struggle really is an open-ended process.) So how are we to think these two opposed processes together? In both cases, the formal break appears as a symbolic act of taking note (registering) that things are already decided; but in the first case, the form precedes the content, i.e. the formal break opens up the process of actual change, while in the second case, the formal break occurs at the end, registering the fact that the work of change is already done. Would it be possible to combine the two into successive stages of one continuous process with the formal break at its beginning and at its end? The first formal break affects only the agents of change who, by way of assuming that the old world is in itself already dead, engage in the work of change; however, this work of change remains subterranean, the hegemonic ideology is blind for it; only when this subterranean work undermines the very foundations of the existing order, everyone, including those in power, realize that their world is lost, and the old order collapses by itself. (Recall the painful process of the disintegration of the Soviet Union: Gorbachev set in motion the process of 'perestroika' in order to save socialism, to make it viable in contemporary world, but his conservative critics were right – the attempt to save socialism was effectively undermining it, and the winners were those who were the first to admit that the game of saving socialism is over.) The formal gesture is thus repeated, the beginning and the end coincide, and the work comes in between. The illusion that pertains to the second formal act is that this act merely registers, takes note of, what already took place (the disintegration of the ancient order). What is thereby overlooked is the 'performative' dimension of this registering: the formal act of taking note of the fall of the ancient order effectively actualizes this fall. Even when the battle is *de facto* lost, this loss has to be registered/assumed as such to become effective.

Brandom is right to point out that 'Geist as a whole has a history, and it is Hegel's view that in an important sense, that history boils down to one grand event. That event – the *only* thing that has ever really happened to Geist – is its structural transformation from a traditional to a modern form.' In a consequently Hegelian way, we should apply this insight also to what Brandom describes as the passage from modernity to postmodernity: postmodernity is not a 'synthesis' of both extremes, traditional realism and modern subjectivism, it is not the unity of both one-sided positions; it is a self-relating repetition of the modernist break, its application to itself, it is modernity brought to conclusion.

So when Brandom evokes 'a hypothetical future third age of Spirit', one should raise the obvious Hegelian question: does such a reading not directly contradict Hegel's emphatic dismissal of 'issuing instructions on how the world ought to be' from the Preface of his *Philosophy of Right*:

> philosophy, at any rate, always comes too late to perform this function. As the *thought* of the world, it appears only at a time when actuality has gone through its formative process and attained its completed state …
> When philosophy paints its grey in grey, a shape of life has grown old, and it cannot be rejuvenated, but only recognized, by the grey in grey of philosophy; the owl of Minerva begins its flight only with the onset of dusk.[21]

Robert Pippin noted that, if Hegel is minimally consistent, this has to apply also to the notion of State deployed in his own *Philosophy of Right*: the fact that Hegel was able to deploy its concept means that dusk is falling on what readers of Hegel usually perceive as a normative description of a model rational state. And the same should hold for any extrapolation of a nonalienated future from present tendencies: such a mode of thinking (the logic of 'now we are in a critical moment of utter alienation, and the possibility is open for us to act as agents of overcoming alienation') is utterly foreign to Hegel who repeatedly emphasizes the retroactive nature of overcoming alienation: we overcome alienation through realizing that we've already overcome it. In other words, nothing 'really changes' in overcoming alienation, we just shift our perspective and gain the insight into how what appears as alienation is the immanent condition of dis-alienation, is in itself already dis-alienation. It is in this sense that, in his 'small' (*Encyclopaedia*) *Logic*, Hegel proposes his own version of *la vérité surgit de la méprise*, ambiguously asserting that 'only from this error does the truth come forth':

> In the sphere of the finite we can neither experience nor see that the purpose is genuinely attained. The accomplishing of the infinite purpose consists therefore only in sublating the illusion that it has not yet been accomplished. The good, the absolute good, fulfills itself eternally in the world, and the result is that it is already fulfilled in and for itself, and does not need to wait upon us for this to happen. This is the illusion in which we live, and at the same time it is this illusion alone that is the activating element upon which our interest in the world rests. It is within its own process that the Idea produces that illusion for itself; it posits an other confronting itself, and its action consists in sublating that illusion. Only from this error does the truth come forth, and herein lies our reconciliation with error and with finitude. Otherness or error, as sublated, is itself a necessary moment of the truth, which can only be in that it makes itself into its own result.[22]

In short, the ultimate deception is not to see that one already has what one is looking for – like Christ's disciples who were awaiting his 'real' reincarnation, blind to the fact that their collective already was the Holy Spirit, the return of the living Christ. Lebrun is thus justified in noting that the final reversal of the dialectical process, far from being a magic intervention of a deus ex machina, is a purely formal turnaround, a shift of perspective: the only thing that changes in the final reconciliation is the subject's standpoint, i.e. the subject endorses the loss, reinscribes it as its triumph. Reconciliation is thus simultaneously less and more than the standard idea of overcoming an antagonism: less, because nothing 'really changes'; more, because the subject of the process is deprived of its very (particular) substance. Recall the paradox of the process of apologizing: if I hurt someone with a rude remark, the proper thing for me to do is to offer him a sincere apology, and the proper thing for him to do is to say something like 'Thanks, I appreciate it, but I wasn't offended, I knew you didn't mean it, so you really owe me no apology!' The point is, of course, that, although the final result is that no apology is needed, one has to go through the entire process of offering it: 'you owe me no apology' can only be said after I *do* offer an apology, so that, although, formally, 'nothing happens', the offer of apology is proclaimed unnecessary, there is a gain at the end of the process (perhaps, even, the friendship is saved).

Out of which error, exactly, does the truth arise? Or, another version of the same question, 'this is the illusion under which we live' – which illusion, exactly? The ambiguity is here radical. The predominant reading would have been the standard idealist-teleological one: the error resides in assuming that the infinite End is not already accomplished, that we are caught in an open-ended struggle with a real substantial enemy. In short, the illusion resides here in the perception of those caught in the struggle who think that the struggle is for the real and not already decided in advance – they don't see that what we, finite agents, perceive as an open struggle is, from the standpoint of the absolute Idea, just a game the Idea is playing with itself. The Idea 'posits' – builds – an external obstacle in order to overcome it and unite with itself ... This, however, is only one aspect of the illusion, and the opposite illusion is no less wrong: the illusion that Truth is already here, that everything is fully predestined, decided in advance, that our struggles are just a game of no substantial importance – in this case, the Absolute remains a Substance which predetermines all subjective agency, it is not yet conceived also as Subject. In other words: to remove the illusion that the infinite goal is not already accomplished, to ascertain that truth is already here, is in itself a performative act: declaring something to be the case makes it the case. So both illusions are worse, to paraphrase Stalin – but how could both opposed versions be wrong? Is it not that either things are predetermined, decided in advance, or not? The solution is retroactivity: Truth is the process of its own becoming, it becomes what it is (or, rather, what it always-already was), not in the sense that it just deploys its immanent potentials, but in the more radical sense of gradually forming (building, constructing) its own 'eternal' past. A thing becomes not what it *is* or what it will be, but what it always-already *was*, its Aristotelian essence (*to ti ēn einai*, 'the what-it-was-to-be', or *das zeitlos-gewesene Sein*, the 'timelessly past being', as Hegel translated it).

The obverse of this vision of a future state beyond alienation is that Brandom gets caught in a spurious infinite of recognition: the gap between intention and consequences of our actions is constitutive, we cannot ever reach full reconciliation, we are condemned to the infinite progress towards overcoming disparity, every agent has to trust forgiveness from the future figures of big Other. At every moment, we build a story of recollection which reconciles us with the past, but

> no such story is final. None anoints as concepts conceptions whose correct (according to the norms they are taken by their users, including the ones producing the retrospective rational reconstruction, to embody) application will not lead to incompatible commitments, the experience of error and failure showing the disparity between what things are for consciousness and what they are in themselves that must be confessed and forgiven anew. Each such story will itself eventually turn out to have crowned a defective conception with the label: what things are *in* themselves, the real concepts. The sense in which there is and can be no finally adequate set of determinate concepts (or conceptions) is visible prospectively, in the space *between* recollections, in the need of each forgiving judge himself to be forgiven in turn.

The recognitive authority of the present judge with respect to past judges is thus conditioned on its recognition by future ones, implying 'an implicit *confession* of the only partial success of each particular exercise of generous recollection': 'Such a confession is an invitation for us who come after him concretely to forgive him for the partial failure of his attempt to forgive, by telling a still better story. He trusts us to continue the conceptually magnanimous enterprise.' Such a simple self-historicization/ self-relativization is thoroughly non-Hegelian – it forgets that one overcomes disparity not by effectively overcoming it but by a shift of perspective which renders visible disparity itself in its positive, enabling dimension.

Here is Brandom's concise description of the progress of knowledge as a continuous revision of what the object is for us: 'one must exhibit the result of one's revision as *finding out* how things all along already were in themselves, what one was really talking and thinking *about*, what one was referring to by deploying the earlier, variously defective senses, the reality that was all along appearing, though in some aspects incompletely or incorrectly.' I find this passage profoundly ambiguous: is it to be read in the standard realist way (we are gradually approaching the object which is out there, the whole time the same), or does the phrase 'one must exhibit the result of one's revision as *finding out* how things all along already were in themselves' indicate a more refined position: 'finding' how the object really is (and always-already was) in itself is a retroactive illusion, a way we necessarily (mis)perceive our process of knowledge:

> One of Hegel's most fundamental ideas is that the notion of content is intelligible in principle only in terms of the sort of *friction* between normative attitudes that shows up in cognitive experience in the collision of incompatible commitments *acknowledged* by one knower, and which we have come to see is rooted in the social-perspectival collision of commitments *acknowledged* and those *attributed* in practical experience of the disparity of Handlung and Tat.

Brandom sees clearly the retroactive nature of the Hegelian teleology, i.e. he is well aware that the rational totality which emerges through historical recollection is a 'retrospectively imputed plan':

> the role of a given event in the evolving plan depends on *what else happens* … As new consequences occur, the plan is altered, and with it the status of the earlier event as aiding in the successful execution of the plan. That status can be altered by other doings, which, in the context of the earlier one, open up some new practical possibilities and close others off. The significance of one event is never fully and finally settled. It is always open to influence by later events.

The unsurpassable case of such a retroactive reversal of contingency into necessity in popular culture remains the ending of *Casablanca*: according to the popular myth, the main actors (Bergman, Bogart) didn't know until the very last days of shooting what the ending would be (will Bergman leave with her husband for Portugal, will she remain in Casablanca with Bogart, or will one of her male partners die?), but once the ending that we know now was chosen all preceding action seemed to lead to it, i.e. it appeared as the only 'natural' ending. What this means is that the progression is '*retrospectively* necessary': 'It is not the case that a given stage could have evolved in no other way than as to produce what appears as its successor.'[23]

It is therefore too simple to just distinguish two ontological levels: natural objects which are what they are independently of how they are 'for us', and spiritual objects which are created through our approach. This is the price that both Pippin and Brandom pay for their 'renormalization' of Hegel as a thinker of discursive recognition: a regression into Kantian dualism of the domain or level of empirical reality and the separate normative domain of rational argumentation. Whatever Hegel is, such dualism is incompatible with his thought.

Healing the wound

Hegel's radical claim about the power of Spirit is that it can make our deeds 'as if they had never happened':

> The wounds of the Spirit heal, and leave no scars behind. The deed is not imperishable; it is taken back by Spirit into itself, and the aspect of individuality present in it, whether as intention or as an existent negativity and limitation, straightway vanishes.[24]

Brandom again puts all his effort into the 'renormalization' of this 'crazy' claim; however, his version of recollection as healing the wounds generates a series of problems. First, in this version, recollection 'ignores expressively retrograde experiences and instead traces out a trajectory of expressively progressive improvements in how things were for us that culminates in the way we currently take them to be in themselves'. But what about extreme self-destructive moments that are part of Hegel's recollective narrative? What about self-destructive revolutionary terror as the outcome of absolute Freedom? What about the absurd infinite judgement 'Spirit is a bone'? They are both a deadlock, clearly superfluous, but precisely as such – as superfluous – they are necessary. We have to commit an error, to make a wrong choice, in order to be able to establish retroactively that it was superfluous to do it. In other words, the Hegelian recollection is not just the narrative structure in its retroactive 'inner necessity', purified of meaningless contingencies. On the contrary, the Hegelian recollection brings life back into a dead scheme by way of resuscitating it 'in its becoming', as Kierkegaard would have put it. It does not reduce the contingency of a process to its notional necessity, it restores the contingent process out of which necessity arose.

But the main point is that, for Hegel, wounds are healed in a much stronger sense than just as steps towards a higher unity: they literally disappear, they are 'undone' – how? Recall Wagner's 'Die Wunde schliesst der Speer nur der Sie schlug' from the finale of *Parsifal* – Hegel says the same thing, although with the accent shifted in the opposite direction: the Spirit is itself the wound it tries to heal, i.e. the wound is self-inflicted. That is to say, what is 'Spirit' at its most elementary? The 'wound' of nature: subject is the immense – absolute – power of negativity, of introducing a gap or cut into the given-immediate substantial unity, the power of differentiating, of 'abstracting', of tearing apart and treating as self-standing what in reality is part of an organic unity. Consequently, the Spirit heals its wound not by directly healing it, but by getting rid of the very full and sane Body into which the wound was cut. It is in this precise sense that, according to Hegel, 'the wounds of the Spirit heal, and leave no scars behind': Hegel's point is not that the Spirit heals its wounds so perfectly that, in a magic gesture of retroactive sublation, even their scars disappear; the point is rather that, in the course of a dialectical process, a shift of perspective occurs which makes the wound itself appear as its opposite – the wound itself is its own healing when perceived from another standpoint.[25]

Does a homologous reversal not define the very core of the Christian experience? When a believer feels alone, abandoned by god, the Christian answer is not that he should purify himself and rejoin god, but that, in this very abandonment, he is already identified with god (the god who is abandoned by itself). It is also in this sense that, from the Christian standpoint, god gives humanity the supreme gift of freedom: when I feel alone, abandoned by god, lacking any protection and support from god, left to myself, to my own devices, I have to turn around the entire perspective and recognize in this lack of support and protection, in this being-left-to-one's-own-devices, the very figure of human autonomy and freedom.

Furthermore, we should test Brandom's reading of forgiveness and reconciliation at history's extreme phenomena: what would it have meant to forgive the Holocaust and get reconciled with it? Can we also imagine that this terrifying 'wound' gets fully healed and disappears by way of becoming a moment of rationally reconstructed history? Should Jews pardon the Nazis because, although in its direct intention the Holocaust meant the total destruction of the Jews, its unintended consequence was the emergence of the state of Israel plus the prohibition of anti-Semitism (in parts of the world, at least)? Or, even more obscenely, should the Jews recognize their own complicity with the Holocaust (Heidegger's reading)? The easy way out is, of course, to claim that the rational recollection of history included only moments which contributed to the progress and ignore blind accidental deadlocks. But this easy way out obviously doesn't work: violent anti-Semitism is all too clearly part of Western spiritual history to be ignored like that, plus the unintended consequence of the Holocaust effectively was some level of ethical progress (higher awareness of the dangers of racism), so that, in a weird way, it did contribute to the ethical progress which wouldn't take place without it. Which means one cannot squeeze out of this deadlock by way of reading the phrase 'wounds of the spirit' literally, as referring openly to spiritual wounds proper (and dismissing the Holocaust as a pathology that doesn't really belong to the domain of spirit): the Holocaust *is* part of the innermost history of our Spirit, of our collective spiritual substance.

Here we can return to our starting point: in his formula of reconciliation between subjective activity and spiritual Substance, Brandom misses an additional reflexive twist, homologous to the passage from determinate negation to negative determination, or to the passage from mediation of immediacy to the immediacy of mediation itself. The best way to clarify this crucial point is by way of addressing the core question of the Hegelian Christology: why does the idea of Reconciliation between God and man (the fundamental content of Christianity) have to appear in a single individual, in the guise of an external, contingent, flesh-and-blood person (Christ, the man-god)? Hegel provides the most concise answer in his lectures on the philosophy of religion:

> Cannot the subject bring about this reconciliation by itself, through its own efforts, its own activity – so that through its piety and devotion it makes its inner [life] conform with the divine idea, and express this conformity through its deeds? And further, is this not within the capability [not merely] of a single subject but of all people who genuinely wish to take up the divine law within themselves, so that heaven would exist on earth and the Spirit would be present in reality and dwell in its community?[26]

Note Hegel's precision here: his question is double. First, the individual's divinization, spiritual perfection; then, the collective actualization of the divine community as 'heaven on earth', in the guise of a community which lives totally in accordance with the divine law. In other words, the hypothesis that Hegel entertains here is the standard Marxist one: why cannot we conceive a direct passage from In-itself to For-itself, from God as full Substance existing in itself, beyond human history, to the Holy Spirit as spiritual-virtual substance, as the substance that exists only insofar it is 'kept alive' by the incessant activity of the individuals? Why not such a direct dis-alienation, by means of which individuals recognize the God qua transcendent substance, the 'reified' result of their own activity?

So why not? Hegel's answer relies on the dialectic of positing and presupposing: if the subject were to be able to do it on its own, through its own agency, then it would have been something merely *posited* by it – however, positing is in itself always one-sided, relying on some presupposition: 'The unity of subjectivity and objectivity – this divine unity – must be a presupposition for my positing.'[27] And Christ as God-man is the externally presupposed Unity/Reconciliation: first the immediate unity, then the mediate one in the guise of the Holy Spirit – we pass from Christ whose predicate is love to love itself as subject (in the Holy Spirit, 'I am where two of you love each other ...').

But even here it may appear that one can counter Hegel with Hegel himself: is not this circle of positing-presupposing the very circle of substance-subject, of the Holy Spirit as a spiritual substance kept alive, effectively existing, arriving at its actuality, only in the activity of living individuals? The status of the Hegelian spiritual substance is properly virtual: it exists only insofar as subjects act as if it exists. Its status is similar to that of an ideological cause like communism or My Nation: it is the 'spiritual substance' of the individuals who recognize themselves in it, the ground of their entire existence, the point of reference which provides the ultimate horizon of meaning to their lives, something for which these individuals are ready to give their lives, yet the only thing that 'really exists' are these individuals and their activity, so this substance is actual only insofar as individuals 'believe in it' and act accordingly. So, again, why cannot we pass directly from spiritual Substance as presupposed (the naive notion of Spirit or God as existing in itself, without regard to humanity) to its subjective mediation, to the awareness that its very presupposition is retroactively 'posited' by the activity of individuals?

Here we reach Hegel's key insight: reconciliation cannot be direct, it has first to generate (appear in) a *monster* – Hegel uses twice on the same page this unexpectedly strong word, 'monstrosity', to designate the first figure of Reconciliation, the appearance of God in the finite flesh of a human individual: 'This is the monstrous [*das Ungeheure*] whose necessity we have seen.'[28] The finite fragile human individual is 'inappropriate' to stand for God, it is '*die Unangemessenheit überhaupt*' (the inappropriateness in general, as such)[29] – are we aware of the properly dialectical paradox of what Hegel claims here? The very attempt at reconciliation, in its first move, produces a monster, a grotesque 'inappropriateness as such'. So, again, why this weird intrusion, why not a direct passage from the (Jewish) *gap* between God and man to the (Christian) reconciliation, by a simple transformation of 'God' from Beyond to the immanent Spirit of Community?

The first problem here is that, in a way, Jews already did it: if there ever was a religion of spiritual community, it is Judaism, this religion which doesn't say a lot about life after death, or even about the 'inner' belief in God, but focuses on the prescribed way of life, of obeying the communal rules; God 'is alive' in the community of believers. The Jewish God is thus both at the same time a transcendent substantial One and the virtual One of spiritual substance. So how is this Jewish community of believers different from the Christian one, from the Holy Spirit?

In order to properly answer this crucial question, one should bear in mind here the properly Hegelian relationship between necessity and contingency. In a first approach, it appears that their encompassing unity is necessity, that is, that necessity itself posits and mediates contingency as the external field in which it expresses-actualizes itself – contingency itself is necessary, the result of the self-externalization and self-mediation of the notional necessity. However, it is crucial to supplement this unity with the opposite one, with contingency as the encompassing unity of itself and necessity: the very elevation of a necessity into the structuring principle of the contingent field of multiplicity is a contingent act – one can almost say: the outcome of a contingent ('open') struggle for hegemony. This shift corresponds to the shift from S to \$, from substance to subject. The starting point is a contingent multitude; through its self-mediation ('spontaneous self-organization'), contingency engenders-posits its immanent necessity, in the same way that Essence is the result of the self-mediation of Being. Once Essence emerges, it retroactively 'posits its own presuppositions', i.e. it sublates its presuppositions into subordinated moments of its self-reproduction (Being is transubstantiated into Appearance); however, this positing is retroactive.

The underlying shift here is the one between *positing presuppositions* and *presupposing the positing*: the limit of Feuerbach-Marxian logic of dis-alienation is that of positing presuppositions: the subject overcomes its alienation by recognizing itself as the active agent which itself posited what appears to it as its substantial presupposition. In religious terms, this would amount to the direct (re)appropriation of God by humanity: the mystery of God is man, 'God' is nothing but the reified or substantialized version of the human collective activity, and so on. What is missing here is the properly Christian gesture: in order to posit the presupposition (to 'humanize' God, reduce him to an expression/result of human activity), the (human-subjective) *positing itself should be 'presupposed', located in God as the substantial ground-presupposition of man, as its own becoming-human/*

finite. The reason is the subject's constitutive finitude: the full positing of presuppositions would amount to subject's full retroactive positing/ generation of its presuppositions, i.e. the subject would be absolutized into the full self-origin.

In his *opus posthumum*, Kant deploys the idea of the self-positing (*Selbstsetzung*) of the pure (transcendental) Self as a passive (recipient) object in the world interacting with other objects: I can be affected by objects, I can perceive them, only insofar as I am myself (also) an object interacting with the objects that affect me. Therefore, in an original act, the pure Self has to posit itself as passive, as a recipient of affections. The twist here is that the pure Self thus has to posit itself as a part of the world constituted by it through transcendental synthesis. Even a naive intuitive approach can perceive the profound truth of this idea: at a certain elementary level, the spontaneity of apperception and the passivity of being affected coincide, i.e. in order for me to be affected, to be a passive recipient, I have 'spontaneously' to posit myself as such, in the same way that, in order to passively enjoy music, I have to 'posit' myself as open/ receptive to music (which is why an animal or a nonmusical person cannot be affected by music). The point is thus more refined than the simple idea that only an object can be affected by another object, so that the pure I also has to be an object in the world: when I perceive objects, it is not just an object interacting with another object but the I itself which is affected; the I itself, as not-object, must therefore self-posit itself as open to being-affected, and the I's perception of itself as an object in the world is just an aspect – an objectivized version – of this spontaneous capacity of the I itself to be affected.

This is why the difference between Substance and Subject has to reflect/ inscribe itself into subjectivity itself as the irreducible gap that separates human subjects from Christ, the 'more than human' monstrous subject. This necessity of Christ, the 'absolute' subject which adds itself to the series of finite human subjects as the supplementary a ($\$+\$+\$+\$+\$...+a$), is what differentiates the Hegelian position from the young Marx-Feuerbachian position of the big Other as the virtual Substance posited by collective subjectivity, as its alienated expression. Christ signals the overlapping of the two kenoses: man's alienation from/in God is simultaneously God's alienation from himself in Christ. So it is not only that humanity becomes conscious of itself in the alienated figure of God, but: in human religion, God becomes conscious of Himself. It is not enough to say that people (individuals) organize themselves in Holy Spirit (Party, community of believers): in humanity, a trans-subjective 'it' organizes itself. The finitude of humanity, of the human subject (collective or individual), is maintained here: Christ is the excess which prohibits simple recognition of collective Subject in Substance, the reduction of Spirit to objective/virtual entity (presup)posed by humanity.

One has to get rid of the old Platonic topos of love as Eros which gradually elevates itself from the love for a particular individual through the love for the beauty of a human body in general and the love of the beautiful form as such to the love for the supreme Good beyond all forms. For true love to emerge, this movement of gradual ascent towards universality has to be supplemented by a sudden descent or fall into singularity: I fall in love also in the ontological sense of falling back into the singularity of a contingent person whom I love (in the same way as, in Christianity, universal god has to fall down into a contingent singular person of Jesus Christ, or in the same way as, in Hegel's theory of monarchy, the universal State has to 'fall down' and embody itself in the contingent person of a monarch). In other words, true love is precisely the opposite of forsaking temporary existence for eternity, it is the move of *forsaking the promise of Eternity itself for an imperfect individual.* (This lure of eternity can have many images, from the postmortal fame to fulfilling one's social role.) What if the gesture of choosing temporal existence, of giving up eternal existence for the sake of love – from Christ to Siegmund in act 2 of Wagner's *Die Walküre*, who prefers to stay a common mortal if his beloved Sieglinde cannot follow him to Valhalla, the eternal dwelling of the dead heroes – is the highest ethical act of them all? The shattered Brunhilde comments on this refusal: 'So little do you value everlasting bliss? Is she everything to you, this poor woman who, tired and sorrowful, lies limp in your lap? Do you think nothing less glorious?' This is why love is love for a Neighbour. When Freud and Lacan insist on the problematic nature of the basic Judeo-Christian injunction to 'love thy neighbour', they are thus not just making the standard critico-ideological point about how every notion of universality is coloured by our particular values and thus implies secret exclusions. They are making a much stronger point on the incompatibility of the idea of the Neighbour with the very dimension of universality. What resists universality is the properly *inhuman* dimension of the Neighbour.

These precise distinctions also enable us to account for the passage of what Hegel called 'objective spirit' to 'absolute spirit' (AS): it is through Christ's mediation that OS changes into AS. There is no Holy Spirit without Christ's mutilated corpse: the two poles, the Universal (the *virtual infinity/immortality* of the Holy Spirit [OS]) and the Particular (the *actual finite/mortal* community of believers [subjective spirit, or SS]) can only be mediated through Christ's monstrous singularity.

We do not pass from OS to AS by way of a simple subjective appropriation of the 'reified' OS by the collective human subjectivity (in the well-known Feuerbach–young Marx pseudo-Hegelian mode: 'the subjectivity recognizes in OS its own product, the reified expression of its own creative power') – this would have been a simple reduction of OS to SS. But we also do not accomplish this passage by way of positing beyond OS another, even more In-itself, absolute entity that encompasses both SS and OS. The passage from OS to AS resides in nothing but the dialectical mediation between OS and SS, in the above-indicated inclusion of the gap that separates OS from SS within the SS, so that OS has to appear (be experienced) as such, as an objective 'reified' entity, by the SS itself (and in the inverted recognition that, without the *subjective* reference to an In-itself of the OS, subjectivity itself disintegrates, collapses into psychotic autism). (In the same way, in Christianity, we overcome the opposition of God as an objective spiritual In-itself and human [believers'] subjectivity by way of transposing this gap into God itself: Christianity is 'absolute religion' only and precisely insofar as in it, the distance that separates God from man separates God from himself [and man from man, from the 'inhuman' in him].)

One can also put it the following way: all that happens in the passage from OS to AS is that one takes into account that 'there is no big Other'. AS is not a 'stronger' absolute entity in comparison with OS, but a 'less strong' one – to reach AS, we pass from reified Substance to a subjectivized virtual substance. AS thus avoids both pitfalls: in it, neither is SS reduced to a subordinate element of the self-mediation of the OS, nor is the OS subjectivized in the Feuerbach–young Marx style (reduced to a reified expression-projection of SS). We reach AS when we (SS) are no longer the agent of the process, when 'it organizes itself' in/through us – however, not in the mode of the perverse self-instrumentalization. Therein resides the pitfall of Stalinism: in Stalinism, the big Other exists, we, communists, are its instruments. In liberalism, in contrast, there is no big Other, all there really is is just us, individuals (or, as Margaret Thatcher put it, there is no such thing as society). A dialectical analysis shows how both these positions rely on the other: the truth of the Stalinism OS is subjectivism (we – the Party, the Stalinist subject – constitute the big Other, we decide what is the 'objective necessity' we pretend to realize); the truth of liberalism is the big Other in the guise of the objective network of rules which sustain the interplay of individuals.

Lacan elaborates the passage from the ontic (factual) to deontic (normative) dimension apropos of his notion of Cause as opposed to causality (the causal network). As he put it in his Seminar XI, *il n'y a de cause que de ce qui cloche*, there is no cause but a cause of something that stumbles/slips/falters[30] – a thesis whose obviously paradoxical character is explained when one takes into account the opposition between cause and causality: for Lacan, they are in no way the same, since a 'cause', in the strict sense of the term, is precisely something which intervenes at the points when the network of causality (the chain of causes-and-effects) falters, when there is a cut, a gap, in the causal chain. In this sense, cause is for Lacan by definition a distant cause ('absent cause', as one used to put it in the jargon of the happy 'structuralist' 1960s and 1970s): it acts in the interstices of the direct causal network. What Lacan has in mind here is specifically the working of the unconscious. Imagine an ordinary slip of the tongue: at a chemistry conference, someone gives a speech about, say, the exchange of fluids; all of a sudden, he stumbles and makes a slip, blurting out something about the passage of sperm in the sexual commerce … an 'attractor' from what Freud called 'an Other Scene' intervened like a kind of gravity, exerting its invisible influence from a distance, curving the space of the speech flow, introducing a gap into it. Back to the relation between factual and normative level, Lacan's formula is thus: a Cause (normative 'attractor' which pushes or obliges us to do things) is operative only when there is a disturbance/cut in the causal network of our reality. Normative dimension is an indicator of the perturbed/perverted texture of reality.

This 'big Other', the spiritual Substance, can also be determined as the domain of 'objective appearances'. When Brandom writes, 'For while something could appear to be red and not really be red, it could not *appear* to appear red and not *really* appear red', he misses the point. From the strict Hegelian perspective, one should say: yes it can, and therein resides the speculative core of Hegel's notion of appearance. Let us take the case of commodity fetishism: 'A commodity appears at first sight an extremely obvious, trivial thing. But its analysis brings out that it is a very strange thing, abounding in metaphysical subtleties and theological niceties.'[31] Marx does not claim, in the usual way of Enlightenment critique, that critical analysis should demonstrate how a commodity – what appears a mysterious theological entity – emerged out of the 'ordinary' real-life process; he claims, on the contrary, that the task of critical analysis is to unearth the 'metaphysical subtleties and theological niceties' in what appears at first sight just an ordinary object. Commodity fetishism (our belief that commodities are magic objects, endowed with an inherent metaphysical power) is not located in our mind, in the way we (mis) perceive reality, but in our social reality itself. In other words, when a Marxist encounters a bourgeois subject immersed in commodity fetishism, the Marxist's reproach to him is not 'The commodity may seem to you to be a magical object endowed with special powers, but it really is just a reified expression of relations between people' but rather, 'You may think that the commodity appears to you as a simple embodiment of social relations (that, for example, money is just a kind of voucher entitling you to a part of the social product), but this is not how things really seem to you. In your social reality, by means of your participation in social exchange, you bear witness to the uncanny fact that a commodity really appears to you as a magical object endowed with special powers.' The same goes for most of us with regard to religious belief: I know there is no god, and there is no god, but my actual behaviour nonetheless bears witness to my unconscious belief in god. It is against the background of such paradoxes that we can give a new twist to Hegel's (in)famous statement 'if facts do not fit the notion, so much worse for the fact': it is a fact that my father is a stupid weakling, but if his symbolic identity defines him as a courageous wise man, so much worse for the facts …

Self-consciousness = Freedom = Reason

All these complications point towards the insufficiency of Brandom's 'renormalized' notion of self-consciousness. Do things stand any better in Robert Pippin's work? In his short but crucial essay on the role of self-consciousness in Hegel's logic,[32] Pippin makes a heroic attempt to 'normalize' (translate into our common understanding) Hegel's craziest speculative principle, according to which 'self-consciousness, freedom and reason are one'. How does Pippin proceed? As expected, he begins by lowering the expectations: the first step in such 'normalization' is to de-ontologize Hegel's logic by way of presenting it as 'something like *an account of all possible account-givings*, a scope that would include everything from ethical justifications to empirical judgements to the concept of explanation presupposed by the Second Law of Thermodynamics' (149). In such a vision of 'deflated Hegel', logic is reduced to a formal analysis of all possible procedures of (implicit or explicit) argumentations: how do we justify our claim that the weather today is cloudy, that not voting in the next elections is the right thing to do, that a certain painting is a great work of art, that quantum physics is true, that creationism is not a science, etc.? And how should our thinking be structured so that all our claims have a normative dimension and include reflexive justification (all our statements, even the most empirical one, never just register a state of things but simultaneously justify themselves)? In his *Hegel's Practical Philosophy*, Pippin calls this 'the capacity of some natural beings to be aware of themselves in a non-observational, but more self-determining way':[33]

> The suggestion Hegel seems to be making is simply that at a certain level of complexity and organization, natural organisms come to be occupied with themselves and eventually to understand themselves in ways no longer appropriately explicable within the boundaries of nature or in any way the result of empirical observation.[34]

> It is the achievement of the sublating relation to nature that constitutes spirit; natural beings which by virtue of their natural capacities can achieve it are spiritual; having achieved it and maintaining it *is* being spiritual; those which cannot are not.[35]

The last quote indicates the thin edge on which Pippin is walking here: although he writes that humans are 'natural beings which by virtue of their natural capacities can achieve' spiritual self-relating, he by no means endorses the Aristotelian view according to which human being is a substantial entity among whose positive features are potentials/powers of spiritual self-relating; for Pippin (following Hegel), spirit is not a substantial entity but a purely processual one, it is the result of its own becoming, it makes itself what it is – the only substantial reality there is is nature. The distinction between nature and spirit therefore does not stem from the fact that spirit is a thing of a different kind from natural things, but rather has more to do with the different sets of criteria that are required for *explaining* them: spirit is 'a kind of norm', 'an achieved form of individual and collective mindedness, and institutionally embodied recognitive relations'. That is to say, free acts are distinguished by the *reason* to which a subject might appeal in *justifying* them, and justification is a fundamentally social practice, the practice of 'giving of and asking for reasons' by participants in a set of shared institutions. Even at the individual level, expressing an intention amounts to 'avowing a pledge to act, the content and credibility of which remains (*even for me*), in a way, suspended until I begin to fulfill the pledge'. It is not until my intention is recognized by others and myself as being fulfilled or realized in my deed that I can identify my act as my own.

Note the radical implication of this position of Pippin's: the subject is constitutively decentred in Lacan's sense, its innermost status as a free agent is decided outside itself, by the social recognition, and retroactively, with a delay, after the (f)act. Justification thus turns out to be more *retro-spective* than prospective, a process in which the agent's own stance on her action is by no means authoritative. (Pippin points out how Hegel's weird repetition apropos of beauty – 'beauty is born of the spirit and born again' – is to be read in the same way, as an indication of the gap between the subject's act and its inscription into the symbolic big Other: a work of art is first created/born by the artist and then re-created/re-born in its social status through its social reception/recognition. Crucial here is the delay between the two, the decentring of the work of art's true meaning with regard to the author's intention: the author/artist himself learns only afterward, from the reception of his or her work, the work's true meaning.) Being an agent, being able to provide reasons to others to justify one's deeds, is thus itself an 'achieved social status such as, let us say, being a citizen or being a professor, a product or result of mutually recognitive attitudes'. This conclusion is more radical than it may appear: objective scientific knowledge is not just an affair between the scientist and impersonal reality but has intersubjective foundation, i.e. when the scientist's propositions are accepted as true, it means they achieved a certain social status, and a subject's position as 'scientist' ultimately functions as a symbolic entitlement grounded in mutually recognitive practices.

We can see now in what precise sense Pippin remains a kind of 'Hegelianized Kantian': the unsurpassable horizon of philosophical reflection is for him self-awareness as a minimal self-relating on account of which we, humans, have to justify with reasons our acts:

> to judge is not only to be aware of what one is judging, but that one is judging, asserting, claiming something. If it were not apperceptive like this, it would be indistinguishable from the differential responsiveness of a thermometer, and thermometers cannot *defend* their claims/readings. But one is not, cannot be, simultaneously judging that one is judging. Rather, judgment somehow *is* the consciousness of judging. These are not two acts, but one. (153)

Pippin's approach is here the very opposite of Kristeva's: the defining feature of subjectivity is for him self-consciousness (in the precise sense of rational self-reflexivity, of how all our relating to reality has to be assumed as such), while Kristeva focuses on the abject as the 'irrational' substance from which subject has to acquire a minimal distance in order to function as subject. My claim is that they both miss negativity as the founding gesture of subjectivity.

In a further development of this basic insight, Pippin demonstrates how such self-consciousness is necessary for the perceiving subject to perform the most elementary distinction between the temporal succession of our perceptions of an object and properties of the object itself. Only a self-conscious subject knows that the succession of his perceptions when he walks around a house are not the succession (or a change) that belongs to the house itself – the house remains the same, there is no change in it. What this means is that 'achieving the unity of self-consciousness *is* differentiating seeming from being':

> Discriminating what belongs together with what, what is connected to what in a temporal order, knowing that the successive perceptions of a house do not count as the perception of a succession in the world, requires an apperceptive unity; it does not just happen to consciousness. What happens is mere succession. Such a unity is possible only selfconsciously and it is the actualization of the power of conceiving. But the unity effected by the power of conceiving (where 'conceiving' means conceiving, not merely thinking together) *is* the representational unity that makes reference to an object possible. Unifying by 'red' achieves the unity that says how things are. It, the rose, belongs with the red things; not with what has seemed red-like to me before. Without this ability to distinguish how things are from how they seem to me, there would be as many 'I's' as arbitrarily associated seemings; and no unity of self-consciousness. Or, achieving the unity of self-consciousness *is* differentiating seeming from being, and so the rules for that distinction, categories, are constitutive of such unity. (147–8)

Pippin makes here the classic Kantian point: the idea of an object's self-identity beyond the ever-changing flux of how it appears to us (we know that we see the same house in sunshine and in rain, from its front and its sides) presupposes the perceiving subject's self-consciousness. Self-consciousness is thus not a second-level consciousness of what I am conscious of (a metaconsciousness in the sense of metalanguage: a consciousness about consciousness) but an ingredient of consciousness (of an object) itself:

> Their all being undertaken self-consciously means no one could be said to 'just' assert, or just believe or just act. Any such undertaking, if self-conscious, must be potentially responsive to the question of 'Why?'; that is, to reasons. (An assertion *is* such a responsiveness;

the latter is not a secondary or even distinct dimension of the former.) And it is at least plausible to say that the greater the extent of such potential responsiveness (or said another way, the greater the self-understanding), the 'freer' the activity, the more I can be said to redeem the action as genuinely mine, back it, stand behind it, as mine. (We thus have that heart of German Idealism cited at the outset, the principle 'that self-consciousness, freedom and reason are one'.) (159)

The link between the three terms – self-consciousness, freedom, reason – now becomes evident: reason is never just an insight into 'objective' necessity, apropos of every fact it always involves a normative elaboration of 'why', and freedom is a 'conceived/understood necessity' – the more answers a subject has to 'why', the more elaborated is his insight into the network of relations within which he dwells, the more he is 'free' in the only meaningful sense of the word. Pippin, of course, here supplements Kant with the Hegelian account of the (transcendental, not empirical) genesis of self-awareness out of the complex social relations focused on mutual recognition: '"Spirit" emerges in this imagined social contestation, in what we come to demand of each other.' The proof of Pippin's Kantianism is that he ends up in standard transcendental dualism: philosophy is reduced to a transcendental analysis of the conditions of account givings and as such totally separated from scientific exploration. Furthermore, in such a transcendentalized Hegel there is no place here for his 'craziest' statement like the one about (North and South) America as a syllogism with a narrow copula uniting its two parts (the narrow distance between the two oceans in Panama). Much more seriously, there is also no place for the key dimension of the Hegelian dialectics of substance and subject. Pippin, of course, does deploy in detail the long and winding process of the subjectivization of substance as a progress in freedom through gradual reflexive assuming of substantial determinations. What he ignores is how subject's distance from substantial being is to be transposed back into substance as its own self-division – the moment of reversal when substance 'bends back into itself' (to use the formulation which Pippin dismisses as an empty metaphor). This weakness goes back to Pippin's first masterpiece, *Hegel's Idealism*, where, in dealing with Hegel's triad of positing, external and determining reflection, he fails to capture the specificity of the determining reflection. Pippin begins with 'the limitations of an exclusively positing and external reflection':

No identity (or identifying rule of reflection, categorial ground rule or qualitative identity) is simply posited; it is 'reflected' in the light of the determinate differences 'presupposed' to require it and it alone. Yet the differences taken to require some sort of conceptual 'identification' are themselves always apprehended *as such*, in a way that already depends on the identification of such differences.[36]

In a somewhat simplified way, the opposition between positing and external reflection is here basically reduced to the opposition between directly asserting ('positing') the identity of an x and bringing out the network of differences implied ('presupposed') by this identity: what x is is determined by a complex network of differential relations – man is not woman, night is not day, etc. He then draws the rather obvious conclusion that the two reflections are mutually dependent: every positing an identity implies a set of differences (to say x is a man means to say x is not a woman, etc.), and every differential relation presupposes the identity of the elements it relates to (the identity of woman should also be posited). The problem is then: are we caught in the 'spurious infinity' of oscillating between these two reflections, or is there a third type of reflection which overcomes this endless oscillation? Here Hegel introduces determining reflection as 'the balanced position that avoids both extremes'[37] – but Pippin's claim is that it doesn't quite do the work:

> To be sure, [Hegel] does keep trying to explain what he means by deter-mining reflection by repeating the 'neither-nor' account … There must be reflection, a self-conscious determination of essence, and it cannot be positing or external reflection, so it must be 'that form of reflection that is neither the one nor the other.' And although it is, I think, fair to argue that it is a typical, serious deficiency of all Hegel's philosophy that he is better at telling us what cannot be an acceptable solution to a problem than he is at describing the details of what can be and is (and that, with his account of 'determinate negation', he sometimes seems to think that the positive answer just *is* the realization of such determinate insufficiency), in this case we need much more than such a programmatic outline of what *would* be an acceptable position … Hegel either just asserts, without explaining very much, the possibility of a position like this: 'In so far, therefore, as it is the positedness that is at the same time reflection-into-self, the determinatedness of reflection is *the relation to its otherness within itself.*' Or he makes use of a strikingly odd metaphor to suggest how this is all supposed to be possible: 'It is *positedness*, negation, which however bends back into itself the relation to other.'[38]

There is a precise critical diagnosis deployed in this passage: (1) Hegel is unable to provide a precise and meaningful determination of determinate reflection – what he does is either just assert its possibility, i.e. provide its formal tautological definition, a kind of programmatic outline, or fill in the conceptual gap with nonconceptual metaphors; (2) this problem with determinate reflection is merely the exemplary case of a serious deficiency of all Hegel's philosophy – he is better at telling us what is not the acceptable solution to a problem than he is at describing the details of what is such a solution ... A lot is at stake in this criticism – to put it bluntly, if it holds, then Hegel's dialectics is fully invalidated, since its key moment, the dialectical reversal ('negation of negation'), is undermined. But is Hegel's oscillation between tautologies and metaphors really the case? Note how Pippin adds a qualification in parentheses: Hegel 'sometimes seems to think that the positive answer just *is* the realization of such determinate insufficiency' – but what if, far from being a minor version of how Hegel tries to squeeze out of a deadlock, the mechanism evoked by Pippin indicates the key structure of a dialectical reversal, the purely formal shift of perspective which makes the subject realize how (what appeared as) the problem is its own solution? This reflexive reversal can be given many names and descriptions, up to the transposition of an epistemological obstacle/antinomy into an ontological feature of the thing itself: what makes insufficiency 'determinate' is that it is not 'external' (merely epistemological) but 'internal' (immanent to the thing itself). Recall the case of reading a classical work of art: 'positing reflection' practises a direct approach to the work, simply describing what it is; 'external reflection' deploys a multiplicity of interpretations, elevating the work into an In-itself eluding interpretations; 'determinate reflection' transposes this multiplicity back into the work itself, as the immanent deployment of its antagonistic potentials. This is how external reflection 'bends back into itself': it bends external determinations back into the thing itself. It doesn't add anything to external reflection – on the contrary, it subtracts from it the presupposed In-itself as the substantial inaccessible core around which subjective interpretations circulate. It is thus wrong to describe the tension between positing and external reflection as the oscillation between the two extremes, and then to search for a solution that would mediate between the two: determinate reflection enacts an even stronger negation of the In-itself than external reflection. External reflection merely posits the In-itself as an inaccessible transcendence, while determinate reflection empties the In-itself of all presupposed substantial content, reducing it to a void.

It is here that the most radical dimension of Hegel's thought, the dimension overlooked by Pippin, enters – that of the reversal of the disparity between subject and substance into the disparity of the substance with itself. This reversal takes place at all levels: subjectivity emerges when substance cannot achieve full identity with itself, when substance is in itself 'barred', traversed by in immanent impossibility or antagonism; the subject's epistemological ignorance, its failure to fully grasp the opposed substantial content, simultaneously indicates a limitation, failure, lack of the substantial content itself; the believer's experience of being abandoned by God is simultaneously a gap that separates God from himself, an indication of the 'unfinished' nature of the divine identity, and so forth. Applied to Pippin's ontological ambiguity, this solution means that the gap that separates the normative from the factual should be simultaneously conceived as the gap immanent to the factual itself. Or, to put it in a slightly different way, while everything is to be mediated/posited by the self-relating void of subjectivity, *this void itself emerges out of the Substance through its self-alienation.* We thus encounter here the same ambiguity that characterizes the Lacanian Real: everything is subjectively mediated, but the subject does not come first – it emerges through the self-alienation of the Substance. In other words, while we have no direct access to the substantial presubjective Real, we also cannot get rid of it. To designate this reflexive move, Hegel uses the unique term *absoluter Gegenstoß* (recoil, counter-push, counter-thrust, or, why not, simply counterpunch) – a withdrawal-from which creates what it withdraws from:

> Reflection therefore *finds before it* an immediate which it transcends and from which it is the return. But this return is only the presupposing of what reflection finds before it. What is thus found only *comes to be* through being *left behind* … The reflective movement is to be taken as an *absolute recoil* [*absoluter Gegenstoß*] upon itself. For the presupposition of the return-into-self – that from which essence *comes*, and *is* only as this return – is only in the return itself.[39]

Absoluter Gegenstoß thus stands for the radical coincidence of the opposites in which the action appears as its own counter-action, or, more precisely, in which the very negative move (loss, withdrawal) generates what it 'negates'. 'What is found only *comes to be* through being *left behind*', and its inversion (it is 'only in the return itself' that what we return to emerges, like nations who constitute themselves by way of 'returning to their lost roots') are the two sides of what Hegel calls 'absolute reflection': a reflection which is no longer external to its object, presupposing it as given, but a reflection which, as it were, closes the loop and posits its presupposition. To put it in Derridean terms, the condition of possibility is here radically and simultaneously the condition of impossibility: the very obstacle to the full assertion of our identity opens up the space for it.

Hegel also uses the expression *absoluter Gegenstoß* – the speculative coincidence of the opposites in the movement by means of which a thing emerges out of its own loss – in his explanation of the category of 'ground/reason' (*Grund*), where he resorts to one of his famous wordplays, connecting *Grund* (ground/reason) and *zu Grunde gehen* (to fall apart, literally 'to go to one's ground'):

> The reflected determination, in falling to the ground, acquires its true meaning, namely, to be within itself the absolute recoil upon itself, that is to say, the positedness that belongs to essence is only a sublated positedness, and conversely, only self-sublating positedness is the positedness of essence. Essence, in determining itself as ground, is determined as the non-determined; its determining is only the sublating of its being determined. Essence, in being determined thus as self-sublating, has not proceeded from another, but is, in its negativity, self-identical essence.[40]

While these lines may sound obscure, their underlying logic is clear: in a relationship of reflection, every term (every determination) is posited (mediated) by another (its opposite), identity by difference, appearance by essence, etc. – in this sense, it 'proceeds from another'. When positedness is self-sublated, an essence is no longer directly determined by an external Other, by its complex set of relations to its otherness, to the environment into which it is emerged – it determines itself, i.e. it is 'within itself the absolute recoil upon itself', the gap or discord that introduces dynamic into it is absolutely immanent.

The only full case of absolute recoil, of a thing emerging through its very loss, is the subject itself, the outcome of its own impossibility. In this precise Hegelian sense subject is the truth of substance: the truth of every substantial thing is that it is the retroactive effect of its own loss. Subject as $ does not pre-exist its loss, it emerges from its loss as a return to itself. In other words, subject is not only always barred, lost, failed, it is a name for such a loss which retroactively creates what is lost.

Reflexivity of the Unconscious

So how does this barred subject stand with regard to the Unconscious? The standard psychoanalytic theory conceives the Unconscious as a psychic substance of subjectivity (the notorious hidden part of the iceberg) – all the depth of desires, fantasies, traumas, etc. In his passing critical remarks on psychoanalysis, Pippin follows this line: for him, the Freudian Unconscious remains a prereflexive determination of the subject, an immediate substantial given, which, as such, already presupposes (and cannot account for) self-consciousness qua self-reflexive accounting for. In short, every (self-)explanation of a subject (say, when a subject claims that his acts were [over]determined by his unconscious) already has to rely on a reflexive self-accounting: the very gesture of accounting for one's acts in terms of unconscious motivations cannot itself be accounted for in terms of unconscious determinism. It may appear that psychoanalysis, the psychoanalytic session, is the unique place where, in the mode of 'free associations', the patient is allowed, enjoined even, to ignore all constraints and 'say it all', with nothing unmentionable – and one could even venture that this is the reason why psychoanalysis is uniquely absent in Muslim countries … However, we should not forget that what we get in 'free associations' is the very shape of our psychic unfreedom, all the constraints and traumas we are not aware of in our normal daily awareness: in 'free associations', we in a way 'freely' confront our unfreedom, we enact or perform it.

Here we come to Lacan's key achievement: breaking with the standard psychoanalytic tradition, he *de-substantializes the Unconscious* (for him, the Cartesian *cogito* is the Freudian subject), thereby bringing psychoanalysis to the level of modern subjectivity. What this means is that he locates into the Unconscious the very reflexive mechanism of self-accounting which, for Pippin, distinguishes self-consciousness. And here, Lacan is much more Hegelian than Pippin himself: for Hegel, 'self-consciousness' in its abstract definition stands for a purely nonpsychological self-reflexive ply of registering (re-marking) one's own position, of reflexively 'taking into account' what one is doing. Therein resides the link between Hegel and psychoanalysis: in this precise nonpsychological sense, 'self-consciousness' is in psychoanalysis an object – say, a tic, a symptom which articulates the falsity of my position of which I am unaware. Say, I did something wrong, and I consciously deluded myself that I had the right to do it; but, unbeknown to me, a compulsive act which appears mysterious and meaningless to me 'registers' my guilt, it bears witness to the fact that, somewhere, my guilt is remarked. This is the function of the Lacanian 'big Other' at its purest: this impersonal, nonpsychological, agency (or, rather, site) of registering, of 'taking note of' what takes place. This is how one should grasp Hegel's notion of the State as the 'self-consciousness' of a people: 'The state is the *self-conscious* ethical substance.'[41] A State is not merely a blindly running mechanism applied to regulate social life, it always also contains a series of practices, rituals and institutions that serve to 'declare' its own status, in the guise of which the State appears to its subjects as what it is – parades and public celebrations, solemn oaths, legal and educational rituals which assert (and thereby enact) the subject's belonging to the State:

> the self-consciousness of the state has nothing mental about it, if by 'mental' we understand the sorts of occurrences and qualities that are relevant to *our own* minds. What self-consciousness amounts to, in the state's case, is the existence of reflective practices, such as, but not limited to, educational ones. Parades displaying the state's military strength would be practices of this kind, and so would statements of principle by the legislature, or sentences by the Supreme Court – and they would be that *even if* all individual (human) participants in a parade, all members of the legislature or of the Supreme Court, were personally motivated to play whatever role they play in this affair by greed, inertia, or fear, *and* even if all such participants or members were thoroughly uninterested and bored through the whole event, and totally lacking in any understanding of its significance.[42]

So it is quite clear to Hegel that this appearing has nothing to do with conscious awareness: it does not matter what individuals' minds are preoccupied with while they are participating in a ceremony, the truth resides in the ceremony itself. Hegel made the same point apropos of the marriage ceremony, which registers the most intimate link of love: 'the solemn declaration of consent to the ethical bond of marriage and its recognition and confirmation by the family and community constitute the formal *conclusion* and *actuality* of marriage', which is why it belongs to 'impertinence and its ally, the understanding', to see 'the ceremony whereby the essence of this bond is expressed and *confirmed* ... as an external formality', irrelevant with regard to the inwardness of passionate feeling.[43] A similar example from Marx: when, in the second chapter of *Capital*, he argues why gold and silver were commodities which lent themselves to be used as general equivalents of all commodities (money), he draws a distinction between *two* use-values of gold, its use-value as a particular commodity and its 'formal' use-value:

> since the difference between the magnitudes of value is purely quanti-tative, the money commodity must be susceptible of merely quantitative differences, must therefore be divisible at will, and equally capable of being reunited. Gold and silver possess these properties by nature.
>
> The use-value of the money-commodity becomes two-fold. In addition to its special use-value as a commodity (gold, for instance,

serving to stop teeth, to form the raw material of articles of luxury, &c.), it acquires a formal use-value, originating in its specific social function.[44]

The properly speculative expression here is 'formal use-value': the difference between exchange-value and use-value as to be reflected into use-value itself, splitting it from within, leading to the rise of a weird use-value the 'use' of which is not its effective practical use but its usefulness to serve as the embodiment of exchange-value. Let us explain this with an example from a different domain. In some Polynesian tribes, if a young man wants to have sex with a girl who publicly rejected him, he is expected to silently crawl into the tent where the girl is asleep and try to force himself on her; the custom is also that he soaks the entire skin of his limbs and body in oil so that if the girl resists and tries to grab him he can easily slip out of her grasp and escape ... Isn't it clear that soaking his skin in oil cannot be fully justified by its actual use-value? Soaking one's skin in oil obviously also displays what Lacan called a 'ritual value': it is an act that is done not only to bring about the desired effect in bodily reality (the slippery skin enabling escape) but also, primarily even, to deliver a message, to declare a subjective stance. I thereby declare to the girl my intention: I am to make love to her, but if she doesn't like it she only has to signal it by way of trying to grab me and I will disappear ... So their interaction is not a rape but a complex sexual ritual. The same holds for a black South African tribe whose members sleep on bare earth; while sleeping, they don't put their head on some firm support (stone or another ersatz of a pillow) – their head rests on the opened palm on the top of a horizontally extended elbow ... without doubt not a very comfortable position. The pragmatic justification is that in this way, since the head comes close to floating in the air, insects and worms who swarm the earth will find it more difficult to reach the face and penetrate ears or other openings there – again, a procedure which obviously doesn't make a lot of sense owing to its ridiculous clumsiness, so we have to add the 'ritual value' of a message and stance displayed by it. In other words, isn't it clear in both cases that what really matters in the performed act is its 'formal use-value': an act clumsily imitates efficiency, but the very clumsiness of its use-value (say, of the oiled skin to enable us to escape from the girl) draws attention to itself as a declaration, as a symbolic performance.

We can thus clearly see the difference between the Kantian transcendental subject and the Freudian subject: contrary to the common notion according to which transcendental subject, the substanceless subject of pure apperception, is a nonpsychological formal function and the Freudian subject an empirical agent of pathological passions (in both Kantian and clinical senses of the term) caught in substantial determinations, the Freudian subject is 'purer' than the transcendental one, a thoroughly de-psychologized X with no determinate ontological status, a virtual entity which never 'is' but will always have been. Furthermore, while the subject of self-consciousness as described by Pippin is engaged in the endless effort of subjectivizing its 'unconscious' substantial determinations, Lacan demonstrates how the Unconscious itself is already thoroughly reflexivized/desubstantialized.

So, to resume, for the 'normativist' Hegelians (Brandom, Pippin, etc.), the central philosophical fact is thus the full autonomy of (subjective) Reason: Reason acts as its own judge, accepting nothing as directly or immediately given. Since every given fact has to be reflexively grounded, accounted for, Reason is the endless process of self-grounding, with no reference to some figure of the external Other (God, Nature) that would serve as a final judge. (Within this perspective, Hegel's Absolute Knowing is reinterpreted in the Kantian way as the inaccessible goal of total reflexive-rational self-grounding.) Consequently, these 'normativist' Hegelians have to reject the three great thinkers of the post-Hegelian 'hermeneutics of suspicion' (Marx, Nietzsche, Freud): they all refer to some prere-flexive substantial Other (Marx's economic base, Nietzsche's Life, Freud's Unconscious) which robs Reason of its autonomy, making it an instrument of this Other (say, ideology serving class interests for Marx), a mere visible top of the iceberg effectively dominated and regulated by its invisible depth … But is this the case? With regard to German Idealism, it can be shown that, from late Fichte onwards, it struggles with how to limit subjectivity without regressing to a precritical (pre-Kantian) realism. As for Marx, when he talks about *political* economy, he thereby signals the subjective core of the 'economic base' which is not an objective process, but a process overdetermined by a political struggle; the critical point made by 'norma-tivist' Hegelians holds only for a vulgar determinist historical materialism. As for the Unconscious, the point made by the 'normativist' Hegelians holds only for the nineteenth-century *Lebensphilosophie* and for Jung (who resubstantialized the Freudian Unconscious), but definitely not for Freud and Lacan. When Lacan repeatedly asserts that *il n'y a pas de grand Autre*, there is no big Other, he means precisely that the Unconscious is not an alienated substance determining subject: the Freudian Unconscious is a name for the inconsistency of Reason itself (Lacan even uses the shortened formula *Ics* which can be read as the condensation of *inconscient* and of *inconsistance*) of reason itself. We should bear in mind that the subtitle of his *écrit* 'The Instance of the Letter in the Unconscious' is 'Reason according to Freud' (*La raison après Freud*), and he writes in it: 'The intolerable scandal when Freudian sexuality was not yet holy was that it was so "intellectual".'[45] The fact of the Unconscious does not imply that Reason is dominated by its Other, but that it is decentred from within.

The same point can also be made in the terms of Malabou's analogy with the structure of earthquakes: the Freudian Unconscious is not the deep hypocentre of the subject's psychic life, but precisely its epicentre. Let's take the case of naming: in a way, we can say that we are all George Kaplans (a name that, by a stupid misunderstanding, gets attached to Roger O. Thornhill – played by Cary Grant – in Hitchcock's *North by Northwest*). At a hotel bar, Thornhill is mistakenly identified by foreign spies as George Kaplan, a mysterious CIA agent, and is treated by them accordingly, totally perplexed by his new situation. Thornhill's predicament is ultimately the predicament of all of us: a name is stuck on me in a contingent way, it has nothing to do with my true nature, at the utmost it is invested with desires and fears of my parents, desires which maybe even do not concern me (say, they name me after a rich uncle to flatter him and get some inheritance from him). However, contingent as it may be, this name marks me, my assuming it involves a kind of investiture, I am burdened with some duty or another form of expectations. Things get interesting when, as expected, the features imposed on me from outside by a name find an echo in deep recesses of my psyche – say, in the case of Thornhill, what if the fact of being (mis)identified as the spy Kaplan aroused in him a series of desires, passions and fears associated with spying (covering up one's identity, trying to penetrate others' secrets, etc.), which were till now resting dormant in the recesses of his mind? However (and now we arrive at the key feature), this resonance does not mean that desires associated with spying were always-already there, lurking deep in me and just waiting for the opportunity to express themselves. What is 'deep in me' is not the Unconscious proper but a mess of the real, and it is the contingent fact of me acquiring a new name (the spy Kaplan, in this case) which performatively forms out of this mess in me a set of desires, fears and passions. In short, to resort to Malabou's analogy with earthquakes, the name Kaplan (which effectively causes an earthquake in Thornhill's identity) is the epicentre of Thornhill's psychic life, the mark of the disturbance that befalls him – what matters, from the Freudian standpoint, is epicentre, much more than the deep 'hypocentre'.

PART TWO

THE DISPARITY OF BEAUTY: THE UGLY, THE ABJECT AND THE MINIMAL DIFFERENCE

4 ART AFTER HEGEL, HEGEL AFTER THE END OF ART

The couple of art and thinking has a long tradition, reaching down to Heidegger's *Dichten und Denken*, but why is religion added as a separate entity? (Hegel himself often treats art and religion as aspects of the same self-deploying entity – for example, ancient Greek art is for him religion in the form of art, religion which finds its appropriate expression in art.) Religion intervenes here as an uncanny intruder, a monstrosity of the supernatural in natural terms. Should the starting point not be religion rather than art? Was what we today consider art not historically first part of a religious or sacred experience? And is the emergence of art in its independence, not as part of the experience of the sacred – a process which reaches its peak only in modernity – strictly correlative to the rise of philosophy and (later) science as an autonomous mode of thinking no longer rooted in religion? Is, then, the very couple of *Dichten und Denken* the outcome of the withdrawal of religious experience?

The progress from art through religion to science moves in the direction of *Ver-Innerung*, of recollection or internalization: it ends when the Spirit no longer needs the external medium of *Vorstellung* to express itself but deals with itself directly in the form of Spirit. This is why every preoccupation with deep mysteries, with unfathomable secrets to be disclosed to the initiated, and so forth is a sign that Spirit has not yet truly found itself: 'The spirit only occupies itself with objects so long as there is something secret, not revealed, in them.'[1] This is why, from a Hegelian standpoint, one should reject absolutely the Schellingian and Heideggerian topic of an impenetrable, self-withdrawing, Ground (*Erde*, Earth, in Heidegger). For Schelling, Reason (*logos*) can only emerge against the background of an obscure and impenetrable *Grund* which can never be sublated in the self-transparency of Reason; for Heidegger, the Platonic metaphysics privileges the Ideal, its self-transparence, and obliterates the self-withdrawal of *Erde*, its nontransparency. What both of them insist on is the unsurpassable character of man's finitude: it is because of this finitude that we are forever caught in struggle, that we can never reach the Absolute at peace with itself (and that this also holds for the Absolute itself which is caught in this struggle). And, from the Hegelian standpoint, one should also reject Schiller's and Schelling's assertion of art as higher than philosophy, as the only adequate rendering of the Absolute, of the harmonious identity of subject and object, ideal and real, freedom and necessity, reflection and spontaneity, activity and passivity (in contrast to philosophy, rational thinking, which privileges the subject and reflection).

With Hegel against Hegel

According to Hegel's (in)famous diagnosis, with the rise of modernity, 'the form of art has ceased to be the supreme need of the spirit': even if excellent works are produced, 'we bow the knee no longer'.[2] This thesis of Hegel's acquired new content with the rise of what he couldn't forecast: the secular capitalist civilization which elevates scientific reason into the highest form of reason (not in the Hegelian sense of *Wissenschaft*, but in the Anglo-Saxon sense of positive science relying on experiments). Today, with the emergence of cognitivism and the brain sciences, the circle is somehow closed, human mind itself has become an object of neurobiology, and although the representatives of the experimental sciences as a rule dismiss Hegel's thought as the high point of speculative madness, as an artistic-obscurantist phenomenon which has nothing to do with science proper, Hegel's thesis that art is no longer the supreme expression of spirit survives this scathing critique. Even cognitivists who admire art or frequently refer to it (Sacks, Damasio) do so with a benevolently condescending attitude – what matters is science, not art.

The Romantic reaction to modern scientific civilization invites us 'to bend the knee anew' (as Pippin wrote apropos of Heidegger)[3]: in what is today often referred to as the 'postsecular' spirit, it endeavours to re-enchant reality, and to elevate art into (one of) the harbinger(s) of the ultimate truth about our lives inaccessible to science. (Another strategy is, of course, to search in the latest sciences themselves for signs of their overcoming of the 'mechanistic paradigm'.) One should be unambiguous here: such re-enchantments are a fake, a pleasing aesthetic game.

How, then, are we to advocate, against Hegel and his diagnostics of the end of art, but nonetheless in the spirit of Hegel, the continuing relevance of art, if we are not allowed to posit an impenetrable Other with which Spirit is caught in an eternal struggle? If there is no impenetrable Other, if Spirit can find itself in itself, in the form of Spirit, why should art persist in its sensuality? The answer is that the struggle should not be conceived as a struggle of Spirit with its Other, but as a thoroughly self-immanent struggle. Spirit is in itself 'barred', hindered, thwarted, and the very objective impenetrable stuff or matter is not what resists concepts but only the secondary materialization of the concept's own inherent blockade. Furthermore, if Spirit is reconciled with itself and thus no longer requires a material embodiment (in the beauty of a work of art), what then to do with bodily reality which continues to exist? Would it not be possible to proceed *a contrario* and to demonstrate the Spirit's indifference towards material reality by way of embodying it not in a beautiful object but in the image of an ugly, weak or distorted body?

Along these lines of reading Hegel against Hegel, Robert Pippin's goal in his *After the Beautiful* is 'to see what Hegel missed, but see it in *his* terms' (61). (The problem with this approach is, of course, how to avoid the naive and thoroughly pre-Hegelian distinction between an empirical, 'historical Hegel' and the 'true Hegel', the Hegel true to his notion or, rather, at the level of his notion: is not, for Hegel, the historical actualization of a notion its truth, the deployment of its actual potentials, so that his mode of thinking totally prohibits all reference to an ideal against its historical realization?) The fundamental limitation of the 'historical Hegel', the 'blind spot in his treatment of modernity', is formulated by Pippin in proto-Marxist terms: it is his 'failure to anticipate the dissatisfactions that this "prosaic" world ... would generate, or his failure to appreciate that there might be a basic form of disunity or alienation that his project could not account for, for which there was no "sublation" or overcoming yet on the horizon' (46). For Pippin, Hegel's thought involves another limitation which concerns the form of art itself: his conclusion – the end of art in its essential role – 'is not motivated by anything essential in Hegel's account and represents a misstep, not an inference consistent with Hegel's overall project' (22–3). So when Hegel correctly claims that in our age, 'art invites us to intellectual consideration',[4] he himself undermines the notion of art as intuitive and affecting, opening up the possibility of a different kind of art, an art which is 'explicitly self-reflexive and exploratory' (42), involving interpretative effort. (And, incidentally, the counterpart of this reflexivization of art is that philosophy itself becomes 'artistic'.) The bad luck with so-called conceptual art (which seems a perfect example of 'art inviting us to intellectual consideration') is that, as a rule, it works only as *hapax*: you do it once, you make your point, and it's over (there is only one *pissoir* for Duchamp, only one white square on black surface with Malevich, we gain nothing by repeating the production of such objects). Hegel's fateful limitation was thus that his notion of art remained within the confines of classical representative art: he was unable to consider the possibility of what we call abstract (nonfigurative) art (or atonal music, or literature which reflexively focuses on its own process of writing, etc.). The truly interesting question here is in what way this limitation – remaining within the constraints of the classical notion of representative art – is linked to what Pippin detects as Hegel's other limitation, his inability to detect the alienation/antagonism which persists even in a modern rational society where individuals attain their formal freedom and mutual recognition. In what way – and *why* – can this persisting unfreedom, uneasiness, dislocation in a modern free society be properly articulated, brought to light, only in an art which is no longer constrained to the representative model? Is it that the modern uneasiness, unfreedom in the very form of formal freedom, servitude in the very form of autonomy, and, more fundamentally, anxiety and perplexity caused by that very autonomy, reaches so deep into the very ontological foundations of our being that it can be expressed only in an art form which destabilizes and denaturalizes the most elementary coordinates of our sense of reality?

The very fact that art plays a key role in an epoch means that in this epoch Spirit is not reconciled with itself – this is why it still needs sensual embodiment (in a work of art). Consequently, Hegel prophesied the end of art because he failed to perceive radical antagonisms which persist in the apparently nonantagonistic, self-reconciled bourgeois society where individuals are condemned to lead a prosaic, everyday life. However, Pippin's critique of Hegelian reconciliation in a modern rational state is deeply ambiguous: does the persistence of art mean that art – authentic and relevant art – is only possible in an unreconciled society, as it sounds when Pippin emphasizes that Hegel did not see the antagonism in modern society, and links this failure to the persistence of art? (Recall the modernist dream of a reconciled society in which art disappears as a separate institution since it overlaps with real everyday life itself.) Or is it that art persists in its very concept even in a fully reconciled society? Or – a third option – is it that the persistence of art signals that reconciliation is not possible for a priori reasons?

What one should further bear in mind is that Hegelian reconciliation is ultimately the reconciliation with failure itself, not a peaceful state in which antagonisms are overcome. The illusion is not that of the enforced 'false' reconciliation which ignores the persisting divisions; the true illusion resides in not seeing that, in what appear to us as the chaos of becoming, the infinite goal *is already realized*: 'In the sphere of the finite we can neither experience nor see that the purpose is genuinely attained. The accomplishing of the infinite purpose consists therefore only in sublating the illusion [or deception: *Täuschung*] that it has not yet been accomplished.'[5] In short, the ultimate deception is not to see that one already has what one is looking for – like Christ's disciples who were awaiting his 'real' reincarnation, blind to the fact that their collective already was the Holy Spirit, the return of the living Christ.

Returning to Pippin, the dissatisfaction in modern prosaic life is what modern art (in painting from Manet to Cézanne, Picasso, etc.) registers. So, again, Hegel's 'greatest failure' is that he

> never seemed very concerned about [the] potential instability in the modern world, about citizens of the same ethical commonwealth potentially losing *so* much common ground and common confidence that a general irresolvability of any of these possible conflicts becomes ever more apparent, the kind of high challenge and low expectations we see in all those vacant looks … He does not worry much because his general theory about the gradual actual historical achievement of some mutual recognitive status, a historical claim that has come to look like the least plausible aspect of Hegel's account and that is connected with our resistance to his proclamations about art as a thing of the past. (69)

And Pippin himself designates as the core of this new dissatisfaction the class division and struggle (here, of course, class is to be opposed to castes, estates, and other hierarchies). A fundamental ambiguity thus characterizes the disturbing and disorienting effect of Manet's paintings: yes, they indicate the 'alienation' of modern individuals who lack a proper place within a society traversed by radical antagonisms, individuals deprived of the intersubjective space of collective mutual recognition and understanding; however, they simultaneously generate and reflect a liberating effect (individuals they depict appear as no longer bound to a specific place in the social hierarchy), as well as an immanently artistic progress in freedom as reflexive awareness of the activity one is involved in. In other words, the modern, 'prosaic' world is the world of the rational state, freedom and mutual recognition (even if this freedom is merely formal, masking deeper class antagonisms), while the premodern universe is the world of hierarchic, nonmutual order. Nicolas Bourriaud wrote in his introduction to Foucault's booklet on Manet:

what vouches for Manet's painting is the definite birth of an individual exiled from his certainties regarding his place in the world ... The viewer is commanded to position himself as an autonomous subject, lacking the possible means to identify himself or to project himself into the artwork he confronts.[6]

For Pippin, the most direct sign of this disorientation is the perplexed gaze of the painted individual, an expression characterized as one of 'looking without seeing': the gaze is directed outside the frame, addressing us, the viewers, but we are treated 'as if invisible or at least indifferent, occupying no important presence in the subject's vacant or bemused look' (48). With this perplexed gaze, Manet is not just a precursor to impressionism, he effectively reaches beyond impressionism and points towards modern art proper (expressionism and abstract painting). The perplexed gaze of the painted individual thus unsettles the viewer as well, making his or her gaze uncertain, simultaneously dislocated (moving, looking at the painting from more than one standpoint since what he sees is impossible to see from one standpoint) and fixed into the unpleasantly exposed position of a voyeur.

However, there is more lurking beneath the surface here. In *The Luncheon on the Grass*, Manet's best-known painting, we see two couples, including two naked women, one in back, knee-deep in water, engaged in what appears a kind of postcoital cleansing (this association was often noted), and a nude in front just sitting on the grass with the expression of 'looking but not seeing'. With whom did the one in back have sex – the silent man or the talking, gesticulating one? Visually, the nude in front and the silent man sitting behind her are a couple, so it must be that the talking man is the one who performed the act and is not flirting with the other woman – or is he covering up his failure to perform the act by his excessive activity? The situation remains ambiguous, but the perplexed, distracted gaze of the naked woman in front remains the gaze of a (sexually) nonsatisfied woman, so that the painting's subtitle could well have been *Il n'y a pas de rapport sexuel*.

Far from being excessive, this reading is confirmed by the general feature of Manet's nude paintings: they are clearly to be conceived as a repetition of classical desexualized nude paintings – a repetition with a twist, of course; that is, what matters is the difference with regard to the classical model. Manet's nude *Olympia* (1863–5) repeats *Reclining Venus* (Ingres, 1822), and what this repetition renders palpable is 'the impossibility (under the emerging conditions of a capitalist society's self-representation) of any continuation of the tradition of the nude in painting, the impossibility, the immediate lack of credibility, of that abstraction from particularity, the desexualizing idealization and so relatively innocent address to the beholder' (77). In short, Manet's Olympia 'is not a nude; she is a naked individual' (77): the same bodily position of the left hand (covering the vaginal area) in Ingres indicates tender shame, while in Manet it designates a prostitute's repose and is as such vulgarly eroticized. All the obscenity of class, power and sex brutally invade the space of the painting, and it is crucial to note that the effect of the repetition of Ingres in Manet is retroactive: it is not only that Ingres's Venus is replaced by a prostitute, it is that Ingres's Venus itself loses its innocence and becomes (visible as) a prostitute.

A further feature which manifests this irruption of obscenity in *Olympia* is the disturbing effect of its light: as Foucault pointed out, there is no discernible source of light within the space depicted by the painting, so that it is as if our gaze at Olympia is the source of the extra-strong light, which means that our possessive erotic gaze makes her visible – in short, we are her customers, our looking at her is like the look of the tourists or potential customers at the prostitutes displayed in the windows in Amsterdam's Red Light district.

The ugly gaze

This brings us back to the topic of the gaze and its vicissitudes in painting. Hegel is fully aware of the disruptive power of the gaze, its exceptional status in the totality of a human body. For Hegel, the form of a human body is

a totality of organs into which the Concept is dispersed, and it manifests in each member only some particular activity and partial emotion. But if we ask in which particular organ the whole soul appears as soul, we will at once name the eye; for in the eye the soul is concentrated and the soul does not merely see through it but is also seen in it. Now as the pulsating heart shows itself all over the surface of the human, in contrast to the animal, body, so in the same sense it is to be asserted of art that it has to convert every shape in all points of its visible surface into an eye, which is the seat of the soul and brings the spirit into appearance. – Or, as Plato cries out to the star in his familiar distich: 'When thou lookest on the stars, my star, oh! would I were the heavens and could see thee with a thousand eyes', so, conversely, art makes every one of its productions into a thousand-eyed Argus, whereby the inner soul and spirit is seen at every point. And it is not only the bodily form, the look of the eyes, the countenance and posture, but also actions and events, speech and tones of voice, and the series of their course through all conditions of appearance that art has everywhere to make into an eye, in which the free soul is revealed in its inner infinity.[7]

A thousand-eyed work of art is thus 'essentially a question, an address to the responsive breast, a call to the mind and the spirit'[8] – a weird metaphor since the breast is not, as one would have expected, the object feeding the subject/mind but the subject itself. The other weird thing is that the image of the thousand-eyed Argus 'is not one of the beautiful but is rather monstrous, ugly even' (101) – so how can such an outstandingly ugly image stand for the metaphor of how a beautiful work of art functions?[9] Let's proceed step by step. First, why *many* eyes? From the Freudian standpoint, there is only one answer possible: in the same way that, according to Freud, the image of multiple penises in a dream signals castration (of the One), thousands of eyes cannot but signal the castration of the (one) Gaze. And the same goes for social life: the principal antagonism, when foreclosed, excluded, returns as a multiplicity. Recall the case of traditional India, where sexual difference is gentrified, its antagonistic edge obfuscated, but it returns in a vast network of hierarchies:

> If any organization is necessarily made up of differences, separations, and oppositions, the caste system, by reason of the endogamy that goes with it and the balance between the two sexes that the latter institutionalizes, seems to translate a difference *elsewhere* by *multiplying* it … The strong caste hierarchy compensates for the man/woman balance introduced by Indian endogamy.[10]

This is the hidden other side of the much-praised balanced relations between the two sexes in Indian society (in contrast to Western patriarchy which oppressed femininity): the fundamental sexual antagonism (the fact that *there is no sexual relationship*) is obfuscated, rendered invisible, but it returns in multiplied form. And does the same not hold for class antagonism which, when occluded by the appearance of class balance (collaboration, mutual support and complementarity – the corporate vision of society as a social body where every organ has its proper role to play), returns in the multiplicity of social separations and hierarchies? (The same goes for the statues and paintings of Indian gods and goddesses with dozens of hands – what this signals is the lack of the one real Hand.) Bourgeois society generally obliterates castes and other hierarchies, equalizing all individuals as market subjects divided only by class difference, but today's late capitalism, with its 'spontaneous' ideology, endeavours to obliterate the class division itself by way of proclaiming us all 'self-entrepreneurs', the differences among us being merely quantitative (a big capitalist borrows hundreds of millions for his investment, a poor worker borrows a couple of thousands for his supplementary education). The expected outcome is that other divisions and hierarchies emerge: experts and nonexperts, full citizens and the excluded, religious, sexual, and other minorities … Therein resides the lie of humanist universalism – or, as Carl Schmitt stated it brutally: 'The one who says "humanity" wants to cheat.' *Cheating* here means simply obfuscating the antagonism in the very core of 'humanity' (and thus covertly taking part by way of privileging one side in the antagonism).

So let us return to the (ugly) gaze that emanates from the painting, in the way the painting we are looking at 'returns the gaze'. Insofar as this gaze, the blind spot of the painting, is an ugly 'phallic' protuberance, an excess that disturbs the painting's harmony (as is the case with Holbein's *Ambassadors*, where the blind spot is the ugly prolonged anamorphic stain in the lower part of the painting), a work of art has to obfuscate this stain in its very heart if it is to become beautiful. This, for Lacan, is beauty: the domesticated ugliness of the gaze – the painter 'gives something for the eye to feed on, but he invites the person to whom this picture is presented to lay down his gaze there as one lays down one's weapons. This is the Apollonian effect of painting. Something is given not so much to the gaze as to the eye, something that involves the abandonment, the *laying down*, of the gaze.' Gaze is disturbing, ugly. 'The problem is that a whole side of painting – expressionism – is separated from this field.'[11]

The image of thousand-eyed Argus is not the only case of ugliness in ancient Greece – there is (at least) also the (in)famous gigantic statue, the 'colossus of Rhodes', which stood above the entrance to the port: it was considered so disgusting with its large genitals etc. that it was taken as a divine punishment when a storm destroyed it. Where does this ugliness in ancient Greek art come from? An answer is provided by Hegel, who does not conceive the ancient Greek miracle as emerging out of nowhere – he is fully aware of the violence of the cut with preceding tradition that enabled it: the Greeks

certainly received the substantial beginnings of their religion, culture, their common bonds of fellowship, more or less from Asia, Syria and Egypt; but they have so greatly obliterated [*getilgt*] the foreign nature of this origin, and it is so much changed, worked upon, turned round, and altogether made so different, that what they, as we, prize, know, and love in it, is essentially their own ... The foreign origin they have so to speak thanklessly [*undankbar*] forgotten, putting it in the background – perhaps burying it in the darkness of the mysteries which they have kept secret [*geheim*] from themselves. They have not only done this, that is they have not only used and enjoyed all that they have brought forth and formed, but they have become aware of and thankfully [*dankbar*] and joyfully placed before themselves this at-homeness [*Heimatlichkeit*] in their whole existence, the ground and origin of themselves.[12]

So there is nothing new for Hegel in the 'Black Athena' thesis – as Rebecca Comay has noted, he even describes the way Greek art relates to its predecessors in terms of a 'conquering' (*siegen*), 'repression' (*zurückdrängen*), 'abolition' (*fortfallen*), 'expunging' (*tilgen*), 'annihilation' (*vertilgen*), 'effacement' (*Auslöschung*), 'erasure' (*Verwischung*), 'stripping away' (*Abstreifung*), 'excision' (*abschneiden*), 'concealment' (*verstricken*) – of what? Of 'the "Orient" or its prehistoric avatar – animal, bodily, ugly, stupid ...'[13] The notion of the Greek miracle as the outcome of organic spontaneous self-generation is thus an illusion grounded on brutal repression – and, as always with Hegel, this repressed origin returns in the fatal flaw of classic Greek art, which is the obverse of its very achievement. And we should not be surprised to learn that this repression takes the form of the exclusion of the gaze: a Greek statue is the perfect human form, the balance of body and spirit – however, as such, it has to be *without gaze*: their eyes are flat, pure surface, not the punctual window into the depth of the soul, since such a crack in the bodily surface would disturb its unity, its harmonious beauty. This is why Greek statues do not yet display subjectivity proper:

> If we compare this vocation of romantic art with the task of classical art, fulfilled in the most adequate way by Greek sculpture, the plastic shape of the gods does not express the movement and activity of the spirit which has retired into itself out of its corporeal reality and made its way to inner self-awareness ... What [these sculptures] lack is the actuality of self-aware subjectivity in the knowing and willing of itself. This defect is shown externally in the fact that the expression of the soul in its simplicity, namely the light of the eye, is absent from the sculptures. The supreme works of beautiful sculpture are sightless, and their inner being does not look out of them as self-knowing inwardness in this spiritual concentration which the eye discloses. This light of the soul falls outside them and belongs to the spectator alone; when he looks at these shapes, soul cannot meet soul nor eye eye.[14]

However, as we have just seen, within Greek art itself, this excluded (foreclosed even) excess of gaze returns as a disturbing multitude: the whole body of a Greek statue becomes a surface with hundreds of eyes. But it is only in later Romantic art that this excess returns – modern subjectivity is the return of the monstrous dimension excluded from ancient Greek harmonious art. This is why the category of beauty is no longer central for modern art: in it, we pass from the Beautiful to (different modalities of) the Sublime.

The first step in this passage is accomplished by Christianity, which brings about the sublime effect in a way exactly opposite to Kant: not through the extreme exertions of our capacity to represent (which nonetheless fails to render the suprasensible Idea and thus paradoxically succeeds in delineating its space), but as it were *a contrario*, through the reduction of the representative content to the lowest imaginable level. At the level of representation, Christ was the 'son of a man', a ragged, miserable creature crucified between two common brigands; and it is against the background of this wretched character of his earthly appearance that his divine essence shines through all the more powerfully. In the late Victorian age, the same mechanism was responsible for the ideological impact of the tragic figure of the 'elephant man', as the subtitle of one of the books about him suggests (*A Study in Human Dignity*): it was the monstrous and nauseating distortion of his body which itself made visible the simple dignity of his inner spiritual life. And was not the same logic an essential ingredient in the tremendous success of Stephen Hawking's *A Brief History of Time*? Would his ruminations on the fate of the universe have been so attractive to the public were it not for the fact that they belonged to a crippled, paralysed body communicating only through the feeble movement of one finger and speaking with an impersonal machine-generated voice? Therein consists the 'Christian Sublime': in this wretched 'little piece of the real' lies the necessary counterpart (the form of appearance) of pure spirituality.

Here we must be very careful not to miss the Hegelian point: what Hegel aims at is not the simple fact that, since the suprasensible is indifferent to the domain of sensible representations, it can appear even in the guise of the lowest representation. Hegel insists again and again that there is no special 'suprasensible realm' beyond or apart from our universe of sensible experience; the reduction to the nauseating 'little piece of the real' is thus *stricto sensu* performative, productive of the spiritual dimension: the spiritual 'depth' is *generated* by the monstrous distortion of the surface. In other words, the point is not merely that God's embodiment in a wretched creature renders visible His true nature by way of the contrast – the ridiculous, extreme discord – between Him and the lowest form of human existence; the point is rather that this extreme discord, this absolute gap, is the divine power of 'absolute negativity'. Both Judaism and Christianity insist on the absolute discord between God (Spirit) and the domain of (sensible) representations; their difference is of a purely formal nature: in the Jewish religion God dwells in an unrepresentable Beyond, separated from us by an unbridgeable gap, whereas the Christian God *is this gap itself*. It is this shift that causes the change in the logic of the Sublime: from a prohibition of representation to an acceptance of the most null representation.

From the sublime to the monstrous

The passage from Greek Beauty to the Christian Sublime and then to the outright explosion of the Ugly as an aesthetic category was first systematically deployed by Karl Rosenkranz, editor and scholar of Hegel, author of his first 'official' biography, although himself a reluctant Hegelian, in his *Ästhetik des Häßlichen* (*Aesthetics of the Ugly*)[15] of 1853. Rosenkranz's starting point is the historical process of the gradual abandonment of the unity of True, Good and Beautiful: not only can something ugly be true and good, but ugliness can be an immanent aesthetic notion, that is, an object can be ugly and an aesthetic object, an object of art. Rosenkranz remains within the long tradition from Homer onwards which associates physical ugliness with moral monstrosity; for him, ugly is *das Negativschöne* (the negatively-beautiful): 'The pure image of the Beautiful arises shining all the more against the dark background/foil of the Ugly.'[16] Rosenkranz distinguishes here between a 'healthy' and a 'pathological' mode of enjoying the Ugly in a work of art: in order to be aesthetically enjoyable and, as such, edifying and permissible, ugliness has to remain as a foil of the beautiful; ugliness for the sake of itself is a pathological enjoyment of art.

Ugliness is as such immanent to Beauty, a moment of the latter's self-development: like every concept, Beauty contains its opposite within itself, and Rosenkranz provides a systematic Hegelian deployment of all the modalities of the Ugly, from the formless chaos to the perverted distortions of the Beautiful. The basic matrix of his conceptualization of the Ugly is the triad of the Beautiful, the Ugly and the Comical, where the Ugly serves as the middle, the intermediate moment, between the Beautiful and the Comical: 'A caricature pushes something particular over its proper measure and creates thereby a disproportion which, insofar as it recalls its ideal counterpart, becomes comical.'[17]

A whole series of issues arises here. First, can this third term not also be conceived as the Sublime, insofar as the ugly in its chaotic and overwhelming monstrosity which threatens to destroy the subject recalls its opposite, the indestructible fact of Reason and of the moral law? What, then, is the triad – the Beautiful, the Ugly and the Comical (Ridiculous), or the Beautiful, the Ugly and the Sublime? It may appear that it depends on what kind of ugliness we are dealing with, the excessive-monstrous one or the ridiculous one. However, excess can also be comical, and *du sublime au ridicule, il n'y a qu'un pas*. The Sublime can appear (turn into) ridiculous, and the ridiculous can appear (turn into) sublime, as we learned from Chaplin's late films.

Second, the notion of the Ugly as the foil for the appearance of the Beautiful is in its very core profoundly ambiguous. It can be read (as it is by Rosenkranz) in the traditional Hegelian way: the Ugly is the subordinated moment in the game the Beautiful is playing with itself, its immanent self-negation which lays the (back)ground for its full appearance. Or it can be read in a much stronger literal sense, as the very (back)ground of the Beautiful which precedes the Beautiful and out of which the Beautiful arises – the reading proposed by Adorno in his *Aesthetic Theory*:

> If there is any causal connection at all between the beautiful and the ugly, it is from the ugly as cause to the beautiful as effect, and not the other way around. If one originated in the other, it is beauty that originated in the ugly and not the reverse.[18]

(In a homologous way, one should turn around the standard Thomist notion of Evil as a privative mode of the Good: what if it is the Good itself which is a privative mode of Evil? What if, in order to arrive at the Good, we just have to take away an excess from the Evil?) Adorno's point here is twofold. First, in general terms, concerning the very notion of art, the Ugly is the 'archaic' or 'primitive', chaotic (Dionysian) life substance which a work of art 'gentrifies', elevates into the aesthetic form, but the price for this is the mortification of the life substance: the Ugly is the force of life against the death imposed by the aesthetic form. Second, with reference specifically to the modern era in which the Ugly became an aesthetic category, Adorno claims that art has to deal with the Ugly 'in order to denounce, in the Ugly, the world which created it and reproduces it in its image'.[19] The underlying premise here is that art is a medium of truth, not just an escapist play of beautiful appearances: in a historical situation in which the Beautiful is irreparably discredited as kitsch, it is only by presenting the Ugly in its ugliness that art can keep open the utopian horizon of Beauty.

A third point that arises is, what if the reversal of the Ugly into the Comical (or the Sublime) does not occur? Herman Parret describes such an option with regard to the Kantian Sublime: if the overwhelming pressure of the Ugly gets too strong, it becomes monstrous and can no longer be sublated/negated into the Sublime. It's thus a question of an acceptable limit:

> there is for Kant a progression from the *colossal* to the *monstrous*, i.e. towards the total annihilation of our faculty of presentation. If the colossal can already be considered a sublime correlate, then it remains certainly inside an acceptable limit; with the monstrous, on the other hand, one has passed beyond the acceptable limit, in full terror and total unpleasure. With the monstrous we are in the margin of the acceptable where the imagination is fully blocked to function. It looks as if the monstrous is the Thing, inexpressible and abyssal. The monstrous does violence to subjectivity without submitting it to any legality.[20]

The Sublime pleasure is a pleasure in unpleasure, while the Monstrous generates only unpleasure – but, as such, it provides enjoyment. In short, what Kant already elaborated in the distinction between pleasure (*Lust*, regulated by the pleasure principle which makes us avoid all painful excess, even the excess of pleasure itself) and enjoyment (*Genuss*, *jouissance*). Therein resides the link between enjoyment and disgust:

> The 'disgust for the object' arises from a certain 'enjoyment' [*Genuss*] in the 'matter of sensation' which distances the subject from its purposiveness. Pleasure [*Lust*] is opposed to 'enjoyment' insofar as 'pleasure is culture' [*wo die Lust zugleich Kultur ist*] ... 'Enjoyment' *in matter*, in contrast, provokes disgust. In addition, this enjoyment of losing oneself in the matter of 'charms and emotions' has a direct impact on the health of our body: it generates disgust which manifests itself in corporeal reactions like nausea, vomiting and convulsions. Pleasure/unpleasure [*Lust/Unlust*] in the feeling of the sublime has nothing to do with that 'enjoyment' [*Genuss*] destructive of culture and generative of disgust.[21]

Which, precisely, is the ontological status of this weird *Genuss* which threatens to drag us into its self-destructive vicious cycle? It is clearly not culture, but it is also not nature, since it is an 'unnatural' excess that totally derails nature – so should we not posit a link, an identity even, between this *Genuss* and what Kant isolated as the 'unnatural' savagery (*Wildheit*) or passion for freedom specific to human nature:

Savagery [or unruliness: *Wildheit*] is independence from laws. Through discipline the human being is submitted to the laws of humanity and is first made to feel their constraint … Thus, for example, children are sent to school initially not already with the intention that they should learn something there, but rather that they may grow accustomed to sitting still and observing punctually what they are told, so that in the future they may not put into practice actually and instantly each notion that strikes them.

Now by nature the human being has such a powerful propensity towards freedom that when he has grown accustomed to it for a while, he will sacrifice everything for it.[22]

In Kant's *Anthropology* we find a long footnote about the scream (*Geschrei*, also 'shrieking', 'fuss', 'yells') of a newborn human being – the first explosion of rage, a reaction to the discovery that its freedom is limited by its bodily constraints. The freedom that explodes in this rage is not so much supernatural but a sign of the passage to a new 'epoch of nature';[23] it bears witness to a conflict between phenomenal bodily reality and the noumenal Real of wild freedom that precedes moral Law. The predominant form of appearance of this weird 'savagery' is passion, an attachment to a particular choice so strong that it suspends rational comparison with other possible choices – when we are in the thrall of a passion, we stick to a certain choice whatever it may cost: 'Inclination that prevents reason from comparing it with the sum of all inclinations in respect to a certain choice is *passion* (*passio animi*).'[24] As such, passion is morally reprehensible, it is 'far worse than all those transitory emotions that at least stir up the resolution to be better; instead, passion is an enchantment that also refuses recuperation … Passions are cancerous sores for pure practical reason, and for the most part they are incurable because the sick person does not want to be cured and flees from the dominion of principles, by which alone a cure could occur.'[25] And, as the subdivision 'On the inclination to freedom as a passion' tells us, 'For the natural human being this is the most violent [*heftigste*] inclination of all.'[26] Passion is as such purely human: animals have no passions, just instincts. The Kantian savagery is 'unnatural' in the precise sense that it seems to break or suspend the causal chain which determines all natural phenomena – it is as if in its terrifying manifestations, noumenal freedom transpires for a moment in our phenomenal universe. Do we not get here even an echo of what Kristeva calls abject? The object of enjoyment is by definition *disgusting*, and what makes it disgusting is a weird superego injunction that appears to emanate from it, a call to enjoy it even if (and precisely because) we find it ugly and desperately try to resist being dragged into it:

Kant insists on the non-representability of ugliness in art: '[in] *disgust* … that strange sensation, which rests on nothing but imagination, the object is presented *as if* it insisted, *as it were*, on our enjoying it even though that is just what we are forcefully resisting.' This is a typically Kantian approach: in a single phrase, there is a *gleichsam* (*as it were*) and an *als ob* (*as if*). The ugly object has no reasonable effect on the *Gemüth*. Instead, an excited and dangerously disconcerted imagination petrifies the subject *in its corporeity*. This is the very essence of disgusting ugliness: it threatens the stability of our corporeity, our body 'forcefully resists' the incitement to enjoy that ugliness deceitfully imposes on us.[27]

This, finally, brings us to the very heart of disgust: the object of disgust 'threatens the stability of our corporeity', it destabilizes the line that separates the inside of our body from its outside. Disgust arises when the border that separates the inside of our body from its outside is violated, when the inside penetrates out, as in the case of blood or shit. It's similar with saliva: as we all know, although we can without problem swallow our own saliva, we find it repulsive to swallow again saliva that was spit into a glass out of our body – again a case of violating the Inside/Outside frontier. What distinguishes man from animals is that, with humans, the disposal of shit becomes a problem: not because it has a bad smell, but because it came out from our innermost. We are ashamed of shit because, in it, we expose/externalize our innermost intimacy. Animals do not have a problem with it because they do not have an 'interior' like humans. One should refer here to Otto Weininger, who designated volcanic lava as 'the shit of the earth' (*Die Lava ist der Dreck der Erde*). It comes from *inside* the body, and this inside is evil, criminal: 'The Inner of the body is very criminal' (*Das Innere des Koerpers ist sehr verbrecherisch*).[28] One should return here to Freud who, in Chapter 4 of 'Beyond the Pleasure Principle', describes how the living substance

floats about in an outer world which is charged with the most potent energies, and it would be destroyed by the operation of the stimuli proceeding from this world if it were not furnished with a protection against stimulation [*Reizschutz*]. It acquires this through its outermost layer – which gives the structure that belongs to living matter – becoming in a measure inorganic, and this now operates as a special integument or membrane that keeps off the stimuli, i.e. makes it impossible for the energies of the outer world to act with more than a fragment of their intensity on the layers immediately below which have preserved their vitality. These are now able under cover of the protecting layer to devote themselves to the reception of those stimulus masses that have been let through. But the outer layer has by its own death secured all the deeper layers from a like fate – at least so long as no stimuli present themselves of such strength as to break through the protective barrier. For the living organism protection against stimuli is almost a more important task than reception of stimuli; the protective barrier is equipped with its own store of energy and must above all endeavor to protect the special forms of energy-transformations going on within itself from the equalizing and therefore destructive influence of the enormous energies at work in the outer world.[29]

Or, as Ray Brassier put it concisely, 'the separation between organic interiority and inorganic exteriority is won at the cost of part of the primitive organism itself, and it is this death that gives rise to the protective shield ... Thus, individuated organic life is won at the cost of this aboriginal death whereby the organism first becomes capable of separating itself from the inorganic outside.'[30]

Disgust arises when the 'dead' barrier is broken and the organic interiority penetrates the surface. One should be clear here and draw all the consequences: the ultimate object of disgust is *bare life itself*, life deprived of the protective barrier. Life *is* a disgusting thing, a sleazy object moving out of itself, secreting humid warmth, crawling, stinking, growing. The birth itself of a human being is an *Alien*-like event: a monstrous event of something erupting out from the inside of a body, a big stupid hairy body crawling around. Spirit is above life, it is death in life, an attempt to escape life while alive, like the Freudian death drive which is not life but a pure repetitive movement. Stephen Mulhall noted apropos of the 'alien' from Ridley Scott's 1979 film of the same name:

> The alien's form of life is (just, merely, simply) life, life as such: it is not so much a particular species as the essence of what it means to be a species, to be a creature, a natural being – it is Nature incarnate or sublimed, a nightmare embodiment of the natural realm understood as utterly subordinate to, utterly exhausted by, the twinned Darwinian drives to survive and reproduce.[31]

This disgust at Life is a disgust at *drive* at its purest. And it is interesting to note how Ridley Scott inverts the usual sexual connotations: Life is presented as inherently *male*, as the phallic power of brutal penetration which parasitizes on the feminine body, exploiting it as the carrier of its reproduction. 'The beauty and the beast' is here the feminine subject horrified at the disgusting immortal Life. There are two properly sublime moments in Jeunet's *Alien: Resurrection* (1997): in the first one, the cloned Ripley enters the laboratory room in which the previous seven aborted attempts to clone her are on display – here she encounters the ontologically failed, defective versions of herself, up to the almost successful version with her own face, but with some of her limbs distorted so that they resemble the limbs of the Alien Thing. This creature asks Ripley's clone to kill her, and, in an outburst of violent rage, the clone effectively destroys the horror exhibition by torching the whole room. Then, there is the unique scene, perhaps *the* shot of the entire series, in which Ripley's clone 'is drawn down into the embrace of the alien species, luxuriating in her absorption into the writhing mass of its limbs and tails – as if engulfed by the very lability of organic being that she had earlier attempted to consume in fire.'[32] The link between the two scenes is thus clear: we are dealing with two sides of the same coin.

The domain where excrements vanish after we flush the toilet is effectively one of the metaphors for the horrifyingly sublime Beyond of the primordial, preontological Chaos into which things disappear. Although we rationally know what goes on with the excrements, the imaginary mystery nonetheless persists – shit remains an excess which does not fit our daily reality, and Lacan was right in claiming that we pass from animals to humans the moment an animal has problems with what to do with its excrements, the moment they turn into an excess that annoys it. The Real in the scene from *The Conversation* (1974) is thus not primarily the horrifyingly disgusting stuff re-emerging from the toilet bowl, but rather the hole itself, the gap which serves as the passage to a different ontological order. The similarity between the empty toilet sink before the remainders of the murder re-emerge from it and Malevich's *Black Square on White Surface* is significant here: does the look from above into the toilet bowl not reproduce almost the same 'minimalist' visual scheme, a black (or, at least, darker) square of water enframed by the white surface of the bowl itself? Again, we, of course, know that the excrements which disappear are somewhere in the sewage network – what is here 'real' is the topological hole or torsion which 'curves' the space of our reality so that we perceive/imagine excrements as disappearing into an alternative dimension which is not part of our everyday reality.

The abyss of the toilet bowl in *Psycho* is a kind of passage to the Other Scene of the unconscious netherworld, so that when, towards the film's end, Lila looks into the bowl and finds there a torn piece of paper with numbers on it, the proof that Marion was there, it is as if a message arrives from the Other Scene. (The same thing occurs in *The Lady Vanishes*, when a slip of paper – a tea bag – appears on the window of the wagon, proving that the lady did exist.) The dark swamp behind the Bates motel in which cars with victims' bodies disappear plays the same role of a gigantic toilet bowl, so that when, in the very last shot of the film, Marion's car is dragged out of the swamp by a cable, it is as if traumatic content buried deep in the unconscious is brought back to daylight.[33]

Hitchcock's obsession with cleansing the bathroom or the toilet after its use is well known, and it is significant that when, after Marion's murder, he wants to shift our point of identification to Norman, he does this with a long rendering of the careful process of cleansing the bathroom – this is perhaps the key scene of the film, a scene that provides an uncanny, profound satisfaction of the job properly done, of things returning back to normal, of the situation being again under control, of the traces of the horrifying netherworld being erased. One is tempted to read this scene against the background of the well-known proposition of Saint Thomas Aquinas according to which a virtue (defined as a proper way to accomplish an act) can also serve evil purposes: one can also be a perfect thief, murderer, blackmailer, one can accomplish an evil act in a 'virtuous' way. What this scene of cleansing the bathroom in *Psycho* demonstrates is how the 'lower' perfection can imperceptibly affect the 'higher' goal: Norman's virtuous perfection in cleansing the bathroom, of course, serves the evil purpose of erasing the traces of the crime; however, this very perfection, the dedication and the thoroughness of his act, seduces us, the spectators, into assuming that, if someone acts in such a 'perfect' way, he should be in his entirety a good and sympathetic person. In short, someone who cleansed the bathroom as thoroughly as Norman cannot be really bad, in spite of his other minor peculiarities ... (Or, to put it even more pointedly, in a country governed by Norman, trains would certainly run on time!) While watching this scene recently, I caught myself nervously noticing that *the bathroom was not properly cleansed* – two small stains on the side of the bathtub remained! I almost wanted to shout: Hey, it's not yet over, finish the job properly![34]

The claim 'this is a beautiful rose' is not the same as the claim 'this rose is beautiful'[35]: the first statement says that this rose is beautiful for a rose, that it actualizes the (limited) beauty-potential of a rose, while the second statement is much stronger, it claims that the very 'absolute' notion of Beauty, Beauty as such, transpires in this rose. Or, to put it in Platonic terms, 'this is a beautiful rose' means that this rose fully and adequately participates in the Idea of rose, while 'this rose is beautiful' means that this rose, even if it is a failure as a rose, participates in the Idea of Beauty. In the same vein, saying 'he is a good torturer' is not the same as saying 'this torturer is good': the proof of the second statement can be the very fact that the first statement is not true, i.e. because this torturer remains a good man, he cannot be a really good torturer. Along these lines, there is something disturbing in Heidegger's proverbial allergy to any mention of moral considerations; in his reading of Plato in the 1931–2 seminar, he even tries to purify the Platonic *to agathon* from all links with moral goodness through a skilful reference to one of the everyday uses of the exclamation 'Good!': '"good!" means: It will be done! It is decided! It has nothing to do with the meaning of *moral* goodness; ethics has ruined the grounding meaning of this word.' One can thus easily imagine, at the conclusion of the Wannsee conference, Heydrich exclaiming: 'Good!' using the term in the 'authentic' Platonic sense ('It will be done! It is decided!') ... And does this same distinction not hold for the fate of all modern art which continues to remain beautiful? It is beautiful art, but no longer in a substantial way: it is not an art which is beautiful, which participates in the idea of Beauty as a mode of appearance of the Absolute.

Hegel's path towards the nonfigurative

How, then, can we think with Hegel against Hegel apropos of art after Beauty? Pippin is right to point out that, in his proclamation of the end of art (as the highest expression of the absolute), Hegel is paradoxically *not idealist enough*. What Hegel doesn't see is not simply some post-Hegelian dimension totally outside his grasp, but *the very 'Hegelian' dimension of the analysed phenomenon.* The same goes for economy: what Marx demonstrated in his *Capital* is how the self-reproduction of capital obeys the logic of the Hegelian dialectical process of a substance-subject which retroactively posits its own presuppositions. However, Hegel himself missed this dimension – his notion of industrial revolution was the Adam Smith-type manufacture where the work process is still that of combined individuals using tools, not yet the factory in which the machinery sets the rhythm and individual workers are de facto reduced to organs serving the machinery, to its appendices. This is why Hegel could not yet imagine the way abstraction rules in developed capitalism: this abstraction is not only in our (financial speculator's) misperception of social reality, but that it is 'real' in the precise sense of determining the structure of the very material social processes: the fate of whole strata of population and sometimes of whole countries can be decided by the 'solipsistic' speculative dance of capital, which pursues its goal of profitability in a blessed indifference to how its movement will affect social reality. Therein resides the fundamental systemic violence of capitalism, much more uncanny than the direct pre-capitalist socio-ideological violence: this violence is no longer attributable to concrete individuals and their 'evil' intentions, but purely 'objective', systemic, anonymous.

And in exact homology to this reign of abstraction in capitalism, Hegel was paradoxically not idealist enough to imagine the reign of abstraction in art. That is to say, in the same way that, in the domain of economy, he wasn't able to discern the self-mediating Notion which structures the economic reality of production, distribution, exchange and consumption, he wasn't able to discern the Notional content of a painting which mediates and regulates its form (shapes, colours) at a level which is more basic than the content represented (pictured) by a painting – 'abstract painting' mediates/reflects sensuality at a nonrepresentative level:

> seeing abstraction as self-conscious, conceptual, not, as with Greenberg, reductionist and materialist. Pollocks and Rothkos are not presentations of paint drips and color fields and flat canvas. They conceptualize components of sensible meaning that we traditionally would not see and understand as such, would treat as given, and this can make sense because the result character of even sensible apprehension, a generalized idealism evident even in the likes of Nietzsche and Proust, has come to be part of the intellectual habits of mind of modern self-understanding, even if unattended to as such. Such is for Hegel the new way nonrepresentational art might matter.[36]

Exemplary here is Kandinsky's *Concerning the Spiritual in Art*, which explores how colours, forms, points, lines, and their interplay directly evoke spiritual inner life (pure emotions), bypassing representative content. One should bear in mind here the gap that separates authentic art from mere decorative art: nonfigurative decorative art also displays the interplay of forms and colours, but this interplay is not a purveyor of a deeper historical Truth. While Kandinsky's text is full of naive theosophical theses, two of his points nonetheless hit the mark, bearing witness to the fact that what he calls 'Spiritual' is also Spirit in the Hegelian sense. First, the progress of art stands for the progress in freedom: 'The greatest freedom of all, the freedom of an unfettered art, can never be absolute. Every age achieves a certain measure of this freedom, but beyond the boundaries of its freedom the mightiest genius can never go. But the measure of freedom of each age must be constantly enlarged.' And second, it is rooted in its historical moment: 'Every artist, as child of his age, is impelled to express the spirit of his age (this is the element of style) – dictated by the period and particular country to which the artist belongs (it is doubtful how long the latter distinction will continue to exist).'[37]

The limitation of figurative art can be deduced already from the deadlocks of Plato's notion of mimesis. Plato's thought mobilizes two panicky fears: the fear of mimesis (of the imitation which makes us confuse the original with an inferior copy), and the fear of music (which, when it is not subordinated to articulated *logos*, threatens to drag us into the self-destructive vortex of its trance). Are these two fears two versions of the same fear? That is to say, is music also a species of mimesis (say, imitating the harmony of divine heavenly spheres, as Plato sometimes put it in his Pythagorean mode), or is it caught into its own antimimetic enjoyment, excluding all relation to an external otherness? And what if music stands for the self-enclosed circulation of drives which sabotages our infinite desire to raise ourselves to the Ideas and constrains us to imperfect copies of the Ideas?[38]

Perhaps one should add to these two a third fear: the fear of sophism, of abstract arguing which loses contact with truth. (This is why the great obsession of Plato's last dialogues is how to clearly distinguish truthful speech from fake sophistry – his dialogue *The Sophist* exemplarily fails in this respect.) In this way, we obtain (yet again) a triad of IRS: the fear of the imaginary power of mimesis, of images reproducing themselves with no regard for the original; the fear of the vortex of the musical Real which threatens to draw us into its abyss, like the crazy dance of the Bacchantes in Euripides' play; the fear of the symbolic reduced to sophistry which disregards truth and aims only at the superficial rhetorical effect.

But why are copies necessarily imperfect? Mimesis seems to fail with regard to the inimitable *je ne sais quoi*, what is in the imitated object 'more than itself', the Lacanian *objet a* which cannot be copied, imitated – we can only copy positive properties, but there is always a mysterious ingredient which seems to elude our grasp … But what if the opposite is the case? What if this elusive *je ne sais quoi* is retroactively created by imitation itself? A voluptuous lady from Portugal once told me a wonderful anecdote: when her most recent lover had first seen her fully naked, he told her that if she lost just one or two kilos, her body would be perfect. The truth was, of course, that had she lost the kilos, she would probably have looked more ordinary – the very element that seems to disturb perfection itself creates the illusion of the perfection it disturbs: if we take away the excessive element, we lose the perfection itself. We can platonize this case as a relationship between the platonic Idea of her perfect body and the reality of a slightly overweight body: the *objet a* is this excess of weight which retroactively creates the Ideal with regard to which every copy fails – if we eliminate the excess, we lose the Ideal itself. And the same goes for mimesis: the excess that eludes imitation is engendered by imitation itself, it does not reside in the imitated Idea.

Between Auschwitz and telenovelas

Hegel, of course, doesn't go in this direction: for him, art after the end of art, art in a reconciled world, has to be comical. What if, however, comedy and radical nonreconciliation do not exclude each other (the reason the best films about the Holocaust are comedies)? Recall how Primo Levi, in *If This Is a Man*, describes the dreadful *selekcja*, the survival examination in the camp:

> The *Blockältester* [the elder of the hut] has closed the connecting-door and has opened the other two which lead from the dormitory and the *Tagesraum* [daily room] outside. Here, in front of the two doors, stands the arbiter of our fate, an SSD subaltern. On his right is the *Blockältester*, on his left, the quartermaster of the hut. Each one of us, as he comes naked out of the *Tagesraum* into the cold October air, has to run the few steps between the two doors, give the card to the SS man and enter the dormitory door. The SS man, in the fraction of a second between two successive crossings, with a glance at one's back and front, judges everyone's fate, and in turn gives the card to the man on his right or his left, and this is the life or death of each of us. In three or four minutes a hut of two hundred men is 'done', as is the whole camp of twelve thousand men in the course of the afternoon.[39]

Right means survival, left means gas chamber. Is there not something properly *comic* in this, the ridiculous spectacle of appearing strong and healthy, of attracting for a brief moment the indifferent gaze of the Nazi administrator who presides over life and death? Here, comedy and horror coincide: imagine the prisoners practising their appearance, trying to hold head high and chest forward, walking with a brisk step, pinching their lips to appear less pale, exchanging advice on how to impress the SS man; imagine how a simple momentary confusion of cards or a lack of attention of the SS man can decide my fate … This 'comical' aspect, of course, causes no laughter – it rather stands for a position beyond comedy and tragedy. On one hand, the so-called Muslim (the 'living dead' in the camp) is so destitute that his stance can no longer be considered 'tragic': there is no dignity in him that is crucial for the tragic position, i.e. he no longer retains the minimum of dignity against the background of which his miserable actual position would have appeared tragic – he is simply reduced to the shell of a person, emptied of the spark of spirit. If we try to present him as tragic, the effect will be precisely comic, as when one tries to read tragic dignity into meaningless idiotic persistence. On the other hand, although the Muslim is in a way 'comic', although he acts in the way that is usually the stuff of comedy and laughter (his automatic, mindless repetitive gestures, his impassive pursuit of food), the utter misery of his condition thwarts any attempt to present and/or perceive him as a 'comic character' – again, if we try to present him as comic, the effect will be precisely tragic, as when the sad sight of someone cruelly mocking a helpless victim (say, putting obstacles in the way of a blind person to see if he will stumble), instead of producing laughter in us, generates sympathy for the victim's tragic predicament. Did not something along these lines happen with the rituals of humiliation in the camps, from the inscription *Arbeit macht frei* above the entrance to the gate at Auschwitz to the music band that accompanied prisoners to work or to the gas chambers? The paradox is that it is only through such cruel humour that the tragic sentiment can be generated. The Muslim is thus the zero-point at which the very opposition between tragedy and comedy, between sublime and ridiculous, between dignity and derision, is suspended, the point at which one pole directly passes into its opposite: if we try to present the Muslim's predicament as tragic, the result is comic, a mocking parody of the tragic dignity, and if we treat him as a comic character, tragedy emerges.

So maybe Hegel, in his tragic vision, was not able to consider the possibility of a horror worse than tragedy and which, precisely for this reason, may give rise to comedy, a laughter which is not done from the position of reconciliation, laughing at the vanity of the conflicts that persist, but a laughter through which the subject's total capitulation and disorientation transpires. In other words, Hegel knew that comedy follows tragedy; what he was not able to imagine is a comedy more horrible than tragedy. So it's not that Hegel jumped too quickly to comedy, to comic reconciliation, and that he should have seen that the tragedy of alienation and antagonism goes on in the modern world. In the modern world, the tragedy passed over to comedy, there is no return to tragic experience, and we should learn to see the horror in terms of comedy, in comedy itself. For Hegel, however, the comedy that fits the modern era concerns what he calls *Humanus*, art without historical Truth, just depicting ordinary life with its irrelevant conflicts and in this way signaling that the Absolute is reconciled with itself. Modern art transcends itself, but

> in this self-transcendence art is nevertheless a withdrawal of man into himself, a descent into his own breast, whereby art strips away from itself all fixed restriction to a specific range of content and treatment, and makes *Humanus* its new holy of holies: i.e. the depths and heights of the human heart as such, mankind in its joys and sorrows, its strivings, deeds, and fates. Herewith the artist acquires his subject-matter in himself and is the human spirit actually self-determining and considering, meditating, and expressing the infinity of its feelings and situations: nothing that can be living in the human breast is alien to that spirit any more. This is a subject-matter which does not remain determined artistically in itself and on its own account; on the contrary, the specific character of the topic and its outward formation is left to capricious invention, yet no interest is excluded – for art does not need any longer to represent only what is absolutely at home at one of its specific stages, but everything in which man as such is capable of being at home.[40]

In this universe where there are no privileged 'great topics' and 'anything goes', all conflict has to remain in the domain of comedy:

> absolute subjective personality moves free in itself and in the spiritual world. Satisfied in itself, it no longer unites itself with anything objective and particularized and it brings the negative side of this dissolution into consciousness in the humor of comedy. Yet on this peak comedy leads at the same time to the dissolution of art altogether. All art aims at the identity, produced by the spirit, in which eternal things, God, and absolute truth are revealed in real appearance and shape to our contemplation, to our hearts and minds. But if comedy presents this unity only as its self-destruction because the Absolute, which wants to realize itself, sees its self-actualization destroyed by interests that have now become explicitly free in the real world and are directed only on what is accidental and subjective, then the presence and agency of the Absolute no longer appears positively unified.[41]

It is interesting to note that the expression *l'art pour l'art* which registers art's full autonomy as an end-in-itself, not serving any broader social purpose, was coined by Hegel's French pupil Victor Cousin, and is the strict obverse of Hegel's thesis on the end of art: it is as if art loses its privileged status of the expression of the Absolute at the very moment when it asserts its full autonomy: when it finally arrives at what it was striving for – the full emancipation from the sacred, from social utility, etc. – the prize becomes worthless, the emancipation of art turns into the emancipation from art. This is one of the ways to understand why Hegel himself characterized art after the end of art as its self-destruction – and is this not what modern art effectively is, caught as it is in a permanent process of self-questioning which goes up to self-annihilation? But we can also understand it in a different way, as the regression of art into superficial comedy. That is to say, does Hegel's description not fit perfectly the universe of today's sitcoms, from *Seinfeld* to Mexican telenovelas? The (social) world is basically reconciled, there are no antagonisms cutting across it, just ordinary people with their everyday, mostly ridiculous complications? The very form of sitcoms seems to evoke the Hegelian 'spurious infinity': there are no big issues, just melodramatic complications which pop up and disappear. So it seems as if Hegel was here ahead of his time: it is only today that reality generated a product that fits his description. And what if this comedy of the prosaic world is the ultimate Christian Sublime, allowing us to see how the Absolute reconciled with itself transpires in everyday irrelevant conflicts?

5 VERSIONS OF ABJECT: UGLY, CREEPY, DISGUSTING

What happens when we stumble upon a decaying human corpse or, a more ordinary case, upon an open wound, shit, vomit, brutally torn-out nails or eyes, even the skin that forms on the surface of warm milk? What we experience in such situations is not just a disgusting object but something much more radical: the disintegration of the very ontological coordinates which enable me to locate an object into external reality 'out there'. The phenomenological description of such experiences is Julia Kristeva's starting point in her elaboration of the notion of *abject*: the reaction of horror, disgust, withdrawal, ambiguous fascination, and so on, triggered by objects or occurrences which undermine the clear distinction between subject and object, between 'myself' and reality 'out there'. Abject is definitely external to subject, but it is also more radically external to the very space within which the subject can distinguish itself from reality 'out there'. Maybe we can apply here Lacan's neologism 'extimate': the abject is so thoroughly internal to the subject that this very overintimacy makes it external, uncanny, inadmissible. For this reason, the status of the abject with regard to the pleasure principle is profoundly ambiguous: it is repulsive, provoking horror and disgust, but at the same time exerting an irresistible fascination and attracting our gaze to its very horror: 'One thus understands why so many victims of the abject are its fascinated victims – if not its submissive and willing ones.'[1] Such a mixture of horror and pleasure points towards a domain beyond the pleasure principle, the domain of *jouissance*: 'One does not know it, one does not desire it, one enjoys in it [*on en jouit*]. Violently and painfully. A passion' (9).

Is then the abject close to what Lacan calls *objet petit a*, the 'indivisible remainder' of the process of symbolic representation which functions as the always-already lost object-cause of desire? *Objet petit a* as the object-cause of desire is, in its very excessive nature, an immanent part of the symbolic process, the spectral/eluding embodiment of lack that motivates desire sustained by the (symbolic) Law. In contrast to *objet a* which functions within the order of meaning as its constitutive blind spot or stain, the abject 'is radically excluded [from the space of symbolic community] and draws me toward the place where meaning collapses' (2): 'Abjection preserves what existed in the archaism of pre-objectal relationship, in the immemorial violence with which a body becomes separated from another body in order to be' (10). The experience of abjection thus comes before the big distinctions between culture and nature, inside and outside, consciousness and the unconscious, repression and the repressed, etc. – abjection stands not for the immersion into nature, the 'primordial Mother', but for the very violent process of differentiation, it is the 'vanishing mediator' between nature and culture, a 'culture in becoming' which disappears from view once the subject dwells within culture. The abject is 'what disturbs identity, system, order. What does not respect borders, positions, rules', but not in the sense of the flow of nature undermining all cultural distinctions; it renders palpable the 'fragility of the law', including the laws of nature, which is why when a culture endeavours to stabilize itself, it does so by way of referring to the laws (regular rhythms) of nature (day and night, regular movement of stars and sun, etc.) (4). The encounter of abject arouses fear, not so much fear of a particular actual object (snakes, spiders, heights, etc.), but a much more basic fear of the breakdown of what separates us from external reality: what we fear in an open wound or a dead body is not its ugliness but the blurring of the line between inside and outside.

The underlying conceptual matrix of the notion of abject is that of a dangerous ground: abject points towards a domain which is the source of our life-intensity – we draw our energy out of it, but we have to keep it at the right distance. If we exclude it, we lose our vitality, but if we get too close to it, we are swallowed by the self-destructive vortex of madness – this is why abjection does not step out of the Symbolic but plays with it from within: 'The abject is perverse because it neither gives up nor assumes a prohibition, a rule, or law; but turns them aside, misleads, corrupts; uses them, takes advantage of them, the better to deny them' (4).

This abjectal excess can also appear in the guise of an 'indivisible remainder' of the Real which resists the process of idealization/symbolization – in this sense, Kristeva mentions the pagan opponents of Western monotheism who praise the notion of remainder as that which prevents the teleological closure of creation, keeping the movement forever open: 'the poet of the *Atharva Veda* extols the defiling and regenerating remainder (*uchista*) as precondition for all form. "Upon remainder the name and the form are founded, upon remainder the world is founded ... Being and non-being, both are in the remainder, death, vigor"' (77).[2] Remainder is here the support of the cyclic notion of the universe: it enables the rebirth of the universe. (We find the last traces of this logic even in the Kaballah, where the evil in our universe is accounted for as the remainder of the previous universes created and then annihilated by god since he was dissatisfied with the result of his creation – remainder thus grounds repeated creation.) Hegel and Christian monotheism are here easy targets: they allegedly tend to abolish the remainder in a complete sublation of the Evil in the Good, in a fulfilled teleology which redeems all previous, lower stages.[3]

Varieties of disavowal

In our daily lives, we deal with abjection in a variety of ways: ignoring it, turning away from it with disgust, fearing it, constructing rituals made to keep it at a distance or constraining it to a secluded place (toilets for defecation, etc.). Disgust, horror, phobia ... there is yet another way to deal with abjection which is to enact an almost psychotic split between abjectal objects or acts and the symbolic ritualization meant to cleanse us of defilement, i.e. to keep the two apart, as if there is no shared space where they may encounter each other since the abject (filth) in its actuality is simply foreclosed from the symbolic. Kristeva evokes the case of castes in India where the strong ritualization of defilement (numerous rituals, prescribed in painful details, that regulate how one should purify oneself)

> appears to be accompanied by one's being totally blind to filth itself, even though it is the object of those rites. It is as if one had maintained, so to speak, only the sacred, prohibited facet of defilement, allowing the anal object that such a sacralization had in view to become lost within the dazzling light of unconsciousness if not of the unconscious. V. S. Naipaul points out that Hindus defecate everywhere without anyone ever mentioning, either in speech or in books, those squatting figures, because, quite simply, no one sees them. It is not a form of censorship due to modesty that would demand the omission in discourse of

a function that has, in other respects, been ritualized. It is blunt foreclosure that voids those acts and objects from conscious representation. A split seems to have set in between, on the one hand, the body's territory where an authority without guilt prevails, a kind of fusion between mother and nature, and on the other hand, a totally different universe of socially signifying performances where embarrassment, shame, guilt, desire, etc. come into play – the order of the phallus. Such a split, which in another cultural universe would produce psychosis, thus finds in this context a perfect socialization. That may be because setting up the rite of defilement takes on the function of the hyphen, the virgule, allowing the two universes of *filth* and of *prohibition* to brush lightly against each other without necessarily being identified as such, as *object* and as *law*. On account of the flexibility at work in rites of defilement, the subjective economy of the speaking being who is involved abuts on both edges of the unnamable (the non-object, the off-limits) and the absolute (the relentless coherence of Prohibition, sole donor of Meaning). (75)

Do we not find similar cases also in Christianity, and in Islam as well? When the (then) Iranian president Ahmadinejad visited New York to attend a session of the UN General Assembly, he was invited to participate in a live debate at Columbia University. When asked about homosexuality in Iran, his reply was rudely mistranslated into English as if he claimed that in Iran they have no problem with homosexuals since there are none there. An Iranian friend (very critical of Ahmadinejad) who was there told me that Ahmadinejad's reply was in reality much more nuanced: what he hinted at was that in Iran they don't talk about homosexuality in public, they condemn it officially and mostly ignore its actual occurrences, thereby 'allowing the two universes of *filth* and of *prohibition* to brush lightly against each other without necessarily being identified as such, as *object* and as *law*'. And does the same not hold for paedophilia in the Catholic Church? Paedophiliac homosexuality is publicly condemned while (until recently, at least) tolerated by being ignored in practice, as if public law and material practice of sinful filth belong to different domains. This logic at work in Hinduism, Islam and Catholicism should not be confused with repression: nothing is 'repressed' or 'unconscious' about filth or homosexuality, the filthy act in question is practised more or less openly and without any qualms, its practitioners are (mostly) not traumatized by their perverse desires or haunted by any deep guilt feelings, they just simply keep the two dimensions apart. Our problem today is that, within the predominant logic of Political Correctness, such a procedure of keeping the two domains apart no longer functions: the PC stance by definition collapses the two dimensions since it aims precisely at directly controlling and regulating 'the body's territory where an authority without guilt prevails, a kind of fusion between mother and nature'. In other words, there is no domain left unseen, ignored by the PC law – its law tolerates no unwritten rules, there is no space here for a transgressive behaviour which violates explicit rules and is precisely as such not only tolerated but even solicited by the law. This is how the paternal prohibition functions:

> In fact, the image of the ideal Father is a neurotic's fantasy. Beyond the Mother … stands out the image of a father who would turn a blind eye to desires. This marks – more than it reveals – the true function of the Father, which is fundamentally to unite (and not to oppose) a desire to the Law.[4]

While prohibiting son's escapades, Father discreetly not only ignores and tolerates them, but even solicits them. It is in this sense that Father as the agent of prohibition/law sustains desire/pleasures: there is no direct access to enjoyment since its very space is opened up by the blanks of the Father's controlling gaze. (And does exactly the same not hold for god himself, our ultimate father? The first commandment says: 'You shall have no other gods before me.' What does the ambiguous 'before me' refer to? Most translators agree that it means 'before my face, in front of me, when I see you' – which subtly implies that the jealous god will nonetheless turn a blind eye to what we are doing secretly, out of [his] sight … In short, god is like a jealous husband who tells his wife: 'OK, you can have other men, but do it discreetly, so that I [or the public in general] will not notice it and you will not put me to shame!') The negative proof of this constitutive role of the Father in carving out the space for a viable enjoyment is the deadlock of today's permissiveness, where the master/expert no longer prohibits enjoyment but enjoins it ('sex is healthy', etc.), thereby effectively sabotaging it.

Is the mechanism described here not a case of so-called fetishist disavowal? Kristeva locates the most radical fetishism, fetishist disavowal, into language itself:

> But is not exactly language our ultimate and inseparable fetish? And language, precisely, is based on fetishist denial ('I know that, but just the same', 'the sign is not the thing, but just the same', etc.) and defines us in our essence as speaking beings. Because of its founding status, the fetishism of 'language' is perhaps the only one that is unanalyzable. (39)

Kristeva locates the fetishist dimension of language into the implicit overcoming of the gap that separates words (signs) from things: 'I know that words are only signs with no immanent relation to things they designate, but I nonetheless … (belief in their magic influence on things).' But where, exactly, is fetishism here? In his classic text, Octave Mannoni distinguishes three modes of *je sais bien, mais quand même …*, and reserves the name 'fetishism' only for the third one.[5] The first mode is the standard functioning of the symbolic order, namely, the relation between the symbolic title of a subject and his/her miserable reality as a person: 'I know very well that this guy in front of me is a miserable stupid coward, but he wears the insignia of power, which means that it is the Law which speaks through him …' Is it, however, accurate to characterize this basic 'alienation' in a symbolic title that changes our perception of an individual as a case of fetishism? Not yet, for Mannoni. Then there is the mode of falling into one's own trap, like a guy who, in order to calm his small child when a storm is ravaging around their house, draws a circle on the floor with a piece of chalk and assures him that one is safe if one stands inside the circle; when, soon thereafter, lightning directly strikes the house, he in a moment of panic quickly steps into the circle, as if being there will protect him, ignoring the fact that he himself concocted the story about the magic property of the circle to calm down the child. For Mannoni, this is also not yet fetishism proper, which only occurs when we have no need for any belief at all: we know how things really stand, plus we have the object fetish with no magic belief attached to it. A foot fetishist has no illusions about feet, plus he simply has a strong libidinal investment in feet, playing with them generates immense enjoyment.

So which among these three versions pertains to language as such? Maybe all three are activated at different levels. First, there is the disavowal that characterizes the symbolic mandate ('I know very well you are a miserable individual, but you are a judge and the authority of the Law speaks through you'). Then, there is the self-deception of a manipulator who as it were falls into his own trap. In his *Anthropology*, Kant explores how the love of the illusion of the good can lead to the love of the good itself: if one loves the illusion of the good and enacts this illusion in social intercourse, one might come to appreciate its worth and to love the good itself for its own sake. Correlatively from the point of view of the spectator, loving the illusion of the good in others may make us be polite in order to become lovable, which, in turn, exercises our self-mastery, leads us to control our passions and, eventually, to love the good for its own sake. In this sense, paradoxically, by deceiving others through politeness and social pretence, we in fact deceive ourselves and transform our pragmatic, polite behaviour into virtuous behaviour.

The difference between this and the first mode of disavowal is obvious: in the first mode, we are dealing with the straight confusion between an object/person and the properties that belong to it only on behalf of its inscription into a symbolic network (to quote Marx, a king is a king only because his subjects treat him as a king, but it appears to them that they treat him as a king because he is in himself a king), while in the second case, the illusion is generated purposefully and consciously (the subject produces an appearance in order to dupe another, and then he ends up falling into his own trap and believing in it himself). One should note how, although the cynical manipulator consciously cheats and is in this sense less naive than the subject of the first mode of disavowal, he ends up believing in a much more direct and naive way: he fully falls into his own trap, in contrast to the first mode in which the subject retains to the end the distance towards his belief ('I know very well it's not true …').

The third mode brings the paradox to its extreme: there is knowledge of how things really stand, this knowledge is assumed with no distance or disavowal, and then there is the fetish-object, its mute presence totally external to the subject's knowledge. As such, a fetish can play the very constructive role of allowing us to cope with the harsh reality: fetishists are not dreamers lost in their private worlds, they are thoroughly 'realists', able to accept the way things effectively are – since they have their fetish to which they can cling in order to cancel the full impact of reality. A psycho-analyst told me the tragic story of a husband, his patient, whose beautiful young wife died of breast cancer three months after she was diagnosed for it; he survived her death without big problems, and was able to talk about her painful dying to his friends without stress. His friends wondered how this was possible: did he not really love her, was he secretly released by her death? Then they got the clue: while talking about her, he would always hold a hamster, his dead wife's favoured pet object, gently playing with it – this hamster was his fetish, a living disavowal of her death, enabling him to rationally accept that she was dead while suspending the symbolic efficiency of this fact. The proof: a year after the wife's death, the hamster also died, and the effect of this *second* death was devastating – the widowed husband immediately suffered a total breakdown and had to be hospitalized after repeated suicide attempts.

In this precise sense, money is for Marx a fetish: I act as a rational, utilitarian subject, well aware how things truly stand – but I embody my disavowed belief in money fetish. So, when we are bombarded by claims that in our post-ideological, cynical era nobody believes in the proclaimed ideals, when we encounter a person who claims he is cured of any beliefs, accepting social reality the way it really is, one should always counter such claims with the question: OK, but where is your hamster? Where is the fetish which enables you to (pretend to) accept reality 'the way it is'? 'Western Buddhism' is such a fetish: it enables you to fully participate in the frantic pace of the capitalist game, while sustaining the perception that you are not really in it, that you are well aware how worthless this spectacle is – what really matters to you is the peace of the inner Self to which you know you can always withdraw.[6] In a further specification, one should note that fetish can function in two opposite ways: either its role remains unconscious – as in the case of the unfortunate husband who was unaware of the fetish-role of the hamster – or you think that the fetish is that which really matters, as in the case of a Western Buddhist unaware that the 'truth' of his existence is the social involvement which he tends to dismiss as a mere game.[7]

Traversing abjection

Until now we have been dealing with the main modes of avoiding the abject. There are, however, two privileged ways of 'traversing' abjection, of going through it and purifying ourselves of it: religion and art (poetic catharsis): 'The various means of *purifying* the abject – the various catharses – make up the history of religions, and end up with that catharsis par excellence called art, both on the far and near side of religion' (17). The whole of modern literature and art, from Artaud to Céline, from Kandinsky to Rothko, confronts and tries to sublimate the abject; following Rilke's famous formula 'beauty is the last curtain before the horrible', it weaves a screen which renders the abject not only tolerable but even pleasurable:

> On close inspection, all literature is probably a version of the apocalypse that seems to me rooted, no matter what its sociohistorical conditions might be, on the fragile border (borderline cases) where identities (subject/object, etc.) do not exist or only barely so – double, fuzzy, heterogeneous, animal, metamorphosed, altered, abject. (207)

In a detailed analysis, Kristeva presents the work of Céline as a long and tortuous confrontation with the abjectal dimension; this is what 'the long voyage to the bottom of the night' (the title of his masterpiece) alludes to – the night is the night of the abject which suspends not only reason but the universe of meaning as such, not only at the level of content (describing the extreme states of dissolution) but also at the level of form (fragmented syntax, etc.), as if some prelinguistic rhythm – 'the 'entirely other' of significance' – is invading and undermining language:

> It is as if Celine's scription could only be justified to the extent that it confronted the 'entirely other' of signifiance; as if it could only be by having this 'entirely other' exist as such, in order to draw back from it but also in order to go to it as to a fountainhead; as if it could be born only through such a confrontation recalling the religions of *defilement*, *abomination*, and *sin*. (149)

Céline carefully walks on the edge of this vortex of ecstatic negativity like the hero of Poe's story on Maelstrom, flirting with it but avoiding complete immersion into it, which would have meant a descent into madness. Here, of course, Kristeva confronts the big problem: one would have expected that such a confrontation with the abject and its libidinal vortex, allowing it to penetrate our universe of meaning, would have a liberating effect, allowing us to break out of the constraints of symbolic rules and to recharge ourselves with a more primordial libidinal energy; however, as is well known, Céline turned into a fully fledged fascist, supporting the Nazis to their very defeat – so what went wrong? At a general level, Kristeva's reply is to avoid both extremes: not only is the total exclusion of the abject mortifying, cutting us off from the source of our vitality (when the abject is excluded, 'the borderline patient, even though he may be a fortified castle, is nevertheless an empty castle' [49]), but the opposite also holds: every attempt to escape the patriarchal/rational symbolic order and enact a return to the prepatriarchal feminine rhythm of drives necessarily ends up in anti-Semitic fascism: 'Do not all attempts, in our own cultural sphere at least, at escaping from the Judeo-Christian compound by means of a unilateral call to return to what it has repressed (rhythm, drive, the feminine, etc.), converge on the same Celinian anti-Semitic fantasy?' (180).

The reason is, of course, that Judaism enacts in an exemplary way the monotheistic rejection of the maternal natural rhythms. However, Kristeva's account of Céline's move to fascism is more complex: the fascist anti-Semitism is not just a regression to the domain of abject, but a regression controlled/totalized by Reason. The return to what Reason has repressed (rhythm, drive, the feminine, etc.) is in itself liberating, it brings about an inconsistent bubble of fresh insights; problems arise when this anarchic schizo-disorder, its mad dance, is totalized through a paranoic stance which totalizes/unifies the entire field, generating a spectral object like 'the Jew' which allegedly explains all antagonisms and dissatisfactions:

> One has to admit that out of such logical oscillations there emerge a few striking words of truth. Such words present us with harsh X-rays of given *areas* of social and political experience; they turn into fantasies or deliriums only from the moment when reason attempts to *globalize, unify*, or *totalize*. Then the crushing anarchy or nihilism of discourse topples over and, as if it were the reverse of that negativism, an *object* appears -- an object of hatred and desire, of threat and aggressivity, of envy and abomination. That object, the Jew, gives thought a focus where all contradictions are explained and satisfied. (177–8)

To clarify this paranoiac totalization (in which it is easy to discern echoes of Deleuze/Guattari's opposition of schizo-analysis and paranoia), let us invoke a couple of cases which exemplify the opposite process, a liberating detotalization of the paranoiac unity. Three decades ago, in Carinthia (Kärnten), Austria's southern province which borders on Slovenia, German nationalists organized a campaign against the alleged Slovene 'threat' under the motto *Kärnten bleibt deutsch!* to which Austrian Leftists found a perfect answer. Instead of rational counterargumentation, they simply printed, in the main newspapers, an advertisement with obscene, disgusting-sounding variations of the nationalists' motto: *Kärnten deibt bleutsch! Kärnten leibt beutsch! Kärnten beibt dleutsch!* etc. Isn't this procedure worthy of the obscene, 'anal', meaningless speech spoken by Hynkel, the Hitler figure in Chaplin's *The Great Dictator*? We should avoid here a fateful conclusion and distinguish this direct penetration of language by obscene enjoyment from the signifying mechanisms of wordplay, displacement and condensation, elaborated by Lacan. Let us take an example from Freud. In a letter to Fliess from 1897, he reports on two sessions with his patient 'E.': the word for beetle, *Käfer*, reminded E. of that for ladybug, *Marienkäfer*, which he associated to overhearing that his deceased mother, Marie, had been undecided about her marriage. Freud noted that in Vienna a woman might be referred to as a 'beetle', and reported that E.'s 'nurse and first love was a French woman':

> Mr E., whom you know, had an anxiety attack at the age of ten when he tried to catch a black beetle, which would not put up with it. The meaning of this attack had thus far remained obscure. Now, dwelling on the theme of 'being unable to make up one's mind', he repeated a conversation between his grandmother and his aunt about the marriage of his

mother, who at that time was already dead, from which it emerged that she had not been able to make up her mind for quite some time; then he suddenly came up with the black beetle, which he had not mentioned for months, and from that to ladybug [*Marienkäfer*] (his mother's name was Marie); then he laughed out loud and inadequately explained his laughter by saying that zoologists call this beetle *septem punctata* or the equivalent, according to the number of dots, although it is always the same animal. Then we broke off and the next time he told me that before the session the meaning of the beetle [*Käfer*] had occurred to him, namely, *que faire?* = being unable to make up one's mind.[8]

So we get here the usual network of overdetermined associations: from the French maid who often didn't know what to do to his mother unable to make up her mind about marrying his father – but the key is that we arrive at the meaning of E.'s anxiety attack not by way of focusing on the associations (even less at the 'deeper psychic meaning') of the image of the beetle. The bridge between explicit content and the unconscious meaning of the scene is provided solely by the signifier (not meaning) '*Käfer*' which sounds like '*que faire?*'. (The further thing to note is that a question ['What to do?'] is embodied in an object [beetle], so that the first gesture of interpretation is to see a question lurking in the fascinating/disgusting object.) These signifying mechanisms remain firmly within the symbolic order and do not enact a regression into what Kristeva calls the Semiotic.

The limitation of Kristeva's theory of the abject resides in the fact that she conceives the symbolic order and abjection as the two extremes between which one has to negotiate a middle way;[9] what she neglects to do is to inquire into *what the symbolic order itself is in terms of the abject*. The symbolic order is not just always-already embedded in the feminine *hora* (or what Kristeva in her earlier work referred to as the Semiotic), penetrated by the materiality of its immanent libidinal rhythms which distort the purity of the symbolic articulations; if it is here, it had to emerge out of *hora* through a violent act of self-differentiation or splitting. Consequently, insofar as we accept Kristeva's term 'abjection' for this self-differentiation, then we should distinguish between *hora* and abjection: abjection points towards the very movement of withdrawal from *hora* which is constitutive of subjectivity. This is why we had to further specify Kristeva's diagnosis: every 'unilateral call to return to what [the Judeo-Christian compound] has repressed (rhythm, drive, the feminine, etc.)' generates fascism (as in Céline's work) not because it regresses from the Symbolic but because it obfuscates abjection itself, the 'primordial repression' which gives rise to the Symbolic. The dream of such attempts is not to suspend the Symbolic, but to have the (symbolic) cake and eat it, i.e. *to dwell in the Symbolic without the price we have to pay for it* ('primordial repression', subject's ontological derailment, antagonism, out-of-joint, the violent gap of differentiation from natural substance) – the ancient dream of a masculine universe of meaning which remains harmonically rooted in the maternal substance of *hora*. In short, what fascism obfuscates (forecloses even) is not the Symbolic as such but the gap that separates the Symbolic from the Real. This is why a figure like that of the Jew is needed: if the gap between the Symbolic and the Real is not constitutive of the Symbolic, if a Symbolic 'at home' in the Real is possible, then their antagonism has to be caused by a contingent external intruder – and what better candidate for this role than Judaism, its violent monotheist assertion of the symbolic Law and rejection of the earth-bound paganism? The Jew as the enemy allows the anti-Semitic subject to avoid the choice between working class and capital: by blaming the Jew whose plotting foments class warfare, he can advocate the vision of a harmonious society in which work and capital collaborate. This is also why Kristeva is right in linking the phobic object (the Jew whose plots anti-Semites fear) to the avoidance of a choice: 'The phobic object is precisely avoidance of choice, it tries as long as possible to maintain the subject far from a decision' (42). Does this proposition not hold especially for political phobia? Does the phobic object/abject on the fear of which the rightist-populist ideology mobilizes its partisans (the Jew, the immigrant, etc.) not embody a refusal to choose – what? A position in the class struggle. This is how anti-Semitism relies on a paranoiac totalization of playing with abjection: the anti-Semitic fetish-figure of the Jew is 'the last thing a subject sees' just before he confronts social antagonism as constitutive of the social body.

Éric Laurent discussed (in his blog post on 'racism 2.0')[10] how the onset of the post-'68 hedonist permissiveness, which was part of the prospect of integrating nations into larger communities held together by the global market, did not give rise to universal tolerance but, on the contrary, triggered a new wave of racist segregation: 'Our future as common markets will be balanced by an increasingly hard-line extension of the process of segregation.'[11] Why? Those who understand globalization as an opportunity for the entire earth to be a unified space of communication, one which brings together all humanity, often fail to notice this dark side of their proposition. Since a Neighbour is, as Freud suspected long ago, primarily a Thing, a traumatic intruder, someone whose different way of life (or, rather, way of *jouissance* materialized in its social practices and rituals) disturbs us, throws the balance of our way of life off the rails, when the Neighbour comes too close, this can also give rise to an aggressive reaction aimed at getting rid of this disturbing intruder. As Peter Sloterdijk put it: 'More communication means at first above all more conflict.'[12] This is why he is right to claim that the attitude of 'understanding-each-other' has to be supplemented by the attitude of 'getting-out-of-each-other's-way', by maintaining an appropriate distance, by implementing a new 'code of discretion'. European civilization finds it easier to tolerate different ways of life precisely on account of what its critics usually denounce as its weakness and failure, namely, the alienation of social life. One of the things alienation means is that distance is included in the very social texture of everyday life: even if I live side by side with others, in my normal state I ignore them. I am allowed not to get too close to others. I move in a social space where I interact with others, obeying certain external 'mechanical' rules, without sharing their inner world. Perhaps the lesson to be learned is that, sometimes, a dose of alienation is indispensable for the peaceful coexistence of ways of life. Sometimes *alienation* is not a problem but a solution.

What, then, is the factor that renders different cultures (or, rather, ways of life in the rich texture of their daily practices) incompatible, what is the obstacle that prevents their fusion or, at least, their harmoniously indifferent coexistence? The psychoanalytic answer is: *jouissance*. It is not only that different modes of *jouissance* are incongruous with each other, without a common measure; the other's *jouissance* is insupportable for us because (and insofar as) we cannot find a proper way to relate to our own *jouissance* – the ultimate incompatibility is not between mine and another's *jouissance*, but between myself and my own *jouissance* which forever remains an extimate intruder. It is to resolve this deadlock that the subject projects the core of its *jouissance* onto an Other, attributing to this Other full access to a consistent *jouissance*. Such a constellation cannot but give rise to jealousy: in jealousy, the subject *creates/imagines a paradise* (a utopia of full *jouissance*) *from which he is excluded*. The same definition applies to what one can call political jealousy, from the anti-Semitic fantasies about the excessive enjoyment of the Jews to the Christian fundamentalists' fantasies about the weird sexual practices of gays and lesbians. As Klaus Theweleit pointed out, it is all too easy to read such phenomena as mere 'projections': jealousy can be quite real and well founded, other people can and do have a much more intense sexual life than the jealous subject – a fact which, as Lacan remarked, doesn't make jealousy any less pathological … Here is Lacan's succinct description of the political dimension of this predicament:

> With our *jouissance* going off track, only the Other is able to mark its position, but only in so far as we are separated from this Other. Whence certain fantasies – unheard of before the melting pot.

Leaving the Other to his own mode of *jouissance*, that would only be possible by not imposing our own on him, by not thinking of him as underdeveloped.[13]

To recapitulate the argument: owing to our impasse with our own *jouissance*, the only way for us to imagine a consistent *jouissance* is to conceive it as Other's *jouissance*; however, Other's *jouissance* is by definition experienced as a threat to our identity, as something to be rejected, destroyed even. With regard to the identity of an ethnic group, this means that 'there is always, in any human community, a rejection of an inassimilable *jouissance*, which forms the mainspring of a possible barbarism'.[14] Lacan here underpins Freud for whom the social bond (group identification) is mediated by the identification of each of its members with the figure of a Leader shared by all: Lacan conceives this symbolic identification (identification with a Master Signifier) as secondary with regard to some preceding rejection of *jouissance*, which is why, for him, 'the founding crime is not the murder of the father, but the will to murder he who embodies the *jouissance* that I reject'.[15] (And, one might add, even the murder of the primordial father is grounded in the hatred of his excessive *jouissance*, his possessing of all women.) Lacan articulates such a group identification in terms of the three temporal phases that characterize what he calls 'logical time':

> This assertion assuredly appears closer to its true value when presented as the conclusion of the form here demonstrated of anticipating subjective assertion:
>
> (1) A man knows what is not a man;
> (2) Men recognize themselves among themselves as men;
> (3) I declare myself to be a man for fear of being convinced by men that I am not a man.
>
> This movement provides the logical form of all 'human' assimilation, precisely insofar as it posits itself as assimilative of a barbarism.[16]

The starting point, what I 'immediately see', is that I don't know who or what I am since my innermost core of *jouissance* eludes me. I then identify myself with others who are caught in the same deadlock, and we ground our collective identity not directly in some Master Signifier but, more fundamentally, in our shared rejection of the Other's *jouissance*. The status of Other's *jouissance* is thus deeply ambiguous: it is a threat to my identity, but at the same time my reference to it founds my identity – in short, my identity emerges as a defensive reaction to what threatens it, or, as we may say apropos of anti-Semitism, what is a Nazi without a Jew? Hitler allegedly said: 'We have to kill the Jew within us.' A. B. Yehoshua provided an adequate comment on this statement:

> This devastating portrayal of the Jew as a kind of amorphous entity that can invade the identity of a non-Jew without his being able to detect or control it stems from the feeling that Jewish identity is extremely flexible, precisely because it is structured like a sort of atom whose core is surrounded by virtual electrons in a changing orbit.[17]

In this sense, Jews are effectively the *objet petit a* of the Gentiles: what is 'in Gentiles more than Gentiles themselves', not another subject that I encounter in front of me but an alien, a foreign intruder, *within* me, what Lacan called *lamella*, the amorphous intruder of infinite plasticity, an undead 'alien' monster who can never be pinned down to a determinate form. In this sense, Hitler's statement tells more than it wants to say: against its intention, it confirms that the Gentiles need the anti-Semitic figure of the 'Jew' in order to maintain their identity. It is thus not only that 'the Jew is within us' – what Hitler fatefully forgot to add is that *he, the anti-Semite, his identity, is also in the Jew.*[18] (And the same holds even for [a certain kind of] anti-racism. The dependence of the Politically Correct anti-racism on what it [pretends to] fight[s], on the first-level racism itself, its parasitizing upon its opponent, is clear: the PC anti-racism is sustained by the surplus-enjoyment which emerges when the PC-subject triumphantly reveals the hidden racist bias on an apparently neutral statement or gesture.)

Another conclusion to be drawn from this intermingling of *jouissances* is that racism is always a historical phenomenon: even if anti-Semitism seems to remain the same through millenia, its inner form changes with every historical rupture. Balibar perspicuously noted that in today's global capitalism in which we are all neighbours to each other even if we live far away, the structure of anti-Semitism is in a way globalized: every other ethnic group that is perceived as posing a threat to our identity functions as a 'Jew' did for the anti-Semite. This universalization reaches is apogee in the unique, exceptional fact that even fervent Zionists themselves construct the figure of the 'self-hating Jew' along the lines of anti-Semitism.

'MOOR EEFFOC'

From here there follows another crucial consequence with regard to Kristeva's theoretical edifice: *hora* (the Semiotic) is not more primordial than the Symbolic but strictly a secondary phenomenon, the return of the presymbolic mimicry (echoes, resemblances, imitations) within the field of symbolic differentiality. Roman Jakobson drew attention to the fact that we can discern overall in our language traces of direct resemblance between signifier and signified (some words signifying vocal phenomena seem to sound like what they signify, sometimes even the external form of a word resembles the form of the signified object, like the word 'locomotive' which resembles the old-fashioned steam locomotive with the elevated cabin and chimney); this, however, in no way undermines the priority and ontological primacy of the differential character of linguistic signifiers (the identity and meaning of a signifier depends on its difference from other signifiers, not on its resemblance to its signified). What we are dealing with in the case of phenomena like these are the secondary mimetic echoes within a field which is already, in its basic constitution, radically different (contingent, composed of differential relations). And the same holds for *hora*, for the immanent rhythm of presymbolic materiality which pervades the Symbolic: what happens first is the violent cut of abjection which gives birth to the Symbolic, and what Kristeva describes as *hora* is a strictly secondary phenomenon of presymbolic mimetic echoes within the symbolic field.

A similar limitation characterizes Catherine Malabou's 'ontology of the accident', which brings negativity to its extreme, in the guise of an external organic or physical catastrophe which totally destroys the symbolic texture of the subject's psychic life, allowing for no interpretation, no symbolic appropriation. Malabou's 'ontology of the accident' is thus

an ontology finally taking into account, as previous orientations have not yet done, explosive events of indigestible, meaningless traumas in which destructive plasticity goes so far as to destroy plasticity itself, in which plasticity is exposed, thanks to itself, to its own disruption … The massive cerebro-lesions of catastrophic neuro-traumas produce the bodies of human organisms living on but not, as it were, living for, that is, not inclining toward future plans, projects … Plasticity (including neuroplasticity) stands permanently under the shadow of the virtual danger of its liquidation.[19]

A materialist notion of humanity should effectively take into account the shadow of a permanent threat to our survival at a multitude of levels, from external threats (an asteroid hitting the earth, volcanic eruptions, etc.) through individual catastrophes like Alzheimer's up to the possibility that humanity will destroy itself as an unintended consequence of its scientific and technological progress. There is, however, a 'catastrophe' which always-already occurred and which is missing from the list of external threats: the 'catastrophe' that is the emergence of subjectivity, of the human mind, out of nature. The exclusion of the Real of *this* 'catastrophe' (what Freud called 'primordial repression') is what introduces the gap that separates the Real from reality – it is on account of this gap that what we experience as external reality always has to rely on a fantasy, and that when the raw Real is forced upon us, it causes the experience of the loss of reality. G. K. Chesterton was on the right track here in his wonderful description of Charles Dickens's realism:

[Dickens] was a dreamy child, thinking mostly of his own dreary prospects. Yet he saw and remembered much of the streets and squares he passed. Indeed, as a matter of fact, he went the right way to work unconsciously to do so. He did not go in for 'observation', a priggish habit; he did not look at Charing Cross to improve his mind or count the lamp-posts in Holborn to practise his arithmetic. But unconsciously he made all these places the scenes of the monstrous drama in his miserable little soul. He walked in darkness under the lamps of Holborn, and was crucified at Charing Cross. So for him ever afterwards these places had the beauty that only belongs to battlefields. For our memory never fixes the facts which we have merely observed. The only way to remember a place for ever is to live in the place for an hour; and the only way to live in the place for an hour is to forget the place for an hour. The undying scenes we can all see if we shut our eyes are not the scenes that we have stared at under the direction of guide-books; the scenes we see are the scenes at which we did not look at all – the scenes in which we walked when we were thinking about something else – about a sin, or a love affair, or some childish sorrow. We can see the background now because we did not see it then. So Dickens did not stamp these places on his mind; he stamped his mind on these places. For him ever afterwards these streets were mortally romantic; they were dipped in the purple dyes of youth and its tragedy, and rich with irrevocable sunsets.

Herein is the whole secret of that eerie realism with which Dickens could always vitalize some dark or dull corner of London. There are details in the Dickens descriptions – a window, or a railing, or the keyhole of a door – which he endows with demoniac life. The things seem more actual than things really are. Indeed, that degree of realism does not exist in reality; it is the unbearable realism of a dream. And this kind of realism can only be gained by walking dreamily in a place; it cannot be gained by walking observantly. Dickens himself has given a perfect instance of how these nightmare minutiae grew upon him in his trance of abstraction. He mentions among the coffee-shops into which he crept in those wretched days 'one in St. Martin's Lane, of which I only recollect it stood near the church, and that in the door there was an oval glass plate with 'COFFEE ROOM' painted on it, addressed towards the street. If I ever find myself in a very different kind of coffee-room now, but where there is an inscription on glass, and read it backwards on the wrong side, MOOR EEFFOC (as I often used to do then in a dismal reverie), a shock goes through my blood.' That wild word, 'Moor Eeffoc', is the motto of all effective realism! it is the masterpiece of the good realistic principle – the principle that the most fantastic thing of all is often the precise fact. And that elvish kind of realism Dickens adopted everywhere. His world was alive with inanimate objects.[20]

Strange realism whose exemplary case – 'the motto of all effective realism' – is a *signifier* MOOR EEFFOC whose lack of meaning (signified) is more than supplemented by a rich condensation of unconscious obscene libidinal echoes (fears, horrors, obscene imaginations), so that it effectively functions as a direct signifier (or, rather, cypher) of *jouissance*, signalling a point at which meaning breaks down! So if we are looking for the traces of *das Ding* in all this, they are not to be found in external reality the way it is independently of our investments into it – say, the way oval glass plates on the doors of coffee-rooms really are – but at those mysterious points within the universe of meaning where meaning breaks down and is overshadowed by a nameless abyss of *jouissance*, and this is why when I stumble upon the meaningless signifier MOOR EEFFOC, 'a shock goes through my blood ...' It may appear that Chesterton is here simply asserting the key role of inner psychic traumas, desires, obsessions, fears, and so forth: 'Dickens did not stamp these places on his mind; he stamped his mind on these places', i.e. certain places impressed him deeply not because of their inherent qualities but because of the intense inner experiences (concerning sin, love, etc.) they served as a pretext and gave birth to ... One can easily imagine here a critic of psychoanalysis like Catherine Malabou sarcastically asking if a devastating catastrophe in 'external reality' like a gigantic tsunami or being exposed to brutal torture also acquires weight only if a previous psychic trauma resonates in it. But are things as simple as that? What makes inanimate objects alive is the way they are enveloped by dreams, which is not the same as that of the famous Freudian dream where the burning cloth on the son's coffin triggers in the sleeping father the terrifying dream-image of his dead son approaching him with 'Father, can't you see I'm burning!' In Freud's case, the dreamer (father) escapes from reality into a dream where he encounters an even more terrifying Real; in Dickens, there is no escape from ordinary reality, a detail of reality itself gets spectralized, is experienced as a moment from a nightmarish dream. Something similar takes place continuously in Kafka's work – Kafka is also a master of 'effective realism'. But let us rather take an unexpected example from cinema.

In James Cameron's *Titanic* there is a short shot from above of an unidentified old couple lying embraced in their bed while the ship is already sinking, so that their cabin is half-flooded and a stream of water is running all around the bed. Although it is meant as a realistic shot, the impression it creates is that of a dream scene – a bed with the tightly embraced couple in the midst of strong flow of water, touchingly rendering the stability of love in the midst of a disaster. This detail in an otherwise average commercial movie bears witness to an authentic cinematic touch, that of making reality appear as a dream scene. A variation of the same motif is those magic moments in some films when it seems as if an entity which belongs to fantasy-space intervenes into ordinary reality, so that the frontier that separates the fantasy-space from ordinary reality is momentarily suspended. Suffice it to recall a scene from *Possessed*, Clarence Brown's melodrama from 1931 starring Joan Crawford. Crawford, playing a poor, small-town girl, stares amazed at the luxurious private train that slowly passes in front of her at the local railway station; through the windows of the carriages she sees the rich life going on in the illuminated inside – dancing couples, cooks preparing dinner, and so on. The crucial feature of the scene is that we, the spectators, together with Crawford, perceive the train as a magic, immaterial apparition from another world. When the last carriage passes by, the train comes to a halt and we see on the observation desk a good-natured drunkard with a glass of champagne in his hand, which stretches over the railing towards Crawford – as if, for a brief moment, the fantasy-space intervened in reality … The great master of such procedure was Krzystof Kieslowski – a part of drab reality all of a sudden starts to function as the 'door of perception', the screen through which another, purely fantasmatic dimension becomes perceptible. What distinguishes Kieslowski is that, in his films, these magic moments of interface are not staged by means of standard Gothic elements (apparitions in the fog, magic mirrors), but as part of an ordinary, everyday reality. In *Decalogue* 6, for example, the brief scene in the post office when Magda, the film's heroine, complains about the money orders is shot in such a way that, several times, we see a person in close-up face-to-face and, behind him or her, on a glass partition dividing the clerks from the customers, a larger-than-life reflection of the face of another person with whom the person we see directly is engaged in conversation. By means of this simple procedure, the spectral dimension is rendered present in the middle of an utterly plain scene (customers complaining about bad service in a drab East European post office).[21]

It is along these lines that we should understand also what Chesterton says about Dickens's eerie realism in which 'the most fantastic thing of all is often the precise fact': 'a shock goes through my blood' when I stumble upon a small material detail which stirs up something in my 'inner life' – not some 'deeper meaning' but something traumatic, nonsymbolizable, ex-timate (external in the very heart of my being). One should emphasize the hyperrealism of such moments: the spectralization of material reality overlaps with full focus on material objects. How is this paradox possible? There is only one solution: external reality itself is not simply 'out there', it is already transcendentally constituted so that it is experienced as such – as 'normal' reality out there – only if it fits these transcendental coordinates.

Let's take a traumatic event like the 9/11 World Trade Center destruction: one should turn around the standard reading according to which the WTC explosions were the intrusion of the Real which shattered our illusory Sphere; quite the contrary, it is prior to the WTC collapse than we lived in our reality, perceiving the Third World horrors as something which is not effectively part of our social reality, as something which exists (for us) as a spectral apparition on the (TV) screen – and what happened on 9/11 is that this fantasmatic screen apparition entered our reality. It is not that reality entered our image: the image entered and shattered our reality (i.e. the symbolic coordinates which determine what we experience as reality). What this means is that the dialectic of semblance and Real cannot be reduced to the rather elementary fact that the virtualization of our daily lives, the experience that we are more and more living in an artificially constructed universe, gives rise to the irresistible urge to 'return to the Real', to regain the firm ground in some 'real reality'. THE REAL WHICH RETURNS HAS THE STATUS OF A(NOTHER) SEMBLANCE: *precisely because it is real, i.e. on account of its traumatic/excessive character, we are unable to integrate it into (what we experience as) our reality, and are therefore compelled to experience it as a nightmarish apparition.* This is what the captivating image of the collapse of the WTC was: an image, a semblance, an 'effect', which, at the same time, delivered 'the thing itself'. This 'effect of the Real' is not the same as what, way back in the sixties, Roland Barthes called *l'effet du réel*: it is rather its exact opposite, *l'effet de l'irréel*. That is to say, in contrast to the Barthesian *effet du réel* in which the text makes us accept as 'real' its fictional product, here, the Real itself, in order to be sustained, has to be perceived as a nightmarish irreal spectre. Usually we say that one should not mistake fiction for reality – recall the postmodern *doxa* according to which 'reality' is a discursive product, a symbolic fiction which we misperceive as a substantial autonomous entity. The lesson of psychoanalysis is here the opposite one: *one should not mistake reality for fiction* – one should be able to discern, in what we experience as fiction, the hard kernel of the Real which we are only able to sustain if we fictionalize it. In short, one should discern which part of reality is 'transfunctionalized' through fantasy, so that, although it is part of reality, it is perceived in a fictional mode – exactly as in our examples from *Titanic*, *Possessed* and Kieslowski, where part of reality is spectralized, acquires dreamlike quality. Much more difficult than to denounce-unmask (what appears as) reality as fiction is to recognize in 'real' reality the part of fiction.

This, then, is what Malabou's critique misses when it accuses psychoanalysis of ignoring the bodily weight of traumatic events, thereby reducing their impact to their stirring up some previous dormant psychic trauma. Let us imagine witnessing or being submitted to extremely brutal torture – precisely because the impact of the scene is so shattering, it would undermine the basic coordinates of what we perceive as 'solid external reality'; the scene would not be experienced as part of ordinary reality but as an unreal, as a nightmarish fiction. The sense of ordinary external reality and extreme trauma are mutually exclusive. This is the ultimate reason why, as Chesterton saw clearly, dream and 'effective realism' go together.

From abjective to creepy

How does the abject relate to subjectivity? Is a subject – which is excessive in its very notion – simply abjective, an outgrowth disturbing the harmony of the world, opening up a gap in its very heart? One has to draw a clear distinction here: 'abjective' is ultimately the inside of a living object (like the depth of Irma's throat from Freud's dream about Irma's injection), while the inside of a subject is 'creepy' – as Adam Kotsko has shown in his *Creepiness*, 'creepy' is today's name for the Freudian 'uncanny', for the uncanny core of a neighbour: every neighbour is ultimately creepy, which is why the title of the book's last subchapter is quite appropriately 'The creepiness of all flesh'. What makes a neighbour creepy is not his weird acts but the impenetrability of the desire that sustains these acts. For example, creepy is not primarily the content of the Marquis de Sade's writings (their content is rather dull and repetitive) but 'why is he doing it?' – everything in Sade is a 'sadist' perversion, everything except his writing, the act of doing it, which cannot be accounted for as a perversion. So the question is: what does a creepy neighbour want? What does he get out of it? An experience, an encounter, gets creepy when we all of a sudden suspect that he is not doing it for the obvious reason one does what he is doing. An example from Kotsko:

> in the case of a sleazy guy who insists on propositioning every woman he meets, the element of enigma may seem to be missing insofar as he clearly wants sex. And yet it seems strange that simply wanting sex would be creepy, because a man who politely asks a woman on a date and then accepts the answer is, all things being equal, not being creepy. What makes the sleazy guy creepy, then, is not that he is simply asking too many women out, but that his constant failure seems to indicate that he *doesn't care* that his methods are ineffective. It's as though he's directly 'getting off' on the very act of approaching women, with no regard for the ostensible goal of sleeping with them. When we recognize this, we can't help but ask, 'What is he *getting* out of this?' Even the most seemingly obvious creepy desire turns out to be enigmatic on closer examination.[22]

Here enters the Lacanian distinction between the object of desire and the object-cause of desire, that which sustains our desire for the object: the creepy effect arises when we perceive that the subject in front of us is doing what he is doing directly for the object-cause of desire, remaining indifferent towards the object of his desire – in short, when there occurs a kind of short circuit between the object and object-cause, so that the object becomes directly the object-cause. For example, what sustains my desire for a woman is the locks in her hair – so what if I simply directly focus on that, forgetting about full sex and finding satisfaction in just caressing her hair? However, there is also a liberating dimension in such an enigmatic intrusion of a gesture with no clear meaning – the condition is that the perverse economy breaks down and the excessive enigmatic gesture remains open and as such provokes a hysterical effect. Kotsko noted apropos of nudity in *Girls*:

> Initially, her nudity was aggressively perverse, but as Lena Dunham's character moves beyond her perverse indulgences in later episodes, her

nudity takes on a variety of new roles. For instance, one scene depicts her getting dressed in the morning after a shower, demonstrating her high level of comfort with her live-in boyfriend. Other nude scenes highlight her vulnerability or other emotional states – but none of them seem to have the primary goal of sexually titillating the viewer, nor (as earlier) of violating their normal expectations of sexual titillation. It's as though the show's excessive and aggressive use of nudity early on had somehow 'de-activated' the customary pop-cultural use of female nudity, opening up a space for a more thorough exploration of what nudity could mean as part of the emotional landscape of a scene.[23]

Such a display is a hysterical gesture at its purest. In the 'revolutionary' 1960s, it was fashionable to assert perversion against the compromise of hysteria: a pervert directly violates social norms, he does openly what a hysteric only dreams about or articulates ambiguously in his/her symptoms. In other words, the pervert effectively moves beyond the Master and his Law, while the hysteric merely provokes her Master in an ambiguous way which can also be read as the demand for a more authentic real Master ... Against this view, Freud and Lacan consistently emphasized that perversion, far from being subversive, is the hidden obverse of power: every power needs perversion as its inherent transgression that sustains it. In the hysterical link, on the contrary, the $ over a stands for the subject who is divided, traumatized, by what for an object she is for the Other, what role she plays in Other's desire: 'Why am I what you're saying that I am?' or, to quote Shakespeare's Juliet, 'Why am I that name?' What she expects from the Other-Master is knowledge about what she is as object (the lower level of the formula). Racine's Phèdre is hysterical insofar as she resists the role of the object of exchange between men by way of incestuously violating the proper order of generations (falling in love with her stepson). Her passion for Hyppolite does not aim at its direct realization/satisfaction, but rather at the very act of its confession to Hyppolite, who is thus forced to play the double role of Phèdre's object of desire and of her symbolic Other (the addressee to whom she confesses her desire). When Hyppolite learns from Phèdre that he is the cause of her consuming passion, he is shocked – this knowledge possesses a clear 'castrating' dimension, it hystericizes him: 'Why me? What for an object am I so that I have this effect on her? What does she see in me?' What produces the unbearable castrating effect is not the fact of being deprived of 'it' but, on the contrary, the fact of clearly 'possessing it': the hysteric is horrified at being 'reduced to an object', that is to say, at being invested with the *agalma* which makes him or her the object of other's desire. In contrast to hysteria, the pervert knows perfectly what he is for the Other: a knowledge supports his position as the object of Other's (divided subject's) *jouissance.*

So far from being a compromiser, the hysterical subject is deeply justified in resisting the temptation of fully throwing herself into pervert transgression: what the hysteric perceives (or, rather, suspects) is precisely the falsity of the pervert's transgression, the way the pervert's activity sustains legal power. Kotsko therefore characterizes hysteria as

> a way of *creeping out the social order itself.* And just as in the case of the individual psyche, the social order is only susceptible to being creeped out due to the creepiness it carries within itself. Under normal circumstances, the social order appears to be obsessive in structure, opting for certain acceptable desires while repressing or excluding others. Yet from the hysteric's perspective, the most salient fact about the social order is the way it is continually setting us up to fail, so that it can even seem that the social order *needs* transgression and the illicit, creepy enjoyment that it provides. The social order's wink and nod of unofficial permission toward our creepy indulgences simultaneously makes social constraints more bearable *and* binds us more closely to the social order insofar as it makes those creepy indulgences possible. In short, the hysteric is uniquely positioned to see that the pervert has a point.[24]

Hysteria is as such always a historical formation: it reacts to the predominant mode of ideological interpellation (identification). This historical approach also allows us to refute the standard argument according to which, in today's permissive era, we no longer get hysterical patients whose symptoms are caused by the oppressed sexuality: what is usually referred to as 'borderline' is precisely hysteria in our time of permissiveness, and the time when the traditional figure of the Master is more and more replaced by the neutral expert legitimized by his (scientific) knowledge:

> Thankfully, the social order no longer explicitly backs women so completely into a corner as in the age of the housewife. Yet women still face conflicting pressures, such as those that Carrie feverishly attempts to navigate in her quest to avoid being 'that girl' in *Sex and the City*. Indeed, some of the contradictions have even been intensified and complicated as, for example, women are expected to excel in professional life while still meeting traditional requirements of motherhood. If anything, women suffer from having *too many* mutually contradictory outlets for their desire. Hence the contemporary manifestation

of hysteria is not the psychosomatic intrusion of the body into the social order – in the face of the impossible demand to 'have it all', the hysteric effectively goes on strike, refusing desire altogether.[25]

The borderline subject is thus *a hysteric without a Master*, a hysteric who is not oppressed by the Master but solicited by some expert-advisor figure to realize all his/her potential and 'have it all', leading a full life. Such a solicitation, of course, immediately acquires the superego-dimension of an inexorable pressure to which the subject can only respond by withdrawing from desire. Is this 'desire on strike' not a perfect formula for 'borderline' as the contemporary form of hysteria?

Many postmodern apologists of capitalism like to present it as a regime of universalized perversion in which 'castration' (antagonism) is successfully suspended, put aside, through the incessant rhythm of polymorphous-perverse expanded self-reproduction. The idea is that, while traditional capitalism still relied on the libidinal economy of paternal authority and the relations of domination and servitude, the 'postmodern' capitalism functions as a post-Oedipal network of self-entrepreneurs each engaged in its own investing and risking, the differences between them only quantitative and not qualitative. From the Lacanian standpoint, one can easily demonstrate that pseudo-Deleuzian anti-Oedipal vision is the fantasmatic core of capitalism, a fantasy that obfuscates the underlying antagonism ('castration', inexistence of class relationship). One should turn around here the standard operation of the critique of binary opposition: it is not that a binary opposition oppresses/totalizes a thriving multiplicity of partial drives (say, the normative heterosexuality totalizing/regulating polymorphous perversity) – on the contrary, partial drives emerge as attempts to obfuscate the basic antagonism (to supplement the absence of sexual relationship). What this means is that there is no happy pre-Oedipal universe of multiform perversity: 'castration' already casts its shadow onto it. The rise of the 'castration-complex' is not just a stage in libidinal development, it is a point at which the antagonism that sustains the entire development explodes openly. (In a similar way, for Lacan, Christianity is the 'true' religion, the religion which brings out the truth obfuscated in other religions.)

Mamatschi!

The exemplary case of creepiness is fantasy itself, the fundamental fantasy which is not yet rendered palpable through 'secondary perlaboration' – and we can be sure that the more 'beautiful' (in a kitschy way) is the surface presentation of a fantasy, the more disturbingly creepy is its inner core. There are moments in sentimental melodramas when one is embarrassed, almost unable to continue watching the scene, not on account of something disturbingly disgusting but on account of the very excessive-kitschy 'beauty' of the scene. Recall one of such moments in *The Sound of Music*: when the von Trapp children had to retire, they perform in front of the large crowd of guests the song 'Aufwiedersehen, Goodbye' full of obscenely embarrassing details which make the scene totally creepy … Crucial is here the dialectical reversal of excessive 'beauty' itself into repulsive creepiness. Just a couple of years after *The Sound of Music*, this kitschy creepiness was brought to extreme with the rise of Heintje, the Dutch-German-English-Afrikaans preteen megastar singer (and actor) from 1968 to 1971, a true voice of the cultural counter-revolution, the reaction to rock, to the spirit of 1968. His voice was a pre-sexual angelic voice, which is why his career went down with mutation – he was a kind of (the closest one can get to the) singing Norman Bates. His two greatest hits form a strange couple: both deal with the abandonment in the relation son/mother, but in the first one son leaves mother, while in the second one he is abandoned by his mother. (In a film clip accompanying the first song, mother is a nun, of course.) So here are the words of the first hit, 'Mama' (1967):

> Mama oh please don't cry
> because your boy must leave you
> Mama oh please don't let the separation grieve you
> You little boy is growing
> but don't be down when he's going
> Nothing can ever replace
> the warmth of your tender embrace.
> Mama the day will come we'll be together once more
> Oh my dear mama then we'll be happy
> and as gay as before.

And here are the words of the second hit, 'Heidschi Bumbeidschi' (1968):

> But Heidschi Bumbeidschi sleeping
> in heaven are the little sheep, the good ones
> They fly along the heavenly canopy
> forgetting the world's pain and worries
> But Heidschi Bumbeidschi boom boom
> But Heidschi Bumbeidschi boom boom

But Heidschi Bumbeidschi, you'll see
how quickly all worries vanish.
And if you are also alone and lonely,
soon the angels will look through the window
Singing Heidschi Bumbeidschi boom boom
Singing Heidschi Bumbeidschi boom boom

But Heidschi Bumbeidschi, sleep long
and if your mother has gone away
and if she has gone and won't come back
and leaves her little boy all alone
But Heidschi Bumbeidschi boom boom

This traditional children's lullaby about a poor child whose mother has abandoned him probably originated in Bohemian Austria in the eighteenth century. 'Heidschi bumbeidschi bum bum' is a nonsense phrase designed to sing children to sleep (in Austrian German, *heidigehen* means to go to sleep).[26] The weird Hölderlinian 'But…', a cut in continuity – things go on, 'but' something happens, a traumatic cut; or, rather, a child is alone, 'but' there is consolation. The wish to fall asleep is, of course, an echo of the wish to self-obliteration. (The underlying negative feature is that there is no father here.)

There is a third song in Heintje's mama-cycle, 'Mamatschi' (Mummy), whose words are worth quoting:

There was once a small boy
Who begged so treacly
Mummy, give me a little horse
A little horse would be my paradise
So the small boy got
A pair of gray horses made of marzipan
And he looks at them, cries and speaks:
'I did not want these kind of horses'

Mummy, give me a little horse
A little horse would be my paradise
Mummy, I did not want these kind of horses

Time passed, the boy wished
Nothing more but a horse from Santa Claus
Then Father Christmas visited him

And gave him what he wanted
On a table stand proudly
Four horses made of varnished wood
And he looks at them, cries and speaks:
'I did not want these kind of horses'

Mummy, give me a little horse
A little horse would be my paradise
Mummy, I did not want these kind of horses

And many years passed
The small boy became a man
Then one day before the gate
Stopped a glorious team of horses
In front of a colourful carriage stood
Four horses, richly decorated and beautiful
They took away his beloved mother
There he was reminded of his youth

Mummy, give me a little horse
A little horse would be my paradise
Mummy, the mourning-horses [*Trauerpferde*] I did not want.

(One should note the obscenity of the signifier 'mamatschi', as is already the case with 'heidschi bumbeidschi.') One shouldn't be afraid here to establish a link with Freud's 'little Hans': usually standard Oedipal reading – the horse feared by Hans is a substitute for the castrating father (big penis, cutting of Hans's small penis); there are, however, two features which undermine this reading. When Hans was about three years and six months old, his *mother* told him not to touch his 'widdler' or else she would call the doctor to cut it off. Furthermore, Hans was most frightened of horses which were drawing heavily laden carts, and, in fact, had seen a horse collapse and die in the street one time when he was out with his nurse. It was pulling a horse-drawn bus carrying many passengers and when the horse collapsed Hans had been frightened by the sound of its hooves clattering against the cobbles of the road. (Recall the Dostoyevsky–Nietzsche echoes of this episode.) So the phobia of Hans is not sustained by the fear of a too strong, animalistic father, but of the weak, dying father.

So if, in the case of Hans, we are dealing with a metaphor (horse stands for father), in 'Mamatschi' horse is a metonymy of the dead mother. There is thus a nice structure of exchange at work in this song: as long as mother is here, the boy gets ersatz horses (marzipan, wood); finally, when he gets the real horses, it is still a '*ce n'est pas ça*', because mother is lost. The impossible incest is to have both: mother *and* the partial object (real horses). But is the underlying idea not that the real desire of the boy was from the very beginning the four horses of the carriage carrying mother's corpse, so that 'Mummy, give me a little horse, A little horse would be my paradise' effectively means 'Mummy, drop dead, that would be my paradise!'

Eisler's sinthoms

The opposition of direct disgust and kitschy creepiness does not cover the entire field: there is another mode of creepiness which we have already touched when we were dealing with Dickens's 'MOOR EEFFOC' – the encounter with the weird materiality of sounds of a word disconnected from its meaning. A similar experience often occurs in our daily lives: there are moments when we all of a sudden become aware of how strange a word really sounds. We thus arrive (not so surprisingly, for a Hegelian) at yet another triad: direct disgust of the Real, its reversal into kitschy creepiness of excessive beauty, and … what?

The spectral materiality we encounter in 'MOOR EEFFOC' is not the direct vocal materiality but something much more weird, a kind of spiritualized materiality which is missed by Foucault, for whom Manet's achievement resides in the 'reinsertion of the materiality of the canvas in that which is represented':[27] the formal properties of the canvas (the horizontal and vertical lines of its border, the texture of the surface, suppression of depth), which traditional art tries to obfuscate, are reflected in the represented content, or, as Lacan would have put it, signifier falls into the signified. But is there not missing here the third level, spiritual materiality? Even if Manet was the first to render palpable the materiality of the surface of a painting undermining the reality of the depicted scene, was he also aware of another materiality beyond (or, rather, beneath) the materiality located in (what we experience as) spatiotemporal reality? The primordial Other of our spatiotemporal bodily reality is not Spirit, but another 'sublime' materiality. Modern art provides perhaps the most pertinent case of this other materiality. When exemplary modernist artists speak about the Spiritual in painting (Kandinsky) or in music (Schoenberg), the 'spiritual' dimension they evoke points towards the 'spiritualization' (or, rather, 'spectralization') of Matter (colour and shape, sound) as such, *outside* its reference to Meaning. Suffice it to recall the 'massiveness' of the protracted stains which 'are' yellow sky in late van Gogh or the water or grass in Munch: this uncanny 'massiveness' pertains neither to the direct materiality of the colour stains nor to the materiality of the depicted objects – it dwells in a kind of intermediate spectral domain of what Schelling called *geistige Körperlichkeit*. From the Lacanian perspective, it is easy to identify this 'spiritual corporeality' as materialized *jouissance*, '*jouissance* turned into flesh'.

Perhaps, in music, we find a homologous effect of 'spiritual corporeality' in (among others) Hanns Eisler's *Fourteen Ways of Describing the Rain* (Op. 70), a twelve-minute exercise in dodecaphony for flute, clarinet, string trio and piano, written as a musical accompaniment to Joris Ivens's documentary *Regen* (*Rain*, 1929), a portrayal of Amsterdam during a rainfall. (Incidentally, Ivens and his collaborator Franken originally commissioned Dutch composer Lou Lichtveld, who wrote a more traditional lyrical score for flute, string trio and harp synchronized to the 1932 version of the film.) Eisler's piece, written in 1941, was premiered in 1944 at Arnold Schoenberg's home in Los Angeles as part of the celebration of Schoenberg's seventieth birthday, and was highly admired by Schoenberg and Adorno who were otherwise opposed to Eisler's Communist political engagement. Two other pieces of Eisler's putatively belong to the same series: the six 'Hölderlin Fragments' from his *Hollywood Songbook* (1942–4, characterized by Matthias Goerne as 'the *Winterreise* of our times'),[28] and his last work, finished a couple of weeks before his death, *Serious Songs* (1962).

Eisler's Hölderlin is not Heidegger's Hölderlin, but a Jacobin one, Hölderlin with Marx, so no wonder that, even before music enters, Eisler reworked the words of the poems in a Brechtian way:

> Omitted or severely restricted are depictions of detail, duplicated expressions, thoughts developed too far, allegories, mythical images or descriptions of nature and landscape, in so far as they do not belong directly to the theme of the poem. Anything atmospheric in the text is also repressed because this the music contributes independently.[29]

However, it is not that the atmospheric excluded from words is allowed to explode in music; quite the contrary, music counteracts the atmospheric content that underlies the words and thus brings out the immanent contradictions in the words – or, to quote Eisler: 'A composer has to view a text in a way full of contradictions. The tragic element is interpreted by me cheerfully … If ever I'm praised for anything, it will be for resisting the text.'[30]

The point is thus not to resist or undermine the explicit text by way of bringing out its implied underground, a procedure often used in melodramas where passions that had to be subdued because of social constraints explode in the accompanying music, like in a scene of two secret lovers meeting in public where they have to behave properly, being observed by others, while their hearts are bleeding. Eisler introduces a further twist into such simple contrapuntal use of music: instead of being simply opposed to the explicit text, the musical line opposes (mocks) this very underground torrent of passions, interpreting the tragic element cheerfully.[31] So it's not that what is repressed, excluded from the domain of words, returns in music; what is inscribed into the music is *the falsity of this repressed content itself* – the music fights against the implied atmospheric mode. This also accounts for what to us, Western listeners, cannot but appear as the 'oriental' sound of Eisler's music: the heavy tragic atmosphere implied by words is countered by ascetically simple and clear playful tones – as if some dreadful content (desperate exchange of persons on the edge of suicide, brutal police questioning ...) is enacted by children as a playful game, with children having no idea of the horrible nature of the events they are talking about. If we apply Benjamin's metaphor of translation as putting together fragments of a broken vessel, we are dealing here with three, not just two, fragments, one of which remains irrepresentable, absent: when the two palpable fragments fit each other, they do not form a harmonious Whole, they just circumscribe the contours of a third invisible fragment. Sometimes, this reversal takes place at the song's end, as is the case in 'Heimat' where music ruins the atmospheric melancholic self-satisfaction. Eisler put to music the first two (out of six) four-line stanzas of Hölderlin's poem, cutting short the second stanza:

Happy does the sailor return to the bright streams
From far off islands, where he has reaped –
I too would like to return to my homeland again.
Oh, how I have woefully reaped.
Your lovely shores, which have raised me,
Oh grant me, you forests of my childhood,
When I return, peace once more again.

(Should one discern in 'reaped' a hint at colonialism?) The key omission is that he dropped the specification of homecoming expected to 'soothe love's sorrow', thereby erasing the romantic motif of a disappointed lover returning home to lick his wounds and find peace and consolation – here is the full second stanza:

River banks whose delights nurtured me,
Can you soothe love's sorrow? And can you,
Forests of my childhood, when I arrive,
Restore to me that peace again?

These words acquire their full meaning only with the music, especially the piano accompaniment which transforms the ending into 'a kind of alienation realized harmonically':[32]

> The arpeggio is marked out by means of a faster tempo and a diminuendo dying away. The harmony of the song precludes any precise analysis because of persistent fluctuations; but the types of chord favored are familiar from functional harmony. The final dissonance is in fact a gentle spreading out of thirds; at the same time it stands out in a telling way because of a substantially higher level of dissonance. The ending is meant to alienate so that the listener finds the whole poem alienating and thereby discovers concealed contemporary relevance.[33]

Compare to this ending of 'Heimat' the final notes of 'An eine Stadt' from the same cycle: 'with the sudden interjection of a completely unrelated and jarring D flat minor chord (marked sffz), this melancholy "winding down" is suddenly scattered like a house of cards.'[34] In this case, the ending is just a dissonant intrusion which shatters us from complacent melancholy, while in 'Heimat' we get the much more radical gesture of corroding melancholic ending from within – how, precisely? In the expression 'alienation realized harmonically', we should, of course, replace 'alienate' with the Brechtian 'extraneate' (render strange, uncommon) – so from what does the final dissonance extraneate the listener? From the self-satisfactory romantic atmosphere of bemoaning the pain of unfulfilled love and hoping that the return home will bring peace – this entire constellation is implicitly denounced as weird and 'unnatural', as a fake, finding enjoyment in brooding in one's own misfortune. And the 'contemporary relevance' becomes clear the moment one recalls that Eisler composed the song in 1942 when Germany was indeed not a place where one should look for a peace restored.

The point of Eisler's extraneation is, of course, not that we should simply drop the longing for a safe home and, in a postmodern mode, opt for nomadic freedom.[35] Now we arrive at the crucial point: this extraneation (*Verfremdung*) in no way implies that Eisler's song advocates a pure rational critical stance which distrusts any atmospheric element or emotion, i.e.

that it simply 'aims at the transmutation of feeling into a distanced objectivity.' The Brechtian extraneation is not just a procedure of acquiring intellectual distance, it is itself an emotion, an atmospheric stance, the 'feeling' that things are weird, out of joint. Therein resides the importance of Eisler's music: it renders the emotional atmosphere which fits the critical stance of extraneation. And although Eisler was a dedicated Communist, this emotion is as far as possible from cheap socialist optimism and trust in a bright future. For Eisler, as for any authentic Communist, revolutionary engagement always occurs against the background of sadness, despair even – despair at all the meaningless suffering that abounds in the long series of catastrophes called 'human history'. This inescapable atmosphere of sadness is grounded in our finitude: there is no way for us to extract ourselves from the texture of history and assume the external position of an agent and observer to whom history is a transparent process.[36] Nowhere is this ontological sadness more clearly expressed than in his *Serious Songs* for baritone and chamber orchestra which accompanies the voice in a Mahlerian mode. Already the motto, based on a fragment from Hölderlin's 'Sophocles', sets the tone:

Many have tried, but in vain,
With joy to express the most joyful;
Here at last, in grave sadness,
Wholly I find it expressed.

The cycle reaches its lowest point in the outrightly pessimistic 'Despair' (words based on Hamerling and Leopardi):

There is nothing worthy of your efforts
And the earth doesn't deserve a sigh.
Pain and boredom are our lot
And the world is dirt, nothing more.
Be calm.

The song that comes next, 'XXth Congress', signals a moment of hope, but with the 'Epilog' (based on Hölderlin again), the dark tone returns with a vengeance:

Come into the clearing, friend, though little shines
here below today, and tightly the heavens enclose us.
It is dim today, the alleys are slumbering.
It seems to be a leaden time [*als in der bleiernen Zeit*].

We should not limit this constellation of small rays of hope that may shine through clouds in a leaden time to the periods of retreat and defeat of the radical emancipatory movement – *every* emancipation has to emerge against the background of despair. This brings us finally back to *Regen*, where the music, instead of corresponding to the mood of each image in the film, pursues an agenda of its own and explores the textures of sadness – not, of course, in the Romantic sense of nature as the mirror of the subject's inner turmoil. In a wonderful phrase, Eisler characterized *Regen* as 'fourteen ways to be sad with decency'.[37] He compared the atmosphere of his piece with Verlaine's poem 'Il pleure dans mon coeur', which compares tears flowing in the heart with drops of rain falling onto a city and ends with the lines: 'It really is the worst pain / Not to know why / Without love and without hatred / There is so much pain in my heart.' It is not only that the depicted external objectivity is rendered as thoroughly indifferent with regard to the rendered emotion; this emotion itself is evoked as an 'abstract' emotion, as an emotion reduced to its pure form, deprived of its pathetic weight – it is at this abstract/formal level that the emotion rendered in music may echo with the emotion associated with the depicted or described external reality. After hearing Eisler's piece, Brecht wrote in his diary that 'it displays something of the Chinese ink drawings'.[38] What this means in the case of *Regen* is that the images and movements that we see on the screen should already be perceived in a reductive mode, reduced to their abstract form with a life of its own, irreducible to a portrait of a city flooded by rain.

These abstract forms (abstract in the sense of abstracted from their representative content) function like a proliferation of what Lacan called *sinthomes*, the elementary patterns of affective intensities. Recall, throughout both parts of Eisenstein's *Ivan the Terrible*, the motif of the thunderous explosion of rage which is continuously morphed and thus assumes different guises, from the thunderstorm itself to the explosions of uncontrolled fury: although it may at first appear to be an expression of Ivan's psyche, its sound detaches itself from Ivan and starts to float around, passing from one person to another or to a state not attributable to any diegetic person. This motif should *not* be interpreted as an 'allegory' with a fixed 'deeper meaning', but as a pure 'mechanical' intensity beyond meaning (this is what Eisenstein aimed at in his idiosyncratic use of the term 'operational'). Other such motives echo and reverse each other, or, in what Eisenstein called 'naked transfer', jump from one to another expressive medium (say, when an intensity gets too strong in the visual medium of mere shapes, it jumps and explodes in movement – then in sound, or in colour ...). For example, Kirstin Thompson points out how the motif of a single eye in Ivan is a 'floating motif', in itself strictly meaningless, but a repeated element that can, according to context, acquire a range of expressive implications (joy, suspicion, surveillance, quasi-godlike omniscience).[39] And the most interesting moments in *Ivan* occur when such motifs seem to explode their preordained space: not only do they acquire a multitude of ambiguous meanings no longer covered by an encompassing thematic or ideological agenda; in the most excessive moments, such a motif seems even to have no meaning at all, instead just floating there as an abstract form, a provocation, as a challenge to find the meaning that would tame its sheer provocative power.[40]

Maybe we should take a risk here and mobilize the ambiguity of the term 'tonality': tonality in the narrow musical sense of the tonal mode of a musical piece, and tonality in the sense of the emotional tone of a situation (the two are already connected in the different tonal modes: the heroic C major, the moody B minor, etc.). So what if we conceive of the atonality of the atonal music in both senses of the term: not only 'not obeying any tonal mode' but also asubjective in the sense of 'deprived of any particular emotional tone'? Or, to put it in Kantian terms, insofar as tonality is vaguely homologous with what Kant calls 'transcendental schematism', what we get in atonality is not a universe without emotions, deprived of emotional atmosphere (*Stimmung*), but pure emotions, emotions which are not yet schematized, attached to particular subjective modes. To make this point somewhat more clear, let us turn to Robert Schumann's *Carnaval* which provides an exemplary case of the Deleuzian rhizomatic structure: its twenty-one sections intertwine in multiple ways, each of them a kind of 'variation' on the others, related to others through melodic or rhythmic echoes, repetitions, and contrasts, whose logic cannot be grounded in a single universal rule. In classical variations (say, in Beethoven's *Diabelli Variations*), we first get the theme 'as such', followed by the multitude of its variations: as one would expect in Schumann, the 'theme' is simply lacking. However – and it is here that Schumann's practice differs from the 'deconstructionist' notion of play of variations without the original – these 'variations' do not all possess equal weight: there is a section which clearly 'sticks out'. The eighth section ('Réplique') is followed by 'Sphinxes', a section which is merely written and cannot be performed. What are these mysterious 'sphinxes'? The subtitle of *Carnaval* is 'Scènes mignonnes sur quatre notes' (Miniature scenes on four notes), and 'Sphinxes' provides these four notes, the musical cipher of *jouissance* which condenses a series of mnemonic associations: the young pianist Ernestine von Fricken, Schumann's girlfriend at the time he composed *Carnaval*, came from the Bohemian town of Asch, a name whose four letters are identical with the only letters of the word 'Schumann' which have note equivalents in German musical terminology (where 'H' stands for B, and 'B' for B-flat). Furthermore, if we read 'As' as A-flat, we get another variant of the musical cipher, so that we obtain three brief series: SCHumAnn (E-flat–C–B–A); ASCH (read as: A-flat–C–B); ASCH (read as: A–E-flat–C–B). In his *Psychanalyser*, Serge Leclaire reports on a psychoanalytic treatment which produced the cipher of enjoyment in his patient: the enigmatic term *poord'jeli*, a condensation of a multitude of mnemonic traces (the patient's love for a girl Lili, a reference to *licorne*, etc. etc.). Do we not encounter something of the same order in Schumann's 'Sphinxes'?

The entire piece thus turns around 'Sphinxes' as its absent, impossible-real point of reference: a series of bare notes without any measure or harmony – to put it in Kantian terms, they are not musically 'schematized', and therefore cannot be effectively performed. 'Sphinxes' are a pre-fantas-matic synthom, a formula of enjoyment, not unlike Freud's formula of trimethilamin, which appears at the end of the dream of Irma's injection. As such, the absence of 'Sphinxes' is structural: if 'Sphinxes' were to be effectively performed, the fragile consistency of the entire piece would fall apart. In short, 'Sphinxes' is the *objet petit a* of *Carnaval*, the section whose very exclusion guarantees the reality of the remaining elements. In some recordings, 'Sphinxes' is effectively performed: less than half a minute of a dozen protracted tones. The effect is properly uncanny, as if we had stepped 'through the looking-glass' and entered some forbidden domain, beyond (or, rather, beneath) the fantasmatic frame – or, more properly, as if we had caught sight of some entity outside of its proper element (like seeing a dead squid on a table, no longer alive and graciously moving in water). For this reason, the uncanny mystery of these notes can all of a sudden change into vulgarity, obscenity even – it is no wonder that the most outstanding proponent of performing 'Sphinxes' was none other than Rachmaninov, one of the exemplary kitsch authors of serious music.[41]

What happens with the rise of modern atonal music is thus the emanci-pation of sounds from tonality: tonality does not simply disappear, it is dispersed and pops up in many inconsistent fragmentary forms against its atonal background which is now visible and palpable as such. In short, what is in Schumann's *Carnaval* a unique, uncanny exception becomes the new rule.

We can now also establish a parallel with the 'spiritual corporeality' in Munch's paintings: the status of 'Sphinxes' in the musical texture of *Carnaval* is the same as that of the anamorphically distorted stains in a Munch painting. That is to say, in the same way that these stains belong to a third level which is neither the direct materiality of colours and shapes nor the represented materiality of the painting's content, the pre-schematized tones of 'Sphinxes' are neither the direct materiality of a sound nor its putative representative content – or, in the case of Eisler's *Regen*, the patterns of the musical form are neither depicting the reality of rain nor can they be reduced to the direct reality of sounds. At this third level, materialism and idealism overlap in a weird version of Platonic materialism: the atonal patterns are in a way immaterial (not yet schematized, pure forms/patterns of rain) and simultaneously more material than sensual objects (not yet included into our subjective experience). This nonschematized *sinthom*, a basic pattern of enjoyment not yet caught in a universe of meaning, is not the presymbolic real, a part of nature that can perhaps be rendered in a genetic code; it is already part of the symbolic process, its immanent zero-level.

6 WHEN NOTHING CHANGES: TWO SCENES OF SUBJECTIVE DESTITUTION

The lesson of psychoanalysis

The stupid commonplace about psychoanalytic treatment is that it has a double goal: to release us from suffering and to bring about our self-knowledge (by making part of our unconscious, of course, connected: we suffer because we don't really know ourselves – or, as the old Platonic and gnostic formula says, suffering accessible to consciousness). The two dimensions are, is caused by our ignorance. But is this view adequate? In a recently published interview with Paul Holdengräber, Adam Phillips said:

> Analysts are people who don't speak on the patient's behalf, don't speak for someone, unlike parents and teachers and doctors and politicians ... Analysis should do two things that are linked together. It should be about the recovery of appetite, and the need not to know yourself ... Symptoms are forms of self-knowledge. When you think, I'm agoraphobic, I'm a shy person, whatever it may be, these are forms of self-knowledge. What psychoanalysis, at its best, does is to cure you of your self-knowledge. And of your wish to know yourself in that coherent, narrative way. You can only recover your appetite, and appetites, if you can allow yourself to be unknown to yourself.[1]

This point is crucial: psychoanalysis does not aim at replacing the false or cyphered self-knowledge with the real one, but at getting rid of the need for self-knowledge, at enabling the patient to act without self-knowledge. Does this bring us back to the ancient wisdom, 'Just do it, don't think about it!' Does it amount to a return to naiveté? The (negative) answer is provided by Phillips's second point about suffering:

> Patients come because they are suffering from something. They want that suffering to be alleviated. Ideally, in the process of doing the analysis, they might find their suffering is alleviated or modified, but also they might discover there are more important things than to alleviate one's suffering.

> INTERVIEWER: Do you feel, in some way, that you have failed when a patient leaves your office feeling better?

> PHILLIPS: … I don't think the project is to make people feel better. Nor is it to make people feel worse. It's not to make them *feel* anything. It's simply to allow them to see what it is they do feel.[2]

Does Phillips contradict himself here? Is making people 'see what it is they do feel' not bringing about a kind of self-knowledge? (An elementary case of 'seeing' would be to discern the ambiguous hatred beneath which the analyst suspects there is hidden love [or vice versa].) The answer is that knowledge gained in analysis is a knowledge to be forgotten, discarded: once I 'see what it is that I feel', I don't go on dwelling in it, I just leave it behind – why? Not because of some decisionist mystique ('to be creative, one should overcome Hamlet-like procrastinations, too much self-analysing, and just do it!') but because the true task of analysis is to open up a void in the midst of our subjectivity: when we discard the knowledge gained in analysis, we open ourselves to this void. Therein resides the link between analysis and love: in love

> we really do know the other person in some profound sense – and also we really don't. And you could think that the fantasy of knowing is spurred by or prompted by something like 'this person has a powerful effect on me and it's so overwhelming that I'm going to manage this through a fantasy of knowledge'. For Proust, for example, knowing people is often very much about dealing with the anxiety that one can't control them.[3]

The paradox here is, of course, that (as the old saying goes) the more we know someone, the more we are forced to admit that we really don't know him/her. Here we should evoke the Rumsfeldian distinction between the known unknowns and the unknown knowns, between what we know that we don't know and what we don't know that we don't know because we are not even aware of that dimension of the object: the more we get to know someone, the more we learn what we don't know about him/her. This is also why, in order to be really close to another person, one has to maintain a certain distance towards him/her, a distance which replicates the unknowable void in the heart of this person. Winnicot's thesis is that the goal for the child is to be alone in the presence of the mother: 'there's something deeply important about the early experience of being in the presence of somebody without being impinged upon by their demands, and without them needing you to make a demand on them.'[4] Maybe the same goes for a love couple: the true test of a relationship comes when the first ecstatic infatuation is over, and the couple has to find a mode to be together without impinging on the other all the time.

And, maybe, this is what we learn in a successful analysis: not how to open up to others and engage with them but how to be alone among them. It is thus easy to see how the two features (abandoning the effort of self-understanding as well as the effort to diminish suffering) are interconnected: they are the two aspects of the same gesture of breaking out of the endless self-probing, of the subject's self-erasure in its dedication to the hard work of fidelity to a task that reaches beyond – political cause, artistic creativity, the building of a love couple.

Recently, I had to undergo the rather unpleasant procedure of colonoscopy in order to check for the signs of colon cancer which had already killed some of my maternal predecessors. After the procedure was over, the examining doctor offered me a small DVD which contained the video recording by the gradual penetration of the mini-camera through the entire length of my colon. I was rather surprised by this offer – what should I do with it? Should I tell my friends who sometimes visit me so that we watch together some old classic movie that I have something much more interesting to show them, a deep journey into the innermost core of my being? And is the practice of endless self-examination, today's version of the ancient motto 'know thyself', not the ideological counterpart of colonoscopy?

This, of course, in no way implies that we should dismiss the entire domain of so-called 'inner experience' as irrelevant; what we should focus on is rather a certain minimal change which amounts to the self-emptying of the subject and is as such profoundly revolutionary. There is a deep irony in the fact that revolution (as a sudden radical change) is usually opposed to evolution (a gradual change): the original meaning of 'revolution' is the circular movement of planets. In short, in an evolution, things change, evolve, they move somewhere else, while in a revolution, they return to the same place – so why did revolution come to mean a radical change? There is nonetheless a deeper meaning in this paradox: in an evolution, things change within the same space of change, while in a revolution, this very space has changed, so that when things return to the same place, this place is no longer the same but is changed radically. This brings us to the notion of minimal change. Kristeva's abject is the Real in the guise of an external abyss that threatens to swallow and dissolve the subject, so the proper dialectical counter-movement would be to focus on a minimal difference – not a gigantic all-shattering dissolution but a minimal change which is no less absolute, a change in which nothing changes in reality, and yet nothing remains the same.

When Kristeva talks about religion and art as reconciliation with the abject through its sublimation, one is tempted to expand her line of thought into a version of what Lacan called 'subjective destitution' (perhaps resonating with what Bataille called *l'expérience intérieure*, or, more generally, what the mystical tradition refers to as Enlightenment, the experience of 'You are that!' – recall also Lacan's insistence on the excremental identity of a saint): a barely perceptive inner shift by means of which the subject fully identifies with the abject, no longer experiencing it as something that causes horror and disgust. Let us analyse two cases, two artistic renderings, of this shift, one from the beginning and one from the end of European modernity: the final scene of Shakespeare's *Richard II*, and Beckett's short play *Not I*.

Music as a sign of love

From the Lacanian standpoint, it is not enough to say that every symbolic representation simply fails, is inadequate to the subject it represents ('words always betray me …'); much more radically, the subject *is* the retroactive effect of the failure of its representation. It is because of this failure that the subject is divided – not into something and something else, but into something (its symbolic representation) and nothing, and fantasy fills the void of this nothingness. And the catch is that this symbolic representation of the subject is primordially *not its own*: prior to speaking, I am spoken, identified as a name by the parental discourse, and my speech is from the very outset a kind of hysterical reaction to being spoken to: 'Am I really then, that name, what you're saying I am?' Every speaker – every name giver – *has* to be named, has to be included into its own chain of nominations, or, to refer to the joke often quoted by Lacan: 'I have three brothers, Paul, Ernest, and myself.' (No wonder that, in many religions, God's name is secret, one is prohibited to pronounce it.) The speaking subject persists in this in-between: prior to nomination, there is no subject, but once it is named, it already disappears in its signifier – the subject never is, it always *will have been*.

It is from this standpoint that one should reread the passages in *Richard II* which turn around *objet petit a*, the object-cause of desire. Pierre Corneille (in his *Médée*, act 2, scene 6) provided its nice description: '*Souvent je ne sais quoi qu'on ne peut exprimer / Nous surprend, nous emporte et nous force d'aimer*' (Often an I-don't-know-what which one cannot express / surprises us, takes us with it and compels us to love). Is this not the *objet petit a* at its purest – on condition that one supplements it with the alternate version: 'and compels us to hate'? Furthermore, one should add that the place of this 'I-don't-know-what' is the desiring subject itself: 'The secret of the Other is the secret for the Other itself' – but crucial in this redoubling is the self-inclusion: *what is enigmatic for the Other is myself*, i.e. I am the enigma for the Other, so that I find myself in the strange position (like in detective novels) of someone who all of a sudden finds himself persecuted, treated as if he knows (or owns) something, bears a secret, but is totally unaware *what* this secret is. The formula of the enigma is thus: 'What am I for the Other? What for an object of the Other's desire am I?'

Because of this gap, the subject cannot ever fully and immediately identify with his symbolic mask or title; the subject's questioning of his symbolic title is what hysteria[5] is about: 'Why am I what you're saying that I am?' Or, to quote again Shakespeare's Juliet: 'Why am I that name?' There is a truth in the wordplay between 'hysteria' and 'historia': the subject's symbolic identity is always historically determined, dependent upon a specific ideological constellation. We are dealing here with what Louis Althusser called 'ideological interpellation': the symbolic identity conferred on us is the result of the way the ruling ideology 'interpellates' us – as citizens, democrats, or Christians. Hysteria emerges when a subject starts to question or to feel discomfort in his or her symbolic identity: 'You say I am your beloved – what is there in me that makes me that? What do you see in me that causes you to desire me in that way?' *Richard II* is Shakespeare's ultimate play about hystericization (in contrast to *Hamlet*, the ultimate play about obsessionalization). Its topic is the progressive questioning by the king of his own 'kingness' – what is it that makes me a king? What remains of me if the symbolic title 'king' is taken away from me?

I have no name, no title,
No, not that name was given me at the font,
But 'tis usurp'd: alack the heavy day,
That I have worn so many winters out,
And know not now what name to call myself!
O that I were a mockery king of snow,
Standing before the sun of Bolingbroke,
To melt myself away in water-drops!

In Slovene translation, the second line is rendered as 'Why am I what I am?' Although this clearly involves too much poetic licence, it does render adequately the gist of it: deprived of its symbolic titles, Richard's identity melts like that of a snow king under sun rays. No wonder that Richard II is so devastated by being deprived of his symbolic title: he embodies the highest reliance on title, the belief that he is the chosen One, destined to wear the royal title. The defining moment of his life occurred when he was only fourteen, at the time of the great peasants' revolt in 1381. The rebels occupied most of London, posing a serious threat to the young king and his councillors who took refuge in the Tower. The king accepted their call to negotiations, and met them on Smithfield in the suburbs of London where he and his small retinue confronted around twenty thousand rebels led by Wat Tyler. In a small unexpected scuffle Tyler was killed and the furious crowd threatened to overrun the king and his men. At that moment of the highest tension, the young Richard did a totally crazy thing: alone, he rode towards the rebels, solemnly shouting: 'I will be your chief and captain, you shall have from me all that you seek.' (Or something along these lines – the reports are conflicting.) The gesture worked, the rebels respectfully withdrew, and the threat was over. One should not miss the precise nature of the king's move: immediately after the death of Tyler, the revolt's leader, he imposed himself not only as the legitimate king but also as the true leader of the rebels themselves who would take care of them – his message was: 'I am your true leader, not your opponent, so it is my duty to protect you, to be the voice of your grievances!'

The hysterical subject is the subject whose very existence involves radical doubt and questioning, his entire being is sustained by the uncertainty as to what he is for the Other; insofar as the subject exists only as an answer to the enigma of the Other's desire, the hysterical subject is the subject par excellence. In contrast to it, the analyst stands for the paradox of the desubjectivized subject, of the subject who fully assumed what Lacan calls 'subjective destitution', that is, who breaks out of the vicious cycle of intersubjective dialectics of desire and turns into an acephalous being of pure drive. With regard to this subjective destitution, Shakespeare's *Richard II* has a further surprise in store for us. Not only does the play enact the gradual hystericization of the unfortunate king; at the lowest point of his despair, before his death, Richard enacts a further shift of his subjective status which equals subjective destitution:

> I have been studying how I may compare
> This prison where I live unto the world:
> And for because the world is populous
> And here is not a creature but myself,
> I cannot do it; yet I'll hammer it out.
> My brain I'll prove the female to my soul,
> My soul the father; and these two beget
> A generation of still-breeding thoughts,
> And these same thoughts people this little world,
> In humours like the people of this world,
> For no thought is contented. The better sort,
> As thoughts of things divine, are intermix'd
> With scruples and do set the word itself
> Against the word:
> As thus, 'Come, little ones', and then again,
> 'It is as hard to come as for a camel
> To thread the postern of a small needle's eye.'
> Thoughts tending to ambition, they do plot
> Unlikely wonders; how these vain weak nails
> May tear a passage through the flinty ribs
> Of this hard world, my ragged prison walls,
> And, for they cannot, die in their own pride.
> Thoughts tending to content flatter themselves
> That they are not the first of fortune's slaves,
> Nor shall not be the last; like silly beggars
> Who sitting in the stocks refuge their shame,
> That many have and others must sit there;
> And in this thought they find a kind of ease,
> Bearing their own misfortunes on the back
> Of such as have before endured the like.
> Thus play I in one person many people,
> And none contented: sometimes am I king;
> Then treasons make me wish myself a beggar,
> And so I am: then crushing penury
> Persuades me I was better when a king;

Then am I king'd again: and by and by
Think that I am unking'd by Bolingbroke,
And straight am nothing: but whate'er I be,
Nor I nor any man that but man is
With nothing shall be pleased, till he be eased
With being nothing. Music do I hear?

(The music plays.)

Ha, ha! keep time: how sour sweet music is,
When time is broke and no proportion kept!
So is it in the music of men's lives.
And here have I the daintiness of ear
To cheque time broke in a disorder'd string;
But for the concord of my state and time
Had not an ear to hear my true time broke.
I wasted time, and now doth time waste me;
For now hath time made me his numbering clock:
My thoughts are minutes; and with sighs they jar
Their watches on unto mine eyes, the outward watch,
Whereto my finger, like a dial's point,
Is pointing still, in cleansing them from tears.
Now sir, the sound that tells what hour it is
Are clamorous groans, which strike upon my heart,
Which is the bell: so sighs and tears and groans
Show minutes, times, and hours: but my time
Runs posting on in Bolingbroke's proud joy,
While I stand fooling here, his Jack o' the clock.
This music mads me; let it sound no more;
For though it have holp madmen to their wits,
In me it seems it will make wise men mad.
Yet blessing on his heart that gives it me!
For 'tis a sign of love; and love to Richard
Is a strange brooch in this all-hating world.

It is crucial to properly grasp the shift in modality which occurs with the entrance of *music* in the middle of this monologue. The first part is a solipsistic rendering of a gradual reduction to nothingness, to the pure void of the subject ($): Richard starts with the comparison of his cell with the world; but in his cell, he is alone, while the world is peopled; so, to solve this antinomy, he posits his thoughts themselves as his company in the cell – Richard dwells in the fantasms generated by a mother (his brain) and father (his soul). The pandemonium he thus dwells in, in which the highest and the lowest coexist side by side, is exemplified by a wonderful Eisensteinian montage of two biblical fragments, 'Come, little ones' (reference to Lk. 18.16, Mt. 19.14, Mk 10.14) counterposed to 'It is as hard to come as for a camel to thread the postern of a small needle's eye' (reference to Lk. 18.26, Mt. 19.24, Mk 10.25). If we read these two fragments together, we get a cynical superego God who first benevolently calls us to come to him, and then sneeringly adds, as a kind of afterthought ('Oh, by the way, I forgot to mention …'), that it is almost impossible to come to Him. The problem with this solution is that, if he with his thoughts is a multitude of people, then, caught in this shadowy unsubstantial world, the substantial consistency of his self explodes, he is forced to play 'in one person many people'. And, he concludes, he effectively oscillates between being a king, a beggar, etc.; the truth of it, and the only peace to be found, is in accepting to be nothing.

In the second part, music as an object enters, a true 'answer of the Real'. This second part itself contains two breaks. First, in his usual rhetorical vein, Richard once again uses this intrusion to form a metaphor: the playing of the music out of tune reminds him how he himself was 'disordered' (out of tune) as a king, unable to strike the right notes in running the country and thus bringing disharmony – while he has great sensitivity for musical harmony, he lacked this sensitivity for social harmony. This 'out of joint' is linked to time – the implication being that, not merely is time out of joint, but time as such signals an out-of-jointness, i.e. there is time *because* things are somehow out of joint. Then, no longer able to sustain this safe metaphoric difference, Richard enacts a properly psychotic *identification with the symptom*, with the musical rhythm as the cipher of his destiny: like an alien intruder, music parasitizes, colonizes him, its rhythm forcing on him the identification with Time, a literal identification, psychotic, where he no longer needs a clock but, in a terrifying vision, he directly *becomes* the clock (in the mode of what Deleuze celebrated as 'becoming-machine'). It is as if Richard is driven to such an extreme of painful madness with this music that, for him, the only way to get rid of this unbearable pressure of music is to directly identify with it … In one of the episodes of the 1945 British horror omnibus *Dead of the Night*, Michael Redgrave plays the ventriloquist who becomes jealous of his dummy, gnawed by the suspicion that it wants to leave him for a competitor; at the episode's end, after destroying the dummy by way of thrashing its head, he is hospitalized; after reawakening from psychic coma, he identifies with his symptom (the dummy), starting to talk and contorting his face like it. Here we get the psychotic identification as the false way out: what started out as a partial object (the dummy is a doll stuck on his right hand, it is literally his hand acquiring an autonomous life, like the hand of Ed Norton in *Fight Club*) develops into a full double engaged in a mortal competition with the subject, and since the subject's consistency relies on this symptom-double, since it is structurally impossible for him to get rid of the symptom, the only way out of it, the only way to resolve the tension, is to directly identify with the symptom, to become one's own symptom – in exact homology to Hitchcock's *Psycho* at the end of which the only way for Norman to get rid of his mother is to identify with her directly, to let her take over his personality and, using his body as a ventriloquist uses his dummy, speak through him.

Finally, there occurs an additional shift towards the end of the monologue, in the last three lines: music, which first is experienced as a violent intrusion that drives Richard to madness, now appears as a soothing 'sign of love' – why this shift? What if it simply stands for the return to real music that he hears: it is a 'sign of love' when separated from the metaphoric dimension of recalling the disharmony of his kingdom. The designation of music as 'a sign of love' has to be understood in its strict Lacanian sense: an answer of the Real by means of which the circular-repetitive movement of drive is reconciled with – integrated into – the symbolic order.

This moment of subjective destitution provides an exemplary case of what event is: not a big spectacular explosion, but just a barely perceptible shift in the subjective position. What happens at this moment of destitution with truth? Apropos of truth, we encounter the same paradox as apropos of *jouissance*: one cannot say all of it, we always miss it, but, simultaneously, *one cannot escape it*, one cannot escape *saying* it – what are the Freudian symptoms if not different forms of how 'I, the truth, speak', of how truth continues to haunt us, to insist and articulate itself behind the speaker's back, unbeknownst to him/her? It is this dimension of the Truth itself speaking behind the speaker's back which is excluded by scientific discourse (which is why Lacan says that science forecloses the dimension of truth). This, of course, in no way implies that the Freudian 'truth' is nonscientifically irrational, 'existential', etc.; that is, Lacan is not mobilizing here the standard opposition between 'objective' scientific knowledge and 'subjective truth': the Freudian subject is for him the subject of modern science, and the 'truth which speaks' behind his back is not a premodern spiritual awareness, but the truth of *this* subject, which is to be articulated in the paradoxes and gaps of scientific formalization itself, elaborated in what Lacan calls the 'logic of the signifier'.

This, however, in no way implies that truth is an all-powerful big Other which pulls the strings behind the subject's back: with the shift in Lacan's teaching which announces itself with his Seminar XI, truth is gradually degraded, its scope and weight constrained at the expense of the real of *jouissance*. In the great opposition between desire and drive, symptom and fantasy, interpretation and construction, truth belongs to the series desire-symptom-interpretation (desire articulates itself in symptoms which are to be interpreted). The series drive-fantasy-construction follows a different logic: fantasy at its most fundamental (the 'fundamental fantasy', precisely) is not to be interpreted but constructed and then 'traversed'; it has to be constructed in the form of 'a-subjective' knowledge which is external to the dimension of truth. (What this means is that the late Lacan rehabilitates a knowledge more radical than truth, a knowledge touching the real.)

As Balmès put it very perspicuously,[6] with a wonderfully appropriate play on words, with the theory of four discourses, where truth is define as a *place* (the place down left, beneath the agent), truth is 'put into its proper place' – one has to read this expression in both of its meanings: (1) truth is finally correctly located, theoretically grasped; (2) truth is contained, limited, it is not the most basic dimension of psychoanalysis. As, again, Balmès noticed, the place of truth in the four discourses should (also) be understood in Hegelian terms of a figure being the 'truth of' another figure, the exposition of its concealed latent structure – in this sense, for example, the fact that, in the discourse of the University, we find at the place of truth the Master Signifier means that the position of the Master is the *truth of* the discourse of the University: its apparently neutral position of knowledge-expertise conceals a dimension of domination. In this sense, also, the fact that, in the Master's discourse, we find at the place of truth $, the divided subject, means that the hysterical 'divided subject' is the *truth of* the Master's discourse. And, again, the place of truth in the discourse of hysteria is *objet a*, which means that the truth of the hysterical subject is the question of what kind of object-cause of desire he is for the other (for his Master) – herefrom the eternal hysterical question-provocation: 'Tell me why you love me!' The analyst assumes this position of *objet a* in order to enable the hysterical patient to clarify his/her desire. So what about knowledge as the truth of the discourse of the analyst? It is precisely a paradoxical knowledge external to the very dimension of truth, the knowledge of the formal coordinates of the fundamental fantasy – and it is a knowledge which is correlative to the *fall* of the 'subject supposed to know'.

This fall of the SStK at the end of the analytic treatment first implies that there is no *subject* to the unconscious knowledge: the unconscious knowledge articulates itself through slips and gaps, behind the subject's back. Then, it implies the end of transference: the insight that the analyst is also not an SStK. But, at its most radical, it concerns not only the analyst, but the Unconscious itself. The Unconscious is for Lacan not a site of profound 'presupposed knowledge', of the truth about himself that is inaccessible to the subject and that has to be brought into the open through the help of the analyst; in other words, it doesn't mean that 'somewhere deep in himself, the subject knows all there is to know, he just has to overcome the obstacles and open himself to the Truth that dwells in the core of his being'. Consequently, the fall of the SStK means the full acceptance of the fact that *the Unconscious itself doesn't know it*, that there is a gap in the symbolic order which is cosubstantial with this order. This is what Lacan means by 'there is no sexual relationship': there is no deep instinctual formula of the harmony between the sexes which should be uncovered, the Unconscious is not a deep-seated wisdom but a big mess, a bricolage of symptoms and fantasies which deal with or cover up this deadlock.

A failed betrayal

If one looks for a homologous subtle subjective shift in contemporary literature, it is a waste of time to peruse the work of James Joyce. One can understand Joyce, with all the obscenities that permeate his writings, as the ultimate Catholic author, 'the greatest visionary of the dark underground of Catholicism, an underground embodying a pure transgression, but one which is nevertheless a profoundly Catholic transgression'.[7] Catholicism is legalistic, and, as Paul knew it so well, the Law generates its own transgression; consequently, the staging of the obscene underground of the Law, the travesty of the Black Mass (or, in Joyce's case, the elevation of Here Comes Everybody into Christ who has to die in order to be reborn as the eternal Life-Goddess, from Molly Bloom to Anna Livia Plurabelle), is the supreme Catholic act.

This achievement of Joyce simultaneously signals his limit, the limit that pushed Samuel Beckett to break with him. If there ever was a kenotic writer, the writer of the utter self-emptying of subjectivity, of its reduction to a minimal difference, it is Beckett. The gap that separates Beckett from Joyce is the gap between the two Reals. The Lacanian Real, in its opposition to the Symbolic, has ultimately nothing whatsoever to do with the standard empiricist (or phenomenological, or historicist, or *Lebensphilosophie*, for that reason) topic of the wealth of reality that resists formal structures, that cannot be reduced to its conceptual determinations – language is grey, reality is green … The Lacanian Real is, on the contrary, even more 'reductionist' than any symbolic structure: we touch it when we subtract from a symbolic field all the wealth of its differences, reducing it to a minimum of antagonism.

Lacan sometimes gets seduced by the rhizomatic wealth of language beyond (or, rather, beneath) the formal structure that sustains it. It is in this sense that, in the last decade of his teaching, he deployed the notion of *lalangue* (sometimes simply translated as 'llanguage') which stands for language as the space of illicit pleasures that defy any normativity: the chaotic multitude of homonymies, wordplays, 'irregular' metaphoric links and resonances … Productive as this notion is, one should be aware of its limitations. Many commentators have noted that Lacan's last great literary reading, that of Joyce to whom his late seminar *Le sinthome*[8] is dedicated, is not at the level of his previous great readings (*Hamlet*, *Antigone*, Claudel's Coûfontaine trilogy). There is effectively something fake in Lacan's fascination with late Joyce, with *Finnegans Wake* as the latest version of the literary *Gesamtkunstwerk* with its endless wealth of *lalangue* in which not only the gap between singular languages, but the very gap between linguistic meaning and *jouissance* seems overcome and the rhizomatic *jouis-sense* (enjoyment-in-meaning; enjoy-meant) proliferates in all directions. The true counterpart to Joyce is, of course, Beckett: after his early period in which he more or less wrote some variations on Joyce, the 'true' Beckett constituted himself through a true ethical act, a *cut*, a rejection of the Joycean wealth of enjoy-meant, and the ascetic turn towards a 'minimal difference', towards a minimalization, 'subtraction', of the narrative content and of language itself (this line is most clearly discernible in his masterpiece, the trilogy *Molloy – Malone Dies – L'innomable*). Beckett is effectively the literary counterpart of Anton Webern: both are authors of extreme modernist minimalism, of subtracting a minimal difference from the wealth of material. So what is the 'minimal difference' – the purely parallax gap – that sustains Beckett's mature production? One is tempted to propose the thesis that it is the very difference between French and English: as is known, Beckett wrote most of his mature works in French (not his mother tongue), and then, desperate at the low quality of translations, translated them himself into English, and these translations are not mere close translations, but effectively a different text.

Beckett's *Texts for Nothing* (first published in French in 1955 as *Nouvelles et textes pour rien*)[9] is the fourth term which supplements the trilogy *Molloy – Malone Dies – The Unnamable*. Beckett himself referred to *Texts* as 'the grisly afterbirth of *L'innomable*', the 'attempt to get out of the attitude of disintegration [of the trilogy] but it failed'.[10] The obvious link is that the first line of the first text ('Suddenly, no, at last, long last, I couldn't any more') echoes the famous last line of *The Unnamable* ('you must go on, I can't go on, I'll go on'), a true Kantian imperative, a paraphrase of Kant's *Du kannst, denn du sollst* (You can, because you must). The voice of conscience tells me 'you must go on'; I reply, referring to my weakness, 'I can't go on'; but as a Kantian, I know this excuse doesn't count, so I nonetheless decide that 'I'll go on', doing the impossible. Is then Beckett's *L'innomable* not to be opposed to Badiou's version of it?[11] For Beckett, *L'innomable* is not the excessive multitude that cannot be forced thoroughly, but the ethical fidelity itself, its persistence embodied in the 'undead' partial object.[12]

Since, for Beckett, what 'must go on' is ultimately writing itself, the Lacanian version of the last line of *The Unnamable* is something that *ne cesse pas de s'écrire*, that doesn't cease writing itself – a *necessity*, the first term in the logical square which also comprises *impossibility* (that which *ne cesse pas de ne pas s'écrire*, doesn't cease not writing itself), *possibility* (that which *cesse de s'écrire*, ceases to write itself), and *contingency* (that which *cesse de ne pas s'écrire*, ceases not writing itself). It is crucial to note here the clear distinction between possibility and contingency: while possibility is the opposite of necessity, contingency is the opposite of impossibility. In Badiou's terms of the attitudes towards a Truth-Event, necessity stands for the fidelity to Truth, impossibility for a situation with no truth, possibility for the possibility of a truth-procedure to exhaust its potentials and to stop, and contingency for the beginning of a new truth-procedure.

So what do *Texts for Nothing* register, a possibility or a contingency? A possibility, definitely – a possibility to 'cease writing', to betray fidelity, to cease going on. The failure of *Texts* is thus good news: *Texts* are failed betrayals, failed attempts to get rid of the ethical injunction. They are a comical supplement to the great triad – an opportunist's attempt to squeeze out of the call of duty, somewhat like Kierkegaard's 'sickness unto death', where a mortal human being attempts to escape immortality, its unbearable ethical burden/injunction. In this sense, *Texts* are an optimistic work – their message is that one cannot but 'go on' as an immortal bodiless drive, as a subject without subjectivity: 'No, no souls, or bodies, or birth, or life, or death, you've got to go on without any of that junk' …

Boulter thus got it right – on condition that we strictly distinguish between subject and subjectivity. The whole of the trilogy can be read as a gradual getting rid of subjectivity, a gradual reduction of subjectivity to the minimum of a subject without subjectivity – a subject which is no longer a person, whose objective correlative is no longer a body (organism), but only a partial object (organ), a subject of *drive* which is

Freud's name for immortal persistence, 'going on'. Such a subject is a living dead – still alive, going on, persisting, but dead (deprived of body) – undead. *Texts* are a comical attempt to resubjectivize this subject – among other things, to provide him with a body, to travel back the road from the Cheshire cat's smile to its full body. Boulter is right to correct Alvarez, who claimed that *Texts* are written in the same 'breathless, bodiless style' as *The Unnamable*:

> One of the things the reader notices about *Texts* from its outset is that the body (of the narrator/narrated) has made an uncanny return from its near obliteration in *The Unnamable*: the narrator of *The Unnamable* is disembodied (it may be that 'he' is merely a brain in an urn). At the very least, the issue of subjectivity is a complex one in the trilogy because the relation between voice (of narrator) and body (of narrator) is continually called into question. We may in fact argue that the trilogy *in toto* is about the dismantling of the physical body: in *Molloy*, the body is ambulatory but weakening; in *Malone Dies* the body is on its last legs, immobile and dying; in *The Unnamable* the physical body may in fact have ceased to be an issue as the narrator floats between personalities and subject positions. All of which is to indicate that in *Texts*, the body has made … an unexpected comeback.[13]

The subject without subjectivity, this 'living dead', is also timeless – when we reach this point, 'time has turned into space and there will be no more time till I get out of here' (note how Beckett here repeats Wagner's precise formula of the sacred space of the Grail's castle from *Parsifal* 'time become here space', which Claude Lévi-Strauss quotes as the most succinct definition of myth). The subject we thus reach, a subject without subjectivity, is a subject which

> cannot maintain with any certainty that the experiences he describes are in fact his own; we have a narrating subject who cannot discern if his voice is his own; we have a subject who cannot tell if he has a body; and most crucially, we have a subject who has no sense of personal history, no memory. We have, in short, a subject whose ontology denies the viability of mourning and trauma, yet who seems to display the viability of mourning and trauma.[14]

Is this subject deprived of all substantial content not the subject as such, at its most radical, the Cartesian *cogito*? Boulter's idea is that, for Freud, trauma presupposes a subject to whom it happens and who then tries to narrativize it, to come to terms with it, in the process of mourning. In the case of the Beckettian narrator, on the contrary,

> there is no hope of establishing a link between his own present condition and the trauma that is its precondition. Instead of having a story seemingly given to him unawares – as in the case of the victim of trauma who cannot recognize his past as his own – the Beckettian narrator can only hope (without hope …) for a story that will reconnect his present atemporal … condition to his past.[15]

This is the division of the subject at its most radical: the subject is reduced to $ (the barred subject), even its innermost self-experience is taken from it. This is how one should understand Lacan's claim that the subject is always 'decentred' – his point is not that my subjective experience is regulated by objective unconscious mechanisms that are decentred with regard to my self-experience and, as such, beyond my control (a point asserted by every materialist), but, rather, something much more unsettling: I am deprived of even my most intimate subjective experience, the way things 'really seem to me', that of the fundamental fantasy that constitutes and guarantees the core of my being, since I can never consciously experience it and assume it. One should counter Boulter's question 'To what extent do trauma and mourning require a subject?' with a more radical one: to what extent does (the very emergence of) a subject require trauma and mourning?[16] The primordial trauma, the trauma constitutive of the subject, is the very gap that bars the subject from *its own* 'inner life'.

Scene from a happy life

This inner and constitutive link between trauma and subject is the topic of what is undoubtedly Beckett's late masterpiece: *Not I*, a twenty-minute dramatic monologue written in 1972, an exercise in theatric minimalism. There are no 'persons' here, intersubjectivity is reduced to its most elementary skeleton, that of the speaker (who is not a person, but a partial object, a faceless MOUTH speaking – an 'organ without a body',[17] as it were) and AUDITOR, a witness of the monologue who says nothing throughout the play; all the Auditor does is that, in 'a gesture of helpless compassion' (Beckett), he four times repeats the gesture of simple sideways raising of arms from sides and their falling back. (When asked if the Auditor is Death or a guardian angel, Beckett shrugged his shoulders, lifted his arms and let them fall to his sides, leaving the ambiguity intact – repeating the very gesture of the Auditor.) Beckett himself pointed to the similarities between *Not I* and *The Unnamable* with its clamouring voice longing for silence, circular narrative and concern about avoiding the first-person pronoun: 'I shall not say I again, ever again.'[18] Along these lines, one could agree with Vivian Mercier's suggestion that, gender aside, *Not I* is a kind of dramatization of *The Unnamable*[19] – one should only add that, in *Not I*, we get the talking partially coupled or supplemented with a minimal figure of the big Other.[20]

Beckettology, of course, did its job in discovering the empirical sources of the play's imagery. Beckett himself provided the clue for the 'old hag', but also emphasized the ultimate irrelevance of this reference: 'I knew that woman in Ireland. I knew who she was – not "she" specifically, one single woman, but there were so many of those old crones, stumbling down the lanes, in the ditches, besides the hedgerows. Ireland is full of them. And I heard "her" saying what I wrote in *Not I*. I actually heard it.'[21] But, replying to the queries, Beckett said: 'I no more know where she is or why thus than she does. All I know is in the text. "She" is purely a stage entity, part of a stage image and purveyor of a stage text. The rest is Ibsen.'[22] As to the reduction of the body of the speaker to a partial organ (mouth), in a letter dated 30 April 1974, Beckett gave a hint that the visual image of this mouth was 'suggested by Caravaggio's *Decollation of St John* in Valletta Cathedral.'[23] As to the figure of the Auditor, it was inspired by the image of a djellaba-clad 'intense listener' seen from a café in Tunis (Beckett was in North Africa from February to March 1972). James Knowlson conjectured that this 'figure coalesced with [Beckett's] sharp memories of the Caravaggio painting', which shows 'an old woman standing to Salome's left. She observes the decapitation with horror, covering her ears rather than her eyes' (a gesture that Beckett added in the 1978 Paris production).[24]

Much more interesting are Beckett's own uncertainties and oscillation with regard to the Auditor (who is generally played by a male, although the sex is not specified in the text): when Beckett came to be involved in staging the play, he found that he was unable to place the Auditor in a stage position that pleased him, and consequently allowed the character to be omitted from those productions. However, he chose not to cut the character from the published script, and left the decision whether to use the character in a production at the discretion of individual producers. As he wrote to American directors David Hunsberger and Linda Kendall in 1986: 'He is very difficult to stage (light – position) and may well be of more harm than good. For me the play needs him but I can do without him. I have never seen him function effectively.'[25] Beckett reinstated the character in the 1978 Paris production, but from then on abandoned it, concluding that it was perhaps 'an error of the creative imagination'.[26] From the Lacanian perspective, it is easy to locate the source of this trouble: the Auditor gives body to the big Other, the Third, the ideal Addressee-Witness, the place of Truth which receives and thereby authenticates the speaker's message. The problem is how to visualize, materialize, this structural place as a figure on the imaginary of the stage: while every play (or even speech) needs it, every concrete figuration is by definition inadequate, i.e. it cannot ever 'function effectively' on stage.

The basic constellation of the play is thus the dialogue between the subject and the big Other, where the couple is reduced to its barest minimum: the Other is a silent impotent witness which fails in its effort to serve as the medium of the Truth of what is said, and the speaking subject itself is deprived of its dignified status of 'person' and reduced to a partial object. And, consequently, since meaning is generated only by means of the detour of the speaker's word through a consistent big Other, the speech itself ultimately functions at a presemantic level, as a series of explosions of libidinal intensities. At the premiere in Lincoln Center, the Mouth was played by Jessica Tandy, the mother from Hitchcock's *The Birds*. Debating the piece with her, Beckett demanded that it should 'work on the nerves of the audience, not its intellect', and advised Tandy to consider the mouth 'an organ of emission, without intellect'.[27]

Where does this bring us with regard to the standard postmodern critique of dialogue which emphasizes its origin in Plato, where there is always the one who knows (even if only that he knows nothing) questioning the other (who pretends to know) to admit he knows nothing? There is thus always a basic asymmetry in a dialogue – and does this asymmetry not break out openly in Plato's late dialogues, where we are no longer dealing with Socratic irony, but with one person talking all the time, with his partner merely interrupting him from time to time with 'So it is, by Zeus!' 'How can it not be so?' and so forth. It is easy for a postmodern deconstructionist to show the violent streak even in Habermas's theory of communicative action which stresses the symmetry of the partners in a dialogue: this symmetry is grounded in the respect of all parts for the rules of rational argumentation, and are these rules really as neutral as they claim to be? Once we accept this and bring it to its radical conclusion – the rejection of the very notion of 'objective truth' as oppressive, as an instrument of domination – the postmodern path to what Lyotard called *le différend* is open: in an authentic dialogue, there is no pressure to reach a final reconciliation or accord, but merely to reconcile ourselves with the irreducible difference of perspectives which cannot be subordinated to any encompassing universality. Or, as Rorty put it: the fundamental right of each of us is the right to tell his/her/their own story of life-experience, especially of pain, humiliation and suffering. But, again, it is clear that people not only speak from different perspectives, but that these differences are grounded in different positions of power and domination: what does the right to free dialogue mean when, if I approach certain topics, I risk everything, up to my life? Or, even worse, when my complaints are not even rejected, but dismissed with a cynical smile? The Left-liberal position is here that one should especially emphasize the voices which are usually not heard, which are ignored, oppressed or even prohibited within the predominant field – sexual and religious minorities, etc. But is this not all too abstract-formal? The true problem is: how are we to create conditions for a truly egalitarian dialogue? Is this really possible to do in a 'dialogic', respectful way, or is some kind of counterviolence needed? Furthermore, is the notion of (not naively 'objective', but) universal truth really by definition a tool of oppression and domination? Say, in the Germany of 1940, the Jewish story of their suffering was not simply an oppressed minority view to be heard, but a complaint whose truth was in a way universal, i.e. which rendered visible what was wrong in the entire social situation.

Is there a way out of this conundrum? What about the dialogic scene of the psychoanalytic session, which weirdly inverts the coordinates of the late Platonic dialogue? As in the latter case, here also one (the patient) talks almost all the time, while the other only occasionally interrupts him with an intervention which is more of a diacritical order, asserting the proper scansion of what was told. And, as we know from the Freudian theory, the analyst is here not the one who already knows the truth and just wisely leads the patient to discover it himself/herself: the analyst precisely doesn't know it, his knowledge is the illusion of transference which had to fall at the end of the treatment.

And is it not that, with regard to this dynamic of the psychoanalytic process, Beckett's play can be said to start where the analytic process ends: the big Other is no longer 'supposed to know' anything, there is no transference, and, consequently, 'subjective destitution' already took place. But does this mean that, since we are already at the end, there is no inner dynamic, no radical shift, possible any more – which would nicely account for the appearance of the circular movement in this (and other) Beckett play(s)? A closer look at the content of the play's narrative, of what is told in this twenty-minute-long monologue, seems to confirm this diagnostic: the Mouth utters at a ferocious pace a logorrhoea of fragmented, jumbled sentences which obliquely tells the story of a woman of about seventy who, having been abandoned by her parents after a premature birth, has lived a loveless, mechanical existence and who appears to have suffered an unspecified traumatic experience. The woman has been virtually mute since childhood apart from occasional winter outbursts, part of one of which comprises the text we hear, in which she relates four incidents from her life: lying face down in the grass on a field in April; standing in a supermarket; sitting on a 'mound in Croker's Acre' (a real place in Ireland near Leopardstown racecourse); and 'that time at court'. Each of the last three incidents somehow relates to the repressed first 'scene' which has been likened to an epiphany – whatever happened to her in that field in April was the trigger for her to start talking. Her initial reaction to this paralysing event is to assume she is being punished by God; strangely, however, this punishment involves no suffering – she feels no pain, as in life she felt no pleasure. She cannot think why she might be being punished but accepts that God does not need a 'particular reason' for what He does. She thinks she has something to tell though she doesn't know what but believes if she goes over the events of her life for long enough she will stumble upon that thing for which she needs to seek forgiveness; however, a kind of abstract nonlinguistic continued buzzing in her skull always intervenes whenever she gets too close to the core of her traumatic experience.

The first axiom of interpreting this piece is not to reduce it to its superficial cyclical nature (endless repetitions and variations of the same fragments, unable to focus on the heart of the matter), imitating the confused mumbling of the 'old hag' too senile to get to the point: a close reading makes it clear that, just before the play's end, there *is* a crucial break, a decision, a shift in the mode of subjectivity. This shift is signalled by a crucial detail: in the last (fifth) moment of pause, the Auditor *doesn't* intervene with his mute gesture – his 'helpless compassion' lost its ground. Here are all five moments of pause:

(1) 'all that early April morning light … and she found herself in the – … what? … who? … no! … she! …' [*Pause and movement 1.*]

(2) 'the buzzing? … yes … all dead still but for the buzzing … when suddenly she realized … words were – … what? … who? … no! … she! …' [*Pause and movement 2.*]

(3) 'something she – … something she had to – … what? … who? … no! … she! …' [*Pause and movement 3.*]

(4) 'all right … nothing she could tell … nothing she could think

... nothing she – ... what? ... who? ... no! ... she! ...' [*Pause and movement 4.*]

(5) 'keep on ... not knowing what ... what she was – ... what? ... who? ... no! ... she! ... SHE! ... [*Pause.*] ... what she was trying ... what to try ... no matter ... keep on ...' [*Curtain starts down.*]

Note the three crucial changes here: (1) the standard, always identical, series of words which precedes the pause with the Auditor's movement of helpless compassion ('... what? ... who? ... no! ... she! ...') is here supplemented by a repeated capitalized 'SHE'; (2) the pause is without the Auditor's movement; (3) it is not followed by the same kind of confused rambling as in the previous four cases, but by the variation of the paradigmatic Beckettian ethical motto of perseverance ('no matter ... keep on'). Consequently, the key to the entire piece is provided by the way we read this shift: does it signal a simple (or not so simple) gesture by means of which the speaker (Mouth) finally fully assumes her subjectivity, asserts herself as SHE (or, rather, as I), overcoming the blockage indicated by the buzzing in her head? In other words, insofar as the play's title comes from the Mouth's repeated insistence that the events she describes or alludes to did not happen to her (and that therefore she cannot assume them in first person singular), does the fifth pause indicate the negation of the play's title, the transformation of 'not I' into 'I'? Or is there a convincing alternative to this traditional-humanist reading which so obviously runs counter the entire spirit of Beckett's universe? Yes – on condition that we also radically abandon the predominant cliché about Beckett as the author of the 'theatre of the absurd', preaching the abandonment of every metaphysical Sense (Godot will never arrive), the resignation to the endless circular self-reproduction of meaningless rituals (the nonsense rhymes in *Waiting for Godot*).

This, of course, in no way implies that we should counter the 'theatre of the absurd' reading of Beckett with its no less simplified upbeat mirror-image; perhaps, a parallel with 'Der Leiermann', the song that concludes Schubert's *Winterreise*, may be of some help here. 'Der Leiermann' displays a tension between form and message. Its message appears to be utter despair of the abandoned lover who finally lost all hope, even the very ability to mourn and despair, and identifies with the man on the street automatically playing his music-machine. However, as many perspicuous commentators have noticed, this last song can also be read as the sign of forthcoming redemption: while all other songs present the hero's inward brooding, here, for the first time, the hero turns outwards and establishes a minimal contact, an emphatic identification, with another human being, although this identification is with another desperate loser who even lost his ability to mourn and is reduced to performing blind mechanical gestures. Does something similar not take place with the final shift of *Not I*? At the level of content, this shift can be read as the ultimate failure both of the speaker (Mouth) and of the big Other (Auditor): when the Mouth loses even the minimal thread of the content and is reduced to the minimalist injunction that the meaningless bubble must go on ('keep on … not knowing what'), the Auditor despairs and renounces even the empty gesture of helpless compassion. There is, however, the opposite reading that imposes itself at the level of *form*: the Mouth emerges as a pure (form of) subject, deprived of all substantial content (depth of 'personality'), and, pending on this reduction, the Other is also depsychologized, reduced to an empty receiver, deprived of all affective content ('compassion', etc.). To play with Malevich's terms, we reach the zero-level of communication – the subtitle of the play's finale could have been 'white noise on the black background of immobile silence' …

In what, then, does this shift consist? We should approach it via its counterpart, the traumatic X around which the Mouth's logorrhoea circulates. So what happened to 'her' on the field in April? Was the traumatic experience she underwent there a brutal rape? When asked about it, Beckett unambiguously rejected such a reading: 'How could you think of such a thing! No, no, not at all – it wasn't that at all.'[28] We should take this statement not as a tongue-in-cheek admission, but literally – that fateful April, while 'wandering in a field … looking aimlessly for cowslips', the woman suffered some kind of collapse, possibly even her death – definitely not a real-life event, but an unbearably intense 'inner experience' close to what C. S. Lewis described in his *Surprised by Joy* as the moment of his religious choice. What makes this description so irresistibly delicious is the author's matter-of-fact 'English' sceptical style, far from the usual pathetic narratives of the mystical rapture: Lewis refers to the experience as the 'odd thing'; he mentions its common location – 'I was going up Headington Hill on the top of a bus'; the qualifications like 'in a sense', 'what now appears', 'or, if you like', 'you could argue that … but I am more inclined to think …', 'perhaps', 'I rather disliked the feeling'.

> The odd thing was that before God closed in on me, I was in fact offered what now appears a moment of wholly free choice. In a sense. I was going up Headington Hill on the top of a bus. Without words and (I think) almost without images, a fact about myself was somehow presented to me. I became aware that I was holding something at bay,

or shutting something out. Or, if you like, that I was wearing some stiff clothing, like corsets, or even a suit of armour, as if I were a lobster. I felt myself being, there and then, given a free choice. I could open the door or keep it shut; I could unbuckle the armour or keep it on. Neither choice was presented as a duty; no threat or promise was attached to either, though I knew that to open the door or to take off the corset meant the incalculable. The choice appeared to be momentous but it was also strangely unemotional. I was moved by no desires or fears. In a sense I was not moved by anything. I chose to open, to unbuckle, to loosen the rein. I say, 'I chose', yet it did not really seem possible to do the opposite. On the other hand, I was aware of no motives. You could argue that I was not a free agent, but I am more inclined to think this came nearer to being a perfectly free act than most that I have ever done. Necessity may not be the opposite of freedom, and perhaps a man is most free when, instead of producing motives, he could only say, 'I am what I do'. Then came the repercussion on the imaginative level. I felt as if I were a man of snow at long last beginning to melt. The melting was starting in my back – drip-drip and presently trickle-trickle. I rather disliked the feeling.[29]

In a way, everything is here: the decision is purely formal, ultimately a decision to decide, without a clear awareness of *what* the subject decides about; it is nonpsychological act, unemotional, with no motives, desires or fears; it is incalculable, not the outcome of strategic argumentation; it is a totally free act, although one couldn't do it otherwise. It is only *afterwards* that this pure act is 'subjectivized', translated into a (rather unpleasant) psychological experience. From the Lacanian standpoint, there is only one aspect which is potentially problematic in Lewis's formulation: the traumatic Event (encounter of the Real, exposure to the 'minimal difference') has nothing to do with the mystical suspension of ties which bind us to ordinary reality, with attaining the bliss of radical indifference in which life or death and other worldly distinctions no longer matter, in which subject and object, thought and act, fully coincide. To put it in mystical terms, the Lacanian act is rather the exact opposite of this 'return to innocence': the Original Sin itself, the abyssal *disturbance* of the primeval Peace, the primordial 'pathological' Choice of the unconditional attachment to some singular object (like falling in love with a singular person which, thereafter, matters to us more than everything else). And does something like *this* not take place on the grass in *Not I*? (The *sinful* character of the trauma is indicated by the fact that the speaker feels punished by God.) What then happens in the final shift of the play is that the speaker *accepts* the trauma in its meaninglessness, ceases to search for its meaning, restores its extrasymbolic dignity, as it were, thereby getting rid of the entire topic of sin and punishment. This is why the Auditor no longer reacts with the gesture of impotent compassion: there is no longer despair in the Mouth's voice, the standard Beckettian formula of the drive's persistence is asserted ('no matter … keep on'), God is only now truly love – not the loved or loving one, but Love itself, that which keeps things going. Even after all content is lost, at this point of absolute reduction, the Galilean conclusion imposes itself: *eppur si muove*.

This, however, in no way means that the trauma is finally subjectivized, that the speaker is now no longer 'not I' but 'SHE', a full subject finally able to assume her Word. Something much more uncanny happens here: the Mouth is only now fully destituted as subject – at the moment of the fifth pause, the subject who speaks fully assumes its identity with Mouth as a partial object. What happens here is structurally similar to one of the most disturbing TV episodes of *Alfred Hitchcock Presents*, 'The Glass Eye' (the opening episode of the third year). Jessica Tandy (again – the very actress who was the original Mouth!) plays here a lone woman who falls for a handsome ventriloquist, Max Collodi (a reference to the author of *Pinocchio*). When she gathers the courage to approach him alone in his quarters, she declares her love for him and steps forward to embrace him, only to find that she is holding in her hands a wooden dummy's head; after she withdraws in horror, the 'dummy' stands up and pulls off its mask, and we see the face of a sad older dwarf who starts to jump desperately on the table, asking the woman to go away … The ventriloquist is in fact the dummy, while the hideous dummy is the actual ventriloquist. Is this not the perfect rendering of an 'organ without bodies'? It is the detachable 'dead' organ, the partial object, which is effectively alive, and whose dead puppet the 'real' person is: the 'real' person is merely alive, a survival machine, a 'human animal', while the apparently 'dead' supplement is the focus of excessive Life.

PART THREE

THE DISPARITY OF THE GOOD: TOWARDS A MATERIALIST NEGATIVE THEOLOGY

7 TRIBULATIONS OF A WOMAN-HYENA: AUTHORITY, COSTUME AND FRIENDSHIP

Why Heidegger should not be criminalized

One of the signs of the ideological regression of our times is the request of the new European Right for a more 'balanced' view of the two 'extremisms', the Rightist one and the Leftist one: we are repeatedly told that one should treat the extreme Left (communism) the same way Europe after World War II was treating the extreme Right (the defeated fascism and Nazism). Upon a closer look, this new 'balance' is heavily unbalanced: the equation of fascism and communism secretly privileges fascism, as can be seen from a series of arguments, the main among which is that fascism copied communism which came first (before becoming a fascist, Mussolini was a socialist, and even Hitler was a national socialist; concentration camps and genocidal violence were practised in the Soviet Union a decade before the Nazis resorted to it; the annihilation of the Jews has a clear precedent in the annihilation of the class enemy, etc.). The point of this argumentation is that a moderate fascism was a justified response to the communist threat (the point made long ago by Ernst Nolte in his defence of Heidegger's 1933 Nazi engagement). In Slovenia, the Right is arguing for the rehabilitation of the anti-communist 'Home Guard' which fought the partisans during World War II: they made the difficult choice to collaborate with the Nazis in order to prevent the much greater absolute Evil of Communism. The same could be said for the Nazis (or fascists, at least) themselves: they did what they did to prevent the absolute Evil of Communism …[1]

But the truly sad thing is that part of the liberal Left is following a similar strategy in its eternal struggle against 'French theory'. Jürgen Habermas remarked apropos of the famous Davos debate between Ernst Cassirer and Martin Heidegger in 1929 that we should rethink the common perception according to which Heidegger was the clear winner: for Habermas, Heidegger's 'victory' was not so much a genuine philosophical victory as the signal of a shift from liberal enlightened humanism to dark authoritarian irrationalism. Cassirer was effectively a figure like Habermas: his thought is simply not strong enough to grasp the horrors that threaten Europe (fascism in his time), in the same way that one looks in vain in Habermas for even the most rudimentary theory of the failure of twentieth-century communism which culminated in Stalinism (if one's knowledge of post-World War II Germany were limited to Habermas's texts, one would never have guessed that there were two Germanys, BRD and DDR …). For Habermas and his followers (like Richard Wolin), it is as if Deleuze, Lacan, Bataille are all proto-fascist irrationalists. They are uneasy even with Adorno and Benjamin who, in their view, often come too close to mystical 'irrationalism', not to mention figures like Rosenzweig, who takes over Heideggerian motifs from a Jewish standpoint. Habermasians commit here the same mistake as those who dismiss Freudian psychoanalysis, a theory about the irrational foundation of human psyche, as in itself irrationalist.

In 2014, a new Heidegger scandal exploded with the publication of the first volumes of the *Black Notebooks* (*Schwarze Hefte*), handwritten notes of his intimate reflections from 1931 until the early 1960s which allegedly confirm his anti-Semitism as well as his continuing fidelity to the Nazi project.[2] (Heidegger himself planned that these notes should be published at the conclusion of the *Gesamtausgabe* of his works, in a gesture which can be read either as a display of frank openness or as a sign of his stubborn commitment to his pro-Nazi views.) Things are actually a bit more complex.

The volumes show that, after 1934, Heidegger effectively cultivated more and more doubts about Hitler and the Nazi regime; however, this growing doubt had the very precise shape of blaming the enemy. What Heidegger reproached Hitler for was not the Nazi stance as such but the fact that the Nazis also succumbed to technological-nihilist *Machenschaft*, becoming like America, Great Britain, France and the Soviet Union, who are thereby always *more* guilty: 'all well-meaning excavation of earlier

Volk-lore, all conventional cultivation of custom, all extolling of landscape and soil, all glorification of the "blood" is just foreground and smokescreen – and necessary in order to obscure what truly and solely *is*: the unconditional dominion of the machination of destruction.'[3] Heidegger's critique of Nazism is thus a critique of the actually-existing Nazism on behalf of its own metaphysical 'inner greatness' (the promise of overcoming modern nihilism). Furthermore, Heidegger's growing reservations about the Nazi regime have nothing to do with the eventual rejection of its murderous brutality; far from denying its barbarism, Heidegger locates in it the greatness of Nazism: 'National Socialism is a barbaric principle. Therein lies its essence and its capacity for greatness. The danger is not [Nazism] itself, but instead that it will be rendered innocuous via homilies about the True, the Good, and the Beautiful.'[4] (The same debate went on at the beginning of modernity when Erasmus of Rotterdam, the Renaissance Catholic polyglot humanist, accused Martin Luther of barbaric primitivism – true, but Luther's break nonetheless opened up the space for modernity.)

Second point: while anti-Semitism persists and survives Heidegger's disenchantment with Nazism, one should note that it doesn't play a central role in Heidegger's thought but remains relatively marginal, an illustration or exemplification of a central scheme which survives without it. However, although one can well rewrite Heidegger's scheme of growing Western nihilism without any mention of Jews, this doesn't mean that 'Jewishness' (*Judentum*) just serves as a misleading example of a certain spiritual stance; such exemplification is never neutral or innocent. Ultimately, one can say the same about Hitler: is the Nazi figure of the Jew not merely an exemplification of the capitalist spirit of inauthentic profiteering and manipulation? In both cases, the 'example' irreducibly colours what it serves as an example of.

What is true is that one can reconstruct from Heidegger's dispersed remarks a consistent 'theory' about the Jews. First, he performs the well-known operation of rejecting primitive biological racism: the question of the role of world Jewry is not a biological-racial question but the metaphysical question about the kind of humanity that, without any restraints, can take over the uprooting of all beings from Being as its world-historical 'task'. European nihilism, our forgetting of Being, culminates in modern *Machenschaft* which 'leads to total deracination, resulting in the self-alienation of peoples',[5] and contemporary Jewry's 'increase in power finds its basis in the fact that Western metaphysics – above all, in its modern incarnation – offers fertile ground for the dissemination of an empty rationality and calculability, which in this way gains a foothold in "spirit", without ever being able to grasp from within the hidden realms of decision'.[6]

'World-Jewry' (*Welt-Judentum*) thus embodies the technological degradation of the totality of Being, which is why, as Heidegger observes in a related text, 'it would be important to enquire about the basis of Jewry's unique predisposition toward planetary criminality.'[7] (And, incidentally, since this 'Jewish worldlessness', their lack of roots in a *Boden*, is counteracted by the Israeli government's endeavour to make out of Israel a proper *Heimat* for the Jewish people, maybe today's Israel would find full approval of Heidegger as an attempt to decriminalize Jewishness …)

So how about the Holocaust? Here things get really dark. As Heidegger observed in 1942, with regard to Jews: 'The highest type and the highest act of politics consists in placing your opponent in a position where he is compelled to participate in his own self-annihilation.'[8] In an obscenely pseudo-Hegelian way, the elimination of European Jews must thus be understood as an act of Jewish 'self-annihilation' (*Selbstvernichtung*): the Holocaust was an act of Jewish 'self-annihilation' insofar as, at Auschwitz and other death camps, the Jews – as the prime movers behind 'machination' and the technological devastation of all of Being – themselves succumbed to industrialized mass murder. In this way, Europe's Jews merely fell prey to forces that they themselves had unleashed, or, as Heidegger states in volume 4 of the *Notebooks*: 'When the essentially 'Jewish', in the metaphysical sense, struggles [*kämpft*] against what is Jewish [*das Jüdische*], the high point of self-annihilation in history is attained.'[9] In short, the Nazis, in organizing the technological annihilation of Jews, merely turned the 'essentially Jewish' stance of *Machenschaft* against the empirical Jews themselves. (Following an old cliché, Heidegger claims that Jews prefer to stay out of sight, manipulating the events behind the scenes and leaving it to other nations, especially to Germans, to shed their blood in real struggles.)

What opened up the space for the Nazi turn in Heidegger's philosophical edifice is relatively easy to discern. *Sein und Zeit* focuses on the individual's authentic existence with its structure of being-towards-death, and the problem it only superficially touches is how to expand the analysis onto collective modes of being, that is, how to think authentic collective being beyond the inauthentic *das Man*, following the anonymous 'one'. It is here that Heidegger 'takes a wrong turn' when he posits as the only way to break out of *das Man* the heroic assuming of one's historical Destiny. What this implies is that Heidegger's edifice cannot be reduced to some Nazi core – it would be absurd to dismiss Left Heideggerians like Caputo and Vattimo as closet fascists or as cases of a simple misreading of Heidegger: Heidegger's edifice is genuinely 'undecidable', open to different political readings. There are even some black activists in the United States and in Africa who, in their reaction to the *Black Notebooks* 'scandal', insisted that a reference to Heidegger helped them to formulate their resistance to global capitalism and its ideological hegemony. And the ongoing attacks on Heidegger aim precisely at closing this undecidability and proving not only that Heidegger's thought is in its very core Nazi (an 'introduction of Nazism into philosophy', as the subtitle of Emmanuel Faye's book on Heidegger says), but that the shadow of the same suspicion falls on all who were influenced by him as well. Markus Gabriel concludes his comment on *Schwarze Hefte* with this:

> Only now can historical-critical research on Heidegger properly begin. Now we have gained the distance needed for this, and we have the texts at our disposal. Furthermore, we should also inquire into the history of Heidegger's enormous influence. No other philosopher exerted with his work such influence from the twenties of the last century – against his will above all on existentialism, deconstruction, psychoanalysis, and the logically educated ontology. We should not close our eyes to all this.[10]

We should not close our eyes – to what? To this Nazi shadow which falls also on the most Left Heideggerians … This old story began in the 1980s when (among others) Lacan was attacked in the United States for his alleged fascist links, and when deconstruction was denounced as a justification of French collaborationism. And, maybe, this brings us to the true stakes of the ongoing attacks on Heidegger: to get rid of the 'French theory' Left by way of imposing on them a gult by association. But the ultimate target here is a tendency within Critical Theory itself: the theoretical complex called 'dialectics of Enlightenment', with its basic premise according to which the horrors of the twentieth century (Holocaust, concentration camps, etc.) are not remainders of some barbaric past but the outcome of the immanent antagonisms of the project of Enlightenment. For Habermasians, such a premise is wrong: the horrors of the twentieth century are not immanent to the project of Enlightenment, but an indication that this project is unfinished. (Incidentally, Adorno and Horkheimer also emphasize that the only way to overcome the deadlock of Enlightenment is through further enlightenment, through enlightened reflection upon these very deadlocks.) We should make one step further here and recognize, in this opposition between Enlightenment as an unfinished project and the dialectic of Enlightnment, the opposition between Kant and Hegel: between the Kantian progress and the Hegelian dialectic of immanent antagonisms.

Against the persistent calls for the direct criminalization of Heidegger's thought, for his simple and direct exclusion from the academic canon, one should insist that he is a true philosophical classic. A direct criminalization of Heidegger's though is an easy way out – it allows us to avoid the painful confrontation with the proper scandal of his Nazi engagement: how was it possible for such a great authentic philosopher to get engaged in this way? When I asked a Heideggerian Jewish friend of mine how Heidegger could remain a key reference for him in view of his anti-Semitism and Nazi sympathies, he mentioned an old Jewish wisdom according to which there are some deep, traumatic insights than can only be formulated by a diabolical person.

The birth of fascism out of the spirit of beauty

If we are in search of the origins of fascism in modern thought, Heidegger is thus an all too easy target – we should look elsewhere, perhaps into the work of one of the most celebrated poets of freedom, Friedrich Schiller. Following Marx, who said that the anatomy of man is the key to the anatomy of monkey, let's begin at the end, with 'The Song of the Bell', the proto-fascist Schiller offering his model of aestheticized politics as the way to overcome revolutionary violence. Then we'll take a look at how Schiller arrived at this point, what antagonisms were obfuscated in this solution.

If there is a song that deserves to be publicly burned Goebbels-style, it is 'The Song of the Bell'. Everything is in it, all the basic coordinates of a fascist-style counter-revolution. It begins with the idealized image of a patriarchal family where man is a benevolent master who goes out, works, and takes risks, bringing home wealth, while the wife stays at home and wisely manages the household:

> The man must go out / Into hostile life, / Must work and strive / And plant and produce, / Calculate, gather, / Must wager and risk, / To hunt for fortune. / There streams to him the endless gift, / The warehouse fills with precious goods, / The rooms grow, the house expands. / And inside rules / The modest housewife, / The children's mother, / And reigns wisely / In the domestic circle, / And teaches the girls, / And guides the boy, / And stirs without end / The industrious hands, / And multiplies the gains / With orderly mind.

What enters then is the key metaphor of blazing fire, the source of productive energy – but only insofar as it is controlled by the man: if it runs out of control, it can bring horror and destruction:

Benevolent is the fire's might, / If the man tames and watches it, / For what he builds, what he creates, / He owes to this heavenly power, / But terrible this heavenly power is, / If she, casting off her shackles, / Strides along on tracks her own / This free daughter of nature. / Beware when she is let loose / Growing without hindrance. / Through the much populated by-streets / Rolls the monstrous blaze!

So where does this explosion come from? The feminization of fire as the 'free daughter of nature' already indicates the answer: when, within the family, mother is no longer loyally subordinated to her husband, when 'the tender bonds of the house are loosened':

Alas! it is the loyal mother, / Which the black prince of shadows / Leads away from the arm of her husband, / Away from the children's tender flock, / Which she bore him while in bloom, / Which she on her faithful breast / With motherly love watched grow – / Alas! the tender bonds of the house / Are loosened evermore, / She now lives in the land of shadows, / She who was the mother of the house, / Now her faithful reign is missing, / Her care watches no more, / In the orphaned place a strange one / Shall direct, lovelessly.

Another metaphoric level is then added: the glowing ore which liberates itself is first equated with the women liberated from family ties, and then the two are equated with the people (citizenry) breaking their chains and liberating themselves:

The master may break the mould / With knowing hand, if the time is right, / But beware when in fiery, spouting brooks / The glowing ore liberates itself! / Blindly raging, with the roar of thunder / It bursts the broken house, / And as out of the maw of Hell / It spews out, igniting destruction; / Where brute force rules mindlessly, / No design can emerge, / When the people liberate themselves, / Then wellbeing can't thrive.

The political stakes are made explicit here: when 'the citizenry, breaking its chains, frightfully seizes arms to help itself', destructive violence explodes:

Freedom and Equality! one hears proclaimed, / The peaceful citizen is driven to arms, / The streets are filling, the halls, / The vigilante-bands are moving, / Then women change into hyenas / And make a plaything out of terror, / Though it twitches still, with panther's teeth, / They tear apart the enemy's heart. / Nothing is holy any longer, loosened / Are all ties of righteousness, / The good gives room to bad, / And all vices freely rule. / Dangerous it is to wake the lion, / Ruinous is the tiger's tooth, / But the most terrible of all the terrors, / That is the man when crazed. / Woe to those, who lend to the eternally blind / Enlightenment's heavenly torch! / It does not shine for him, it only can ignite / And puts to ashes towns and lands.

The French Revolution is thus feminized: the figure that embodies revolutionary terror is a woman changed into a madly laughing hyena. Plus, in the standard early liberal Enlightenment way, the full light of Reason should be constrained to the educated few: if Enlightenment's heavenly torch is allowed to shine directly on the poor uneducated crowd who are condemned to eternal blindness, we get 'the most terrible of all the terrors' … Schiller passes over the details of how one should crush this revolutionary explosion, and moves directly on to the idealized image of the collective production process which runs organically and harmoniously after order is restored:

Thousands of busy hands stir, / Help each other in happy union, / And in this fiery movement / All powers become known. / The master stirs and journeyman too / Within the holy protection of freedom. / Everyone enjoys his place, / Offering defiance to contemptors. / Work is the adornment of the burgher, / Blessing the reward for toil. / If dignity honours the king, / We are honoured by industriousness of hands.

Although freedom is restored here, it is the protective freedom in which 'everyone enjoys his place' – one is free insofar as one fully identifies with a specific place within the organic Whole. What such a vision prohibits is any kind of direct link between the individual and the universal dimension, bypassing the particular: the perfect utopian image of such freedom is the harmonious collaboration of individuals in an organically structured hierarchic Whole.

One should also note here that the same feminization of the revolutionary fury took place in the German conservative reaction to the October Revolution: we regularly encounter the myth of a wild Bolshevik woman, promiscuous and cruel, in *Freikorps* memoirs of the defenders of the eastern borders of Germany after the Great War:

Anti-Bolshevism, anti-Semitism and a distinct hate for the other woman characterize these texts. The women of the enemy army are described as savage and uncivilized female warriors. These women took a very active part in the 'butcheries', thus wrote Georg Heinrich Hartman in his description of the time he spent in a *Freikorps*, published in 1929. The texts display an intense feeling of revulsion against Communist women, who, according to Klaus Theweleit's psychoanalytical study of the *Freikorps*-literature, symbolized 'a horror' that 'had no name in the language of the soldierly man'. 'At the hands of seductively smiling, gun-toting women' one received 'the longest death ... the most bitter and the most cruel which one could suffer', wrote the *Freikorps* author Thor Goote. At the same time, these descriptions of the other women are ambivalent: the sensuality and the sexual prowess imputed to them are seductive and tempting. The way in which these descriptions are placed in the texts illuminates their function as a legitimization for the following violent excesses. Communist and Latvian women are desired but at the same time mutilated beyond recognition. The depictions of their executions are bloody, cruel and sadistic; they refer to the dangers of desire. Sexuality here uncovers the instable process of the construction of borders.[11]

Back to Schiller, is the ultimate laughing hyena not Caroline von Schlegel, the promiscuous Jacobin who wrote in 1799: 'Yesterday at noon we almost fell from our chairs, we laughed so much at a poem by Schiller on the bell.'[12] No wonder she was referred to in the circle of Schiller's friends as the 'Dame Lucifer' or 'the Evil [or Misfortune: *das Übel*]' ... How did Schiller arrive at this point? Let's move from this end point back to the beginning: in his first big success, *The Robbers*, Schiller already deals with the topic of 'The Song of the Bell', the danger of excessive unconstrained freedom. While he condemns the revolutionary attempt to 'maintain law by lawlessness', that is, to impose a new, just law through 'illegitimate' change, Schiller symptomatically fails to raise the obvious question: But what if it is the existing law itself which maintains itself by lawlessness? What if the restoration of the 'majesty of the law' restores also its lawless dark side? Furthermore, while, in his final speech, Karl, the play's hero, generously offers himself as the exemplary victim ready to declare before all mankind how inviolable that majesty of the law is, he passes over in silence the true sacrificial offering: his love Amalia, who convinces him to kill her. Although the logic of her demand seems rational (he cannot leave his gang and she cannot live without him), the killing remains a weird act branded by mysterious ambiguity, a true symptomal point of the play.[13] A woman is here an obstacle to men's murderous gang, an agent of the stability of a home, not the revolutionary woman-hyena as in 'The Song of the Bell': revolutionary violence is here male bonding without women who stand for order and stability, not the murderous excess embodied in a free woman. The murder of the woman who disturbs male collaboration belongs to the antifeminist space of 'The Song of the Bell'; it is precisely the moment Schiller passes over in silence in the poem, as the means to restore harmonious order – so it is as if the repressed of the poem returns here, in the opposite constellation where the woman should have been celebrated … Does this weird return not indicate that there is somethimg deeply wrong in the entire logic that underlies Schiller's work? To cut a long story short, is the implication of the weird killing of the woman not that the lawless male bonding (in *The Robbers*) is the obscene obverse of the noble male friendship and collaboration celebrated in 'The Song of the Bell'? So how do we pass from the one to the other?

The answer is provided by Schiller's 'Ode to Joy' where, in a clear reversal of *The Robbers*, he asserts the brotherhood of man bonded by friendship as opposed to the gang of outlaws:

> Be embraced, millions!
> This kiss to the entire world!
> Brothers – above the starry canopy
> A loving father must dwell.
> Whoever has had the great fortune,
> To be a friend's friend,
> Whoever has won the love of a devoted wife,
> Add his to our jubilation!
> Indeed, whoever can call even one soul
> His own on this earth!
> And whoever was never able to must creep
> The account of our misdeeds be destroyed!
> Reconciled the entire world!

No wonder this poem provided the words for the anthem of the European Union: it describes the vision of global reconciliation with all debts written off – except those owed to big banks, as in the case of Greece, but the Greeks are then offered the choice of creeping away tearfully from the European circle … The difference from *The Robbers* is that, in contrast to the gang led by a rebel against his father, here the circle of friends is sustained by the belief that 'above the starry canopy a loving father must dwell'. We get here Schiller's dream: a fraternal bond of friendship under the protective care of a benevolent father – an impossible combination, for sure, and this impossibility explodes in (is the theme of) *Don Carlos*,

Schiller's masterpiece which brings all these motifs together: friendship, love, political power and freedom.[14]

Don Carlos between authority and friendship

At the beginning of the play, King Philip and his son don Carlos are rivals for the affections of Queen Elisabeth of Valois, but when Philip meets Carlos's friend the Marquis of Posa, he feels that he has found a true friend for the first time in his life. In a new love triangle, don Carlos and Philip are rivals for Posa's love and friendship; however, Posa cares more about achieving political freedom in the rebellious Netherlands, and when his ruthlessly manipulative plan fails he sacrifices himself in order to save Carlos. Philip is affected more seriously by Posa's betrayal than he is by Elisabeth's presumed infidelity. At the end of act 4 the audience is informed by Count Lerma that 'Der König hat / Geweint' ('The king has wept') (lines 4464–5). In an ingenious cinematic detail, we never see Philip crying, it is just reported as an *hors-champ* detail, which makes it all the more effective. Later, in act 5, scene 9, after the Marquis of Posa has died at his orders, Philip confesses that he loved him: 'I loved him, loved him a lot … He was my first love.' One should bear in mind here that, in a normally functioning monarchy, the problem of the humanization of authority (of how to provide the monarch with ordinary human features) doesn't arise: for a true king, a patronizing friendship with selected courtiers is part of his image.[15]

It would be totally wrong to read this love in homosexual terms: the topic is that of friendship, friendship of equals in the sense of full mutual recognition and trust. The main tension of the play, its principal contradiction, to use the old Maoist term, is between (male) friendship and (political) power, while the topic of love remains at the level of comical intrigues; the king steals the bride from his son and then indulges in another affair, etc. Marcel Reich-Ranicki noted apropos of *Don Carlos* that one cannot take fully seriously a drama in which the plot relies on a love letter reaching a wrong addressee, and there are even three such letters in Schiller's play (Carlos's letter to the queen reaches Princess Eboli, the king's letter to Eboli reaches Posa, Posa's letter to the Dutch rebels is intercepted by the king's police). Don Carlos, who is the focus of love intrigues, 'might have been more successful as a comic figure.'[16] He is thoroughly immersed in the tensions of friendship and love, that is, he oscillates between two particular contents, which is why he doesn't participate in any authentic tragic conflict. Posa is also outside the tragic conflict: he oscillates between Carlos and Philip, but at a purely tactical level, i.e. he has to choose whom to manipulate through friendship for his universal political cause. The only properly tragic character in the play is the king (as in *Antigone* where the only tragic character is Creon, not Antigone): Posa moves at the level of the universal, he is fully dedicated to his cause; don Carlos moves at the level of conflicting particulars; only the king is torn between the Universal and the Particular, State and friendship. The queen is also identified with the political cause (freedom for the Dutch), and her message to don Carlos is to pass from the Particular (his love for her) to the Universal (political freedom), so the ideal emancipatory couple would have been the one of Posa and the queen.

In contrast to this sometimes ridiculous melodramatic imbroglio, the play's three crucial scenes all concern friendship and power. The first scene is the long conversation between the king and Posa in act 3. Posa tells him (twice) 'Ich kann nicht Fürstendiener sein' ('I cannot be a servant of princes'), and it is precisely through this asserion of autonomy that he seduces Philip into friendship. Immediately using this friendship, Posa asks Philip to grant his subjects *Gedankenfreiheit*, the freedom of thought – he wants to use Philip immediately for his political cause. Predictably refusing this, Philip asks Posa to meet with Carlos and Elisabeth and find out their true intentions, enlisting him in his private affairs: 'Marquis, so far / You've learned to know me as a king; but yet / You know me not as man.' Posa warns Philip that the price for being the king is that, since friendship requires mutual recognition of friends as equals, he has to remain alone in a friendless world: 'Once degrade mankind, / And make him but a thing to play upon, / … You thus become / A thing apart, a species of your own. / This is the price you pay for being a god.' Furthermore, Posa reminds Philip that in a monarchy, not only can the king not have friends but friendship is thwarted even among his subjects: since they fear the authority, they are suspicious of each other and pushed into egotism, each possessed by fear and care for himself: 'I dearly love mankind, / My gracious liege, but in a monarchy / I dare not love another than myself.' What Schiller stages here is the fundamental deadlock of the relationship between Master and Servant analysed a decade later in the famous chapter of Hegel's *Phenomenology*: the Servant's recognition of the Master is worthless since the Servant is not recognized by the Master as an equal. Does this mean that Schiller is ready to renounce monarchy? As we have already seen, his solution is the utopia of the friendly bond of equals dominated by a loving father (Master) who 'above the starry canopy must dwell'. In the famous declaration of his view of god, Posa further elaborates this vision:

Look round on all the glorious face of nature,
On freedom it is founded – see how rich,
Through freedom it has grown. The great Creator
Bestows upon the worm its drop of dew,
And gives free-will a triumph in abodes
Where lone corruption reigns. See your creation,
How small, how poor! The rustling of a leaf
Alarms the mighty lord of Christendom.
Each virtue makes you quake with fear. While he,
Not to disturb fair freedom's blest appearance,
Permits the frightful ravages of evil
To waste his fair domains. The great Creator
We see not – he conceals himself within
His own eternal laws. The sceptic sees
Their operation, but beholds not Him.
'Wherefore a God!' he cries, 'the world itself
Suffices for itself!' And Christian prayer
Ne'er praised him more than doth this blasphemy.

Schiller's formula of how to combine the reign of the Father-God with the freedom of His creatures is to render the Father invisible. This God is neither the Pascalean *deus absconditus*, the obscure withdrawn god whose impenetrable will causes anxiety among his subjects, nor the God of deism who just triggers the mechanism of the world and then lets it roll itself: Schiller's God is acting all the time, but hidden behind his own laws. In contrast to the Christian god, a visible master who lives in fear, alarmed by the prospect that his subjects might misuse the freedom of their will, but at the same time allowing the evil to happen in the world in order to maintain the appearance of freedom, the true Creator lies concealed behind the immanent growth of creation, so that the more we are bewildered by the autonomous growth of the world, ignoring God, the more we praise God, his creativity. The political equivalent of this vision would be a benevolent paternal ruler who allows his subjects all their freedom, wisely steering their activity in order to prevent freedom to run amok and turn into a self-destructive fury. But does this idea work, theologically and politically?

With Posa himself, the advocate of this view, things quickly take a wrong turn. After his first plan of how to use his influence on the king fails, he decides to sacrifice himself: he writes a letter to William of Orange in Brussels, the leader of the Protestant rebellion there, knowing that it will be intercepted and brought to King Philip. He will be arrested, but suspicion will be diverted from Carlos who should escape to the Netherlands and lead the rebellion. After Posa is shot down, he tells Carlos with his dying words to save himself by way of escaping. But instead of escaping, Carlos wants to confront his father courageously out of fidelity to Posa: when Philip and his noblemen arrive, Carlos blames his father for ordering Posa's murder. (There is a nice ethical paradox at work here: in refusing to escape out of fidelity to Posa, don Carlos precisely betrays his friendship with Posa – he betrays the true point of Posa's friendship/sacrifice out of friendship.) Carlos's accusations are interrupted by the news that the people are rioting, clamoring to see him. Upon hearing the word 'rebellion', Philip is overcome by panic; he surrenders his royal insignia, faints, and is carried out.

When Philip divests himself of the royal insignia, he offers them to his son don Carlos whom he considers the leader of the rebellion, provoking him to take the insignia and become the new king, but the hysterical don Carlos is not ready or able to do it. In this act, Philip realizes his earlier declaration to Posa: 'Marquis, so far / You've learned to know me as a king; but yet / You know me not as man.' Now everyone around him can see and know him as a man – but what, precisely, does one see? Recall the classic scene (so powerfully staged by Shakespeare in his *Richard II*) of the deposed king, a king deprived of his royal title: all of a sudden the charisma dissipates and we have in front of us a weak and confused man ... But are we 'really' just what we are, miserable individuals? What remains of Richard II after he is deprived of his insignia of royal power? Not an ordinary miserable person but a subject *traumatized by the void of what he is now.*[17] When he is deprived of his royal title, his bodily and psychic existence appear to him broken, inconsistent, lacking any firm ground or foundation, so that it is as if his symbolic insignia were not masking the miserable reality of a person to whom these insignia were attributed but the void or gap of subjectivity, of the Self irreducible to physical or psychic properties. And it is, of course, the same with Philip deprived of his insignia: we do not see an ordinary human being but, precisely, an extraordinary – crippled, panicked – human being. How, then, do the insignia of power transubstantiate our miserable bodily reality into the vehicle of another dimension, so that what we 'really are' is magically transformed into a medium of power? The paradox is that it is only against the background of insignia (whatever they are, from those of a king to those of an office cleaner) that a subject's immediate reality is made visible as that of an 'ordinary person': how we perceive a person's direct reality, the reality of his or her actual properties, is always-already mediated through the lenses of the insignia. If a king is crippled, it is not the same thing as a beggar who is crippled.

Back to *Don Carlos*: after the rebellion is crushed, the king survives, remains in power, but as a broken man and a broken king. What Philip loses when he renounces his insignia (and what he remains deprived of even after he later regains his insignia) is his main royal prerogative, his capacity to decide, to confer the performative dimension on his counsellors' advices, to make them *acts*. Hegel described this unique position of a king in clear terms:

> In a fully organized state, it is only a question of the highest instance of formal decision, and all that is required in a monarch is someone to say 'yes' and to dot the 'i'; for the supreme office should be such that the particular character of its occupant is of no significance ... In a well-ordered monarchy, the objective aspect is solely the concern of the law, to which the monarch merely has to add his subjective 'I will'.[18]

This 'highest instance of formal decision', this pronouncement of S_1, a Master Signifier, which supplements the series of S_2, of the knowledgeable proposals of his advisors and ministers, is what Philip is now deprived of, and this is why he sends for the Grand Inquisitor – not for advice about how to make the right decision but to *decide* instead of him. In the great confrontation between the broken king and the Inquisitor, the latter reprimands Philip for his leniency towards Posa which put in danger the very survival of monarchy. Philip asks him to decide Carlos's fate and the Inquisitor decrees that Carlos must die.

This deeply disturbing dialogue between the king and the Inquisitor opens up upon a totally new terrifying, post-tragic, domain. The deadlock in which the king finds himself can be resolved only by the Inquisitor who enters almost as a deus ex machina, absent until now in the play.[19] The Inquisitor is blind but as such all-seeing and all-knowing – his blindness stands for his total ignorance of human passions and affairs, people are for him just numbers to be manipulated from a cold distance: 'KING. I sought a human being. GRAND INQUISITOR. How! human beings! What are they to you? / Cyphers to count withal – no more! Alas! / ... An earthly god must learn to bear the want / Of what may be denied him. When you whine / For sympathy is not the world your equal? / What rights should you possess above your equals?' The castrative dimension of supreme power is here clearly stated: the monarch 'must learn to bear the want / Of what may be denied him.'

The Inquisitor knows in advance the answers to the questions he asks: 'INQUISITOR. What was the reason for this murder? KING. 'Twas a fraud unparalleled – INQUISITOR. I know it all.' Far from being the remainder of some dark past, the Inquisitor is the most modern figure in the play; he stands for the agency which takes over when the king's authority disintegrates – in short, he stands for the big Other of the state bureau-cracy, a pure superego-knowledge, not a crazy brutal Master. Apropos of Posa, the Inquisitor emphasizes precisely this complete knowledge: 'All his life is noted / From its commencement to its sudden close, / In Santa Casa's holy registers.' And when Posa is killed on the king's orders, the Inquisitor deplores merely the spontaneous and brutal character of Posa's death: Posa 'is murdered – basely, foully murdered. / The blood that should so gloriously have flowed / To honour us has stained the assassin's hand.' When he decides for the king, the Inquisitor does not simply appropriate the prerogative of the king, he is not a new S_1 (Master), but an S_2 without S_1 – the very definition of modern bureaucracy. Already the reasoning of the Inquisitor, the way he answers Philip's queries, is subtle in an obscene way, a model case of senseless bureaucratic legalism. In in order to calm the king's conscience troubled with how one can 'justify / The bloody murder of one's only son?' the Inquisitor draws a weird parallel with God who sacrificed Christ, his own son, in order to redeem humanity: 'To appease eternal justice God's own Son / Expired upon the cross.' But if we draw this parallel to the end, what we get in *Don Carlos* is something like God asking the Holy Spirit for permission/decision to deliver Christ to his death.

In contrast to the Inquisitor, the King-Master doesn't 'know it all', but in an ambiguous way, leaving to others (his faithful servants) to do discreetly the dirty job that has to be done but which cannot be admitted publicly. When, in the autumn of 1586, Queen Elizabeth I was under pressure from her ministers to agree to the execution of Mary Stuart (the topic of another of Schiller's plays), she replied to their petition with the famous 'answer without an answer': 'If I should say I would not do what you request I might say perhaps more than I think. And if I should say I would do it, I might plunge myself into peril, whom you labour to preserve.'[20] The message was clear: she was not ready to say that she doesn't want Mary executed since saying this would be saying 'more than I think' – while she clearly wanted her dead, she did not want to publicly assume upon herself this act of judicial murder. The implicit message of her answer is thus a very clear one: if you are my true faithful servants, do this crime for me, kill her without making me responsible for her death, i.e. allowing me to protest my ignorance of the act and even punish some of you to sustain this false appearance.

Stalin as anti-Master

However, at a more radical level, ignorance is the condition of an act: in the moment of madness when one decides to act, one has to obliterate the complexity of a situation, reducing it to a simple gesture. This is what bureaucracy tries to avoid: its proper mode of functioning is not to decide but to persist forever in an in-between state, sliding from one to another temporary measure. The Swiss bureaucracy provides an exemplary case of this avoidance of a final decision. A foreigner who wants to teach in Switzerland has to appear before a state agency called *Comité de l'habitant* and to apply for a *Certificat de bonne vie et moeurs*; the paradox, of course, is that nobody can *get* this certificate – the most a foreigner can get, in the case of a positive decision, is a paper stating that he is *not to be refused* the Certificat – a double negation which, however, is not yet a positive decision.[21] This is how Switzerland likes to see a poor foreign worker: your stay there can never be fully legitimized; the most you can get is the admission which allows you to dwell in a kind of in-between state – you are never positively accepted, you are just not yet rejected and thus retained with a vague promise that, in some indefinite future, you stand a chance ...

On a different level, we encounter the same procrastination, the same postponing of a final decision, in the Stalinist bureaucracy. This may sound strange: was it not the case that the Stalinist regime didn't have any difficulty deciding the death of hundreds of thousands? However, upon a closer look, we can immediately discern a structural inability to stabilize the interminable search for traitors. The double bind that pertains to the very notion of superego is best embodied in the fate of Stalin's ministers of the interior: Yezhov, Yagoda, Abakoumov. There was constant pressure on them to discover ever new anti-socialist plots, they were always reproached for being too lenient, not vigilant enough; the only way for them to satisfy the demand of the Leader was thus to invent plots and to arrest innocent people – however, this way, they were laying the ground for their own violent demise, since their successor was already at work, collecting evidence of how they were actually counter-revolutionary agents of imperialism killing good dedicated Bolsheviks ... The victim's innocence is thus part of the game, it enables the self-reproducing cycle of revolutionary purges which 'eat their own children'. This impossibility to achieve the 'proper measure' between lack and excess (of zeal in the fight against counter-revolution) is the clearest index of the superego-functioning of the Stalinist bureaucracy: we are either too lenient (if we do not discover enough traitors, this proves our silent support for counter-revolution) or too vigilant (which, again, makes us guilty of condemning dedicated fighters for socialism). This codependence of lack and excess is, perhaps, the core of what we call 'modernity'.

Why, then, was Stalin not a Master proper? A Master performs an act, and an act always involves a radical risk – what Derrida, following Kierkegaard, called the madness of a decision, a step into the open with no guarantee about the final outcome:

> The moment of *decision as such*, what must be just, *must* always remain a finite moment of urgency and precipitation; it must not be the conse-quence or the effect of ... theoretical or historical knowledge, of ... reflection or ... deliberation, since the decision always marks the inter-ruption of the juridico-, ethico-, or politico-cognitive deliberation that precedes it, that *must* precede it. The instant of a decision is a madness, says Kierkegaard.[22]

Why? Because an Act retroactively changes the very coordinates into which it intervenes. This lack of guarantee is what the critics cannot tolerate: they want an Act without risk – not without empirical risks, but without the much more radical 'transcendental risk' that the Act will not only simply fail, but radically misfire. In short, to paraphrase Robespierre, those who oppose the 'absolute Act' effectively oppose the Act *as such*, they want an Act without the Act. What they want is homologous to the 'democratic' opportunists who, as Lenin put it in the fall of 1917, want a 'democratically legitimized' revolution, as if one should first organize a referendum, and only then, after obtaining a clear majority, seize power ... It is here that one can see how an Act proper cannot be contained within the limits of democracy (conceived as a positive system of legitimizing power through free elections). The Act occurs in an emergency when one has to take the risk and act without any legitimization, engaging oneself in a kind of Pascalean wager that the Act itself will create the conditions of its retroactive 'democratic' legitimization. So the point is not that an act is totally irrational, a rupture in the nexus of causality: an act is done for reasons, but it retroactively determines these reasons – or, to put it in theological terms, there are reasons, but in order to see or understand them you have to believe in the act, you have to take sides.

It is agains this background that Jean-Claude Milner tries to reconstruct the genesis of Stalinism.[23] His starting point is a statement by Saint-Just from 1794: 'Ceux qui font des révolutions ressemblent au premier navigateur instruit par son audace' ('Those who make revolutions resemble a first navigator, who has audacity alone as a guide').[24] The explorer discovers what no one has seen before. There is no previous map of the political regions that he enters. This ignorance is particularly true of those who do not participate in the exploration. They cannot see what the revolutionaries see. Of course, the latter do not occupy a higher position than the former. Nevertheless their political perceptions are radically different. Moreover, there is no previous theoretical or practical science of revolution that could be common to the revolutionaries and their non-revolutionaries counterparts. Consequently no one but revolutionaries themselves may express a judgment on their choices.

So there is no revolutionary tradition: 'every revolution is a type in itself'. The consequence of this fact is that, with respect to himself, 'the revolutionary subject is defined by his "non-knowledge". He does not know what he will discover.'

So how do we come from this nonknowledge that characterizes a revolutionary to the Stalinist Leader? Milner evokes here the classic Marxist thesis that, in capitalism, the impersonal power of capital rules; he draws from this the conclusion that the anticapitalist revolutionary process has to rehabilitate personal power:

> since the industrial capitalism, as theorized by Marx, allows only impersonal power, there is no place for a personal power in the modern world, except among those who fight against the industrial capitalism. But such fighters are called revolutionaries. Conclusion: according to Stalin, only the revolutionary may hold a personal power. When translated in Machiavelli's vocabulary, this conclusion becomes: only the revolutionary may be a Prince in the modern world. In other words, the revolutionary is the Prince who decides on the revolution.

Next conclusion: since the Machiavellian prince is by definition a single person, 'there is only one revolutionary Leader in a given revolutionary situation. A revolutionary party should be a device that, at each level of decision, produces the required unicity of the corresponding revolutionary Prince. Such is the organization of a communist party; it is called "democratic centralism".' But how does a Leader legitimize his authority? It cannot be his knowledge which authorizes him, because a revolutionary doesn't know and can only rely on his audacity. In Descartes, we already find the principle of legitimization of the prince: in Part III of his *Discourse on Method*, he mentions the example of travelers who, when they have lost their way in a forest, ought not to wander from side to side, far less remain in one place, but proceed constantly towards the same side in as straight a line as possible, without changing their direction for slight reasons, although perhaps it might be chance alone which at first determined the selection; for in this way, if they do not exactly reach the point they desire, they will come at least in the end to some place that will probably be preferable to the middle of a forest.[25]

Does the same not hold also for the revolutionary Leader? What matters is not the *specific* direction he imposes on the Party, but the mere formal fact that it is *one* consistent direction. Eventual opposition against him is not wrong for the reasons of content, but simply because (as the Stalinists like to put it) it threatens the unity of the Party.

The next consequence: although the Leader doesn't know, he has to appear with regard to his followers as the (only) one who knows. However, since the Leader's supposed knowledge has no positive content, it can only be determined negatively, by the nonknowledge of his followers:

> Stalinists considered their own non-knowledge as a legitimation of Stalin's leadership. Such is their definition. For example, the German/Soviet pact came as an unjustifiable surprise for those who, in Western Europe, had considered the USSR to be the last refuge against Nazism. Some members of the European Communist parties broke their allegiance; many sympathizers were shocked. But a true Stalinist would conclude on the contrary that his own inability to understand Stalin's decision was the ultimate proof of Stalin's superior knowledge. The line of reasoning was not 'Stalin is right although we do not understand', but 'We do not understand, therefore Stalin is right'.

This is why a true Leader does not give well-grounded directives – if he were to do so, if reasons for his decisions were to be rationally grounded, he would expose himself to the endless process of arguments and counterarguments. (So when a Leader gives directives, there has to be an impenetrable arbitrary element in them – say, in his directives for the growth of agriculture, there has to be an item for which there is no obvious reason, like 'only persons older than forty-five can grow cucumbers'.) It is in this sense that Stalinism 'combines a dimension of knowledge with a dimension of non-knowledge', but in a way different from Marxist and Leninist tradition. To elaborate this difference, Milner refers to Lacan's distinction between S_1 and S_2:

S_1 is the *signifiant-maître*; as indicated by its index, it is structurally first. Each utterance of S_1 functions as if it were unprecedented. S_2, on the other hand, is knowledge, *le savoir*; as indicated by its index, it is structurally second. S_1 functions as the *signifiant-maître* as long as it is excepted from knowledge; by uttering that *signifiant*, the subject asserts that it is the name of everyone's ignorance, including his own. Among the verbal tenses, it is disconnected from all past tenses. S_2, by contrast, is crucially connected with a past tense: it is still already known.

S_1 stands for the ungrounded revolutionary decision that is ultimately sustained only by its own audacity, and S_2 stands for the entire domain of our experience of reality, of historical and scientific knowledge of reality. The big dream of Marxist revolutionary theory is, of course, 'to do the impossible: to close the gap between S_1 and S_2,' – to ground revolutionary decisions and politics in positive knowledge of reality. That's why Marxism 'connects a bundle of features to the notion of revolution: the overthrow of the former ruling class, the dictatorship of the proletariat, the appropriation of all means of production, etc.'.

Marx had already tried to build

> a scientific theory of revolutions, as certain and as extensive as Darwin's theory of the origin of species. Lenin at least thought so, witness his celebrated formulation 'The Marxist doctrine is omnipotent because it is true'. Thus Marxism-Leninism is based on the following axiomatic statement: *there is no place for any non-knowledge in revolutionary actions.* A Lacanian would translate: thanks to Marx, S_1 and S_2 are one.

Stalinism does the same, but in a radically different way: 'In Stalin's version of such a revolution, he concentrates in his own person S_1 and S_2. He blends them together. He knows what was already known, in its entirety. He also knows what cannot be known by anyone but himself: what the revolution should do in order to continue.' In what, precisely, does this difference reside? In every revolution, ungrounded decisions sooner or later generate obscure situations in which the 'cognitive mapping' provided by theory (knowledge) crumbles and revolutionary agents are brutally confronted with their nonknowledge:

> During the French Revolution itself, it is easy to recognize the moments in which the most rational and the most courageous among the revolutionaries despaired. Most of them were competent and cultured,

but no historical precedent in history, no scientific discovery, and no philosophical argument could help them. The same can be said about Lenin. Whoever has read his works cannot but admire his intelligence, his encyclopedic culture and his ability to invent new political concepts. Nonetheless, his own writings show a growing uncertainty about the situation that he himself had created. Right or wrong, the NEP was not only a turning point; it implied a severe self-criticism, bordering on a renegation. At least, it proved that Lenin had been confronted by his own lack of knowledge in the field of political economy, where, as a Marxist, he was the most sure of himself; he was indeed discovering a new political country.

Without any explicit critique of Lenin, of course, Stalin 'understood intuitively' that such a grounding of revolution in scientific understanding of reality has to fail; and in the early 1920s, it was as if the entire Soviet reality this cognitive disorientation: one wild improvisation followed another and, as Lenin himself wrote, the Bolsheviks committed 'all possible mistakes'. How did Stalin cut short this confusion? How did he bring together S_1 and S_2, the real of the revolutionary act embodied in the Leader's unpredictable decisions and the knowledge of complex processes that compose social reality? On the one hand, he presented itself as the absolute bearer of objective knowledge: the Soviet revolutionary process followed objective laws of history, it was a process that should and could be studied from a cold scientific distance, and Stalin's policy was just the result of the political application of this knowledge, everything happened in reality … However, this domain of the objective knowledge of reality was at the same time totally subjectivized, effectively functioning as a series of arbitrary decisions, nothing was firm in reality, even the past could be at any time rewritten the way it fitted the present political requirements. There is thus no longer a properly dialectical tension between S_1 and S_2, the two levels directly collapse, which de facto means that (social) reality dissolves and collapses into the Real. In other words, Stalin understood that

> a revolution has something to do with the real, rather than with the imaginary mixture of past events and past assessments that is called 'reality'. Lenin and all true Marxist-Leninists treated the revolution as a reality. More generally, they seem to have had no sense of the real difference between the real and reality. Stalin is but the symptom of what happens when the real comes back in a world that denies it: it destroys all reality.

Again, what this means in practice is that the actual content of the 'knowledge' promulgated by Stalin is a weird mixture of paranoiac constructs and of radically unprincipled opportunism – the anti-Semitic conservative Tchaikovsky is proclaimed the greatest Russian composer and elevated into an untouchable icon, planned economy is combined with the utmost brutality of competitive exploitation of workers, and so forth. An extreme example of this dissolution of reality is provided by Anna Larina, Bukharin's widow, who in her memoirs reports one of Stalin's most surprising remarks: at a meeting of the Central Committee just prior to his arrest, Bukharin was complaining about the attacks against him by other members and reminded them indignantly what he had done for the Revolution; Stalin replied with indifference that nobody had done more for the Revolution than Trotsky, and yet he is now justly treated as the lowest traitor.[26] So it is not that while Trotsky, at the level of reality, did great things, he now lost his way and has to be liquidated; his present conflict with Stalin (the real of the situation) obliges us to rewrite the past and present even his key role in the October Revolution and the ensuing civil war as a mask covering the reality of his treasons and sabotages.

Although Stalin's power is often presented as the power of an absolute monarch, we have to oppose here the figure of the Stalinist Leader to the Hegelian Monarch: Hegel's solution is precisely the opposite one, it is to maintain the maximum distance between S_1 and S_2: the king is the formal point of subjective decision, but he is as such reduced to someone whose job is purely ceremonial; he has to sign documents proposed by his advisers who stand for knowledge.

Schiller versus Hegel

Back to *Don Carlos*, the true counterpart of the Inquisitor is thus not Philip but – who? None other than Posa. When the king is betrayed by Posa, he merely gets his own message back from him: he thought that, while he remains a king, Posa is now his equal, a friend to whom he is bound by mutual recognition, but he discovers that in the same way he looked down upon others, Posa now looks down upon him, just exploiting him for his own political purposes. And Posa is fully justified to ruthlessly manipulate his friendship with don Carlos and Philip in order to realize his political goal. Even when he sacrifices himself to save don Carlos (by way of sending a secret letter to the Dutch rebels he knows will be intercepted), he doesn't do this out of friendship but again for a political purpose (to enable don

Carlos to escape and lead the Dutch rebellion). There effectively is a weird parallel between Inquisitor and Posa: they are both cold functionaries fully dedicated to their cause, the only difference is that, while the Inquisitor is the functionary of the existing order, Posa is, to quote Reich-Ranicki, 'the functionary of the revolution' – in short, a kind of proto-Leninist.

Schiller's effort is to keep at a distance this friendless world whose two faces are the Inquisitor and Posa; he desperately tries to save friendship, although he is fully aware that the fraternal bond of friendship has to be discreetly controlled by a Master who has to remain friendless, as is made clear in a short poem 'Die Freundschaft' (Friendship), written after *Don Carlos* and which recapitulates the king's deadlock in the play, the need of an absolute Master for equal friends bound by mutual recognition. Here is the poem's original version of 1782:

> Friendless was the great world-master
> Felt a lack – and so created spirits,
> Blessed mirrors of his own blessedness
> But the highest being still could find no equal.
> From the chalice of the whole realm of souls
> Foams up to *him* – infinitude.

Schiller describes here a lonely Creator who cannot overcome the gap that separates Him from his creation: the spirits He creates remain his own mirror images, shadowy insubstantial others, so He remains alone, caught in his own narcissistic game. Interestingly, the last two lines are quoted at the very conclusion of Hegel's *Phenomenology*, but they are slightly changed; what is the meaning of this change? The standard approach to Hegel is that the Idea can afford extreme self-externalization since it is merely playing a game with itself, knowing full well that, at the end, it will safely return to itself, reappropriating its otherness. The difference between Hegel and Schiller is that Hegel fully endorses this view of the Absolute encountering only its own shadows and thus playing a narcissistic game with itself, while Schiller saw the deadlock of the Absolute: it cannot find any equal, so it remains lonely … But does this (standard) objection hold? Was Hegel not fully aware of the deadlock of a Master position? To clarify this point, let us take a look at the conclusion of Hegel's *Phenomenology*, in which a dense description of Absolute Knowing is 'sutured' by a quote from Schiller:

> The *goal*, Absolute Knowing, or Spirit that knows itself as Spirit, has for its path the recollection of the Spirits as they are in themselves and as they accomplish the organization of their realm. Their preservation,

regarded from the side of their free existence appearing in the form of contingency, is History; but regarded from the side of their ... comprehended organization, it is the Science of Knowing in the sphere of appearance: the two together, comprehended History [*begriffene Geschichte*], form alike the inwardizing-memory [*Erinnerung*] and the Calvary of absolute Spirit, the actuality, truth, and certainty of its throne, without which it would be lifeless and alone. Only

> from the chalice of this realm of spirits
> foams forth for Him his infinitude
> [aus dem Kelche dieses Geisterreiches
> schäumt ihm seine Unendlichkeit].[27]

The last two lines are a (subtly transformed) quote from Schiller's poem – so what does Hegel achieve with theses changes? When Hegel quotes the same two lines again in his *Philosophy of Religion*, he supplements them with another poetic quote, the two lines from Goethe's 'An Suleika' (from *West-östlicher Divan*) where, apropos of the torment of the endless striving of love, Goethe writes: 'Ought such torment to afflict us, / since it enhances our desire?'[28] The link between the two quotes is clear: what appears in the 'chalice of this realm of spirits' is, as Hegel says two lines before, the 'Calvary of absolute Spirit', and insofar as the Spirit is able to recognize in this path of torment his own infinitude, traversing this path brings joy, that is, pleasure in pain itself.

If we read the infinite 'foaming forth' from the chalice of spirits in this way, as the repetitive movement of the drive, then it also becomes clear how we can read it in a nonnarcissistic way, not as the philosophical covering up of the gap (conceded by Schiller) that separates the divine Absolute from the realm of finite spirits. In Hegel's version, God is not just playing a game with Himself, pretending to lose Himself in externality while fully aware that He remains its master and creator: infinity is *out there*, and this 'out there' is not a mere shadowy reflection of God's infinite power. In short, the divine Absolute is itself caught up in a process it cannot control – the Calvary of the last paragraph of the *Phenomenology* is not the Calvary of finite beings who pay the price for the Absolute's progress, but *the Calvary of the Absolute itself*. One should note how Hegel says here the exact opposite of the famous passage on the cunning of reason from his *Philosophy of History*:

> The special interest of passion is thus inseparable from the active development of a general principle: for it is from the special and determinate

and from its negation, that the Universal results. Particularity contends with its like, and some loss is involved in the issue. It is not the general idea that is implicated in opposition and combat, and that is exposed to danger. It remains in the background, untouched and uninjured. This may be called the *cunning of reason*, – that it sets the passions to work for itself, while that which develops its existence through such impulsion pays the penalty and suffers loss. For it is *phenomenal* being that is so treated, and of this, part is of no value, part is positive and real. The particular is for the most part of too trifling value as compared with the general: individuals are sacrificed and abandoned. The Idea pays the penalty of determinate existence and of corruptibility, not from itself, but from the passions of individuals.[29]

Here we get what we expect the 'textbook Hegel' to say: Reason works as a hidden substantial power that realizes its goal by deftly exploiting individual passions; engaged individuals fight each other, and through their struggle the universal Idea actualizes itself. The conflict is thus limited to the domain of the particular, while the Idea 'remains in the background, untouched and uninjured', at peace with itself, as the calm of the true universality: subjects are reduced to instruments of historical substance. This standard teleology is, however, totally rejected by what Hegel sees as the fundamental lesson of Christianity: far from remaining 'in the background, untouched and uninjured', *the Absolute itself pays the price, irretrievably sacrificing itself.*

We should remember here that Schiller was the main proponent of the German aesthetic reaction to the French Revolution: his message was that, in order to avoid the destructive fury of the Terror, the revolution should occur with the rise of a new aesthetic sensibility, through the transformation of the state into an organic and beautiful Whole (Lacoue-Labarthe located the beginnings of fascism in this aesthetic rejection of the Jacobin Terror).[30] Since Hegel clearly saw the necessity of the Terror, his reference to Schiller could be paraphrased as: *only from the chalice of this revolutionary Terror foams forth the infinitude of spiritual freedom.* (And, taking a step further, we can even propose a paraphrase concerning the relationship between Phenomenology and Logic: *only from the chalice of phenomenology, which contains the Calvary of the Absolute Spirit, foams forth the infinitude of logic, pure logic.*)

This brings us back to Schiller's aestheticization of politics which should protect us from revolutionary terror: with regard to the French Revolution, he 'expresses the wager of an entire generation: we don't need *that* kind of revolution. Only through *aesthetic* revolution can we forestall the explosion of politics into terror. Only through beauty do we inch our way towards freedom.'[31] This is how fascism begins – in contrast to Hegel who does not forestall explosions of terror but accepts the necessity of passing through it. In other words, Schiller – although he presents himself as the poet of freedom – effectively pleads for the restoration of a discreet, benevolent Master who can only prevent the explosion of politics into terror. There are two modes of 'ugly' freedom that Schiller rejects: the destructive revolutionary freedom and the 'mechanical' chaos of unorganic market relations where each individual pursues only egotist goals. They are perceived as the two sides of the same process which can be countered only through the aestheticization of politics. It is this aestheticization which renders Schiller blind to the new forms of domination which, already in his lifetime, began to replace the classic disposition of power which is sustained by symbolic castration.

The self-debased authority

More precisely, what Schiller was not able to see is how contemporary authority is split into two: on one hand a pure blind knowledge (embodied in the Inquisitor), and on the other hand a friendly boss 'like us', with all ordinary human weaknesses – the necessity of this second figure is what Schiller couldn't see. The only 'castration' he clearly saw was the alienation of the monarch who is unable to engage in authentic friendship.

Symbolic castration is the price to be paid for the exercise of power. How, precisely? One should begin by conceiving of phallus as a signifier – which means what? From the traditional rituals of investiture, we know the objects which not only 'symbolize' power, but put the subject who acquires them into the position of effectively *exercising* power – if a king holds in his hands the sceptre and wears the crown, his words will be taken as the words of a king. Such insignia are external, not part of my nature: I don them; I wear them in order to exert power. As such, they 'castrate' me: they introduce a gap between what I immediately am and the function that I exercise (i.e. I am never fully at the level of my function). This is what the infamous 'symbolic castration' means: not 'castration as symbolic, as just symbolically enacted' (in the sense in which we say that, when I am deprived of something, I am 'symbolically castrated'), but the castration which occurs by the very fact of me being caught in the symbolic order, assuming a symbolic mandate. Castration is the very gap between what I immediately am and the symbolic mandate which confers on me this 'authority'. In this precise sense, far from being the opposite of power, it is synonymous with power; it is that which confers power on me. And one has to think of the phallus not as the organ which immediately expresses the vital force of my being, my virility, and so on, but, precisely, as such an insignia, as a mask which I put on in the same way a king or judge puts on his insignia – phallus is an 'organ without a body' which I put on, which gets attached to my body, without ever becoming its 'organic part', namely, forever sticking out as its incoherent, excessive supplement.

However, this gap between the symbolic title (its insignia) and the miserable reality of the individual who bears this title tends to function today in a radically different way: it underwent a weird reversal noted by Badiou apropos of Jean Genet's *Le Balcon*:

> We encounter here an imaginary feature of democracy. Democracy means precisely that there are no costumes. Inequality no longer wears a costume/dress. There are dramatic, gigantic inequalities, but their laicization leaves them without a costume.[32]

On a simple descriptive level, this means that, in a democratic-egalitarian society, masters (those who exert power over others) no longer have to wear insignia or costumes that would performatively constitute them as bearers of power: they can dress and act 'naturally' like everybody else, renouncing all dignity. The message of the way they dress and act is: 'See, we are common people like you, with all weaknesses, fears, and limitations like everyone else!' – in short, their 'castration' is no longer covered up by the splendour of their insignia but is openly displayed. However, this 'honest' operation should in no way deceive us: for all their common appearance they continue to assert their full power, perhaps even more directly than the traditional master: 'Let the image be castrated in all possible ways, while I can do more or less whatever I want ... In a strange reversal of the classic logic of castration (as a means to access symbolic power), we are dealing here with the castration of the symbolic (public) image as a means to execute and perpetuate limitless power.'[33]

Castration (the display of weakness) thus 'becomes part of the public image', but not in the simple and straightforward sense that it simply masks the actual exercise of ruthless power – the point is rather that *this mask of castration is the very means (instrument, mode) of how power is exercised.*[34] The mystification is here redoubled: beneath the gesture of demystification ('You see, I dropped all masks and costumes, I am an ordinary guy like you!'), the exercise of power (which is a symbolic fact, not a 'real' property of its agent) remains intact. When confronted with a boss who talks and acts as an ordinary man, his subordinate would thus be fully justified in addressing him with a paraphrase of the well-known Marx Brothers phrase: 'Why are you talking and acting as an ordinary man *when you really are just an ordinary man*?' (The paradox is that, if the agent of power were to put on the masks of insignia, this would not increase his power but undermine it, making it appear ridiculously pathetic.) The matrix of *je sais bien mais quand même* is here given a specific twist formulated by Zupančič: it is no longer just 'I know very well that you are an ordinary weak guy like me, but I still accept you as a master', it is rather something like 'I know very well you are a miserable weak guy like me, and for that very reason I can continue to obey you like my master'. Knowledge is here not an obstacle to be suspended but a positive condition of the functioning of what it discloses in its gesture of 'demystification'. The mystification persists not in spite of its denunciation but *through it, because of it.* (In a strictly homologous way, Freud demonstrates how repression can persist through the very knowledge [conscious awareness] of the repressed content – repression remains active even when we 'know it all'.)

So, back to *Don Carlos*: Philip is at the end of the drama not just playing castration in order to retain his full actual power, he really *is* broken and impotent – Schiller wasn't yet able to imagine the figure of a Master who rules through a display of his castration. What he wasn't able to imagine is the totally new link between authority and friendship that we can observe in today's power figures: a Master who claims he is 'our pal', who renounces his insignia and presents himself as our equal friend while retaining all his authority with the help of this very self-debasement. In other words, what Schiller was not able to think is the reversal of the status of castration in the functioning of power: in the traditional power, castration that sustains it resides in the fact that the phallic insignia which provide power are decentred with regard to the subject; in contemporary power, the castration that sustains power is the very fact of being deprived of the insignia of power. (Today, the implicit defence of Barack Obama against his Leftist critics also involves a kind of display of castration: when he is accused of not closing Guantanamo, of allowing the use of drones, etc., his [unspoken but clear] message is 'I am simply helpless here, that is how the state functions ...' – but who is playing a game here?)

This paradox characterizes cynicism as the hegemonic form of today's ideology: in it, the fetishist denial acquires a new form – it is no longer the belief which persists in our actual practice in spite of our knowledge (I know very well, but nonetheless ...), like 'I know there is no god, but I continue to participate in religious rituals out of respect for my culture'. In today's cynicism, the disavowal (of knowledge) is not embodied in a fetish-object; things are brought to a self-referential extreme, so that the fetish (which enables us to disavow knowledge) is knowledge itself – knowledge functions as the obstacle which prevents ... what? Seriously accepting and assuming knowledge itself. It is true that we didn't really learn from Snowden (or from Manning) anything we didn't already presume to be true – but it is one thing to know it in general, and another to get concrete data. It is a little bit like knowing that one's sexual partner is playing around – one can accept the abstract knowledge of it, pain arises when one learns the steamy details, when one gets pictures of what they were doing. This is why the most perfidious defence of those in power is not to deny the Wikileaks accusations but to say: 'We are not naive, we already knew or suspected all of this. Do you really think we are so stupid that we didn't know it all along? So why all the fuss about it?' With this operation, those who disclosed the problematic data that should worry and annoy us become themselves a source of annoyance. So if we all already knew it, who didn't know it? The Lacanian answer is: the big Other. If the big Other doesn't know it, we can act as if we also don't know it. A similar strategy is at work in apologizing where a quick admission can serve as an excuse to avoid a real apology ('I said I'm sorry, so shut up and stop annoying me!'). Along these lines, one can imagine a new version of Freud's old example of a dreamer whose answer to 'Who was that woman in your dream?' is 'I don't know who that woman was, but I am sure it was not my mother!' But what if the dreamer admits all too willingly 'It was my mother, of course!', hoping that with this fast admission the fact will be dealt with and one can pass to other less sensitive topics?

So, to recapitulate, the basic fetishism which structures the way we relate to a person of authority was described long ago by, among others, Marx: a king is a king because we treat him like a king, but it appears to us that we treat him as a king because he is in himself a king. However, beneath this basic fetishist reversal, there is another, more tricky one: the illusion that, beneath the costume of power which confers on a person their charisma, there is just an ordinary person like ourselves. Recall how, on the back cover of a book, we often find beneath the decription of the topic and content of the book some personal details about the author, something like: 'In her free time, Miss Highsmith grows tulips and collects rare silver coins.' Such a list of personal features not only does not defetishize the writer but is *the very operator of his or her fetishization*. Lacan cunningly subverted this procedure: those who knew him personally were desperately looking for small private details, signs of humanity, so that they would be able to say, 'you know, behind the arrogant posture of his performances he is a nice warm guy like us' – but the big surprise was that in private he behaved exactly in the same way as in public ... (The same held for Stalinist leaders: archives demonstrate that among themselves they did not use another language, cynical and frank, but exactly the same jargon as in their public performances.) So where is the Real here where public posture coincides with the private self behind it? In between the two terms of the tautological repetition. In the case of a modern boss who appears as if he is an ordinary guy like us (and effectively *is* that), the two sides nonetheless do not collapse into one: the in-between is (the illusion of) his power. Or, in the inverted case of Lacan, his subjectivity is the abyss in-between the two same staged performances.

There is a (slightly brutal) experiment one can perform on a friendly child. I approach him with a mask on, and he gets frightened; then I pull the mask off and show him my stupid face which is well known to him, and he (hopefully) smiles; then I put the mask on again and he is terrified again although he knows very well what is beneath the mask – and he is right, since the mask engenders a third reality, a 'ghost in the mask' which is not the face hidden beneath it. This X the child is afraid of is the abyss of the pure subject (not to be confused with the personality expressed in a face). This is also the reason why wearing a burqa is so unbearable for (some of) us in the West: not because the face remains hidden so that we do not know with whom we are dealing, but because we in a way 'see' the void behind the naked face, this ultimate mask. When, in 2010, the French government prohibited wearing a burqa in public, what could not but strike the eye was the ambiguity of the critique of the burqa: it moved at two levels. First, the prohibition of the burqa was presented as a defence of the dignity and freedom of the oppressed Muslim women – it is unacceptable that, in a secular France, any woman has to live a hidden life secluded from public space, subordinated to brutal patriarchal authority. Second, however, as a rule the argument then shifted towards the anxieties of non-Muslim French people: faces covered by the burqa do not fit with the coordinates of French culture and identity, they 'intimidate and alienate non-Muslims'. Some French women have even suggested that they perceive the wearing of a burqa as *their own* humiliation, as being brutally excluded, rejected from a social link.

This brings us to the true enigma here: why does the encounter with a face covered by a burqa trigger such anxiety? Is it that a face so covered is no longer the Levinasian face – that Otherness from which the unconditional ethical call emanates? But what if the opposite is the case? From a Freudian perspective, the face is the ultimate mask that conceals the horror of the Neighbour-Thing: the face is what makes the Neighbour *le semblable*, a fellow-man with whom we can identify and empathize. (Not to mention the fact that, today, many faces are surgically modified and thus deprived of the last vestiges of natural authenticity.) This, then, is why the covered face causes such anxiety: because it confronts us directly with the abyss of the Other-Thing, with the Neighbour in its uncanny dimension. The very covering-up of the face obliterates a protective shield, so that the Other-Thing stares at us directly (recall that the burqa has a narrow slit for the eyes; we don't see the eyes, but we know there is a gaze there). Alphonse Allais presented his own version of Salome's dance of seven veils: when Salome is completely naked, Herod shouts 'Go on! On!' expecting her to take off also the veil of her skin. We should imagine something similar with the burqa – the opposite of a woman removing her burqa to reveal her face. What if we go a step further and imagine a woman 'taking off' the skin of her face itself, so that what we see beneath is precisely an anonymous dark smooth burqa-like surface with a narrow slit for the gaze? Maybe, this would be the ultimate terrifying example of what Schiller imagined as a woman-hyena.

But why should the figure of the laughing hyena be that of a woman? What Schiller was not able to see is how a laughing and self-debasing hyena is also a transitional figure in the passage from the reign of a Sovereign to the rule of the Inquisitor. In a unique moment in *Star Wars III: Revenge of the Sith*, we get a glimpse of this figure. We should bear in mind the (somewhat awkward) Hegelianism of the first three instalments of the *Star Wars* saga: as in G. K. Chesterton's *The Man Who Was Thursday* where the master-mind criminal is revealed to be none other than god himself, we gradually discover that senator Palpatine, the leader of the Republic (Chancellor of its Senate) in its war against the separatist federation, is none other than Darth Sidious, the mysterious supreme Sith lord who pulls the strings behind the separatists – in fighting the separatists, the Republic is fighting itself, which is why the moment of its triumph and the defeat of the separatists is the moment of the Republic's conversion into the evil Empire. In the middle of the film, when Palpatine reveals himself to Anakin (the future Darth Vader) as the Sith lord Darth Sidious, Anakin reports his treachery to Mace Windu, a Jedi knight, who subdues Palpatine in a lightsabre duel. Seeing Palpatine threatened and humiliated by Mace Windu, Anakin intervenes on Palpatine's behalf, allowing him to kill the Jedi Master.

What one should focus on here is the transformation of Palpatine's face during this interchange. After being exposed to brutal energy-shocks from

Windu's lightsabre, the skin of his face gradually turns hard and crinky, as if corrugated, changing it into a crocodile-head surface. But the change is also the one in his attitude: when Palpatine is under duress, his face gets deformed, twisted, expressing Palpatine's fear of pain and death, like an evil child in panic, and the moment Anakin cuts off Windu's hand and thus immobilizes him, Palpatine attacks him, frying him with rays of Force with childish pleasure – a true laughing hyena. Palpatine seizes power at this very moment of 'total helplessness. One can see he knows he's won in that very moment. He's already looking forward to the moment when he can throw back his hood in the Senate and display his horribly mutilated scrotum-like head.'[35] So it is only after this passage through utter loss of all dignity, after his symbolic authority is thoroughly debased, that Palpatine can re-emerge as what he really was: Darth Sidious, the lord of Darkness – or, in Schiller's terms, the crippled old Inquisitor who holds all the reins of power. His ridiculous weakness is not an obstacle to his power but its very resort.

8 IS GOD DEAD, UNCONSCIOUS, EVIL, IMPOTENT, STUPID ... OR JUST COUNTERFACTUAL?

On divine inexistence

In the New Testament, Jesus is not called 'Son of God', but much more regularly 'Son of Man' – why? The key is provided by the ironic fact that, owing to his immaculate conception, Jesus is precisely *not* a son of man, a human being whose father was a man. This is why the designation does not say 'a son of man' (which would have simply meant a human being born of human parents) but 'THE son of man': the designation is not a predicate stating a fact, a property, it functions as a symbolic *title* (like a king who is 'gracious, good, and wise', even if he is a creepy idiot).[1] He is not a man who has the honorific title 'Son of God' (as many figures in the Bible do), but *a god who has the title 'Son of Man'*. This is why Paul, in an unusual formulation, doesn't call Jesus *the* Christ (as a title, messiah), but simply 'Jesus Christ', as if 'Christ' is his surname. In other words, if Jesus were to be a Scandinavian where the family name is usually formed by adding a 'son' to the father's name, his complete name (along the model of 'Charles "Lucky" Luciano', i.e. of a nickname [title] inserted between the given name and the family name), Jesus would not be 'Jesus "Christ" Josephson', but 'Jesus "Josephson" Christ.'

This is why Christ's death and resurrection in the Holy Spirit are not the same as, say, the death of the individual Julius Caesar and his 'resurrection' in the guise of the universal symbolic title 'caesar'. One can say that, precisely prior to his death, as a living Teacher, Christ remained all too 'universal', delivering a universal message (of love, etc.) and 'exemplifying' it with his behaviour and acts. With his death, Christ is no longer just a bearer of a message, he himself *is* the message. It is only in his death on the Cross that Christ – up to that point a man who was a divine messenger – directly became God, i.e. that, in Hegelese, the gap between the universal content and its representation was closed:

> Without Judas, Christ would only be a Buddha or a prophet like others. He would have communicated till his old age a sublime teaching of generosity and peace, but he would not have 'revealed' in a human body and behaviour the invincible power of humble Love faced with absurdity, violence and death.[2]

With regard to this figure of Christ, reference to the universe of commodities also enables us to reactualize Marx's old idea that Christ is like money among men – ordinary commodities: in the same way money as universal equivalent directly embodies/assumes the excess ('value') that makes an object a commodity, Christ directly embodies/assumes the excess that makes the human animal a proper human being. In both cases, then, the universal equivalent exchanges/gives itself for all other excesses – in the same way money is the commodity 'as such', Christ is man 'as such'; in the same way that the universal equivalent has to be a commodity deprived of any use value, Christ has taken over the excess of sin of *all* men precisely insofar as he was the pure one, without excess, simplicity itself.

The death of Christ is a temporal event, and, as such, contingent – it could easily not have happened. But it is at the same time a necessary event – it is a temporal event which, once it happened, retroactively created its own necessity, through a weird reversal described by Dupuy: 'if an outstanding event takes place, a catastrophe, for example, it could not not have taken place; nonetheless, insofar as it did not take place, it is not inevitable. It is thus the event's actualization – the fact that it takes place – which retroactively creates its necessity.'[3] Dupuy provides the example of the French presidential elections in May 1995; here is the January forecast of the main polling institute: 'If, on next May 8, Ms. Balladur is elected, one can say that the presidential election was decided before it even took place.' If – accidentally – an event takes place, it creates the preceding chain which makes it appear inevitable: *this*, not the commonplaces on how the underlying necessity expresses itself in and through the accidental play of appearances, is *in nuce* the Hegelian dialectics of contingency and necessity.

The same goes for the October Revolution (once the Bolsheviks won and stabilized their hold on power, their victory appeared as an outcome and expression of a deeper historical necessity), and even of Bush's much contested first US presidential victory (after the contingent and contested Florida majority, his victory retroactively appears as an expression of a deeper US political trend). In this sense, although we are determined by destiny, we are nonetheless *free to choose our destiny* – and this is also how we should approach the ecological crisis: not to 'realistically' appraise the possibilities of the catastrophe, but to accept it as destiny in the precise Hegelian sense: like the election of Balladur, 'if the catastrophe happens, one can say that its occurrence was decided before it even took place'. Destiny and free action (to block the 'if') thus go hand in hand: freedom is at its most radical the freedom to change one's destiny. *This* freedom is the message of Christ – the contingent free act that can change necessity.

According to Matthew 27.19, Pilate's wife (anonymous in the Gospels, in later tradition called Procla [Procula] or sometimes Claudia) sent a message to her husband asking him not to condemn Christ to death: 'While Pilate was sitting in the judgment hall, his wife sent him a message: "Have nothing to do with that innocent man, because in a dream last night, I suffered much on account of him."' Some theologians (Luther among them) argued that the dream was sent by the devil in an attempt to thwart the salvation that was going to result from Christ's death: it was part of the 'divine economy' that Christ had to die, this was planned from the beginning, Christ discreetly ordered Judas to betray him, and so on; Procla's intervention – an act of goodness – as well as Pilate's oscillations are thus acts which threaten the fulfilment of the divine economy. One can also imagine a similar scenario of some partisan of Christ overhearing Judas's dealing with the Romans and trying to prevent the act of handing Christ over to the Romans; at the last minute, he is pulled aside by Christ and Judas who whisper to him angrily: 'You idiot, you are out of your depth here, so stop, don't mess with things which are far beyond you!' However, a much more adequate approach would be here to grasp these very obstacles to the fulfilment of the divine plan as an immanent part of this plan, in a way similar to what goes on in Wagner's *Parsifal*. The enigma of *Parsifal* is: what are the limits and contours of a ceremony? Is the ceremony only that which Amfortas is unable to perform, or is part of the ceremony also the spectacle of his complaint and resistance and final acceptance to perform the ceremony? In other words, are Amfortas's two great complaints not highly ceremonial, ritualized? Is not even the 'unexpected' arrival of Parsifal to replace him (who nonetheless arrives just in time, i.e. at just the moment when the tension is at its highest) part of a ritual?

This brings us to another aspect of the Christian truth: we are dealing here with a universal truth whose truth-value hinges on the agent and moment of its enunciation. In his admirable text on Hitchcock's *Vertigo*, Jean-Pierre Dupuy deployed a temporal logical paradox:

> An object possesses a property x until the time t; after t, it is not only that the object no longer has the property x; it is that it is not true that it possessed x at any time. The truth-value of the proposition 'the object O has the property x at the moment t' therefore depends on the moment when this proposition is enunciated.[4]

One should note here the precise formulation: it is not that the truth-value of the proposition 'the object O has the property x' depends on the time to which this proposition refers – *even when this time is specified, the truth-value depends on the time when the proposition itself is enunciated.* Or, to quote the title of Dupuy's text, 'when I die, nothing of our love will ever have existed'. Think about marriage and divorce: the most intelligent argument for the right to divorce (proposed, among others, by none other than the young Marx) does not refer to common vulgarities in the style of 'like all things, love attachments are also not eternal, they change in the course of time', etc.; it rather concedes that undissolvability is in the very notion of marriage. The conclusion is that divorce always has a retroactive scope: it means not just that marriage is now annulled, but something much more radical – a marriage should be annulled because *it never was a true marriage.* (And the same holds for Soviet communism: it is clearly insufficient to say that, in the years of the Brezhnev 'stagnation', it 'exhausted its potentials, no longer fitting new times'; what its miserable end demonstrates is that it was a historical deadlock *from its very beginning.*)

And the same holds for Christianity and its truth: Christ died contingently, it could have not happened, but once he died his death was predestined, he was born to die – this is how we pass from Jesus of Nazareth to Jesus Christ, from the Palestinian revolutionary preacher to universal Redeemer, from a noble individual spreading a great message to the individual whose ultimate message is the very fact of his existence. This is what Paul saw clearly: Christ's sayings and acts become true only with the Event of Death/Resurrection. Aslan relies all too simply on the standard opposition between the original historical 'Jesus of Nazareth' (the revolutionary messianic preacher who wanted to raise the Jews against the Roman oppressors as well as against their own corrupt priest, establishing an egalitarian Jewish kingdom of God on earth) and the Paulinian 'Jesus Christ' (the redeemer who, by means of his death on the Cross, gave a chance to all of humanity, and whose Kingdom is not of this world). What Aslan excludes (and what accounts for the deep ambiguity of the Paulinian theology) is the (rather obvious) third option: a Christ who is universalist and at the same time aiming at (universal) emancipation on this earth, a Christ whose death on the Cross does not signal renunciation to this world but functions as a founding gesture of universal mobilization. This is why radical political movements, with their elementary move of 'sublating' their dead hero in the living spirit of the community, resemble so much the Christological resurrection – the point here is not that they function like 'secularized Christianity', but, on the contrary, that the resurrection of Christ itself is their precursor, a mythic form of something which reaches its true form in the logic of emancipatory political collective.

Where, then, are we to look for the resources of this mobilization? Recall the famous lines from Matthew 21.12-13: 'And Jesus went into the temple of God, and cast out all them that sold and bought in the temple, and overthrew the tables of the moneychangers, and the seats of them that sold doves, And said unto them, It is written, My house shall be called the house of prayer; but ye have made it a den of thieves.' Can we imagine Jesus entering the New York Stock Exchange and scattering all the digital machinery there, cutting off all the cables, or, more appropriate to our times, as the ultimate hacker planting a virus which would cause a short circuit and paralyse the entire digital support of stock-exchange trading?

But such an approach is all too direct. That is to say, the first paradox of the materialist critique of religion is that, sometimes, it is much more subversive to undermine religion from within, accepting its basic premise and then bringing out its unexpected consequences, than to deny outright the existence of god. There is a popular New Age short story about a diehard atheist who, after dying in an unexpected traffic accident, reawakens after death and discovers that, basically, the spiritualist worldview was right: there is god or some higher power (which is indifferent to the plight of the souls), our souls survive our earthly death and dwell in a weird limbo-state where they can communicate with other souls as well as observe life on earth, and so forth. The atheist is extremely displeased by this outcome, his narcissism is deeply wounded – his atheist view was so perfect and convincing, how could he have been so wrong? Gradually, however, after getting over the first shock, he starts to carefully observe his new reality and adapts his materialism to new conditions: he was basically right, his existence after his death also has its own materiality, he can feel and touch objects, etc., it is just that this materiality is composed of totally different subatomic particles. But then he stumbles upon the true unpleasant surprise: in this new reality, conscious beings do not have sexual organs or orientation, there is friendship and sympathy but no sexuality, no sexual love, and also no ethics and morality except the most basic utilitarian stance of not hurting others too much. Getting desperate, he kills himself, but he is reawakened into the same boring reality, so what to do? Talking to other souls, he discovers that almost all of them are caught in the same despair, and that a kind of weird religion is emerging among them based on obscure rumours that, if you kill yourself in a very specific way, you are not reawakened but ... There are two schools of thought among undead souls: according to one of them, you really and forever die, disappearing into nothingness, while according to the other school, it is only after this second death that you reach true eternity and blessing.

This story fits perfectly the materialist procedure of the immanent self-undermining of a religious edifice – the claim that god is evil or stupid can be much more unsettling than the claim that there is no god since the first claim destroys the very notion of divinity. Let's take another example, *The Rapture* (1991, written and directed by Michael Tolkin, who also wrote the scenario for Altman's *The Player*) in which Mimi Rogers superbly plays Sharon, a young LA woman who works during the day as a phone operator endlessly repeating the same questions in a small cubicle among dozens of others, while in the evenings she engages in swinging orgies. (It can even be said that the film is ultimately 'about Mimi Rogers' face. Its transformations, its naked pain, its fearless openness.'[5]) Bored and dissatisfied at leading such an empty life, Sharon becomes a member of a sect which preaches that the end of times and the Rapture are imminent; turning into a passionate believer, she begins to practise a new, pious lifestyle, gets married to Randy, one of her previous swinging partners, and has a daughter Mary with him. Six years later, when Randy, now also a devoted Christian, is shot to death by a madman, this senseless catastrophe makes her and her daughter even more convinced that the Rapture is soon approaching. Sharon believes god told her to go with Mary to a nearby desert camping place and wait there until the two are taken into heaven where they will be united with Randy. Foster, a well-meaning, nonbelieving patrol officer, takes care of them there during their long wait when they run out of food. Mary gets impatient and proposes to her mother that they simply kill themselves in order to go to heaven and join Randy immediately. After a couple of weeks, Sharon also loses patience, decides to do the unspeakable and follows Mary's advice to stop her suffering; however, after shooting Mary, she is unable to take her own life afterwards, knowing that suicides are not allowed into heaven. She confesses her act to Foster, who arrests her and takes her to a local jail.

Until this point, the story moves along 'realist' lines, and one one can easily imagine a possible 'atheist' ending: bitter and alone, deprived of her faith, Sharon realizes the horror of what she had committed, and is maybe saved by the good policeman … Here, however, events take a totally unexpected turn: in the jail cell, Rapture happens, literally, in all naivety, including bad special effects. First, deep in the night, Mary appears with two angels, and then, early in the morning, while Sharon sits in her cell, a loud trumpet blast is heard all around and anounces a series of supranatural events – prison bars fall down, etc. Escaping from the jail, Sharon and Foster drive out into the desert, where signs of Rapture multiply, from dust storms up to the horsemen of the apocalypse running after and around the car. The message of god is something like: 'Look, man, you read the Bible, you think I didn't mean what I said in it? I *told* you it would be like this, so don't whine about it now. You *knew* what you were getting into. Pay up.'[6] So it is the exact opposite of the common idea that we should not take divine declarations too literally, that we should learn to discern in them their deeper metaphoric meaning. Ordinary people mostly believe at this level: when asked if they really think that two thousand years ago a son of god was walking around Palestine, they would say that while this is of course in all probability not literally true, there is for sure some higher power which softly takes care of us … The lesson of *The Rapture* is that this very metaphoric approach, the search for some deeper meaning, is a trap.

Next, Sharon and Foster are both 'raptured', transported to a purgatory-like landscape where Mary approaches them from heaven and pleads with Sharon to accept god, to declare that she loves god – by just doing this she will be able to join Mary and Randy in heaven. Foster, although until now an atheist, quickly seizes the opportunity, says that he loves god and is allowed entrance to heaven, but Sharon refuses, saying that she cannot declare her love for a god who acted so cruelly towards her family for no reason at all. When Mary asks her if she knows for how long she will be confined to the purgatory, condemned to be there alone, Sharon replies: 'Forever'. In short, Sharon realizes that she 'wasted her life appeasing someone who is only toying with her feelings; this would be easier to dismiss if we discovered that God did not exist',[7] i.e. that Sharon was just caught into her own delirious imagination. But she persists in renouncing a god who is real and really

a narcissist, giving us life for the sole purpose of demanding unconditional love in return, no matter how much damage his demands have inflicted on human lives. The film posits the theory that God is undeserving of our love even if he does exist, that he is in no way any less fallible to pettiness and power trips than the human beings he created. Like many humans, God lives by a set of rules and laws that he applies arbitrarily at his own moral convenience. Tolkin illustrates this by showing the non-believing cop immediately being accepted into heaven by declaring his love for God in a last ditch effort to be saved. He's merely saying what God wants to hear to save his own skin.[8]

God obviously doesn't care if you really mean it when you declare that you love him – as the case of Foster demonstrates, you just have to say it. (On a closer look, we can see that things are here more ambiguous: maybe Foster deserves to be taken into heaven more than Sharon since he demonstrated love and care for his neighbours.) Such an indifferent and narcissistic god is part of the Christian tradition: for Nicolas Malebranche, in the same way that the saintly person uses the suffering of others to bring about his own narcissistic satisfaction in helping those in distress, God also ultimately *loves only himself*, and merely uses man to promulgate his own glory. Malebranche here draws a consequence worthy of Lacan's reversal of Dostoyevsky ('*If God doesn't exist, then nothing is permitted*'): it is not true that, if Christ had not come to earth to deliver humanity, everyone would have been lost – quite the contrary, *nobody* would have been lost, i.e. *every* human being had to fall so that Christ could come and deliver *some* of them. Malebranche's conclusion here is properly perverse: since the death of Christ is a key step in realizing the goal of creation, at no time was God (the Father) happier then when he was observing His son suffering and dying on the Cross.

Sharon's resistance to God, her refusal to declare her love for him, is thus an authentic ethical act. It would be totally wrong to say that she rejects the *false* god and that, in an authentically Christian version of the film, the true Christ should appear at the end, proclaim her a true believer precisely because she refused to declare that she loves the false god. (Along the lines from the New Testament, in which Christ explains that whenever there is love between his followers, he will be there – god should not be loved, he *is* love.) The true temptation to be resisted is thus to declare our love for a god who doesn't deserve it *even if he is real*. For a vulgar materialist, all this cannot but appear as a pseudotopic, an empty mental experiment; however, for a true materialist, it is only in this way that we really renounce god – by way of renouncing him not only insofar as he doesn't really exist, but even if he is real. In short, the true formula of atheism is not 'god doesn't exist' but 'god not only doesn't exist, he is also stupid, indifferent, and maybe outright evil' – if we do not destroy the very fiction of god from within, it is easy for this fiction to prolong its hold over us in the form of disavowal ('I know there is no god, but he is nonetheless a noble and uplifting illusion').

For Gnostics, the God of the Old Testament is somewhat of a cosmic clown, neither ultimate nor good (many Gnostic documents invert the meaning of Old Testament stories in order to ridicule him). This lesser evil god, the demiurge of our material world, created the universe in order to keep the mortals in bondage in material matter and prevent the pure spirit souls from ascending back to the one true god after the death of the physical bodies. Deliverance from this entrapment in the material form is attainable only through special knowledge, and Christ was the divine redeemer who descended from the spiritual realm to reveal the knowledge necessary for this redemption. In standard Christianity the problem of Evil is ethical and concerns the pure Spirit itself: Evil is a category of spirit, it designates an egotist spirit which has sinned against the good Creator, turned itself against creation and is focused only on itself; there is nothing immanently evil in the material world, nature in itself can even be beautiul in an innocent way, only the Spirit brings evil into it. In Gnosticism, on the contrary, the problem is one of knowledge, and Evil is the material world as such which keeps the spirit in chains.

From such a perspective, bad guys systematically turn out to be good guys: the snake in paradise who tempts the first couple to eat the apple from the tree of knowledge is interpreted as the agent of wisdom who tries to awaken the couple from their ignorance and slavery to the evil Creator; the doubtful Thomas makes it clear that human knowledge is not a fixed dogma but a continuous process of search; the prostitute Mary Magdalene who reigns in bed stands for the unification of man and god; up to Judas himself who, by 'betraying' Jesus, enables him to free himself from the prison of his earthly/bodily existence. This means that the whole view of Crucifixion changes: it is no longer the unbearably painful spectacle of the Son of God paying for our sins but a comedy staged for the ignorant, a spectacle observed by the mocking Christ from above, from a safe distance: 'Never have I suffered in any way, nor have I been distressed. And this people has done me no harm.' 'I did not die in reality, but in appearance.' Those 'in error and blindness ... saw me; they punished me. It was another, their father, who drank the gall and vinegar; it was not I. They struck me with the reed; it was another, Simon, who bore the cross on his shoulder. I was rejoicing in the height over all ... And I was laughing at their ignorance.'

The further consequence of this view of Christ (which we find also in contemporary New Age teaching) is that one has to separate Jesus from the Christ: for Valentinus, for example, Christ, an immaterial spiritual agent, descended on Jesus, a material human person, at his baptism, and left Jesus's body before his death on the Cross ... No wonder that Irenaeus, in his *Against Heresies*, insists that Jesus was, is, and always will be the Christ.

As for the feminist potentials of Gnosticism, it is sufficient to recall the concluding lines from the Gospel of Thomas:

> Simon Peter said to them, 'Let Mary leave us, for women are not worthy of life.' Jesus said, 'I myself shall lead her in order to make her male, so that she too may become a living spirit resembling you males. For every woman who will make herself male will enter the kingdom of heaven.'

Male thus remains the standard, only a woman who makes herself male will be redeemed – these lines effectively sound as an ironic reversal of Paul's famous claim that, in Christ, there are no Jews and Greeks, no men and women: yes, there are no men and women since the only women allowed in have to be remade into men … The counterfactual notion of god that we should oppose to Gnosticism is the evil Demiurge, with no other, higher, god at his side – it's simply that our Creator is evil, period.

So what does the idea that god has to die in itself, not just for us, effectively amount to? For decades now, a classic joke has been circulating among Lacanian psychoanalysts: a man who believes himself to be a grain of seed is taken to the mental institution where the doctors do their best to finally convince him that he is not a grain but a man; however, when he is cured (convinced that he is not a grain of seed but a man) and allowed to leave the hospital, he immediately comes back trembling with fright – there is a chicken outside the door and he is afraid that it will eat him. 'Dear fellow,' says his doctor, 'you know very well that you are not a grain of seed but a man.' 'Of course I know that,' replies the patient, 'but does the chicken know it?' Therein resides the true stake of psychoanalytic treatment: it is not enough to convince the patient about the unconscious truth of his symptoms, the Unconscious itself must be brought to assume this truth. And does exactly the same not hold for the Marxian commodity fetishism? Here is the very beginning of the famous subdivision 4 of Chapter 1 of *Capital*, on 'The Fetishism of the Commodity and its Secret':

> A commodity appears at first sight an extremely obvious, trivial thing. But its analysis brings out that it is a very strange thing, abounding in metaphysical subtleties and theological niceties.[9]

These lines should surprise us, since they invert the standard procedure of demystifying a theological myth, of reducing it to its terrestrial base: Marx does not claim, in the usual way of Enlightenment critique, that the critical analysis should demonstrate how what appears a mysterious theological entity emerged out of the 'ordinary' real-life process; he claims, on the contrary, that the task of critical analysis is to unearth the 'metaphysical subtleties and theological niceties' in what appears at first sight just an ordinary object. In other words, when a critical Marxist encounters a bourgeois subject immersed in commodity fetishism, the Marxist's reproach to him is not 'The commodity may seem to you to be a magical object endowed with special powers, but it really is just a reified expression of relations between people'. The Marxist's actual reproach is, rather, 'You may think that the commodity appears to you as a simple embodiment of social relations (that, for example, money is just a kind of voucher entitling you to a part of the social product), but this is not how things really seem to you – in your social reality, by means of your participation in social exchange, you bear witness to the uncanny fact that a commodity really appears to you as a magical object endowed with special powers'. Alenka Zupančič goes here to the end and imagines a brilliant example that refers to God himself:

> In the enlightened society of, say, revolutionary terror, a man is put in prison because he believes in God. By various means, but above all by means of an enlightened explanation, he is brought to the knowledge that God does not exist. When he is freed, the man comes running back and explains how scared he is of being punished by God. Of course he knows that God does not exist, but does God know too?[10]

It is in this precise sense that the current era is perhaps less atheist than any prior one: we are all ready to indulge in utter scepticism, cynical distance, exploitation of others 'without any illusions', violations of all ethical constraints, extreme sexual practices, etc. – protected by the silent awareness that the big Other is ignorant about it.

Counterfactuals

This paradox can be perfectly formulated in terms of counterfactuals. Dupuy returns again and again to the distinction between the two types of conditional proposition, counterfactual and indicative: 'If Shakespeare did not write *Hamlet*, someone else did it' is an indicative proposition, while 'If Shakespeare had not written *Hamlet*, someone else would have done it' is counterfactual. The first one is obviously true, since it starts from the fact that *Hamlet* is here, was written, and someone had to write it. The second one is much more problematic, since it presupposes that there was a deeper historical tendency/necessity pushing towards a play like *Hamlet*, so even if Shakespeare were not to write it, another writer would have done it.[11] In this case, we are dealing with a rather crude historical determinism reminding us of what Georgi Plekhanov, in his classic text on the role of individuals in world history, said about Napoleon: there was a deeper historical necessity of the passage from Republic to Empire, so if, owing to some accident, Napoleon were not to have become the emperor, another individual would have played his role. Is exactly the same distinction not at work in how we consider Stalinism? For many, the rise of Stalinism was necessary, so that even without Stalin or in the case of his early accidental death, another leader would have played his role, maybe even Trotsky, his great opponent. For Trotskyites, but also many others like Kotkin, the role of Stalin's contingent person was crucial: no Stalinism without Stalin, i.e. if Stalin were to have disappeared from the historical scene in the early or mid-1920s, things like the forced collectivization and the practice of the 'construction of Socialism in one country' would not have taken place.

Was then the rise of Stalinism a simple accident, the actualization of one of the historical possibilities that were lying dormant within the situation after the victory of the October Revolution? Dupuy proposes here a more complex logic, the logic of retroactively transforming an accidental act into the expression of a necessity: 'necessity is retrospective: before I act, it was not necessary that I act as I do; once I have acted, *it will always have been true* that I could not have acted otherwise than I did.'[12] Stalin could have died or he could have been deposed, but once he won, his victory retroactively became necessary. It is the same with Julius Caesar crossing the Rubicon: he could have acted otherwise, but once he did it, crossing the Rubicon became his fate, he retroactively became (pre) destined to do it. This properly dialectical relationship between necessity and contingency is radically different from Plekhanov's determinism: the point is not that if Caesar were not to accomplish the fateful first step from the Republic to the Empire, there would have been another person to serve as the vehicle of this historical necessity – Caesar made a contingent choice which retroactively became necessary. That is to say, we, of course, cannot change the past causally, at the level of facts, we cannot retroactively undo what actually happened, but we can change it counterfactually. In Hitchcock's *Vertigo*, the past is also changed in this way. What Scottie first experiences is the loss of Madeleine, his fatal love; when he recreates Madeleine in Judy and then realizes that the Madeleine he knew already was Judy pretending to be Madeleine, what he discovers is not simply that Judy is a fake (he knew that she is not the true Madeleine, since he recreated a copy of Madeleine out of her), but that, *because she is not a fake*

– she is Madeleine – Madeleine herself was already a fake. His discovery thus changes the past: he discovers that what he lost (Madeleine) never existed.

Especially today, in our Politically Correct times, a seduction process always involves the risky move of 'making a pass' – at this potentially dangerous moment, one exposes oneself, one intrudes into another person's intimate space. The danger resides in the fact that if my pass is rejected, it will appear as a Politically Incorrect act of harassment; so there is an obstacle I have to overcome. Here, however, a subtle asymmetry enters: if my pass is accepted, it is not that I have successfully overcome the obstacle – what happens is that, retroactively, I learn that *there never was an obstacle to be overcome*.[13] Do we not find a homologous paradox of asymmetrical choice in the Gospel according to John, when Christ says he did not come to judge but to save, rejection of judgement – don't judge (others) for you will yourself be judged? The text then goes on:

> Whoever believes in him is not judged [*ou krinetai*], but whoever does not believe is judged [*kekritai*] already, because he has not believed in the name of the only Son of God. And this is the judgment: the light has come into the world, and people loved the darkness rather than the light because their works were evil. (Jn 3.18-19 ESV)

The temporality is here crucial: there is no present moment of judgement when you are judged – you either are not judged or you have already been judged. What is excluded is to be judged innocent, the same as in Dupuy's example of seduction: either you fail and the obstacle remains in force (you are rejected as a harrassing intruder) or there was no obstacle – what is excluded is to successfully overcome/force the obstacle. And, incidentally, exactly the same asymmetry is at work in the Hegelian dialectical process: the subject either stumbles upon an insurmountable obstacle or he realizes that there is no obstacle at all, that what appeared to him as an obstacle is the very condition of his success.

There is another, tragic version of changing the past. When we learn that a flight we planned to take but postponed the trip at the last minute (or simply missed the flight) has crashed, killing all passengers, we cannot but experience a dreadful feeling of 'My god, if I had taken that flight, I would have died!' … Dupuy mentions a wonderful case of his own daughter who took the AF flight 447 from Rio de Janeiro to Paris on 31 May 2009, one day before the plane on the same flight crashed into the Atlantic; after hearing of the crash, his reaction was: 'Had she delayed the flight by a day she would have been counted among the victims …' Seeking to relieve his anxiety, his daughter told him: 'But Dad, if I'd flown the next day the crash wouldn't have occurred!'[14] However, there is a dark obverse of Dupuy's case. On 2 September 1998, the Swissair flight 111 from JFK to Geneva crashed into the Atlantic Ocean southwest of Halifax, and all 229 people on board died. The investigation took over four years, and it disclosed that the inflammable material used in the aircraft's structure allowed a fire to spread beyond the control of the crew, resulting in a loss of control and the crash of the aircraft. After bringing out a series of wrong moves by the pilots and the ground control, a report in the National Geographic Air Crash Investigation series ends by raising the question: if the pilots had avoided all mistakes, what then? The sad answer is: the flight was doomed from the beginning, no correct moves would have made a difference. So it is not that 'if the pilots had acted differently, the tragedy would have been avoided' – the counterfactual past possibility is retroactively cancelled. This is how past can be changed counterfactually: when we learn that the flight was doomed from the beginning, nothing changes at the level of (past) facts, what changes is just counterfactual possibilities.

The Hegelian repetition which sublates a contingency into universal necessity thereby changes the past (not factually, of course, but in its symbolic status). The French Revolution became a world-historical event with a universal significance only through its repetition in Haiti where the black slaves led a successful rebellion with the goal to establish a free republic like the French one; without this repetition, the French Revolution would have remained a local, idiosyncratic event. The same holds today for the Syriza government in Greece: it will become a universal event only if it triggers a process of its 'repetitions', of similar movements taking over in other countries; otherwise, it will just remain a local Greek idiosyncrasy. What this means is that, in both cases, a repetition did (or will) retro-actively change the event from a particular idiosyncrasy into a universal truth-event.

The past thus retroactively becomes what it was 'in itself': retroactivity is not a simple illusion; the true illusion, the true retroactive projection, is rather the notion of an indifferent 'most real' with no opening towards the future. In other words, our point is not that reality is in-itself open/undecidable, and that its closure is a mere retroactive projection. Let us take J. B. Priestley's *Time and the Conways*, a play from 1937. Its first act is set in the Conway house in 1919 on the night of the birthday of one of the daughters, Kay; act 2 moves to the same night in 1937 and is set in the same room in the house; act 3 then returns to 1919 seconds after act 1 left off. In the first act we meet the Conway family; the atmosphere is one of festivity as the family celebrates the end of the war and looks forward to a great future of fame, prosperity and fulfilled dreams. Act 2 plunges us into the shattered lives of the Conways exactly eighteen years later. Gathering in the same room where they were celebrating in act 1, we see how their lives have failed in different ways. As the act unfolds, resentments and tensions explode and the Conways are split apart by misery and grief. Act 3 returns us to the continuation of the same evening of 1919 and owing to the fact that we see how the seeds of the downfall of the Conways were being sown even then, their enthusiasm appears all the more desolate ... The past is thus 'in itself' pregnant with future and as such undecidable, open – it is only in its future, retroactively, that it becomes the past it 'always-already was' (i.e. that, in our example, the fate of the Conways appears as doomed).

The same sad lesson is rendered in Roland Suso Richter's *The I Inside* (2004, based on Michael Cooney's play *Point of Death*). Simon Cable, the survivor of a near-fatal car accident, wakes up in a hospital bed with no memory of the last two years. Determined to figure out how and why he got there, he soon discovers that his brother Peter has been killed and that he's married to a woman named Anna whom he doesn't recognize and who seems to know more than she's letting on about Cable's situation. He's also haunted by Peter's girlfriend Claire who claims she's his lover. As Simon tries to unravel the mystery of his brother's death, he switches back and forth between the present – 2002 – and the accident which took place two years earlier. In the last scene, Simon visits Peter who reveals to him the secret: all three of them (Simon, Peter and Claire) died in the car accident, and all we have seen until now – the dying Simon's confused visions – were actually his desperate attempts to avoid accepting the unavoidable fact that he is dead. We then jump to the scene of the accident and see how doctors who were trying to reanimate Simon finally decide to cut short their endeavour – a sign that Simon finally accepted his death. With this final revelation, all different versions of what went on, which form the bulk of the film, are denounced as counterfactual possibilities and are thus retroactively cancelled.

Retroactivity, omnipotence and impotence

Predestination (2014, based on Robert Heinlein's short story 'All You Zombies', written and directed by Michael and Peter Spierig) explores the paradox of time travel: the story's tragic hero is gradually revealed to be a self-created entity trapped within a closed loop in time; his three main embodiments are a nameless temporal agent (played by Ethan Hawke) whose mission is to stop crimes before they happen, Jane (an androgynous writer known as 'The Unmarried Mother') and the Fizzle Bomber (who explodes bombs which kill thousands to prevent even greater catastrophes); plus there is Mr Robertson, the Temporal Bureau's mysterious boss.[15] This story instantiates the so-called predestination paradox, in which a time traveller (entity, object or information) exists within a closed loop in time where the chain of cause–effect events runs in a continuously repeating circular pattern: in the guise of John, the temporal agent is the cause of his own birth and has to travel back in time and have sex with himself (as Jane) from the past, giving birth to a child who travels back in time and grows up to become them. This loop is closed in the same way in which the Oedipus story and the story about the 'appointment in Samarra' are closed: any attempt by the time traveller to change events in the past would subsequently result in that person playing a role in creating the event they are trying to prevent, not changing it. Events are thus predestined to happen the same way over and over again: John wants to save Jane from all the heartache caused by her mysterious lover, only for John to fall in love with Jane and cause the same situation he tried to prevent. John's very future depends upon him travelling back to the past, ensuring he gets his younger female self, Jane, pregnant, and then (as temporal agent) stealing her child, travelling with her back to 1945 and dropping her off at an orphanage where she will grow up to become them. She is forced to repeat the process over and over again inside an endless loop, or else cease to exist. Therefore, Jane, John, the temporal agent and the Fizzle Bomber all turn out to be the same person caught inside a closed time loop, with the temporal agent becoming the Fizzle Bomber after his decommission in the 1970s.

It is not clear, at the end of the movie, if the time loop continues or whether Hawke manages to break the loop and split it into alternative timelines (as in the many-worlds theory of the collapse of quantum oscillations) – both versions can be supported. On the one hand, a predestination paradox states that if time travel were possible, it would be impossible to change the past, and any attempt to do so would become the precipitating event for the change we are trying to make (imagine a time traveller going back in time to save a friend from being hit by a car, only to discover he is the man driving the car that killed his friend). (The reverse also holds: the event can happen only if we try to avoid it – only in this way does Oedipus kill his father or the servant meet Death.) The Bomber in the film sharpens this paradox: he commits crimes (explosions triggered by him kill people, to prevent greater crimes) and ends up doing what he is trying to prevent, like Pétainists in France who were arresting Jews and delivering them to Nazis to prevent Nazis doing this more brutally, and at the end doing all the job for them. (Or like the obsessive subject who never directly performs sex as such but just engages in sex to train himself for the real sex; or like writers who write endless preparatory versions of a story, never the story itself. The shocking discovery to be made is that this preparatory activity – sex, writing – is already the thing itself. Perhaps, we, humans, cannot ever do directly the thing itself.) The film ends with this paradox: the temporal agent confronts the Bomber, his future self, and kills him to prevent him killing thousands; however, as the Bomber warns him, in this way the agent just makes it certain that he will become the Bomber – the only way to really cut the loop would have been for the agent to let the Bomber live, become friendly with him, and convince him of the futility of his murderous acts. So already at a purely formal level, in killing the Bomber, the agent obeys the latter's logic – he kills in order to prevent a greater killing.

The extreme version of the temporal loop is the craziest theory in atomic physics: according to it, our entire universe consists of only one atom which travels back in time infinitely, encountering and interacting with itself in its previous versions. On the other hand, the many-worlds theory would claim that every time we travel back in time and actually manage to change events, we are only ever managing to create a new, alternate timeline. So how are we to choose between these two options? The first thing to do is to note how sexual difference overdetermines the opposition between temporal loop and linear time: the loop is feminine and the linear time masculine. This is why, if one takes a closer look at the story line of *Predestination*, it immediately becomes clear that the focal point of the story, the agent of the series of metamorphoses, is not the temporal agent but Jane. Jane is extraordinary, a strong, ultra-intelligent hermaphrodite, and her change of sex from female to male after she gives birth is a real transformation in real linear time. It is thus Jane who will keep impregnating herself and then stealing her own baby and sending it back in time to become her forever. After she becomes a man she will get her face blown off; then, with her face repaired, she will look like the temporal agent (Hawke) and eventually go crazy from time travelling too much and become the Bomber.

One should nonetheless note that this maternal loop is not complete, wholly self-enclosed – Mr Robertson, the mysterious boss of the Temporal Bureau, is external to it, he is not just another version of the same person. The boss stands for science, for the invention of time travel in 1981, which only rendered possible Jane's self-impregnating circular movement. But is then the temporal loop really eternal, without beginning and end? Is it not that, in our linear time, Jane couldn't have been sent back before 1981 when time travel was invented, so she had to exist in 1981 in order to be sent back? But what if even in her existence before 1981 she was sent there from the future? What one should bear in mind is that if the temporal loop is broken it is retroactively undone, i.e. *it was never operative*. (Such a temporal causality loop exists separate from ordinary space-time: while time repeats itself within the closed loop, for those people outside the loop time continues in a normal, linear manner. This does not mean that linear time is the only reality, and that temporal loops are just imagined circles which don't exist in 'actual' reality: the continuous flow of actual reality itself is an illusion since it can sustain itself only through temporal loops.)

Since, however, there is no time travel in our world, we should raise a simple question: is there a phenomenon in our reality which echoes the temporal loop? A phenomenon which allows us, in some qualified sense, to change the past, a phenomenon whose basic principle is that of retroactivity? The answer is no surprise: the symbolic order which has no outside (once we dwell within it) since it always presupposes itself. (One should add the Hegelian Spirit which is the result of itself, of its own activity.) Recall the structuralist idea that one cannot think the genesis of the symbolic (order) – one should note here, as a curiosity, that in 1866, the Société linguistique de Paris formally prohibited to its members any research into the origins of language, claiming that it exceeds the cognitive capacities of men: 'The society will not admit any communication which concerns the origins of language.'[16] The symbolic order is, once it is here, always-already here, one cannot step outside it, all one can do is to tell myths about its genesis (which Lacan engages in occasionally). Recall the wonderful title of Alexei Yurchak's book about the last Soviet generation: *Everything Was Forever, Until It Was No More* – the point we are looking for is its exact inversion of this rupture: nothing of it (the symbolic order) was here, until all of it was all of a sudden *always-already here*. The problem here is the emergence of a self-relating 'closed' system which has no outside: it cannot be explained from outside because its constitutive act is self-relating, that is, the system fully emerges once it starts to cause itself, to posit its presuppositions in a closed loop. So it's not just that the symbolic order is all of a sudden fully here – there was nothing, and a moment later it is all here – but that there is nothing and then, all of a sudden, it is as if the symbolic order was *always-already here*, as if there was never a time without it. Language has no externality because there is no metalanguage: we cannot step outside of language and draw a line of separation between language and reality external to it since our approach to reality is always-already mediated through language, this self-relating totality. But the other side of this circularity of the symbolic order, of the fact that it has no outside, is that reality is totally indifferent towards it, nonaffected by it, with no relation towards it. Magic is precisely the illusion of words directly affecting things – it is only with science that language touches the real: scientific inventions enable us to generate new entities that previously did not exist in reality. Therein resides the monstrosity of science: it enables us to construct new 'unnatural' (inhuman) objects which cannot but appear to our experience as freaks of nature (gadgets, genetically modified organisms, cyborgs, etc.). The power of human culture is not only to build an autonomous symbolic universe beyond what we experience as nature, but to produce new, 'unnatural' natural objects which materialize human knowledge. We not only 'symbolize nature', we as it were denaturalize it from within. Such moments when 'the word becomes flesh' are truly terrifying.

How far does the power of retroactivity reach? In his essay on the Ratman case ('Notes upon a Case of Obsessional Neurosis', 1909), Freud describes a wonderful compulsive act of his patient:

> One day, when he was out with her [his lady] in a boat and there was a stiff breeze blowing, he was obliged to make her put on his cap, because a command had been formulated in his mind that *nothing must happen to her*. This was a kind of obsession for protecting, and it bore other fruit besides this … On the day of her departure he knocked his foot against a stone lying in the road, because the idea struck him that her carriage would be driving along the same road in a few hours' time and might come to grief against this stone. But a few minutes later it occurred to him that this was absurd, and he was obliged to go back and replace the stone in the original position in the middle of the road.[17]

When he 'spontaneously' kicked the stone to the middle of the road, Ratman thereby articulated his aggressivity towards the lady. The reason he immediately afterwards returns the stone to its previous place is not simply the insight into the exaggerated, absurd even, nature of his fear, but a deeper suspicion that his kicking the stone displays his aggressivity towards the lady; so he puts the stone back to erase the trace of his desire. In short, we can understand Ratman's meaningless double gesture only if we include the level of desire: the point of putting back the stone is to 'correct' a disturbance in reality into which his desire inscribed itself. And, as is always the case with obsessional rituals, this erasure spectacularly fails: after it occurred to Ratman that his fear that his lady might come to grief agaist this stone is absurd, *why did he feel obliged to go back and replace it to the original position?* Why didn't he simply leave the stone where it landed when he kicked it, off the road, and just laugh at the absurdity of his act? Isn't this compulsion to put the stone back to its original position a proof of the libidinal investment in it, a monument to Ratman's desire to hurt his lady? In short, isn't his act of putting the stone back, i.e. his effort to erase the traces of his desire, the only proof of this desire?

This mechanism of undoing is characteristic of obsessional neurosis, along with isolation. It involves a process of 'negative magic' that tends to undo what has been done: when an action is undone by a second action, it is as if neither had occurred, whereas in reality both have taken place. In 'Inhibitions, Symptoms and Anxiety' (1926), Freud points out the difference between undoing and repression: repression merely obfuscates a traumatic event which remains there, while the obsessive ceremony strives not only to prevent the appearance of a traumatic event but to undo it, which is 'irrational' and magical. How does this obsessive undoing relate to so-called empty gestures, offers which are rejected, proclaimed super-fluous, but which precisely as such fulfil their function?

When, after being engaged in a fierce competition for a job promotion with my closest friend, I win, the proper thing to do is to offer to retract, so that he will get the promotion, and the proper thing for him to do is to reject my offer – this way, perhaps, our friendship can be saved. What we have here is symbolic exchange at its purest: a gesture made to be rejected. The magic of symbolic exchange is that, although at the end we are where we were at the beginning, there is a distinct gain for both parties in their pact of solidarity. This paradox is brought to a climax in a scene from the English working-class drama *Brassed Off* in which the hero accompanies home a pretty young woman who, at the entrance to her flat, asks him: 'Would you like to come in for a coffee?' To his answer – 'There is a problem – I don't drink coffee' – she retorts with a smile: 'No problem – I don't have any ...' The immense, direct erotic power of her reply resides in how, through a double negation, she articulates an embarrassingly direct sexual invitation without ever mentioning sex: when she first invites the guy in for a coffee and then admits she has no coffee, she does not cancel her invitation, she just makes it clear that the first invitation for a coffee was a stand-in (or pretext), indifferent in itself, for the invitation to sex.

Although there is a purely formal similarity between these cases of 'offers meant to be rejected' and the obsessional undoing of the past (in both cases, the first gesture is undone or rejected, so that the final result is zero), there is a basic difference between the two series. In the first series the past is not undone, the whole procedure – making the offer and rejecting it – is fully admitted since it 'makes sense', the sense of asserting basic benevolence of both partners, while in the case of obsessional undoing, there is a magic component at work, the second gesture tries literally to undo the first one, to bring things back to the state prior to it. We are thereby in the midst of a theological problematic: how far does divine omnipotence reach? Can god not only perform miracles in the present but also undo factual past, can he make it that what effectively happened in the past never happened? In his Seminar X, on anxiety (1962–3), Lacan tackles this topic by way of providing one of the clearest definitions of what atheism means from the psychoanalytic standpoint; he begins with

> a question which was raised in what I could call the heated circles of analysis, the ones in which there still lives the movement of a primary inspiration, namely whether the analyst ought or ought not to be an atheist and if the subject, at the end of analysis, can consider his analysis terminated if he still believes in God … Whatever an obsessional testifies to you in his remarks, if he has not been routed out of his obsessional structure, you can be quite persuaded that qua obsessional he still believes in God, I mean that he believes in the God that everybody or almost everybody in our cultural arena, in the God that everybody believes in without believing in him, namely this universal eye that is brought to bear on all our actions … Such is the veritable dimension of atheism: the one which is supposed to have succeeded in eliminating the phantasy of the Omnipotent … The existence therefore of the atheist in the true sense can only be conceived of in effect at the limit of an ascesis, which indeed, as it appears to us, can only be a psychoanalytic ascesis, I mean the ascesis of an atheism conceived of as a negation of this dimension of presence, at the basis of the world of omnipotence.[18]

The 'eliminating the phantasy of the Omnipotent' is what will become, a year later (in Seminar XI), 'traversing the fantasy'; how? It is not enough to simply assume that there is no omnipotent/omnivoyant Other? The inner link between omnipotence and impotence is a much more twisted one: the spectre of omnipotence arises out of the very experience of impotence, and this paradoxical reversal of omnipotence in impotence is what characterizes the phallic signifier, the instrument of potency, of vitality, and simultaneously the signifier of castration, which is why the phallus never appears except as lack, and this is its link with anxiety. And all of this means that the phallus is called on to function as an instrument of potency. Now potency, I mean what we are speaking about when we speak about potency, when we speak about it in a fashion which vacillates about what is involved – for it is always to omnipotence that we refer ourselves; now that is not what is involved, omnipotence is already the slippage, the evasion with respect to this point at which all potency fails – one does not demand potency to be everywhere, one demands it to be where it is present. It is precisely because it fails where it is expected that we begin to foment omnipotence. In other words: the phallus is present, it is present everywhere where it is not up to it.[19]

In short, the spectre of omnipotence arises when we stumble upon the limitation of the Other's potency: *toute-puissance* (omnipotence) is *toute-en-puissance* (all-in-potentiality), the actualization of its power/potency is always constrained:

> Omnipotency is for Lacan not a kind of maximum, apex, or even infinitization of potency – to what one often reduces it in order to deny its actual existence – but a beyond of potency which only appears in the latter's failure. It does not appear on the slope of impotence but on the slope of what remains 'all in potency', without ever passing over into the dimension of an act which belongs to the domain of some determinate potency/power.[20]

In every field of normativity there is a blind spot of facticity, a point at which the opposition of factuality and normativity breaks down and factuality pops up in the midst of a normative order (even in Kantian ethics, this facticity arises in the guise of what Kant calls the inexplicable 'fact of reason'). In theology, this blind spot appears as the abyss of the divine omnipotent will which is not bound by any laws, not even the (natural and moral) laws he himself imposed on the created world; in psychoanalysis, it appears in the guise of the capricious 'primordial (pre-Oedipal) mother' to whose whims the small child is exposed without any protective screen of laws; in the legal social order, it is the capriciousness of sovereign power noted, among others, by Jean Bodin, who wrote that 'the sovereign prince cannot bind himself, even if he wishes. For this reason edicts and ordinances conclude with the formula 'for such is our good pleasure', thus intimating that the laws of a sovereign prince, even when founded on truth and right reason, proceed simply from his own free will.'[21] Every legal power, no matter how 'democratic' it appears, no matter how much it is constrained by laws and regulations, has to be sustained by an underground echo of 'But ultimately, they can do whatever they want with us!' – without this echo, power simply loses its authority. Does the same not hold for the divine Predestination? God's decision to save some of us and to condemn others for eternity is not 'founded on truth and right reason' (how could it be when we were not even created when this decision was made?), it was made simply *for such was His good pleasure* ... Such experience of omnipotence is rooted in the small child's dependency on his/her mother, the first love object which has the inexplicable power of arbitrarily providing or withdrawing pleasure and objects which satisfy the child's needs. Insofar as the child cannot guess why mother decided to do this and not that when his/her very survival depends on such impenetrable decisions, s/he cannot but experience her as an omnipotent agent. In the same way, the protestant God of Predetermination is an agent of pure caprice, with his omnipotence the mode of appearance of the fact that he himself doesn't know what he is doing. Already towards the end of his Seminar V, 'Formations of the Unconscious', which was delivered five years earlier (1957–8), Lacan outlined the contours of this link between omnipotence and impotence, describing how such a total dependency on the omnipotent mother which cannot but cause anxiety is overcome when the child notices that this omnipotent (M)Other is itself 'symbolized', subordinated to an 'Other of the Other', that it itself obeys a Law:

> no mental life could be organized, which corresponds to what we are given in experience, to what experience articulates in analysis, if there is not a beyond of this Other primordially placed in the position of omnipotence ... with the ambiguity of promise and of refusal that is contained in this term. That there is I might say, the Other of this Other, namely what permits this other locus of the word, which the subject perceives it as itself symbolised, namely that there is this Other of the Other.[22]

For those who know Lacan, it is impossible to miss the irony of the last sentence: the 'Other of the Other' designates exactly what later becomes 'there is no Other of the Other'. In both cases, the point is that the Other is in itself 'castrated', incomplete, thwarted, far from a perfectly organized symbolic network or machine:

> Only the Other is not that. It is precisely not purely and simply the locus which is this something perfectly organised, fixed, rigid. It is an Other which is itself symbolised. This is what gives it its appearance of

liberty. It is a fact that it is symbolised, and that what happens at this level of the Other of the Other, namely of the father in this instance, of the locus where the law is articulated from the point of the perspective of the one who depends on an Other; this Other is itself subjected to signifying articulation, more than subjected to signifying articulation, marked by something which is the denaturing effect – let us strongly underline it – of our thinking, of this presence of the signifier ... of this effect of the signifier on the Other as such, of this mark of it that it was subjected to at this level. It is this mark that represents castration as such.[23]

Is Lacan's target here not his own elevation of the Symbolic into a perfect machine which regulates the entire space of subjective experience, the elevation which provides the tonality of the Seminars II and III? Exemplary here is the true hymn to structural overdetermination from the beginning of his 'Seminar on "The Purloined Letter"' which opens his *Écrits*:

I am, of course, aware of the importance of imaginary impregnations in the partializations of the symbolic alternative that give the signifying chain its appearance. Nevertheless, I posit that it is the law specific to this chain which governs the psychoanalytic effects that are determinant for the subject – effects such as foreclosure (*Verwerfung*), repression (*Verdraengung*), and negation (*Verneinung*) itself – and I add with the appropriate emphasis that these effects follow the displacement (*Entstellung*) of the signifier so faithfully that imaginary factors, despite their inertia, figure only as shadows and reflections therein.[24]

Le Gaufey's formula is '*la toute-puissance sans tout-puissant*':[25] omnipotency is a fact of the symbolic universe in which we can retroactively change the past, and the proper atheist/materialist position is not to deny omnipotence but to assert it without an agent that sustains it (God or another omnipotent Entity) – but is this enough? Do we not have to take a further step and assert the thwarted (inconsistent, constrained) character of the big Other qua depersonalized structure? And it is precisely this inconsistency/limitation of the big Other that resubjectivizes it in the sense of raising the question: 'But what does the Other want?' And, of course, in a Hegelian way, this enigma of the Other's desire is an enigma for the Other itself. Only at this level do we reach 'symbolic castration' which does not stand for the subject's 'castration', for his/her being at the mercy of the big Other, for his/her depending on its whims, but for the 'castration' of this Other itself. The barred Other is thus not just the depersonalized Other but also the bar which cracks this depersonalized Other itself.[26]

The twelfth camel as one of the names of god

Does the same counterfactual logic not sustain the famous joke from Lubitsch's *Ninotchka*: "'Waiter! Get me a cup of coffee without cream!' 'I'm sorry, sir, we have no cream, only milk, so can it be a coffee without milk?'"? At the factual level, coffee remains the same coffee, but what we can change is to make the coffee without cream into a coffee without milk – or, more simply even, to add the implied negation and to make the plain coffee into a coffee without milk, as in Robert Schumann's *Humoreske* with its famous 'inner voice' (*innere Stimme*) added by Schumann (in the written score) as a third line between the two piano lines, higher and lower: as the vocal melodic line which remains a nonvocalized 'inner voice' (which exists only as *Augenmusik*, music for the eyes only, in the guise of written notes). This absent melody is to be reconstructed on the basis of the fact that the first and third levels (the right- and the left-hand piano lines) do not relate to each other directly; that is, their relationship is not that of an immediate mirroring: in order to account for their interconnection, one is thus compelled to (re)construct a third, 'virtual' intermediate level (melodic line) which, for structural reasons, cannot be played. Schumann takes this use of the absent melody to an apparently absurd level of self-reference when, later in the same fragment of *Humoreske*, he repeats the same two actually played melodic lines, yet this time the score contains no third absent melodic line, no inner voice – so that what is absent here is the absent melody, absence itself. How are we to play these notes when, at the level of what is actually to be played, they repeat the previous notes exactly? The actually played notes are deprived only of what is not there, of their constitutive lack. Consequently, when we suspend the symbolic efficiency of the inexistent 'third melody', we do not simply return to the explicit line; what we get is a double negation – in terms of the Lubitsch joke, we do not get straight coffee, but a no-no-milk coffee; in terms of Schumann's piece, we do not get a straight melody, but a melody which lacks the lack itself, in which the lacking 'third line' is itself lacking. We thus pass from the counterfactual statement 'If we were to have cream (but we do not have it) I would have served you coffee without cream' to the factual statement 'If you ask for coffee without milk (but you did not) I can serve it to you'.

This is how we can change the counterfactual past: the same plain coffee changes from 'without cream' to 'without milk', and the 'without' functions here in the precise mode of what Hegel calls 'determinate negation': it concerns what is negated in 'plain coffee', cream or milk. The political implications are far-reaching here: 'determinate negation' in a political process means that it is not enough to directly assert universality against particular identity – the specific path to universality matters: *which* particularity is negated in a new universality? If, in a conflict between universality of human rights and black identity, the universality is directly the white liberal one, then blacks are called to join it, to sacrifice part of themselves. The white-liberal universality is therefore falsely universal, which is why universality had to proceed as growing out of the Black Power process. The paradox is thus that the overcoming of black identity politics has to proceed as a double negation: yes, one should negate exclusive black particularity, but one should simultaneously negate the hegemonic white universality which secretly privileges whites. Say, in France today, the true representative of *égalité/liberté* is not a pure Frenchman, a Frenchman *sans phrase*, advocating universal citizenship and exerting pressure on African immigrants to abandon their local customs and integrate themselves into the French way of life, but precisely those immigrants who want to be part of French society as equals and reject anti-immigrant populists – they are literally more French than Frenchmen themselves. What this means at a more general level is that the missed opportunities of our life, what we failed to do, are part of the identity of our life: to 'know myself' is not only knowing about what I did, it includes what I failed to do. Commenting on Randall Jarrell's line 'The ways we miss our lives are life', Adam Phillips said:

> What's painful about it? It could be extremely comforting, couldn't it? It could be a way of saying, Actually, that's what life is, it's the lives you don't have. As if to say, Don't worry, because that's what a life is. Or just that missing all our supposed other lives is something modern people are keen to do. We are just addicted to alternatives, fascinated by what we can never do. As if we all had the wrong parents, or the wrong bodies, or the wrong luck.[27]

Maybe we should redefine a 'rich life' along these lines: it is not the life I actually live but my actual life together with all alternate lives that I miss while I live this one life, it's the panoply of all possible lives which defines my situation. Vladimir Sharov's novel *Before and During* deploys crazy variations on the Russian history of the nineteenth and twentieth centuries: Leo Tolstoy's twin brother is eaten by the writer in his mother's womb and is then reborn as Leo's son; a self-replicating Madame de Staël becomes the lover of the philosopher-hermit Nikolai Fyodorov, who claims the task of humanity is physical resurrection; and so on. Sharov is totally justified in emphasizing that we are not dealing here with alternate histories but with additional layers of the actual history itself: 'I write the entirely real history of thoughts, intentions and beliefs. This is the country that existed. This is our own madness, our own absurd.'[28]

A person's actual life is thus a kind of two-dimensional surface on which the three-dimensional multiplicity of what might have happened to him/her is superposed over his/her actuality. In a similar vein, relying on the Kaballah notion of created reality as a 'broken vessel' that needs to be put together by believers, Walter Benjamin, in his early essay 'The Task of the Translator', used it to discern the inner working of the process of translation:

> Just as fragments of a vessel, in order to be articulated together, must follow one another in the smallest detail but need not resemble one another, so, instead of making itself similar to the meaning of the original, the translation must rather, lovingly and in detail, in its own language, form itself according to the way of signifying [*Art des Meinens*] of the original, to make both recognizable as the broken parts of a greater language, just as fragments are the broken parts of a vessel.[29]

The movement described here by Benjamin is a kind of transposition of metaphor into metonymy: instead of conceiving translation as a metaphoric substitute of the original, as something that should render as faithfully as possible the meaning of the original, both original and its translation are posited as belonging to the same level, parts of the same field (in the same way that Claude Lévi-Strauss claimed that the main interpretations of the Oedipus myth are themselves new versions of the myth). The gap that, in the traditional view, separates the original from its (always imperfect) translation is thus transposed back into the original itself: the original itself is already the fragment of a broken vessel, so that the goal of the translation is not to achieve fidelity to the original but to supplement the original, to treat the original as a broken fragment of the 'broken vessel' and to produce another fragment which will not imitate the original but will fit it as one fragment of a broken Whole may fit another. What this means is that a good translation destroys the myth of the original's organic Wholeness, it renders this Wholeness visible as a fake. One can even say that, far from being an attempt to restore the broken vessel, translation is the very act of breaking: once the translation sets in, the original organic vessel appears as a fragment that has to be supplemented – breaking the vessel *is* its opening to its restoration.

In the domain of telling stories, a gesture homologous to translation would have been a change in the plot of the original narrative which makes us think 'it is only now that we really understand what the story is about'. Zachary Mason's *The Lost Books of the Odyssey*[30] contains a series of variations on Homer's 'official' story presented as fragments from the (recently discovered) vast chaotic mess of legends out of which Homer cut out and refashioned his epic poem: Odysseus returns home to Ithaca and finds that, following the ancient custom, Penelope married another man who is a good king; Polyphemus really was a quiet farmer who found Odysseus and his men in his cave, stuffing their faces with his provisions; the old Odysseus visits again the ruins of Troy and finds it has become a market town, where there are vendors and actors working the crowd, 'aping famous Greeks and Trojans'; and so forth. These (imagined) variations should not be read as distortions of some lost primordial original, but as fragments of a totality which would have consisted in the matrix of all possible (in the sense in which Lévi-Strauss claims that interpretations of the Oedipus myth, including that of Freud, are part of the myth). Should we then endeavour to reconstruct the full matrix? What we should do is rather to locate the traumatic point, the antagonism, which remains untold and around which all variations and fragments circulate.

Raymond Khoury's *The Templar Salvation* (2010) presents an interesting variation on the basic motif of religious thrillers: the secret document that threatens to destroy Christianity if rendered public is here the collection of all texts – gospels, letters, ruminations, and other fragments – which were not included in the Bible when the emperor Constantine established Christian orthodoxy. The hypothesis of the novel is that Constantine ordered all these excluded documents to be burned, fearing that such an inconsistent mess would fuel endless quarrels of interpretation, but Constantine's advisor Hosius refused to carry out his order and stashed them in a safe, secret place where they are discovered by Templars ... Even in fictional terms, one should not overestimate such a discovery: *The Templar Salvation* can be read as an exemplary case of restoring the 'broken vessel', of relocating the Bible into the complex and inconsistent network of variations out of which it was selected, so that the truth does not reside in any single version but in the very superposition of incompatible versions. (This, of course, has nothing to do with any kind of postmodern relativism and plurality of truths: the superposition of incompatible versions always points towards a singular oppressed/excluded traumatic truth.) However, as for the predominant tendency of the rediscovered documents, we get the standard mess of gnostic inner spirituality (god is deep in your soul, etc. – the line which later culminates in the Cathar movement) and of social-revolutionary messianism (Christ wanted to establish the Kingdom of God – a Jewish state freed from Roman domination – on this earth), the two extremes that the church tried to repress. (Incidentally, what about a much more dark version in which the hidden manuscripts demonstrate that Christ was a brutal egotist prone to violent outbursts, something like an ancient Rasputin displaying a mixture of sanctity and obscenity, or that he was a puppet secretly supported by Romans in their effort to undermine Jewish institutions?) One is almost tempted to say that the church was basically right in this choice: the two rejected choices stand for the alternative of gnostic universalism limited to inner life, and of radical social transformation limited to one's own ethnic group. What about a universalism which is asserted at the level of actual social life, as the emancipation of humankind in its entirety, not just of a particular ethnic group? The true distinction takes place here: between the universality of a hierarchic social institution (church), and the no-hierarchic universality whose model is the rejects.

But is the supreme case of a 'broken vessel' not the Seven Last Words of Christ? (1) *Father, forgive them, for they know not what they do* (Lk. 23.34); (2) *Truly, I say to you, today you will be with me in paradise* (Lk. 23.43); (3) *Woman, behold your son: behold your mother* (Jn 19.26-27); (4) *My God, my God, why have you forsaken me* (Mt. 27.46 and Mk 15.34); (5) *I thirst* (Jn 19.28); (6) *It is finished* (Jn 19.30); (7) *Father, into your hands I commit my spirit* (Lk. 23.46). The most stupid thing imaginable one can do with them is what Franco Zefirelli and Mel Gibson did in their kitsch cinematic versions: they use all of them, with Christ pronouncing one after the other while dying on the Cross – the effect is one of a ridiculous and suffocating excess, there is too much of it, as in some Hollywood films or classic operas where the dying hero miraculously goes on talking, delivering his message in its entirety although he should have dropped dead a long time ago. Instead of striving for this kind of unification, one should treat the seven last words as what they call in quantum physics the superposition of multiple quantum states, as synchronous alternate versions which are in a way 'all true' – their truth does not reside in a single narrative or in conceiving the seven versions as fragmentary remainders of a consistent single original; it resides in the way the seven versions resonate among themselves, interpreting each other. This, perhaps, is also the ultimate lesson of Christianity: Judaism conceives our universe as a broken vessel, that is, as the result of a cosmic catastrophe, with the endless task to gather the broken pieces and reconstruct the universe as a harmonious Whole, while Christianity, at its most radical, conceives the act of breaking itself as the outburst of divine creativity. As is often the case, it was G. K. Chesterton who made this point clearly and with a direct reference to broken vessel:

> It is the instinct of Christianity to be glad that God has broken the universe into little pieces ... All modern philosophies are chains which connect and fetter; Christianity is a sword which separates and sets free. No other philosophy makes God actually rejoice in the separation of the universe into living souls.[31]

So what if we apply Benjamin's notion of translation to the very relationship between god and man, to the notion that man was made in the likeness of god? Instead of making himself similar to god, man must rather, lovingly and in detail, in his own way, form himself according to the way of god, to make both recognizable as the broken parts of a greater vessel. The gap that, in the traditional view, separates the perfect god from his (always imperfect) human image is thus transposed back into god itself: god himself is imperfect, already the fragment of a broken vessel, so that he needs man to supplement his imperfection, and the goal of humanity is not to achieve fidelity or likeness to god but to supplement god, to treat god as a fragment of the 'broken vessel' and to make itself into another fragment which will not imitate god's perfection but will fit it as one fragment of a broken Whole may fit another. The topic of the divine Trinity, of Christ's doubt on the Cross, and other similar motifs, clearly indicate that in Christianity, the 'broken vessel' is not only the created reality which fell from god and lost its perfection – *the ultimate broken vessel is god himself.* Father, Son, and the Holy Spirit should thus be conceived as three fragments of the vessel whose unity is forever lost.

Furthermore, it is crucial to link this specific notion of the counterfactual to Lacan's distinction, developed in his Seminar XX, 'Encore', between phallic *jouissance* and the other (feminine) *jouissance*: only phallic enjoyment is (f)actual, actually existing, while the other (feminine) *jouissance* is counterfactual:

It is the enjoyment which is not required / doesn't fail [*il ne faut pas*] that I believed I could call conditional. This suggests to us, for it to be used, the protasis, and the apodosis. It is: if it were not for that, things would have gone better – conditional in the second part. Material implication, which the Stoics realized was perhaps what was most solid in logic.

Enjoyment then. How are we going to express what is not required / does not fail in its regard, if not by the following. If there were an enjoyment other than phallic … if there were another one, it would not be required / it would be false that it should be this one … The first part – if there were another of them – designates something false: there is no other of them than phallic enjoyment. It is then false that there is another. Which does not prevent what follows – namely, that it must not be that one – from being true. You know that it is quite correct, that when the true is deduced from the false, it is valid, the implication works. The only thing that cannot be admitted is that from the true there follows the false … Suppose that there is another one, but precisely there is not, and, at the same time, it is not because there is not and that it is from this that there depends the *it is not required*.[32]

(It is easy for a careful reader to discern here the paradoxical prohibition of something which is already in itself impossible: *jouissance féminine* doesn't exist, and nonetheless it is not required.) Do Lacan's formulas of sexuation also not point in the same direction? 'There is no x which is not subordinated to the phallic function', i.e. there is no exception at the factual level, all positively existing enjoyment is phallic. What makes the situation 'feminine' is just the non-all of its (actual) elements, i.e. the fact that they cannot be totalized, that they are never 'all' – why? Because they are always supplemented by the superposition of counterfactuals, of what may have been if it were … (but it's not). Exactly the same holds also for God who, for Lacan, possesses not actual existence but counterfactual ex-sistence – *l'inexistence divine*, as Quentin Meillassoux put it: god qua real is like the impossible *jouissance*: it never was here *and* we cannot get rid of it, or, in the case of god, there is not god *and* it continues to haunt us in its very inexistence.

Dupuy often mentions the ancient story of the twelfth camel: an Arab merchant dies and leaves to his three sons eleven camels, with the precise instructions on how to distribute them: the first son gets half of the camels, the second one-third, and the third one-sixth. So how to do it when 11 is not divisible by 2, 3 or 6? A wise judge proposes the solution: he will add just to the sum a camel of his own. Now we have twelve camels and the first son gets six, the second three, and the third two, together eleven; the judge then takes back the camel he added, so that he is not at a loss … (Niklas Luhmann has written a book on this.) The key feature is here that one can also merely imagine the twelfth camel – it needn't exist in reality. And is god not something like the twelfth camel, is the twelfth camel not one of the names for god, a lie (a nonexisting entity) which makes things clear? So does god exist or not? It does not exist as a fact, but it inexists counterfactually, which does not meant that it is simply an illusion: it is the paradox of an illusion which is immanent to reality itself, a counterfactual immanent to factuals, to our symbolic universe:

> It is really fabulous that the function of the other, of the other as locus of the truth, and in a word of the only place, even though an irreducible one, that we can give to the term of Divine Being, of God to call him by his name. God is properly the locus where, if you will allow me the term, there is produced the *dieu*, the *dieur*, the *dire*, for a trifle, *dire* gives us *Dieu*.
>
> As long as something is said, the God hypothesis will be there. And it is precisely as trying to say something that there is defined the fact that, in short, there can be no true atheists other than theologians. Namely, those who speak about God.[33]

It is in this sense that Lacan speaks of the 'God hypothesis' (ironically referring, of course, to Lamarck's famous reply to Napoleon, that in his theory of nature he had no need for such a hypothesis) – in the same sense in which Badiou talks about the 'Communist hypothesis'. This is why it is not enough for a materialist to deny god's existence, he must also qualify his counterfactual ex-sistence: if there were a God (which there is not), he would not have been a being of supreme Good, a beautiful illusion, but an evil, cruel, ignorant God – this is the point made by *The Rapture*.

A truth that arises out of a lie

The epistemological lesson of this paradox of counterfactuals is thus a weird one: it is not only that one can deduce a true statement from a false premise (what already the ancient Stoics knew); in some precisely defined cases, it is only if we take as our starting point a false premise that we can clearly see the true in its proper contours, or, to make the same point in different terms, it is only from a counterfactual premise that we can grasp the truth of the factual. The big problem of the cognitive process is thus not simply to get rid of the lies and illusions, but how to select the right lie, a lie which eventually can enable us to arrive at the truth – if we want to go directly for truth, we lose the truth itself. In Robert Harris's *The Ghost* (filmed by Polanski), a ghostwriter for Adam Lang, the UK former prime minister modelled on Tony Blair, discovers that Lang was planted in the Labour Party and manipulated all along by the CIA; the *New York Observer* commented that the book's 'shock-horror revelation' was 'so shocking it simply can't be true, though if it were it would certainly explain pretty much everything about the recent history of Great Britain'. Do we not find here a perfect example of counterfactual statement: 'If Blair were to be a CIA agent – which he was not – it would explain everything about recent UK politics'? In other words, the plot of *The Ghost* is the perfect case of a lie, a false premise, which enables us to see the truth of the Blair years, a counterfactual premise which renders palpable actual truth.[34]

So what happens when we reject this detour through a lie and want to stick to pure factual truth? The outcome is a psychotic rejection of the proper symbolic dimension. Recall the well-known Italian expression *se non e vero, e ben'trovato* – '(even) if it is not true, it is well-found (it hits the mark)'. In this sense, anecdotes about famous persons, even when invented, often characterize the core of their personality more appropriately than the enumeration of their real qualities – here also, lie is a path towards truth or, as Lacan put it, 'truth has the structure of a fiction'. There is a wonderfully obscene Serbo-Croat version of this expression which perfectly renders the protopsychotic rejection of the symbolic fiction: *se non e vero, jebem ti mater!* 'Jebem ti mater' (pronounced 'yebem ti mater', meaning 'I'll fuck your mother') is one of the most popular vulgar insults; the joke, of course, relies on the perfect rhyme, with the same accents and number of syllables, between *e ben'trovato* and *jebem ti mater*. The meaning thus changes into the explosion of rage in the incestuous direction, attacking the other's most intimate primordial object: 'It better be true – if it is not true, I'll fuck your mother!' These two versions thus clearly enact the two reactions to what literally turns to be a lie: its furious rejection, or its 'subl(im)ation' into a 'higher' truth. In psychoanalytic terms, their difference is the one between foreclosure (*Verwerfung*) and symbolic transubstantiation.[35]

Yet another example of a lie which renders the truth visible concerns political jokes in late communist regimes. One of the popular myths in Eastern Europe was that there was a department of the secret police whose function was (not to collect, but) to invent and put in circulation political jokes against the regime and its representatives, as they were aware of jokes' positive stabilizing function (political jokes offer to ordinary people an easy and tolerable way to blow off steam, easing their frustrations). Attractive as it is, this myth ignores a rarely mentioned but nonetheless crucial feature of jokes: they never seem to have an author, as if the question 'who is the author of this joke?' were an impossible one. Jokes are originally 'told', they are always-already 'heard' (recall the proverbial 'Did you hear that joke about …?').[36] Therein resides their mystery: they are idiosyncratic, they stand for the unique creativity of language, but are nonetheless 'collective', anonymous, authorless, all of a sudden here out of nowhere. The idea that there has to be an author of a joke is properly paranoiac: it means that there has to be an 'Other of the Other', of the anonymous symbolic order, as if the very unfathomable contingent generative power of language has to be personalized, located into an agent who controls it and secretly pulls the strings … However, although the idea of a secret department fabricating political jokes is false at the factual level, it renders visible the truth about the stabilizing role of these jokes, about how the transgression enacted by telling them was a false one.

Is not the Idea of communism also such a lie (a false utopian notion) which enables us to see the truth about the existing capitalist system and its antagonisms? Yes, but in a very specific way. The traditional Marxist notion of communism is false in the sense that it remains immanent to the capitalist universe. Every historical situation contains its own unique utopian perspective, an immanent vision of what is wrong with it, an ideal representation of how, with some changes, the situation could be made much better. When the desire for a radical social change emerges, it is thus logical that it first endeavours to actualize this immanent utopian vision – and this endeavour is what characterizes every authentic emancipatory struggle. So the critics of communism were in a way right when they claimed that the Marxian communism is an impossible fantasy; what they did not perceive is that the Marxian communism, this notion of a society of pure unleashed productivity outside the frame of capital, was a fantasy inherent to capitalism itself, the capitalist inherent transgression at its purest, a strictly ideological fantasy of maintaining the thrust to productivity generated by capitalism, while getting rid of the 'obstacles' and antagonisms that were – as the sad experience of the 'really existing capitalism' demonstrates – the only possible framework of the effective material existence of a society of permanent self-enhancing productivity. This, however, should not seduce us into abandoning the very idea of communism – on the contrary, this idea should be conceived in a strict Hegelian sense, as a notion which transforms itself in the course of its actualization.

The divine death drive

So where does this bring us with regard to materialist theology? If one wants to engage seriously – which means from the standpoint of radical emancipatory politics – in the topic of the intersection between theology and politics, one should definitely leave behind the standard Marxist patronizing stance towards religion as an imaginary supplement destined to render bearable the misery of our actual lives, and which, as such, can be of some use to mobilize the poor in the Third World countries of Latin America, but has no place in the innermost structure of emancipatory politics. The question to be raised is: is there a religious dimension in the very core of every radical emancipatory project? There are two main answers: the first one is the standard secular-liberal reproach to Marxism that it is nothing more than a secularized religion of deliverance, and the second one Walter Benajmin's notion of the 'weak messianic force', of revolution as retroactive redemption of past failures. Is there a third option? Perhaps the path was shown by Rowan Williams who, commenting on the work of four British Catholic novelists – O'Connor, Percy, Spark and Ellis – wrote:

> All four create a world in which the secular majority account of what is going on is severely relativized, but there is no simple alternative that anyone can step into by a single decision or even a series of decisions. The 'religious' dimension of these fictions lies in the insistent sense of incongruity, unmistakable even if no one within the fiction can say what we should be congruent *with*.[37]

The term 'negative theology' is used to designate the idea that god cannot be described by any positive determinations, so we can only circumscribe his place in a negative way – god is neither infinite nor finite, neither ideal nor real, neither being nor nonbeing, and so on. But what if, in contrast to this notion of god as a pure In-itself beyond all categorial determinations, we locate negativity into god himself, positing that the experience of the divine is, at its most elementary, a negative experience in the sense described by Williams, the experience of the out-of-jointness of our lives? At its most radical, religion is thus not the opium of the people (the opium of and for the people is today, as they say, more and more opium itself, drugs), but an awareness of incongruity and/or inconsistency of existing positive reality. This negative dimension, the awareness of the basic out-of-jointness of our situation, has priority over the positive content located into a Beyond and which aims at restoring the 'broken vessel'. The opposition between religion and evolutionary materialists like Richard Dawkins is thus not simply the opposition between idealism and materialism; what Dawkins and his partisans advocate is a kind of commonsense realism which claims that there is a full self-sufficient reality which can be understood scientifically, while religion is ultimately an empty superstition which obfuscates the clear view of positive reality. In contrast to this assertion of positive reality, the core of religious experience resides in the insight into the 'broken' character of our world, its inconsistency (this insight should not be confounded with Gnosticism which asserts some higher reality which was lost when our fallen world emerged). The basic religious experience is thus effectively opposed not only to naive scientific materialism but, more fundamentally, to the notion of reality which runs from Spinoza through Nietzsche up to Foucault and Deleuze, and which emphasizes the absolute self-immanence of reality: there is no lack in reality, reality is the fullness of the productive process of Life. The Absolute is not a transcendent entity, but the immanent life-force of the wealth of reality, and all appearance of some transcendent power which controls, regulates, and oppresses the immanent flow of life is engendered by the self-reversals of this life process itself.

Such a view is not necessarily materialist: the immanent Absolute can also be spiritualized, which is why religion proper should be thoroughly opposed to any notion of enchanted reality which characterizes so-called spiritual materialism. Tolkien's Middle-Earth is materialist: an enchanted world full of magic forces, evil and good spirits, etc., but strangely *without gods* – there are no transcendent divine entities in Tolkien's universe, all magic is immanent to matter, a spiritual power that dwells in our terrestrial world. And the opposite also holds: the basic religious experience of the out-of-jointness of our world does not necessarily (or even primarily) imply the assertion of some higher spiritual reality, it can be also formulated in materialist terms. Rowan Williams wrote apropos of Dostoyevsky's *Notes from the Underground*:

> The right-minded liberal of his time assumes that when human beings are authoritatively shown what is good for them, they will want it and choose it; but the fact is that human beings are not so constructed ... People will not readily accept any would-be definitive account of what is in their interest ... In other words, part of the distinctively human is the capacity for perversity, addictions, self-sacrifice, self-destruction and a whole range of 'rationally' indefensible behaviours. Remove this capacity and two things result: the distinctively human disappears and

is replaced by a pattern of ordered but mechanical interactions; and violence is canonized as the means of social rationalization – because the amputation of irrational human needs or wants can only be effected by force.[38]

Naive and simplistic as this view may sound, it fully resonates with today's predominant normativity of enlightened hedonism: pleasures are allowed, promoted even, insofar as they serve healthy reproduction (the 'sex is good for health' stance), and experts who know what is good for us are thereby justified in regulating our lives – a regulation which can go up to the amputation of those of our needs which are perceived as irrational and dysfunctional (just think about the anti-smoking legislation). The dimension which resists this regulation – what Williams designates as 'the capacity for perversity, addictions, self-sacrifice, self-destruction and a whole range of "rationally" indefensible behaviours' – is the very dimension of irreducible self-sabotaging, of the 'pursuit of unhappiness', that Freud designated as the domain of the death drive, of the weird overlapping between negativity and inertia that we encounter in a paradigmatic way in Hamlet. Hamlet doesn't kill Claudius when he sees him praying since if he were to do it at that moment, he would not strike at more than what is here, at that X that makes Claudius a king. This is also a problem – maybe even *the* problem – of revolutionaries: how not only to overturn power, but strike at what is more than mere power as a fact, thus preventing the ancient regime from returning in a new guise? It is this uncertainty which propels Hamlet to procrastinate the act (of revenge), i.e., to use Hegel's term, to *tarry* with the negative. Negativity is usually thought of as a dynamic entity consisting of struggles, cuts, and other modes of negation, but, as Cutrofello pointed out, what makes Hamlet a unique figure is that it stands for tarrying with the negative: Hamlet treats negativity itself as an expression of the melancholic inertia of being.

Perhaps, the first move of what one can call 'materialist theology' should be to discern this dimension of death drive in divinity itself. Postmodern philosophers from Nietzsche onwards as a rule prefer Catholicism over Protestantism: Catholicism is a culture of external playful rituals in contrast to the inner sense of guilt and the pressure of authenticity that characterize Protestantism; we are allowed to just follow the ritual and ignore the authenticity of our inner belief … However, this playfulness should not deceive us: Catholicism is resorting to such subterfuges to save the divine big Other in his goodness, while the capriciously 'irrational' Predestination in Protestantism confronts us with a god who is ultimately not good and all-powerful but stained by the indelible suspicion of being stupid, arbitrary, or even outright evil. The dark implicit lesson of Protestantism is: if you want god, you have to renounce (part of the divine) goodness. Along these lines, the most radical reading of the Book of Job was proposed in the 1930s by the Norwegian theologian Peter Wessel Zapffe, who accentuated Job's 'boundless perplexity' when God himself finally appears to him: expecting a sacred and pure God whose intellect is infinitely superior to ours, Job 'finds himself confronted with a world ruler of grotesque primitiveness, a cosmic cave-dweller, a braggart and blusterer, almost agreeable in his total ignorance of spiritual culture … What is new for Job is *not* God's greatness in quantifiable terms; that he knew fully in advance … what is new is the qualitative baseness.'[39] In other words, God – the God of the real – is like the Lady in courtly love, it is *das Ding*, a capricious, cruel master who simply has no sense of universal justice. God-the-Father thus quite literally doesn't know what he is doing, and Christ is the one who does know it, but is reduced to an impotent, compassionate observer, addressing his father with 'Father, can't you see I'm burning?' – burning together with all the victims of the father's rage. Christopher Hitchens's title *God Is Not Great* thus literally applies to Jesus: he is not a great divine king but a miserable wandering preacher whose place was among the destitute. Only by falling into his own creation and wandering around in it as an impassive observer can god perceive the horror of his creation and the fact that he, the highest lawgiver, is himself the supreme criminal. Since God-the-demiurge is not so much evil as a stupid brute lacking moral sensitivity, we should forgive him because he doesn't know what he is doing. In the standard onto-theological vision, only the demiurge elevated above particular reality sees the entire picture, while particular agents caught in struggles get only partial misleading insights; in the core of Christianity we find a different vision – the demiurge elevated above reality is a brute unaware of the horror he is creating, and only when he enters his own creation and experiences it from within, as its inhabitant, can he see the nightmare he fathered. (It is easy to discern in this vision the old literary motif of a king who occasionally dresses up as an ordinary man and mingles with the poor to get a taste of how they live and feel.) It is here that the god of the Real returns with a vengeance in the very heart of Christianity. This dark excess of the ruthless divine sadism – excess over the image of a severe, but nonetheless just, God – is a necessary negative, an underside, of the excess of Christian love over the Jewish Law: love which suspends the Law is necessarily accompanied by the arbitrary cruelty which also suspends the Law. The external difference between Law and love, the excess of love over Law, is thus necessarily reflected within the space of the Law as the passage from just Law to arbitrary/cruel Law (of

Predestination): the arbitrariness of the (in)justice of the cruel God and the arbitrariness of mercy which suspends the Law are two faces of the same gesture of overcoming the Law.[40]

Is this arbitrary God of Terror to whose whim we are delivered not God himself as a creep, the creepy God? Does the way he acts, he treats us, not continuously raise the question: 'What is He getting out of it?' And, furthermore, is this God, a God reduced to the empty point of abstract capricious negativity, not homologous to the terror of the absolute freedom in Hegel's account of the French Revolution? In Hegel's passage from the revolutionary Terror to the Kantian morality: the utilitarian subject of the civil society, the subject who wants to reduce the State to the guardian of his private safety and well-being, has to be crushed by the Terror of the revolutionary State which can annihilate him at any moment for no reason whatsoever (which means that the subject is not punished for something he did, for some particular content or act, but for the very fact of being an independent individual opposed to the universal) – this Terror is his 'truth'. So how do we pass from revolutionary Terror to the autonomous and free Kantian moral subject? By what, in more contemporary language, one would have called full identification with the aggressor: the subject should recognize in the external Terror, in this negativity which threatens all the time to annihilate him, the very core of his (universal) subjectivity, i.e. he should fully identify with it. And, in a homologous way, that's why absolute subordination to God is a step towards freedom: it constitutes me as a universal subject no longer identified with my 'pathological' features.

Recall the strange fact, regularly evoked by Primo Levi and other Holocaust survivors, on how their intimate reaction to their survival was marked by a deep split: consciously, they were fully aware that their survival was a matter of meaningless accident, that they are not in any way guilty for it, that the only guilty perpetrators are their Nazi torturers; at the same time, they were (more than merely) haunted by the 'irrational' guilt feeling, as if they survived at the expense of others who died there and are thus somehow responsible for their death – as is well known, this unbearable guilt feeling drove many of them to suicide. This guilt feeling displays the agency of the superego at its purest: the obscene agency which manipulates us into a spiralling movement of self-destruction. Back to the procedure of *selekcja* in Auschwitz described by Primo Levi: do we not get here close to the arbitrary procedure of Predestination? Is the scene staged around 'the man who comes around' from Johnny Cash's song not the ultimate *selekcja* with regard to which even the Auschwitz *selekcja* is a relief? The Final Judgement is in Cash's song not 'deconstructed', it is not transformed into an endlessly postponed horizon, an event that is always-to-come: the Final

Judgement takes place here and now, but as an obscene travesty of divine justice, an act performed by a crazy god who resembles the Nazi selector in Auschwitz.

As some commentators noted, the reasoning 'God decides who to free and who to blame; those who believe in Jesus will be saved and will escape punishment' is inconsistent: if our salvation depends on our belief in Jesus, then he doesn't have to make any decision but just to follow his insight. This inconsistency can be explained away if we endorse the rather terrifying premise that the all-powerful god has the capacity to freely and arbitrarily determine our beliefs. Cash's god effectively is a 'God of Terror', not just in the sense of the arbitrariness of Predestination and the nightmarish quality of the Last Judgement, but at a more visceral level indicated by a passage from Matthew which is as a rule ignored by the Christian tradition. Here is how Matthew describes the redemptive death of Christ:

> Jesus, when he had cried again with a loud voice, yielded up the ghost … and the earth did quake, and the rocks rent; and the graves were opened; and many bodies of the saints which slept arose, and came out of the graves after his resurrection, and went into the holy city, and appeared unto many. (Mt. 27.50-53)

We can easily see from these lines why, in the opening credits of the 2004 remake of *Dawn of the Dead*, Cash's song accompanies a 'documentary' mixture of news reports and home videos in order to provide a quick exposition of a zombie outbreak gone global and catastrophic:

> It is easy to see why it has made so many parish priests nervous; identifying the Christian mystery with an apocalyptic zombie attack is not exactly soothing Easter-morning sermon fare. That the world should shudder at the alleged Messiah's death seems appropriate, after all – something *evil* has been done! – but that the *saints*, the hallowed departed, should come shambling out of their graves? The incongruity jars us.
>
> The risen Jesus of Christianity is himself the ultimate profane obscenity, the ultimate returning horror – not a ghost, but reanimated flesh, crawled out from the grave three-days rotten, demanding that we slide our fingers along and into his suppurating wounds, demanding (if translators were more honest with the original Greek) that we '*chomp down*' on his flesh and '*guzzle*' his blood. Christ demands of each of his followers that they become necrophagic fetishists; Christians who justify their ludicrous anti-Semitism by characterizing Jewish people as

'Christ-killers' should keep in mind: the Jews may have killed God, *but the Christians ATE him.*

'Holy shit!' then, is not just a curse; it is, collapsed into two words, *the whole of the Christian project*: the deification of the excremental remainder, the glorification of a newborn king laid in a trough, and the apotheosis of a naked criminal, nailed to a plank outside the city limits – 'the stone the builders rejected has become the corner stone' (Acts 4:11), they claim – and claim in triumph. To 'sanctify' Christ – to make him clean, and well-mannered, and meek, is to forget the key message of his ministry. It is to forget the man who came not to bring peace, but a sword; it is to forget the man who flipped tables in the Temple, who back-talked the Roman oppressors ... and whose final promise was to return to bring the earth to judgment, once there was no more room in Hell, and walk the earth again.[41]

The authentic Christian notion of Ressurection should be totally cleaned of this obscene topic – what 'God is love' means is: 'No one has ever seen God; but if we love one another, God lives in us and his love is made complete in us' (Jn. 4.12, New International Version). There is a double movement of *Aufhebung* here: (1) the singular person of Christ is sublated in his resurrected identity as the Spirit (Love) of the community of believers; (2) the empirical miracle is sublated in the higher 'true' miracle (the true miracle is not the dead Christ walking around, but the love in the collective of believers). When the believers gather, mourning Christ's death, their shared spirit *is* the resurrected Christ. Recall how the front page of the first issue of *Charlie Hebdo* after the Paris killings was the drawing of Mohammad holding a placard 'Je suis Charlie' – would not the appropriate image of Christ be a drawing of him holding a placard 'Je suis athée', 'I am atheist'?

It is against the background of this dark topic that we should read Jesus's statement: 'Not that which goeth into the mouth defileth a man; but that which cometh out of the mouth, this defileth a man' (Mt. 15.11). Another version: 'There is nothing from without a man, that entering into him can defile him: but things which come out of him, those are they that defile the man' (Mk 7.15). In a clear break from the Jewish (but also pagan) notion of pollution coming from without, of the pure Self corrupted by reality, Christianity conceives the Self itself as the source of corruption. We should thus turn around the notion of a Self which desperately strives to avoid being contaminated by external filth – this noncontaminated Self *is* evil as such.

Hegel discerns this notion of the Self as evil in its very form in the biblical narrative of the creation of man which contains what he calls a 'marvelous, contradictory feature': on the one hand, man before the fall, man in paradise, was to live eternally (since it is sin that leads to death, man without sin was in a state of immortality); on the other hand, however, it is stated that man would be immortal if he ate from the tree of life – the tree of knowledge – hence if he transgressed the prohibition, in short if he sinned. Man would thus accede to divine perfection only by sinning, that is, by carrying out the forbidden act of knowledge. Furthermore, the knowledge that would separate him from his natural, animal, and mortal state, enabling him to reach, through thought, purity and freedom, is fundamentally sexual knowledge. It takes only one further step to suppose that the invitation to perfection is also an invitation to sin, and conversely; perhaps official theology does not take that step, but the mystic grants himself the fathomless depravity of doing so. This motif of man's total subordination to god, far from necessarily sustaining a vision of slavery and subordination, can also sustain a project of universal emancipation, as it does in Sayyid Qutb's *Milestones* where he deploys the link between universal human freedom and human servitude to god:

A society in which sovereignty belongs exclusively to Allah and finds expression in its obedience to the Divine Law, and every person is set free from servitude to others, only then does it taste true freedom. This alone is 'human civilization', because the basis of human civilization is the complete and true freedom of every person and the full dignity of every individual in the community. On the other hand, in a society in which some people are lords who legislate and others are slaves who obey them, there is no freedom in the real sense, nor dignity for the individual.

It is necessary to understand the point that legislation is not limited only to legal matters, since some people do in fact assign this narrow meaning to the *Shari'ah*. The fact is that attitudes, the way of living, values, criteria, habits, and traditions are all legislated and affect people. If a particular group of people forges all these chains to imprison others in them, it will not be a free society. In such a society some people have the position of authority, while others are subservient to them. This society will be backward, and in Islamic terminology is called a *jahili* society.

An Islamic society is unique in so far as in it authority belongs to Allah alone, and man, freeing himself from servitude to other human beings, serves only Allah, attaining the real and complete freedom, the focus of human civilization, to this society, human dignity and honor are sacrosanct in law prescribed by Allah. Man, as the vicegerent of Allah on earth, attains a position even higher than that of the angels.

In a society based on the concept, belief, and way of life, originating from Allah, man's dignity is held inviolable to the highest degree: no one is a slave to another, as they are in societies in which the concepts, beliefs, and way of life originate from human sources. In the former society, man's noblest characteristics – both spiritual and intellectual – find fullest expression, while in a society based on color, race, nationalism, or other similar bases, these degenerate into fetters for human thought and a means for suppressing nobler human attributes and qualities. All men are equal regardless of their color, race, or nation, but when they are deprived of spirit and reason they are also divested of their humanity. Man is able to change his beliefs, thinking, and attitude toward life, but he is incapable of changing his color and race, nor can he decide in what place or nation he is to be born. Thus it is clear that a society is civilized only to the extent that human associations are based on a community of free moral choice, and a society is backward in so far as the basis of association is something other than free choice.[42]

(Note, however, the symptomatic absence of a term in this series of natural properties of a human being: one cannot change colour, race or nation, but also gender, so why does a free society not include the equality of men and women?) Qutb's underlying premise is that, insofar as we, humans, act 'freely' in the sense of just spontaneously following our natural inclinations, we are not really free but enslaved to our animal natures – we find this same line of reasoning already in Aristotle who, referring to slavery as an example to illustrate a general ontological feature, wrote that, left to themselves, slaves are 'free' in the sense that they just do what they want, while free men follow their duty – and it is this very 'freedom' which makes slaves slaves:

all things are ordered together somehow, but not all alike – both fishes and fowls and plants; and the world is not such that one thing has nothing to do with another, but they are connected. For all are ordered together to one end, but it is as in a house, where the freemen are least at liberty to act at random, but all things or most things are already ordained for them, while the slaves and the animals do little for the common good, and for the most part live at random; for this is the sort of principle that constitutes the nature of each.[43]

(From today's hindsight, one should of course add that, in between slaves/animals and humans, there is what Kant called the 'savagery' [*Wildheit*] proper to the human animal before it gets civilized/disciplined, i.e. what

Freud called death drive.) In spite of all that is deeply problematic in the quoted passage, is there not a grain of truth in it, i.e. does this characterization of slaves not provide a good determination of today's consumerist slavery where I am allowed to act at random and 'do what I want', but remain precisely as such enslaved to the stimuli of commodities?

Back to Aristotle and Qutb: Aristotle's advantage is (from our standpoint, at least) that he refers to the sense of ethical duty, not subordination to god, as the agency which constrains our animal freedom; however, the advantage of Qutb is that he envisages universal (also social and economic) freedom, universal absence of any masters. What Qutb proposes is a kind of symbolic exchange homologous to the one described in the famous lines from Racine's *Athalie*: 'Je crains Dieu, cher Abner, et je n'ai point d'autre crainte' (I fear God, my dear Abner, and have no other fears) – all fears are exchanged for one fear, it is the very fear of God which makes me fearless in all worldly matters. For Qutb, my sole master is god, so not only do I have no other masters but my servitude to god is the negative quarantee of the rejection of all other (earthly, human) masters – or, as we can put it more daringly, the only positive content of my subordination to god is my rejection of all earthly masters.[44]

The deposed god

But is this dark god the last word of Christianity? It is the ultimate version of the transcendent God-in-itself, and one has to go through it to reach the core of the Christian atheism. Jean-Luc Marion developed this point in detail: I only exist through being loved by the Other (God, ultimately). This, however, is not enough – God himself only exists through ex-sistence, as the effect of men's referring to him (in the blockbuster *Clash of the Titans*, Zeus is right to complain that if men stop praying to gods and celebrating them in their rituals, gods will cease to exist). Such a properly comical notion of a God who depends on human approbation is, as one would expect it, evoked by Kierkegaard who, in his *Concept of Anxiety*, describes in a mockingly anti-Hegelian way how Simon Tornacensis (the thirteenth-century scholastic theologian from Paris) 'thought that God must be obliged to him for having furnished a proof of the Trinity … This story has numerous analogies, and in our time speculation has assumed such authority that it has practically tried to make God feel uncertain of himself, like a monarch who is anxiously waiting to learn whether the general assembly will make him an absolute or a limited monarch.'[45]

We should also bear in mind that we are dealing here with a properly dialectical mediation of knowing and being in which being itself hinges on (not-)knowing. As Lacan put it long ago, god doesn't know he is dead (that's why he lives) – in this case, existence hinges on not-knowing, while in Christianity god learns that he is dead. However, already the logical 'god of philosophers' is a dead god, although in a different way, so maybe Tornacensis was wrong or at least he should be read in a more ambiguous way: if a philosopher proves the existence of god, is the god who comes to exist in this way not a dead god? So, maybe, what god really dreads is the very success of the proof of his existence, and the situation is here the same as in the well-known anecdote about the Hearst editor: God fears that the proof of his existence will fail, but he fears even more that it will *not* fail. In short, god's impasse is that he is either alive (but as such caught in a terrifying suspension about his existence) or existing, but dead.

Kierkegaard of course dismisses the attempts to logically demonstrate the existence of god as absurd and pointless logical exercises (his model of such professorial blindness for the authentic religious experience was Hegel's dialectical machinery); however, his sense of humour cannot withstand the wonderful image of a god in anxiety, dreading for his own status as if it depends on the logical exercises of a philosopher, as if the philosopher's reasoning has consequences in the real, so that, if the proof fails, god's existence itself is threatened. And one can go even further in this line of Kierkegaardian reasoning: what undoubtedly attracted him to the remark of Tornacensis was the blasphemous idea of a god himself in anxiety.

The divine impasse thus resides in the fact that the god whose existence is proven is like a monarch whom the assembly makes an absolute one: the very form of confirming his absolute power (it depends on the whim of the assembly) undermines it. The political parallel is here crucial, since Kierkegaard himself resorts to the comparison of god and king: god exposed to the philosopher's wit and whimsy is like a king exposed to the wit and whimsy of a popular assembly. But what is his point here? Is it simply that, in both cases, we should reject liberal decadence and opt for absolute monarchy? What complicates this simple and apparently obvious solution is that, for Kierkegaard, the (properly comical) point of the Incarnation is that that god-king becomes a beggar, a low ordinary human. Would it thus not be more correct to conceive Christianity as the paradox of God's abdication – god steps down to be replaced by the assembly of believers called the Holy Spirit? Recall again 'The Glass Eye' episode from *Alfred Hitchcock Presents* in which a lone woman falls for a handsome ventriloquist; when she gathers the courage to approach him alone in his quarters, she declares her love for him and steps forward to embrace him, only to find that she is holding in her hands a wooden dummy's head. As she withdraws in horror, the 'dummy' stands up and pulls off its mask, and we see the face of a sad older dwarf who starts to jump desperately on the table, imploring the woman to go away. Is this not the perfect rendering of an 'organ without bodies'? It is the detachable 'dead' organ, the partial object, which is effectively alive, and whose dead puppet the 'real' person is: the 'real' person is merely alive, a survival machine, a 'human animal', while the apparently 'dead' supplement is the focus of excessive Life … And is something similar not at work in the very heart of Christianity? 'God is dead' means that we have to abandon (or, rather, turn around) the common notion of Christ as God-the-Father's puppet, someone through whom/ which the transcendent God is speaking and addressing us, his believers. The insight of Christianity is that the transcendent God is dead, that the only living being is the son, and that God-the-Father is a big dead puppet through whom/which the son is speaking, so that when the son himself dies, nothing remains – nothing which is another name of freedom.

This is why authentic religion is incompatible with direct knowledge or unconditional certainty; radical doubt is its innermost component, and the believer him/herself is again and again surprised at unexpected signs of divine presence or intervention ('miracles').[46] This is how one should read Kierkegaard's point that 'a miracle is only a sign that has to be interpreted and therefore … a merely ambiguous indication': already the Jansenists made the same point when they insisted that miracles are not 'objective' miraculous facts which demonstrate the truth of a religion to everyone – they appear as such only to the eyes of believers; to nonbelievers, they are mere fortuitous natural coincidences. This theological legacy survives in radical emancipatory thought, from Marxism to psychoanalysis.

Jean-Claude Milner[47] articulated the difference between truth and exactitude (in the sense of *adequatio*, coincidence between words and things, between a statement and the designated state of things) as a distinction between substantive and predicate. When a statement is exact, it means that it fits its external measure, and, as such, it is true – being true is here a predicate. Truth, on the other hand, is a substantive, an agent – truth itself speaks, as in Lacan's famous prosopopoeia: 'Men, listen, I am telling you the secret. I, truth, speak … The discourse of error – its articulation in action – could bear witness to the truth against the apparent facts themselves … Whether you flee me in deceit or think you can catch me in error, I will catch up with you in the mistake from which you cannot hide.'[48] This does not mean that one should elevate truth into an authentic mode of existential engagement against true (statements) as a mere exact report on external facts. The domain of truth hides its own traps and dangers when it is disconnected from exactitude (conformity with facts), as Lacan makes it clear when he provides three telling examples of truth: 'the world market in lies, the trade in all-out war, and the new law of self-criticism'.[49] One should take into account here that these words were written at the height of the Cold War and refer to the emerging media-manipulations in reporting on facts, to the rhetoric of the Cold War with regard to the danger of self-destruction of humanity in an all-out atomic war, and to the Stalinist confessions in mock trials. To limit ourselves to the last example, Stalinist confessions clearly relied on truth against exactitude, even at the price of a ridiculous ignorance of facts: what mattered was the accused victim's confession which was considered to overcome all factual inconsistencies. (Say, when, in one of the big Moscow trials, the prosecutor claimed that a meeting took place on a small provincial airport in Norway between one of the accused and Trotsky, who used this opportunity to deliver to the accused orders to organize a murder of Stalin, no one was bothered when Western journalists checked the facts and discovered that this airport was abandoned and out of use for years before the meeting was supposed to take place – what mattered was the 'inner truth' of the accusation, not simple facts.) The Russian language has two words for 'truth' which perfectly render this distinction: *istina* (the simple exactitude of reported facts) and *pravda* (the 'deeper' ethico-political truth); it is significant that the title of the main official Soviet daily newspaper was *Pravda*, not *Istina*. For example, the celebration of the big successes of Soviet agriculture was 'true' even if some (at least) of the statistics were falsified since it expressed the progressive stance of trust in Socialist progress, while the public disclosure of these statistical errors, even if exact, would not be 'true' since it would run against the historical progress and 'objectively' support capitalist propaganda ...

Does this mean that we should simply endorse the empiricist distrust of Truth and remain wary of the 'totalitarian' dangers of Truth? Things are much more complex.[50] The refrain of an old German communist song from the 1930s is '*Die Freiheit hat Soldaten!*' (Freedom has its soldiers!). It may appear that such an identification of a particular unit as the military instrument of Freedom itself is the very formula of the 'totalitarian' temptation: we do not just fight for (our understanding of) freedom, we do not just serve freedom, it is freedom itself which immediately avails itself of us ... The way seems open to terror: who would be allowed to oppose freedom itself? However, the identification of a revolutionary military unit as a direct organ of freedom cannot simply be dismissed as a fetishistic short circuit: in a pathetic way, this *is* true of the authentic revolutionary explosion. What happens in such an 'ecstatic' experience is that the subject who acts is no longer a person, but, precisely, an *object*. And it is precisely this dimension of identifying with an object which justifies the use of the term 'theology' to describe the situation: 'theology' is here a name for what is, in a revolutionary subject, beyond a mere collection of individual humans acting. This ecstatic subjective stance is not to be confused with the standard logic of symbolic mandate which relies on the institutional cover: when a judge speaks, no matter how corrupt he may be as a private person, Law itself (the big Other) speaks through him.

In the above-quoted passage, Lacan evokes yet another case of the Truth which speaks, the case proper to psychoanalysis: when I commit a slip of the tongue and say something other than what I wanted to say, and this other message tells the truth about me that I am often not ready to recognize, then one can also say that in my slip the truth itself spoke, subverting what I wanted to say. There is truth (a truth about my desire) in such slips even if they contain factual inexactitude – say, an extremely simple example, when the moderator of a debate, instead of saying 'I am thereby opening the session!' says 'I am thereby closing the session!' he obviously indicates that he is bored and considers the debate worthless … Lacan's notion of 'I, truth, speak' is this marginalist one, in contrast to the charisma and dignity of a symbolic institution speaking through me: I am spoken, the truth speaks, and it is in this sense that 'the discourse of error – its articulation in action – could bear witness to the truth against the apparent facts themselves'. This is why psychoanalysis shows that 'one is digressive whether or not one wants to be. Indeed, the digressions one is unaware of are the most telling.'[51] Digressions are ambiguous: a digression can be an avoidance of a dangerous topic (when I approach it, I quickly move to another topic), but it also can be a roundabout way to approach what it really matters when I realize that a direct approach gets stuck. The lesson of psychoanalysis is, of course, that the two opposite procedures often overlap: I want to avoid a sensitive topic, but in my very attempt to move somewhere else truth catches up with me, I inadvertently say something crucial about what I wanted to avoid.

It is easy to see how truth is characterized by the same paradox as *jouissance*: it is simultaneously impossible to arrive at it and impossible to get rid of it. On the one hand, for structural reasons, we cannot ever tell the whole truth, one can only half-say (*mi-dire*) it, as Lacan famously states at the beginning of his *Television*. This, however, in no way brings us to postmodern relativism which allows us to formulate only dispersed fragments of truth: truth is at the same time something we cannot get rid of, since no matter how much we want to obliterate it it catches up with us and we inadvertently articulate it through our very attempts to evade it. Back to Stalinism: the great public building projects in the Soviet Union of the 1930s often put on the top of a flat multistorey office building a gigantic statue of the idealized New Man or a couple; in the span of a few years, the tendency to flatten more and more the office building (the actual working place for the living people) became clearly discernible, so that it changed more and more into a mere pedestal for the larger-than-life statue. Does this external, material feature of architectural design not render visible the 'truth' of the Stalinist ideology in which actual, living people are reduced to instruments, sacrificed as the pedestal for the spectre of the future New Man, an ideological monster which crushes under his feet actual living men? The paradox is that were anyone in the Soviet Union of the thirties to say openly that the vision of the Socialist New Man was an ideological monster squashing actual people, they would have been immediately arrested – it was, however, allowed, encouraged even, to make this point via architectural design … Again, 'the truth is out there'. It is not simply that ideology also permeates the alleged extra-ideological strata of everyday life: this materialization of ideology in external materiality renders visible inherent antagonisms which the explicit formulation of ideology cannot afford to acknowledge – it is as if an ideological edifice, if it is to function 'normally', must obey a kind of 'imp of perversity', and articulate its inherent antagonism in the externality of its material existence.

In short, *moi, la vérité, je parle* … but what does the truth say? Lies, basically, i.e. statements which are not true: truth is delivered through hysterical symptoms, slips of the tongue, and other forms of what is, as to its literal meaning, a lie. What kind of a notion of God fits a Truth which speaks? In his Seminar XX, 'Encore', Lacan warns against a too simplistic atheism: he says that while god doesn't exist (in the sense of an absolute Entity dwelling somewhere out there independently of us, humans), he nonetheless ex-sists. This ex-sistence, of course, can be understood in different ways, imaginary (god doesn't exist in himself, but only outside himself, as humanity's imaginary projection), symbolic (god ex-sists in human practices and rituals which refer to him, as a symbolic Cause kept alive through human activity), real – the meaning emphasized by Lacan (god is the impossible/real, purely virtual point of reference which resists symbolization, like the unbearable intensity of the *jouissance féminine*). But we can cut short the looming debate and simply posit that God ex-sists outside himself in our practice of love – not in our love for him, but our love for our neighbours (as Christ put it to his disciples, when there is love among you, I am there). What this means is that man and god are caught in a circle: a religious man perceives god as the presupposition of his entire life, but this presupposition is posited by his serving god and has no meaning outside this relationship. This is why Kierkegaard has to insist on God's thorough 'desubstantialization' – God is 'beyond the order of Being', He is nothing but the mode of how we relate to him, i.e. we do not relate to him, he *is* this relating:

> God himself is this: *how* one involves himself with Him. As far as physical and external objects are concerned, the object is something else than the mode: there are many modes. In respect to God, the *how* is the what. He who does not involve himself with God in the mode of absolute devotion does not become involved with God.[52]

The Christian passage to Holy Spirit as Love is to be taken literally: God as the divine *individual* (Christ) passes into the purely *nonsubstantial link* between the individuals. This is why if aliens were to land on Earth, we can be certain that they would not know about Christ, Christ is exclusively a part of human history – but this is not an argument that Christ is just a human creation/projection or, even worse, that there is one divine Absolute which appears in multiple ways to different groups of people (or other rational beings). And this is also why the genuine dimension of Christian doubt does not concern the existence of God, i.e. its logic is not 'I feel such a need to believe in God, but I cannot be sure that he really exists, that he is not just a chimera of my imagination' (to which a humanist atheist can easily respond: 'then drop God and simply assume the ideals God stands for as your own'), which is why a Christian subject is indifferent towards the infamous proofs of God's existence. Recall Brecht's famous Herr Keuner anecdote about the existence of god:

> Someone asked Herr Keuner if there is a God. Herr Keuner said: I advise you to think about how your behaviour would change with regard to the answer to this question. If it would not change, then we can drop the question. If it would change, then I can help you at least insofar as I can tell you: You already decided: You need a God.[53]

Brecht is right here: we are never in a position to directly choose between theism and atheism, since the choice as such is already located within the field of belief (in the sense of our practical engagement). What an authentic believer should do here is to shift the accent of Brecht's anecdote: from God to God's ex-sistence which is fully compatible with materialism. This is why doubt is immanent to an authentic religion: not abstract intellectual doubt about god's existence, but doubt about our practical engagement which makes god himself ex-sist.

This doubt is brought to extreme in Christianity where (as Chesterton pointed out) not only do believers doubt God, God himself gets caught in doubt (in his 'Father, why have you abandoned me?' Christ himself commits what is for a Christian the ultimate sin: he wavers in his faith) – and Chesterton is fully aware that we are thereby approaching 'a matter more dark and awful than it is easy to discuss … a matter which the greatest saints and thinkers have justly feared to approach. But in that terrific tale of the Passion there is a distinct emotional suggestion that the author of all things (in some unthinkable way) went not only through agony, but through doubt.'[54] What god doubts about and dreads is that the bond of human engagement which makes him ex-sist will be broken, and there is no true atheism which does not go through this experience. Even the most ruthless rejections of religious faith are often secretly biased with regard to religion. Say, there is a deep necessity, not just a personal idiosyncrasy, in the fact that Sam Harris ends his scathing critique of religious faith with the antimaterialist concession (elaborated by David Chalmers) that consciousness may be a rudimentary phenomenon of its own; plus he is quick to concede two exceptions to his overall condemnation of religion. First, he praises spiritual mysticism – spiritual experiences are a fact which should be closely studied: 'Mysticism is a rational experience. Religion is not.'[55] Second, a closer looks also renders visible Harris's covert Jewish bias: 'Judaism is a far less fertile source of militant extremism. Jews tend not to draw their identity as Jews exclusively from the contents of their beliefs about God. It is possible, for instance, to be a practicing Jew who does *not* believe in God. The same cannot be said for Christianity and Islam.'[56]

One should add at least two things to this: (1) de facto, the same goes for the majority of Christians today; (2) Harris relies on an all-too-primitive notion of belief – as if 'believing' simply means 'taking it to be factually true'. What lurks in the background here is the standard Jewish argument for the unique character of Judaism: only Judaism keeps open the enigma of the Other, it doesn't obfuscate the anxiety when we encounter god – 'What does he want from us?' Christianity covers up this abyss by way of providing a soothing answer: god loves us, we can be sure of his care and mercy … (The atheist-Christian radical answer is that the message of Christianity is not the love but the death of god. Christian love is the love of the community of believers ['Holy Spirit'] after the death of god, not the love of a transcendent god for humanity.) We should imagine an interrogation of Christ similar to the final dialogue in Wilder's *Some Like It Hot*: 'You are a loser crucified by the establishment!' 'But I accepted my death for your benefit.' 'You cannot really help us!' 'But you have all my sympathy in your suffering.' 'What this means is that you are not a real God!' 'Well, nobody is perfect ...' And even Christ's sympathy for us sinners should not be sentimentalized – as for Christ forgiving us our sins, remember what Ford Madox Ford wrote in his *Parade's End*: the true cruelty is to forgive someone without mercy. This is how Christ does it: just brutally forgiving us, with no sentimentality, no place for expressions of gratitude.

At the most basic level, Harris dismisses religious faith as epistemological nonsense out of sync with our present knowledge of the world: every religion involves accepting as truth statements which are obviously incompatible with what we know, i.e. statements which obviously could only have been generated in a society much more primitive than ours. When dealing with religion, we are thus obviously ready to suspend our normal standards of veracity: who, when dealing with everyday reality, would accept stories about water changing into wine, about birth without impregnation, etc.? In this discrepancy, he sees the main danger for the survival of humanity: the prospect of nuclear weapons in the hands of the Muslim fundamentalists means that the means of our destruction will be at the disposal of the people who mentally belong to the fourteenth century. The worst, for Harris, is the enlightened, 'tolerant' view which tells us that, on account of religious freedom, we should not prevent others displaying any beliefs they want, and the concomitant claim that terrorist fundamentalism is a terrible perversion of the great authentic religions. Harris asks here the pertinent question: why then do we have only Muslim (and, to a smaller extent, Hindu) terrorists? Say, the suffering of the Tibetans is no less terrible than the plight of the Palestinians, and yet there are no Tibetan terrorists ...

The problem with religions is obviously that they cannot all be true – with the wonderful exception of the partisans of the New Age Wicca faith, according to whom Christians go to heaven when they die, Vikings go to Valhalla, Buddhists are reincarnated, Muslim martyrs get their seventy virgins, and so forth, while atheists sleep their Big Sleep. So why didn't God make up his mind and reveal Himself once and for all, instead of confusing honest believers? The solution is to historicize all religious narratives, perceiving them as expressions of some underlying transcendent divinity ('we all, each in our way, talk about the same God ...'). (Schelling is here unique: the history of religions is for him the immanent history of the Divinity itself, its self-development.) And the next logical step is the rather obvious one: secular humanism as the common denominator of all religions, i.e. the idea that all religions are 'expressions' of the deepest human cravings and fears at the different stages of the development of humanity. In the same way that Marx, in his analysis of the 1848 French revolution, claimed that Republic was the only form in which the two groups of royalists (Orleanists and Bourbons) could exert their common rule, i.e. that to be a republican is the only way to be a royalist 'as such', to be a secular humanist is the only way to be religious 'as such', without subscribing to a particular religion: to paraphrase Marx, religion 'as such' is the anonymous faith of the atheist humanist. The task is to drop this very form of religion that persists in secular humanism – but with an unexpected twist: what if the same holds also for atheism? There are different kinds of atheism, and to be a Christian is the only way to be an atheist 'as such' since only in Christianity does god himself cease to believe in himself.

This is why all attempts to thoroughly 'defetishize' religion, to conceive a god 'beyond the order of being', a god who is pure relational Otherness and not the Supreme Being, the all-powerful regulator of the universe, are condemned to fail. Among the latest attempts in this direction, Markus Gabriel posited that religion

> arises from the need to return to ourselves from a maximal distance. The man is able to distance himself from himself to such an extent that he can understand himself only as a vanishing point in infinity. When we return to ourselves from this distance, the question arises if our life still has any meaning or if our hopes for a meaning are dissolved like a drop in the ocean of the infinite. Religion is therefore a return to ourselves from the infinite, from what is thoroughly not at our disposal and unchangeable; at stake in it is that we don't get completely lost.[57]

The first modern proponent of such a view was Schleiermacher, the father of philosophical hermeneutics, for whom god is a name for our yearning for the Infinite which can only find its proper expression in feelings and is therefore betrayed the moment we ontologize its object; Gabriel's supreme example is, as one can expect, the usual suspect for such an approach, Kierkegaard who defined god as the fact 'that everything is possible':

> What he means thereby is that we encounter go or the divine when reach the maximal distance and experience that everything is possible. At the existential level, in our life experience, this appears as losing the ground under our feet which occurs when we understand that we could have assumed totally different ways of life … According to Kierkegaard's analysis, god is our assuming a maximal distance towards ourselves.[58]

Such a notion of god effectively seems free of every fetishization – 'god' just names a specific feature of our spiritual self-relating:

> In every self-description, we also display a normative self-under-standing, a mode and way of how we want to be. Kierkegaard calls this insight 'god', and we can agree with him insofar as religion relates to human spirit which open itself up to something which is not at our disposal.[59]

Gabriel brings this stance to its extreme: if we 'defetishize' god in this way so that 'god' no longer names a supreme entity the reference to which explains everything (since he created all reality), then the true meaning of religion is simply that there is no god:

> Religion is the opposite of an explanation of the world ... We could also say in a slightly provocative way that the meaning of religion resides in the insight that there is no god, that god is not an object or super-entity which guarantees the meaning of our life.[60]

In short, insofar as 'god' is a name for the immanent decentrement of human subjectivity, and insofar as every positive notion of god (as the highest Being, etc.) already fills in this gap of decentrement, we are compelled to conclude that the only authentic radical materialism is this zero-form of theology, the assertion of 'pure' decentrement without any divine entity covering it up. (This brings us back to Rowan Williams's definition of the most elementary religious dimension as the experience of out-of-jointness of our existence.) But if we go so far, why then should we continue to call what religion refers to 'god'? To put this question another way, how exactly do we come back to ourselves from the maximal distance in religion? Note Gabriel's ambiguity: god, the divine, is for him 'our assuming a maximal distance towards ourselves' and at the same time the 'return to ourselves from a maximal distance'. So what if we simply do *not* return to ourselves but fully accept that we are just a 'vanishing point in infinity', 'an insignificant speck of dust on a small planet'? Or, more precisely, what if our 'return to ourselves' resides precisely in our fully assuming this fact, in the spiritual stance which expresses such assuming – something like feeling the awe apropos of the infinity of the universe (which Kant mentions when he talks about the sky above us with all its stars blinking)? Such a stance should not be reduced to scientific objectivism since it involves a profound 'mystical' experience of the abyss in which we dwell – in it, we effectively 'lose the ground under our feet' ...

Is then (what we usually refer to as) religion not precisely a defence against this radical experience of abyss, an attempt to obfuscate this void of infinity by way of imagining a personalized supreme Being, a 'super-entity which guarantees the meaning of our life'?

This stance is not scientific objectivism where science erases itself (as Lacan put it, science forecloses subject): scientific objectivism presupposes an invisible subject who as it were observes reality from nowhere (or, as we say, from an objective distance). In other words, scientists who advocate scientific objectivism somehow presuppose that the autonomous subject is still here, freely arguing and experimenting. The true question apropos of scientific objectivism which claims that our Self doesn't really exist, that it is just the 'user's illusion' generated by our brains: is it possible to *live* in our daily experience the fact that Self doesn't exist? The positive answer to this question was provided by contemporary German philosopher and brain scientist Thomas Metzinger[61] who claims that in Buddhist enlightenment the Self directly, in its innermost self-experience, assumes its own nonbeing, i.e. recognizes itself as a 'simulated self', a representational fiction. Such an enlightened awareness is no longer self-awareness: it is no longer I who experience myself as the agent of my thoughts; 'my' awareness is the direct awareness of a self-less system, a self-less knowledge. In short, there effectively *is* a link, or at least a kind of asymptotic point of coincidence, between the position taken by radical brain sciences and the Buddhist idea of 'an-atman' (of the Self's inexistence): Buddhism provides a kind of subjective eventalization of scientific cognitivism: the Event which takes place when we fully assume the results of brain sciences is the Event of enlightenment, the attainment of Nirvana, which liberates us from the constraints of our Self as an autonomous substantial agent.

There is a further problem with Gabriel's version of Kierkegaard: far from limiting himself to a purely relational notion of god (god as the extreme of our spiritual self-relating), Kierkegaard locates the uniqueness of Christianity in its evental character: while (most) other religions search for a direct contact with some transhistorical Eternity in which we get rid of our temporal and bodily limitations, the fundamental premise of Christianity is that we only have access to god through Christ, through assuming an absurd belief that, two thousand years ago, god incarnated himself in an earthly individual – this and *only* this is how, in Christianity, we return to ourselves from the abyssal infinity of the universe. If, then, for Kierkegaard, there is no authentic Christianity outside this absurd belief in a particular event which took place at a precise moment in time and place in our reality, does this mean that Kierkegaard is simply inconsistent or self-contradicting, that he 'regresses' from pure spiritual self-relationality to the most crude objectivism? Or is the opposition of a purely spiritual-relational god and the 'fetishized' notion of god as a super-agent not an all too rude one? Do we not find in Kierkegaard yet another case of the Hegelian infinite judgement 'spirit is a bone'? God, the desubstantialized pure self-relationality, coincides with a miserable individual walking around Palestine two thousand years ago ... The truly difficult thing is not to get rid of the 'fetishizing' of god but to grasp the inner necessity of the incarnation of the purely spiritual self-relationality in a single contingent individual.

G. K. Chesterton was thus right (as he usually is) when he wrote: 'I believe in preaching to the converted, for I have generally found that the converted do not understand their own religion.'[62] This misunderstanding is brought to extreme in Christianity where the large majority of believers do not understand the atheist core of Christianity.

9 JECT OR SCEND? FROM THE TRAUMATIZED SUBJECT TO SUBJECT AS TRAUMA

The parallax of drive and desire

Among the root words with multiple prefixes, two stand out: JECT ('thrown': subject, object, project, inject, interject, reject, abject, eject, deject ...) and SCEND ('climb': transcend, ascend, descend). Instead of getting lost in the multitude of prefixes and their complex logic (say, the ambiguity of 'object': a thing in front of us, a goal, and an obstacle), we should perhaps focus on the root words themselves: does the couple JECT and SCEND not render the minimal form of drive and desire? 'Drive' stands for the 'throw' that derails peaceful stability, while 'desire' stands for the effort of ascending towards a goal out of reach. Do we not find this tension already in the work of the first two big classics of philosophy? The couple of Plato and Aristotle seems to point forward to the Freudian (or, rather, Lacanian) opposition of desire (the search for the eluding transcendent object) and drive (satisfaction in the immanent movement). And, effectively, is Aristotle's notion of an activity which brings pleasure in itself not opposed to the Platonic notion of pleasure as something that signals the overcoming of a lack or obstacle? For Aristotle, true pleasure does not arise from filling a lack (like eating or drinking in order to quell hunger or thirst), it is rather a positive pleasure in an activity which does not serve an external goal (its supreme human example is the philosopher's pleasure in thinking):

> Aristotle grants pleasure an ontological dignity by rethinking it according to *energeia*, a category that escapes the Platonic opposition between movement and rest. *Energeia* is a neologism derived from the word *ergon*, or work, and is usually translated as activity or actuality; its fullest expression consists in activities that are complete (at rest) in themselves, i.e. those whose end does not lie in any external accomplishment but in their own performance. 'There is not only an activity of movement but an activity of immobility [*energeia akinesias*], and pleasure is found more in rest than in movement' (*NE* 1154b27–28).[1]

But does this supreme pleasure in an activity which has its end in itself (from dancing to thinking) not find its counterpart in a much more perverse example of *energeia akinesias*, that of the obsessional pseudoactivity where I am active (hyperactive, even) all the time not in order to achieve something but precisely to make sure that nothing will change? This is what one can call *false activity*: people not only act in order to change something, they can also act in order to prevent something from happening, i.e. so that *nothing will change*. Therein resides the typical strategy of the obsessional neurotic: he is frantically active in order to prevent the real thing from happening. Say, in a group situation in which some tension threatens to explode, the obsessional talks all the time, tells jokes, and so on, in order to prevent the awkward moment of silence which would compel the participants to openly confront the underlying tension. This is why, in psychoanalytic treatment, obsessional neurotics talk all the time, overwhelming the analyst with anecdotes, dreams, insights: their incessant activity is sustained by the underlying fear that, if they stop talking for a moment, the *analyst* will ask them the question that truly matters – in other words, they talk in order to keep the analyst immobile. In this weird *energeia akinesias*, the subject is hyperactive in order to guarantee the immobility of the situation. Upon a closer look, we can soon see how difficult it is to clearly separate the 'good' *energeia akinesias* from the 'bad' one: what if god himself, the supreme agent of *energeia akinesias* for Aristotle, keeps the entire universe in movement just to prevent any real change in it?

Such weird redoublings and reversals indicate that the couple of desire and drive not only plays a central role in the Freudian edifice, but is also much more complex and ambiguous than it may appear: we are dealing with an antagonism proper, that is, the two terms cannot be brought to a common denominator, nor do they supplement each other since each term seems to corrode the other from within. We can perceive this antagonism very clearly when we reformulate it in terms of desire and its satisfaction (enjoyment). The retroactive illusion through which a contingent encounter creates its own necessity ('all my life I was waiting for it, I was predestined to it') is at work also when we stumble upon an unexpected enjoyment: we first experience enjoyment as a disturbing intrusion, and then we create a desire for it, a lack presumed to be filled by it, so that the excess is renormalized:

> Was the lack really there prior to its filling? Or is it something that is supposed after the fact, post festum? What if the lack were a retrospective creation which served to explain and 'ontologically' justify the uncanny experience of a joy that was not sought after or expected? This is the special quality of sublimated pleasure, its unique existential and temporal logic: it takes the form of a surplus that is not 'wanted' – no preceding desire corresponds to its arrival – yet is nevertheless enjoyed. It is like an answer without a question, to turn around the old philosophical cliché of the question without an answer … The wayward answer in search of a question, an answer that forces a new question precisely because it does not quite fit into any previously existing ones, or maybe even an answer that does not need a question at all. The strangeness of this experience is such that one tends to resolve its incongruity by re-inscribing it into the standard logic of lack and fulfillment. What is found turns out to be what one had been looking for all along. This fantasy of a predestined match is precisely a retroactive illusion, a domestication of the oddness of the initial encounter, the fateful meeting of an unwanted satisfaction with an imperceptible desire.

Maybe this provides us even with one of the possible definitions of fantasy: not just the answer to the question *Che vuoi?*, to the enigma of what the other wants, but also the question that provides the frame, the coordinates of understanding, for the odd excess of enjoyment. Furthermore, does the same not hold for the subject itself? Although the standard association would have been the one of subject with question and of object with answer (subject inquires into reality, searching for objects which provide answers), for Lacan, subject is an *answer* of the real while object, in its obscure impenetrability, is an enigma, a question addressed to the subject. (More generally, subject qua answer of the real is *ce qui du réel pâtit du signifiant*, an answer of the real of the body to its colonization by the signifying order.)

In another variation on this motif, Lévi-Strauss characterized the incest prohibition as an answer without question: the rise of this prohibition was an answer, the resolution of a problem, but it is not clear to which question it was an answer, which problem it was meant to resolve: all attempts to provide the question, the reasons enumerated (from biological ones – incest prevents genetic variations necessary for the evolution of a species – to sociocultural ones – prohibition of incest is the other side of marrying a woman from outside, belonging to another family or tribe, which thus grounds extended network of social links) are obviously insufficient insofar as they are all ultimately circular, i.e. they only work as questions if the answer is already here. Once the prohibition of incest is here, one can rationalize it, but the idea that one can imagine a situation in which an individual or group ponders what to do to resolve a deadlock and then decides to impose the prohibition of incest is the same absurdity as the naive explanation of the origins of language that one finds in Friedrich Engels:

> the development of labour necessarily helped to bring the members of society closer together by increasing cases of mutual support and joint activity, and by making clear the advantage of this joint activity to each individual. In short, men in the making arrived at the point where *they had something to say* to each other. Necessity created the organ; the undeveloped larynx of the ape was slowly but surely transformed by modulation to produce constantly more developed modulation, and the organs of the mouth gradually learned to pronounce one articulate sound after another.[2]

In short, speech emerged when 'men in the making arrived at the point where *they had something to say* to each other' – as if the very notion of 'having something to say' does not already presuppose that language is here ... We thus arrive at a weird loop where the two excesses/lacks supplement each other without ever finding a common space to balance each other: there is a lack (propelling desire, a lack that in a way 'is' the desiring subject) which cannot ever be filled in by an object (desire is by definition unsatisfied, it always wants something more, something else, it never gets 'that'); there is an excess (of satisfaction), a disturbing intrusion of enjoyment, which throws the subject off its rails and is unable to find its adequate place in the subject's universe. These two excesses cannot find a shared space of balance because they are the same element in two modes, giving birth to the impossible dream of harmoniously supplementing each other. Schuster is right to emphasize that this gap or failure to match question and answer, desire and enjoyment-in-drive, subject and object, far from being an unresolved of psychoanalytic theory, is in a way its own solution, namely, a basic positive insight of psychoanalytic theory, a feature that characterizes its object itself, the structure of the human psyche.

Desire is related to interpretation as drive is to sublimation: the fact that sublimation is, as a rule, mentioned together with drive, not with desire – Freud never speaks of the 'sublimation of desire', nor does he ever speak of the 'interpretation of drive' but always links interpretation to desire – bears witness to a profound theoretical necessity. The title of Lacan's seminar from 1958–9 ('Desire and Its Interpretation') is to be taken as a direct assertion of their ultimate identity: desire coincides with its own interpretation. When the subject endeavours to interpret (its own or, originally, the Other's) desire and never finds the ultimate point of reference, when it forever slides from one reading to another, this very desperate attempt to arrive at 'what one really wants' *is desire itself.* (Insofar as the coordinates of desire are provided by the 'fundamental fantasy', and insofar as this fantasy emerges as an attempt to provide an answer to the enigma of *Che vuoi?*, of the Other's desire, in short: as the interpretation of this desire, of what the Other 'effectively wants from me', desire as such is sustained by interpretation.)

Deleuze himself found it too difficult to tarry with this gap of his, and he succumbs to the temptation to fill in this gap when he deploys how desire emerges out of drives and their antagonism (or how the molar emerges out of the molecular, or how representation emerges out of productive presence). True, one can 'deduce' desire out of the deadlock of the circular movement of drives: desire resolves the debilitating deadlock of drives caught in their endless loop by way of externalizing the goal into a transcendent lost object that forever eludes the subject's grasp. However, the opposite deduction is, if anything, even more convincing: does drive not emerge as an attempt to turn failure into success? So that while desire again and again misses its goal, full enjoyment, drive emerges when this repetitive failure, the endless circulation around the lost object, itself turns into a source of satisfaction. One should thus reject this temptation to reduce one of the poles to its opposite, and to persist in the absolute parallax between the two.

Therein resides the difference between Deleuze and Lacan. For Deleuze, everything begins with 'organs without bodies', the chaotic multiplicity of asubjective intensities, concentrated patterns of enjoyment; they form the primordial transcendental process of passive synthesis out of which subject gradually emerges through active synthesis. Passive synthesis is thus a process which precedes the subject/object distinction, the opposition of subject and external objective reality; as such, passive synthesis involves a subjectivization without (or, rather, prior to) subject – Lacan also characterizes the circular movement of drives as involving an acephalous subjectivization without subject.

Lacan's basic approach here is a different one: his point is not to locate the starting point in the swarm of drives circulating around primitive *objets a*, and to provide a transcendental deduction of the fully constituted (desiring) subject out of it. For him, the couple of asubjective phenomenona (the primordial fantasy kernels, patterns of enjoyment, which cannot be subjectively assumed) and empty (barred) subject ($) – $ and *a* – always go together: whenever we have asubjective phenomena the void of the pure subject already has to be here, i.e. the subject of the unconscious (*cogito*, $) and the swarm of headless drives are always correlated. This weird couple subverts the Aristotelian couple of soul and body (soul as the immanent form of the body), as well as the transcendental couple of subject and object facing each other.

The antagonism of drives that Deleuze locates at their most elementary level (and which triggers the development towards desire/lack/subject) is the one between organs without body (OwB) and body without organs (BwO), the empty/flat surface, the oneness prior to the imaginary identification with the mirror image, the ground for all later syntheses. We arrive at BwO when we subtract from a desiring machine all its organs/parts (partial objects), so that, in contrast to all holistic organicism, BwO is not more but *less* than the sum of its parts. From the Lacanian pespective, however, BwO is ultimately another name for subject ($) as the void of radical negativity correlative to the swarm of drives. Let us elaborate in greater detail this convoluted structure.

Immortality as death in life

Deleuze often varies the motif of how, in becoming posthuman, we should learn to practise 'a perception as it was before men (or after) … released from their human coordinates':[3] those who fully endorse the Nietzschean 'return of the same' are strong enough to sustain the vision of the 'iridescent chaos of a world before man'.[4] The standard realist approach aims at describing the world, reality, the way it exists out there, independently of us, observing subjects. But we, subjects, are ourselves part of the world, so the consequent realism should include us in the reality we are describing, so that our realist approach should include describing ourselves 'from the outside', *independently of ourselves*, as if we are observing ourselves through inhuman eyes. What this inclusion-of-ourselves amounts to is not naive realism but something much more uncanny, a radical shift in the subjective attitude by means of which we become strangers to ourselves.

Although Deleuze here resorts openly to Kant's language, talking about the direct access to 'things (the way they are) in themselves', his point is precisely that one should subtract the opposition between phenomena and things-in-themselves, between the phenomenal and the noumenal level, from its Kantian functioning, where noumena are transcendent things that forever elude our grasp. What Deleuze refers to as 'things in themselves' is in a way *even more phenomenal* than our shared phenomenal reality: it is the impossible phenomenon, the phenomenon that is excluded from our symbolically constituted reality. The gap that separates us from noumena is thus primarily not epistemological, but practico-ethical and libidinal: there is no 'true reality' behind or beneath phenomena, noumena are phenomenal things which are 'too strong', too intens(iv)e, for our perceptual apparatus attuned to constituted reality – epistemological failure is a secondary effect of libidinal terror; that is, the underlying logic is a reversal of Kant's 'You can, because you must!': 'You cannot (know noumena), because you must not!' Imagine someone being forced to witness a terrifying torture: in a way, the monstrosity of what he saw would make this an experience of the noumenal impossible-real that would shatter the coordinates of our common reality. (The same holds for withessing an intense sexual activity.) In this sense, if we were to discover films shot in a concentration camp among the *Musulmannen*, showing scenes from their daily life, how they are systematically mistreated and deprived of all dignity, we would have 'seen too much', the prohibited, we would have entered a forbidden territory of what should have remained unseen. (One can well understand Claude Lanzmann, who said that if he were to stumble upon such a film, he would destroy it immediately.) This is also what makes it so unbearable to witness the last moments of people who know they are shortly going to die and are in this sense already living-dead – again, imagine that we would have discovered, among the ruins of the Twin Towers, a video camera which magically survived the crash intact and is full of shots of what went on among the passengers of the plane in the minutes before it crashed into one of the towers. In all these cases, it is that, effectively, we would have seen things as they are 'in themselves', outside human coordinates, outside our human reality – we would have seen the world with inhuman eyes. (Maybe the US authorities do possess such shots and, for understandable reasons, are keeping them secret.) The lesson is here profoundly Hegelian: the difference between the phenomenal and the noumenal has to be reflected/transposed back into the phenomenal, as the split between the 'gentrified' normal phenomenon and the 'impossible' phenomenon.

The gap between $ and life-enjoyment (whose most elementary form is the circular movement of drives) implies that subject stands for death in life, that it stands at a distance towards life, for its denaturalization, and what this denaturalization of life means is that the will to live is not, as a long line of thinkers from Aristotle to Spinoza presumed, a spontaneous natural impetus (or *conatus*) but something towards which the subject already entertains a minimal distance: subject and its life

> do not form an organic unity. Instead this innermost drive is felt as an external compulsion, as a foreign element in which one has become entangled. Which is why it can appear as a terrible bother and a drudgery, a series of chores to be carried out: thinking, speaking, traveling, working, copulating, and so on – I'd rather not. Life does not immediately identify with itself, but is something separated from the subject that is compelled to live it ... For the human being, life does not present itself as a self-evident inner power but as a commandment and a duty. Freud writes, 'To tolerate life remains, after all, the first duty of all living beings.' This should be read literally: to live is not a natural and spontaneous *energeia* but a duty, a superego imperative, even the most fundamental one. Vitalism is the formula of the superego.

Insofar as to live means to follow a superego injunction, and insofar as superego is an agency which operates beyond the pleasure principle (even if we understand superego in Lacan's sense, as the imperative 'Enjoy!', enjoyment is to be opposed here to pleasure), life itself functions beyond the pleasure principle – but how, precisely? In Lacanese, the Freudian pleasure principle is 'non-all': there is nothing outside it, no external limits, and yet it is not all, it can break down. Deleuze drew the ultimate consequence of this notion of death drive: death drive is 'the transcendental conditions of the pleasure principle', it accounts for 'how the psyche is constituted such that it can be ruled by pleasure and unpleasure (with the twist in the story being that what makes possible the pleasure principle's reign also undermines it from within)':

> The death drive is 'beyond' the pleasure principle, but again this does not mean that it is located somewhere else. The death drive is not a separate power that fights against or opposes life, but rather what de-naturalizes or de-vitalizes the flux of life. It takes away the self-evidence of that powerful compass of nature, the orientation provided

by feelings of pleasure and pain. If the unconscious is the distortion, the glitch, the deviation of consciousness, the death drive is the skew of Eros, the twist that makes of life not a direct expression of vital forces but the deviation of the negative: instead of a perseverance in being a 'failing not to be'.

So it is not that subject is secretly dominated by some perverse tendency to sabotage its pleasures; the point is that, in order for the subject to search for pleasures and avoid unpleasures, it already has to stand at a certain distance towards life, and this distance itself has to be inscribed into the functioning of the pleasure principle as its incompleteness, as its inconsistency. Nowhere is this immanent inconsistency of the pleasure principle more clearly displayed than in the work of the Marquis de Sade in which full pleasure in life overlaps with the most rigorous Kantian ethics. The greatness of Sade is that, on behalf of the full assertion of earthly pleasures, he not only rejects any metaphysical moralism but also fully acknowledges the price one has to pay for it: the radical intellectualization–instrumentalization– regimentation of the (sexual) activity intended to bring pleasure. Here we encounter the content later baptized by Marcuse 'repressive desublimation': after all the barriers of sublimation, of cultural transformation of sexual activity, are abolished, what we get is not raw, brutal, passionate, satisfying animal sex, but, on the contrary, a fully regimented, intellectualized activity comparable to a well-planned sporting match. The Sadean hero is not a brute animal beast, but a pale, cold-blooded intellectual much more alienated from the true pleasure of the flesh than is the prudish, inhibited lover, a man of reason enslaved to the *amor intellectualis diaboli* – what gives pleasure to him (or her) is not sexuality as such but the activity of outstripping rational civilization by its own means, i.e. by way of thinking (and practising) to the end the consequences of its logic. So, far from being an entity of full, earthly passion, the Sadean hero is fundamentally apathetic, reducing sexuality to a mechanical planned procedure deprived of the last vestiges of spontaneous pleasure or sentimentality. What Sade heroically takes into account is that pure bodily sensual pleasure and spiritual love are not simply opposed, but dialectically intertwined: there is something deeply 'spiritual', spectral, sublime, about a really passionate sensual lust, and vice versa (as the mystical experience teaches us), so that the thorough 'desublimation' of sexuality also thoroughly intellectualizes it, changing an intense pathetic bodily experience into a cold, apathetic mechanical exercise.

Sade thus consequently deployed the inherent potential of the Kantian philosophical revolution – but how, precisely? The first association here is, of course: what's all the fuss about? Today, in our postidealist Freudian era, doesn't everybody know what the point of the 'with' in 'Kant with Sade' is – the truth of Kant's ethical rigorism is the sadism of the Law, i.e. the Kantian Law is a superego agency that sadistically enjoys the subject's deadlock, his inability to meet its inexorable demands, like the proverbial teacher who tortures pupils with impossible tasks and secretly savours their failings? Lacan's point, however, is the exact opposite of this first association: it is not Kant who was a closet sadist, it is Sade who is a closet Kantian. That is to say, what one should bear in mind is that the focus of Lacan is always Kant, not Sade: what he is interested in are the ultimate consequences and disavowed premises of the Kantian ethical revolution. In other words, Lacan does not try to make the usual 'reductionist' point that every ethical act, as pure and disinterested as it may appear, is always grounded in some 'pathological' motivation (the agent's own long-term interest, the admiration of his peers, up to the 'negative' satisfaction provided by the suffering and extortion often demanded by ethical acts); the focus of Lacan's interest rather resides in the paradoxical reversal by means of which desire itself (i.e. acting upon one's desire, not compromising it) can no longer be grounded in any 'pathological' interests or motivations and thus meets the criteria of the Kantian ethical act, so that 'following one's desire' overlaps with 'doing one's duty'. Suffice it to recall Kant's own famous example from his *Critique of Practical Reason*:

> Suppose someone asserts of his lustful inclination that, when the desired object and opportunity are present, it is quite irresistible to him; ask him whether, if a gallows were erected in front of the house where he finds this opportunity and he would be hanged on it immediately after gratifying his lust, he would not then control his inclination. One need not conjecture very long what he would reply.[5]

Lacan's counterargument here is that we certainly *do* have to guess what his answer may be: what if we encounter a subject (as we regularly do in psychoanalysis) who can only fully enjoy a night of passion if some form of 'gallows' is threatening him, i.e. if, by doing it, he is violating some prohibition? Mario Monicelli's *Casanova '70* (1965) with Virna Lisi and Marcello Mastroianni hinges on this very point: the hero can only retain his sexual potency if doing 'it' involves some kind of danger. At the film's end, when he is on the verge of marrying his beloved, he wants at least to violate the prohibition of premarital sex by sleeping with her the night before the wedding – however, his bride unknowingly spoils even this minimal pleasure by arranging with the priest for special permission for the two of them to sleep together the night before, so that the act is deprived of its transgressive sting. What can he do now? In the last shot of the film, we see him crawling on the narrow porch on the outside of the high-rise building, giving himself the difficult task of entering the girl's bedroom in the most dangerous way, in a desperate attempt to link sexual gratification to mortal danger ... So, Lacan's point is that if gratifying sexual passion involves the suspension of even the most elementary 'egotistic' interests, if this gratification is clearly located 'beyond the pleasure principle', then, in spite of all appearances to the contrary, we are dealing with an ethical act, and his 'passion' is *stricto sensu* ethical.

The crucial clue that allows us to discern the contours of 'Sade in Kant' is the way Kant conceptualizes the relationship between sentiments (feelings) and the moral law. Although Kant insists on the absolute gap between pathological sentiments and the pure form of moral law, there is one a priori sentiment that the subject necessarily experiences when confronted with the injunction of the moral law, the pain of humiliation (because of man's hurt pride, due to the 'radical evil' of human nature); for Lacan, this Kantian privileging of pain as the only a priori sentiment is strictly correlative to Sade's notion of pain (torturing and humiliating the other, being tortured and humiliated by him) as the privileged way of access to sexual *jouissance* (Sade's argument, of course, is that pain is to be given priority over pleasure on account of its greater longevity – pleasures are passing, while pain can last almost indefinitely). Why does cliterodectomy cause such consternation? Because it provides a clear case of how even the most brutal deprivation of the means of pleasure (cutting of the clitoris) can function as a means of generating specific *jouissance*. What is so disturbing about cliterodectomy is not the extremely brutal nature of this operation and its obvious role as an instrument of male domination; nor is it the fact that some women at least value their social acceptance so much that they are ready to accept cliterodectomy as a moment of their full entrance into society. The truly disturbing thing is that they may enjoy it.

A recent publicity spot for upper-class eco-friendly tourism proposes that what we should be doing is 'exploring ways of blending luxury and sustainability', and it clearly designates its addressees: 'For hedonists with a conscience'. There is nothing truly paradoxical in this link between apparent opposites: 'hedonist with a conscience' is one of the most succinct definitions of the predominant type of subjectivity we are interpellated into today. In this type, pleasure principle and reality principle are harmoniously blended, and what is excluded from this space of 'hedonism with conscience' is not only *jouissance* itself in its excessive character, but also the ethical dimension proper – duty in its Kantian, unconditional sense. In short, what is excluded is the domain designated by Lacan's formula *Kant avec Sade*, the uncanny domain in which desire and law coincide, in which the ultimate categorical imperative is 'do not compromise your desire'.

This link can be further substantiated by what Lacan calls the Sadean fundamental fantasy: the fantasy of another, ethereal body of the victim, which can be tortured indefinitely and nonetheless magically retains its beauty (see the standard Sadean figure of a young girl sustaining endless humiliations and mutilations from her deprived torturer and somehow mysteriously surviving it all intact, in the same way Tom and Jerry and other cartoon heroes survive all their ridiculous ordeals intact). Doesn't this fantasy provide the libidinal foundation of the Kantian postulate of the immortality of the soul endlessly striving to achieve ethical perfection, i.e. is not the fantasmatic 'truth' of the immortality of the soul its exact opposite, the immortality of the body, its ability to sustain endless pain and humiliation? Judith Butler pointed out that the Foucauldian 'body' as the site of resistance is none other than the Freudian 'psyche': paradoxically, 'body' is Foucault's name for the psychic apparatus insofar as it resists the soul's domination. That is to say, when, in his well-known definition of the soul as the 'prison of the body', Foucault turns around the standard Platonic-Christian definition of the body as the 'prison of the soul', what he calls 'body' is not simply the biological body, but is effectively already caught in some kind of presubjective psychic apparatus.[6] Consequently, don't we encounter in Kant a secret homologous inversion, only in the opposite direction, of the relationship between body and soul: what Kant calls 'immortality of the soul' is effectively the immortality of the other, ethereal, 'undead' body?

This redoubling of the body into the common mortal body and the ethereal undead body brings us to the crux of the matter: the distinction between the two deaths, the biological death of the common mortal body and the death of the other 'undead' body; it is clear that what Sade aims at in his notion of a radical Crime is the murder of this second body. Sade deploys this distinction in the long philosophical dissertation delivered to Juliette by Pope Pius VI, part of book 5 of *Juliette*:

> there is nothing wrong with rape, torture, murder, and so on, since these conform to the violence that is the way of the universe. To act in accordance with nature means to actively take part in its orgy of destruction. The trouble is that man's capacity for crime is highly limited, and his atrocities no matter how debauched ultimately outrage nothing. This is a depressing thought for the libertine. The human being, along with all organic life and even inorganic matter, is caught in an endless cycle of death and rebirth, generation and corruption, so

that 'there is indeed no real death', only a permanent transformation and recycling of matter according to the immanent laws of 'the three kingdoms', animal, vegetable, and mineral. Destruction may accelerate this process, but it cannot stop it. The true crime would be the one that no longer operates within the three kingdoms but annihilates them altogether, that puts a stop to the eternal cycle of generation and corruption and by doing so returns to Nature her absolute privilege of contingent creation, of casting the dice anew.

What, then, at a strict theoretical level, is wrong with this dream of the 'second death' as a radical pure negation which puts a stop to the life cycle itelf? In a superb display of his genius, Lacan provides a simple answer: 'It is just that, being a psychoanalyst, I can see that the second death is prior to the first, and not after, as de Sade dreams it.' (The only problematic part of this statement is the qualificaion 'being a psychoanalyst' – a Hegelian philosopher can also see this quite clearly.) In what precise sense are we to understand this priority of the second death – the radical annihilation of the entire life cycle of generation and corruption – over the first death which remains a moment of this cycle? Schuster points the way: 'Sade believes that there exists a well-established second nature that operates according to immanent laws. Against this ontologically consistent realm he can only dream of an absolute Crime that would abolish the three kingdoms and attain the pure disorder of primary nature.' In short, what Sade doesn't see is that there is no big Other, no Nature as an ontologically consistent realm – nature is already in itself inconsistent, unbalanced, destabilized by antagonisms. The total negation imagined by Sade thus doesn't come at the end, as a threat or prospect of radical destruction, it comes at the beginning, it always-already happened, it stands for the zero-level starting point out of which the fragile/inconsistent reality emerges. In other words, what is missing in the notion of Nature as a body regulated by fixed laws is simply *subject itself*: in Hegelese, the Sadean Nature remains a Substance, Sade continues to grasp reality only as Substance and not also as Subject, where 'subject' does not stand for another ontological level different from Substance but for the immanent incompleteness–inconsistency–antagonism of Substance itself. And, insofar as the Freudian name for this radical negativity is death drive, Schuster is right to point out how, paradoxically, what Sade misses in his celebration of the ultimate Crime of radical destruction of all life is precisely the death drive:

> for all its wantonness and havoc the Sadeian will-to-extinction is premised on a fetishistic denial of the death drive. The sadist makes

himself into the servant of universal extinction precisely in order to avoid the deadlock of subjectivity, the 'virtual extinction' that splits the life of the subject from within. The Sadeian libertine expels this negativity outside himself in order to be able to slavishly devote himself to it; the apocalyptic vision of an absolute Crime thus functions as a screen against a more intractable internal split. What the florid imagination of the sadist masks is the fact that the Other is barred, inconsistent, lacking, that it cannot be served for it presents no law to obey, not even the wild law of its accelerating auto-destruction. There is no nature to be followed, rivaled or outdone, and it is this void or lack, the non-existence of the Other, that is incomparably more violent than even the most destructive fantasm of the death drive. Or as Lacan argues, Sade is right if we just turn around his evil thought: subjectivity is the catastrophe it fantasizes about, the death beyond death, the 'second death'. While the sadist dreams of violently forcing a cataclysm that will wipe the slate clean, what he does not want to know is that this unprecedented calamity has already taken place. Every subject is the end of the world, or rather this impossibly explosive end that is equally a 'fresh start', the unabolishable chance of the dice throw.

It was already Kant who had characterized a free autonomous act as an act which cannot be accounted for in the terms of natural causality, of the texture of causes and effects: a free act occurs as its own cause, it opens up a new causal chain from its zero-point. So insofar as 'second death' is the interruption of the natural life cycle of generation and corruption, no radical annihilation of the entire natural order is needed for this – an autonomous free act already suspends natural causality, and subject as $ already is this cut in the natural circuit, the self-sabotage of natural goals. The mystical name for this end of the world is 'night of the world', and the philosophical name, radical negativity as the core of subjectivity. And, to quote Mallarmé, a throw of the dice will never abolish the hazard, i.e. the abyss of negativity remains forever the unsublatable background of subjective creativity. We may even risk here an ironic version of Gandhi's famous motto 'be yourself the change you want to see in the world': the subject is itself the catastrophe it fears and tries to avoid. And is the lesson of Hegel's analysis of the French revolutionary terror not exactly the same (which is why the parallel between Sade's absolute crime and revolutionary terror is well grounded)? Individuals threatened by the Terror have to grasp that this external threat of annihilation is nothing but the externalized/fetishized image of the radical negativity of self-consciousness – once they grasp this, they pass from revolutionary Terror to the inner force of the moral Law.

Although Catherine Malabou is an excellent reader of Hegel, it seems that even she misses this Hegelian point in her critique of Freud who, according to her, cannot think the 'destructive plasticity', that is, the subjective form assumed by the very destruction of the self, the direct form of death drive: 'It is as if there is no intermediary between the plasticity of the good form and elasticity as the mortifying erasure of all form. *In Freud, there is no form of the negation of form*.'[7] In other words, Freud fails to consider

the existence of a specific form of psyche produced by the presence of death, of pain, of the repetition of a painful experience. He should have rendered justice to existential power of improvisation proper to an accident, to the psyches deserted by pleasure, in which indifference and detachment win over links, and which nonetheless remain psyches. What Freud is looking for when he talks about the death drive is precisely the form of this drive, the form he doesn't find insofar as he denies to destruction its own specific plasticity ... The beyond of the pleasure principle is thus the work of the death drive as the giving-form to death in life, as the production of those individual figures which exist only in the detachment of existence. These forms of death in life, fixations of the image of drive, would be the 'satisfying' representatives of the death drive Freud was for such a long time looking for far away from neurology.[8]

These figures are 'not so much figures of those who want to die as figures of those who *are already dead*, or, rather, to put it in a strange and terrible grammatical twist, who *have already been dead*, who "experienced" death'.[9] The strange fact is that, although it is impossible to miss the Hegelian resonances of this notion of 'negative plasticity', of the form in which destructivity/negativity itself acquires positive existence, Malabou – the author of a groundbreaking book on Hegel – not only totally ignores Hegel in *Les nouveaux blessés*, but even gives here and there hints that this negative plasticity is 'non-dialectizable' and, as such, beyond the scope of Hegelian dialectics. Malabou sees here not only a task for psychoanalysis, but also a properly *philosophical* task to reconceptualize the notion of subject so that it will include this zero-level of the subject of death drive: 'the only philosophical issue is today the elaboration of a new materialism which precisely refuses to envisage any, even the smallest, separation not only between brain and thought, but also between brain and the unconscious.'[10] Malabou is right to emphasize the philosophical dimension of the new autistic subject: in it, we are dealing with the zero-level of subjectivity, with the formal conversion of the pure externality of meaningless real (its brutal destructive intrusion) into the pure internality of the 'autistic' subject detached from external reality, disengaged, reduced to the persisting core deprived of its substance. The logic is here again that of the Hegelian infinite judgement: the speculative identity of meaningless external intrusion and of the pure detached internality – it is as if only a brutal external shock can give rise to pure interiority of subject, of the void that cannot be identified with any determinate positive content.

The properly philosophical dimension of the study of post-traumatic subject resides in this recognition that what appears as the brutal destruction of the subject's very (narrative) substantial identity is the moment of its birth. The post-traumatic autistic subject is the 'living proof' that subject cannot be identified (does not fully overlap) with 'stories it is telling itself about itself', with the narrative symbolic texture of its life: when we take all this away, something (or, rather, *nothing*, but a *form* of nothing) remains, and this something is the pure subject of death drive. If one wants to get an idea of the elementary, zero-level, form of subjectivity, one has to take a look at autistic monsters. The Lacanian subject as $ is thus a response *to/ of* the real: a response *to* the real of the brutal meaningless intrusion – a response *of* the real, i.e. a response which emerges when the symbolic integration of the traumatic intrusion fails, reaches its point of impossibility. As such, the subject at its most elementary effectively is 'beyond unconscious': the empty form deprived even of unconscious formations encapsulating a variety of libidinal investments.

We should thus apply even to the post-traumatic subject the Freudian notion that a violent intrusion of the real counts as trauma only insofar as a previous trauma resonates in it – *in this case, the previous trauma is that of the birth of subjectivity itself*: a subject is 'barred', as Lacan put it, it emerges when a living individual is deprived of its substantial content, and this constitutive trauma is repeated in the present traumatic experience. This is what Lacan aims at with his claim that the Freudian subject is none other than the Cartesian *cogito*: the *cogito* is not an 'abstraction' from the reality of living, actual individuals with the wealth of their properties, emotions, abilities, relations; it is, on the contrary, this 'wealth of personality' which functions as the imaginary 'stuff of the I', as Lacan put it; the *cogito* is, on the contrary, a very real 'abstraction' – an 'abstraction' which functions as a concrete subjective attitude. The post-traumatic subject, the subject reduced to a substanceless empty form of subjectivity, is the historical 'realization' of *cogito* – recall that, for Descartes, *cogito* is the zero-point of the overlapping of thinking and being at which the subject in a way neither 'is' (he is deprived of all positive substantial content) nor 'thinks' (his thinking is reduced to the empty tautology of thinking that it thinks).[11]

The predominant notion of subjectivity today is the one at work in the Habermasian project of the mutual recognition of free responsible agents … what disappears in this project is the antagonistic core of subjectivity, a traumatic disturbance inscribed into the very notion of subject from Kant to Hegel – as Finkelde put it, the true meaning of 'excessive subjectivity' is that *subjectivity is as such an excess*. Intersubjectivity engaged in the game of mutual recognition is ultimately a defence formation, an attempt to contain the excess of subjectivity.

So when Malabou claims that the post-traumatic subject cannot be accounted for in the Freudian terms of the repetition of a past trauma (since the traumatic shock erases all traces of the past), she remains all too fixed on the traumatic content and forgets to include in the series of past traumatic memories the very erasure of the substantial content, the very subtraction of the empty form from its content. In other words, precisely insofar as it erases the entire substantial content, the traumatic shock *repeats* the past, i.e. the past traumatic loss of substance which is constitutive of the very dimension of subjectivity. *What is repeated here is not some ancient content, but the very gesture of erasing all substantial content.* This is why, when one submits a human subject to a traumatic intrusion, the outcome is the empty form of the 'living-dead' subject, but when one does the same to an animal, the result is simply total devastation: what remains after the violent traumatic intrusion onto a human subject which erases all its substantial content is the pure form of subjectivity, the form which already must have been there. It is in this precise sense that subjectivity and mortality are closely linked, although in a sense that totally differs from the standard Heideggerian topic of finitude. In his rejection of the thought of finitude, Badiou asserted that

> death is something that *happens to you*; it is not the immanent unfolding of some linear programme. Even if we say that human life cannot go beyond a hundred and twenty years, for biological, genetic etc. reasons, death as death is always something that *happens to you*. One great thinker on death is La Palice. A truth we get from La Palice is that 'a quarter an hour before his death, he was still alive'. That isn't at all absurd or naïve. It means that 'a quarter an hour before death' he wasn't what Heidegger sees as 'a quarter hour before death' – he wasn't 'a-being-toward-death' ever since his birth. 'A quarter of an hour before his death' he was alive, and death *happens* to him. And I would maintain that death always comes from the outside. Spinoza said something

excellent on that score: 'Nothing can be destroyed except by an external cause' ... This means that death is in a position of radical exteriority: we would not even say that a human reality, a *Dasein*, is mortal. Because 'mortal' means to say that it contains the virtuality of death in an immanent fashion. In truth, all that is is generically immortal, and then death intervenes.[12]

Crucial here is the mention of Spinoza, and here one should oppose Spinoza to Hegel: while for Spinoza, every destruction comes from outside, thwarting every organism's immanent tendency to reproduce and expand its life power, for Hegel, negation is immanent, inscribed into the innermost identity of every living being, so that every destruction is ultimately self-destruction. To avoid misunderstanding, Hegel would have agreed that there is no deeper meaning in death, that death comes as a radically external meaningless contingency – but it is precisely as such that it corrodes from within the very core of human identity and its universe of meaning. Furthermore, like Badiou, Hegel asserts infinity/immortality, but for him, immortality emerges precisely through 'tarrying with the negative', through its immanent ovecoming: only a being which is not constrained by its mortality can relate to its death 'as such'. This overcoming is paradoxically a form of 'death in life': a human being overcomes its mortality through gaining a distance towards its life-substance (for example, through its readiness to risk its life for some spiritual cause). Hegel's name for this dimension is negativity, and Freud's name is death drive. Immortality is death in life, a deadly force that acquires control over the living substance, or, as Paul would have put it, Spirit is the death of flesh.

One should strictly oppose here subjectivity and the soul of living beings: 'The Notion is not merely *soul*, but free subjective Notion that is for itself and therefore possesses *personality* – the practical, objective Notion determined in and for itself which, as person, is impenetrable atomic subjectivity ... It contains *all* determinateness within it.'[13] The distinction between Soul and Subject is crucial here: Soul is the Aristotelian immanent ideal form/principle of an organism, the immaterial 'life force' that keeps it alive and united, while Subject is antisoul, the point of negative self-relating which reduces the individual to the abyss of a singularity at a distance from the living substance that sustains it. That's why, for Hegel, a notion comes to exist as such, 'for itself', in its opposition to its empirical instantiations, only insofar as it is located in an 'impenetrable atomic subjectivity'. His point here is not a commonsense vulgarity according to which in order for universal thoughts to exist, there has to be an empirical subject that does the thinking (therein resides the endlessly boring motif of the critics of

Hegel from young Marx onwards: 'thoughts don't think themselves, only concrete living subjects can think …'). While Hegel is fully aware of this dependence of thoughts on a thinking subject, his point is a more precise one: what kind of subject can do this 'abstract' thinking (in the common sense of the term: thinking of formal thoughts purified of their empirical wealth – say, thinking of a 'horse' in abstraction from the wealth of content of empirical horses)? His answer is: a subject which is itself 'abstract', deprived of the wealth of empirical features, reduced to its 'impenetrable atomic' singularity. This may sound weird and counterintuitive: is Notion in its universality not the very opposite of atomic impenetrability? However, 'abstraction' can be performed in two ways (or, rather, in two directions): erasure of all particular features in order to obtain the abstract form (say, the universal 'horse' as such), end erasure of all particular features (qualities) in order to obtain the pure singularity of the thing in question (a pure 'this' or X without properties), and Hegel's point is that subjectivity emerges when such singularity becomes 'for itself': a subject is for itself the abyss of a pure X at a distance from all its properties. Both 'abstractions' are strictly correlative: universal form can emerge as such only in an entity which is for itself reduced to the impenetrable abyss of pure singularity. More precisely, the impenetrable atomic singularity is not something external to the Notion, it is Notion itself in its 'oppositional determination', Notion as actually existing singularity – in this sense Hegel wrote that Self is a pure Notion. The Cartesian name for this singularity is *cogito*: the Self reduced to the evanescent punctuality of the act of thinking.

The troubles with finitude

When Badiou opposes the life of a human animal oriented towards 'servicing of the goods' and the life defined by the fidelity to an Event, one should raise the key question: how should animal life be transformed so that it can sustain the consequences of an Event, i.e. what happens to a human animal when it turns into a subject? The Hegelo-Lacanian reply is here: death drive, i.e. human animal has to integrate the dimension of death, it has to become a 'living dead', at a distance from life. In other words, the eventual level does not simply add itself to animal life as another dimension, its arrival distorts, transforms animal life at its innermost. At this point, one has to make a choice between idealism and materialism: is the distortion of the human animal the effect of an Event, the way an Event inscribes itself into the order of animal life (idealist version), or does the distortion of the human animal come first, opening up the space for the possible emergence of an Event (materialist version)?

The axiom of the philosophy of finitude is that one cannot escape finitude/mortality as the unsurpassable horizon of our existence; Lacan's axiom is that, no matter how much one tries, one cannot escape immortality. But what if this choice is false? What if finitude and immortality, like lack and excess, also form a parallax couple, what if they are the same from a different point of view? What if immortality is an object that is a remainder/excess over finitude, what if finitude is an attempt to escape from the excess of immortality? What if Kierkegaard was right here, but for the wrong reason, when he also understood the claim that we, humans, are just mortal beings who disappear after their biological death as an easy way to escape the ethical responsibility that comes with the immortal soul? He was right for the wrong reason insofar as he equated immortality with the divine and ethical part of a human being – but there is another immortality. What Cantor did for infinity, we should do for immortality, and assert the multiplicity of immortalities; the Badiouian noble immortality/infinity of the deployment of an Event (as opposed to the finitude of a human animal) comes after a more basic form of immortality which resides in what Lacan calls the Sadean fundamental fantasy: the fantasy of another, ethereal body of the victim, which can be tortured indefinitely and nonetheless magically retains its beauty. In this form, the comical and the disgustingly-terrifying (recall different versions of the 'undead' – zombies, vampires, etc. – in popular culture) are inextricably connected. The same immortality underlies the intuition of something indestructible in a truly radical Evil. In the classic German poem about two naughty children, Wilhelm Busch's 'Max und Moritz' (first published in 1865), the two children are constantly acting in a disgraceful way against respected authorities, until, finally, they both fall into a wheat mill and come out cut into tiny grains – but when these grains fall on the floor, they form a shape of the two boys: '*Rickeracke! Rickeracke! / Geht die Mühle mit Geknacke. / Hier kann man sie noch erblicken, / Fein geschroten und in Stücken.*' In the original illustration, their shapes are obscenely sneering, persisting in their evil even after their death … Adorno was right when he wrote that when one encounters a truly evil person, it is difficult to imagine that this person can die. We are of course not immortal, we all (will) die – the 'immortality' of the death drive is not a biological fact but a psychic stance of 'persisting beyond life and death', of a readiness to go on beyond the limits of life, of a perverted life force which bears witness to a 'deranged relationship towards life'. Lacan's name for this derangement is, of course, *jouissance*, excessive enjoyment, whose pursuit can make us neglect or even self-sabotage our vital needs and interests. At this precise point, Lacan radically differs from the thinkers of finitude for whom a human being is a being-towards-death, relating to its own finitude and unavoidable death: it is only through the intervention of *jouissance* that a human animal becomes properly mortal, relating to the prospect of its own extinction. Lacan notes apropos of the 'life and death dialogue' how 'it only acquires the character of a drama from the moment when enjoyment [*jouisssance*] intervenes. The vital point ... is the deranged relationship to one's own body called enjoyment':[14]

> If an animal is eating [stuffing itself: *bouffe*] regularly, it is clear that this happens because it doesn't know the enjoyment of hunger. The one who speaks – this is what psychoanalysis teaches us – colors with enjoyment all its [vital] needs, that is to say, that by means of which it defends itself against death.[15]

One should take here 'enjoyment of hunger' quite literally: what if, as part of a complex ritual, hunger itself becomes libidinally invested? What if, in a typical reversal, preparation to eat provides more pleasure than the act of eating itself? Robert Brandom uses the same example of hunger to illustrate the structure of what he calls 'erotic awareness':

> Erotic awareness has a tripartite structure, epitomized by the relations between *hunger, eating*, and *food*. Hunger is a desire, a kind of *attitude*. It immediately impels hungry animals to respond to some objects by treating them *as* food, that is, by *eating* them. *Food* is accordingly a *significance* that objects can have to animals capable of hunger. It is something things can be *for* desiring animals. *Eating* is the activity of taking or treating something *as* food. It is what one must *do* in order in practice to be attributing to it the desire-relative erotic significance of *food*.[16]

But does this structure really deserve to be called 'erotic'? Doesn't eroticism proper emerge only when the aim of our activity doesn't directly overlap with its goal – in the case of hunger, when postponing the act of eating itself brings pleasure? To put it another way, when Brandom writes: 'That practical identification, through risk and sacrifice, with one element of what he is for himself at once expresses and constitutes the Master as in himself a geistig, normative being, and not just a desiring, natural one',[17] should we not raise the obvious question: but what if this 'element' is (an object of) desire itself? What if someone is ready to risk and sacrifice everything for his/her desire, including all his/her natural interests? Therein resides the point of Lacan's '*Kant avec Sade*'. And what if, in an additional moment of perversion, an object causes our desire precisely because it involves risk and sacrifice? Owing to his ignorance of this aspect of desire, Brandom ultimately fails in his endeavour to provide 'a non-reductive account of how we should understand the place of norms in the natural world': he remains here an idealist. When he describes the passage from (animal) desire to (symbolic) recogntion, he ignores the key (Freudian) materialist question: how desire itself has to be fundamentally transformed (from satisfaction to its postponement, etc.) to be able to sustain recognition.[18]

We can immediately see how the cliché about 'deadly incestuous *jouissance*' which burns us if we come too close to it totally misses this link of death and *jouissance*. The point is not that *jouissance* has to be kept at a certain distance, otherwise it would kill us; the point is that we *are* already dead, in the precise sense in which Lacan reinterpreted Sade's notion of the 'second death': subject (written by Lacan as $, the barred subject) is in a way the survivor of its own death, i.e. even when it is biologically still alive (attached to a living body), it is caught in the vicious cycle of *jouissance* which functions at a distance from life, which is never synchronized with life rhythm. Our self-perception as mortal beings, our relating to the prospect of our death, is grounded in this discord/excess of *jouissance* – which makes us aware of our biological finitude.

Lacan did not arrive at this insight directly; first, he conceived awareness of mortality as an effect of our dwelling in the symbolic order: for a being-of-language, its biological life gets denaturalized, caught into a symbolic rhythm which followed its own rules, and 'death drive' is here interpreted as this autonomous functioning of the symbolic order at a distance from life, with no mention of the excess of *jouissance*. This brings us back to the phallic signifier in which omnipotency overlaps with impotence, or, even more radically, in which the 'thrust of life' overlaps with death drive: the phallic signifier stands for potency, live thrust, but potency within the domain of the signifier, which means: of the symbolic death, of the subordination of life to a dead symbolic machine:

> This articulation by Freud of the death instinct is the articulation of a position essential to an animal being who is caught up and articulated in a signifying system which permits him to dominate his immanence as a living being, and to perceive himself as already dead … There is no experience of death, of course, which can correspond to it, and this is the very reason that it is symbolised in a different fashion. It is symbolised on this point and on this precise organ where there appears in the most obvious fashion the thrust of life. That is the reason that

it is the phallus in so far as it represents simply the rise of vital power which takes its place in the order of signifiers, in order to represent for the human individual in his existence that which is marked by the signifier, that which is struck by the signifier with this essential caducity in which there can be articulated the signifier itself, this lack of being whose dimension the signifier introduces into the life of the subject.[19]

So how does 'the rise of vital power take its place in the order of signifiers'? It takes its place on the very edge where the Imaginary touches the Real, as the experience of life in its horror and disgust:

The famous trauma from which we started, the famous primitive scene, what is it, if it is not precisely something which enters into the economy of the subject, and which operates at the heart, at the horizon of the discovery of the unconscious, always as a signifier, a signifier in so far as it is defined in its incidence as I began to articulate it above, namely that life, I mean the living being grasped as living, qua living, but with this separation, this distance which is precisely what constitutes this autonomy of the signifying dimension, the trauma or the primitive scene. What is it therefore if not this life which grasps itself in a horrible perception of itself, in its total strangeness, in its opaque brutality as pure signifier of an existence intolerable for life itself, once it separates itself from it to see the trauma and the primitive scene. This is what appears of life to itself as signifier in the pure state, namely as something which cannot yet in any fashion be resolved, be articulated.[20]

The Real in its most terrifying dimension, as the primordial abyss which swallows everything, dissolving all identities, is a figure well known in literature in its multiple guises, from Poe's Maelstrom and Kurtz's 'horror' at the end of Conrad's *The Heart of Darkness* to Pip from Melville's *Moby Dick* who, cast to the bottom of the ocean, experiences the demonic God:

Carried down alive to wondrous depths, where strange shapes of the unwarped primal world glided to and fro before his passive eyes ... Pip saw the multitudinous, God-omnipresent, coral insects, that out of the firmament of waters heaved the colossal orbs. He saw God's foot upon the treadle of the loom, and spoke it; and therefore his shipmates called him mad.[21]

What is crucial here is that Lacan counterintuitively characterizes this experience as the one that renders 'signifier in the pure state': it is not, as it may appear, simply the experience of some presymbolic primordial Real Thing but already the obverse, the other side, of symbolic castration – and vice versa, we do not experience 'signifier in the pure state' when we encounter a pure symbolic formation like a mathematic formula but precisely when we confront the Real at its most raw. Why? The fact that, in this experience, we are not directly immersed into the Real but that the Real appears as something absolutely foreign/repellent – this fact already implies that we are already subjected to symbolic castration which entails the loss of the immediate identification with life. Once we are in the Symbolic the ultimate trauma is life itself.

Lacan's name for finitude is (symbolic) castration, and his name for immortality is death drive. They are the two sides of the same operation, i.e. it's not that the substance of life, the immortal Jouissance-Thing, is 'castrated' by the arrival of the symbolic order. As in the case of lack and excess, the structure is that of parallax: the undead Thing is the remainder of castration, it is generated by castration, and vice versa, there is no 'pure' castration, castration itself is sustained by the immortal excess which eludes it. This codependence of lack and excess was clearly described in Deleuze's *The Logic of Sense*, where he develops how a symbolic order always implies the minimal difference between a structural place and the element that occupies (fills out) this place: an element is always logically preceded by the place in the structure it fills out. We are dealing here with two series (or, rather, levels), the 'empty' formal structure (signifier), and the series of elements filling out the empty places in the structure (signified); the paradox consists in the fact that these two series never overlap: we always encounter an entity that is simultaneously – with regard to the structure – an empty, unoccupied place and – with regard to the elements – a rapidly moving, elusive object, an occupant without a place.[22] We have thereby produced Lacan's formula of fantasy $\$<> a$, since the matheme for the subject is $\$$, an empty place in the structure, an elided signifier, while *objet a* is, by definition, an excessive object, an object that lacks its place in the structure. Consequently, the point is not that there is simply the surplus of an element over the places available in the structure or the surplus of a place that has no element to fill it out. An empty place in the structure would still sustain the fantasy of an element that will emerge and fill out this place; an excessive element lacking its place would still sustain the fantasy of some yet unknown place waiting for it. The point is, rather, that the empty place in the structure is strictly correlative to the errant element lacking its place: they are not two different entities, but the front and the back of one and the same entity, that is, one and the same entity inscribed onto the two surfaces of a Moebius strip.

So it's not that first there is an ideal, complete symbolic structure out of which a key signifier is subtracted; this subtraction itself creates the structure. The structure is here the one of 'one-less-plus-*a*', which means that this lack is only as surplus – we don't get first a lack which is then eventually filled in. One should thus resist the temptation to conceive excess-object as filling in the lack, as if one can entertain the vision of a heroic confronting of the pure lack not yet filled in by object. The difference between lack and excess-object is purely topological: excess-object *is* the same as lack, its other side, there is no lack without object. (Here we encounter a nice case of the Hegelian distinction between Understanding and Reason: Understanding is not able to grasp this purely topological distinction of lack and excess, so it conceives them as external, not as identical, and searches for an excess that would fill in the lack.)

Language exists because there is no binary signifier – or, as Alenka Zupančič put it succinctly, 'language is nothing but a reply to a missing signifier, to a signifier which is not there'.[23] This determination is, of course, tautological and circular: language emerges out of the lack of something that belongs to language itself. What this means is that the external limit of language is simultaneously its internal limit: the limit between language and its Outside (reality or whatever), between words and things, is always simultaneously internal to language, it curtails language from within, makes it non-all, unable to signify fully – whatever is said in a language always circulates around an unsayable core. The signifying order is thus characterized by its own impossibility, it functions as its own obstacle.

What this means is that language is not simply composed of signifiers, i.e. the presence (or, rather, efficient functioning) of signifiers is not a sufficient ground for the occurrence of language. What has to occur is a signifier less, a signifier missing at its place, where it is expected – it is only such a lack of a signifier which awakens the human animal from its indifference and pushes it to speak (and enjoy), and sexual difference is a consequence of this 'ontological deficit' (Zupančič). Recall the well-known case of the language of bees: when they are searching for flowers, one bee can signal to others the exact location of a nearby blossoming bush (direction and distance) by means of a complex codified dance – but this is not yet language proper for the simple reason that the code followed by a bee is in itself complete, with no signifier lacking in it.

So, again, language arises not when there are signifiers but when a signifier lacks, stays out, and it is through this missing signifier that the chain of signifiers subjectivizes itself – more precisely, the lack of a signifier is always registered in a chain by a paradoxical reflexive signifier which represents this lack itself, and in this sense a signifier represents the subject (lack) for other signifiers. This lack/surplus is in itself asexual, and it is subjectivized in two ways, masculine and feminine, which is why sexual difference is a feature of subjectivity as such, not secondary – or, rather: sexual difference is secondary, but 'subject' is the very name for this secondariness. Sexual difference is thus not a pure difference between the two types which is never perfectly actualized, it is *this imperfection itself*, two ways/modes to deal with it, with the lack of the binary signifier: 'if we were to be able to say what Man and Woman mean, they would have been One and the same – that is to say, the binary signifier. It's only that, in this case, we wouldn't be talking at all.'[24] This is what Lacan aims at with his axiom 'There is no sexual relationship'. The point is not that the universe is the field of an eternal struggle between the two opposed cosmic principles (yin and yang, light and darkness, spirit and matter, and other versions of the sexualized cosmology) which cannot ever be harmonized but that, precisely, there is only One – the Other one (what Lacan calls the 'binary signifier') is missing: no 'vaginal signifier' supplements the phallic signifier. But now comes the real paradox: this lack of the 'binary signifier' doesn't imply a 'phallogocentric monotheism', the reign of the One; on the contrary, it curtails from within the One itself – there is no One precisely because there is only One without its complementary counterpart, the Other (one) which makes it One.

We have to differentiate two modalities here, along the lines of Lacan's subtle distinction between 'doesn't exist' and 'there is no' (*il n'y pas*): god doesn't exist (but there is a God who doesn't exist), while there is no sexual relationship. Something that doesn't exist can be efficient, it can leave traces in (symbolic) reality. God doesn't exist, but its inexistence leaves traces in our reality. More precisely, God qua Cause is a retroactive effect of its own traces-effects, in the same way that a political cause only exists in the series of its effects: communism only exists insofar as there are individuals fighting for it (or attacking it), motivated by it in their activity. So the idea that something exists because something else doesn't/cannot exist could be read at two levels: first, god ex-sists (or inexists) because there is no sexual relationship; then, our ordinary reality exists because god doesn't exist. There is a God-Woman because there is no sexual relationship, and this God-Woman doesn't exist but merely inexists.

Materialism or agnosticism?

In his detailed reading of Lacan, Lorenzo Chiesa[25] interprets Lacan's position in a different way: not as a direct assertion of materialism but as a specifically qualified agnosticism. He grounds his reading in some passages from Lacan's seminars which point in this direction, and the whole point is how to read such passages. One has to agree with Chiesa that Lacan often gets caught in a rhetorical trap, conceding something that he shouldn't, but Chiesa and I locate this excess differently. For Chiesa, it is Lacan's positioning of the difference already into the prehuman nature (lamella as real, not just retroactive myth; lack in nature) which is problematic since it obfuscates nature's indifference; for me, it is Lacan's agnostic allowances (maybe, who knows, there is sexual relationship in nature, there is soul which survives death, there is god …) which are his illegitimate concessions. Already the programmatic 'Rapport de Rome' concludes with Indian wisdom from the Upanishads:

> When the Devas, the men, and the Asuras were finishing their novitiate with Prajapati, as we read in the first Brahmana of the fifth lesson of the Brihadaranyaka Upanishad, they begged him, 'Speak to us'. 'Da', said Prajapati, god of thunder. 'Did you hear me?' And the Devas answered, saying: 'Thou hast said to us: Damyata, master yourselves' – the sacred text meaning that the powers above are governed by the law of speech. 'Da', said Prajapati, god of thunder. 'Did you hear me?' And the men answered, saying: 'Thou hast said to us: Datta, give' – the sacred text meaning that men recognize each other by the gift of speech. 'Da', said Prajapati, god of thunder. 'Did you hear me?' And the Asuras answered, saying: 'Thou hast said to us: Dayadhvam, be merciful' – the sacred text meaning that the powers below resound to the invocation of speech. That, continues the text, is what the divine voice conveys in the thunder: Submission, gift, grace. Da da da. For Prajapati replies to all: 'You have heard me'.[26]

And then we have 'Encore' with its famous references to the ineffable *jouissance féminine* located in the mystical sphere outside the symbolic:

> There is an enjoyment, let us say the word, of her own [*à elle*], of this her who does not exist, who does not signify anything. There is an enjoyment, there is an enjoyment for her of which perhaps she herself knows nothing; except that she experiences it. She knows that. She knows it, of course, when it happens. It does not happen to all of them.[27]

To add insult to injury, Lacan even couldn't resist the temptation to include his own *Écrits* into this series: 'all these mystical jaculations which are in short some of the best things one can read – right at the bottom of the page, put a note: add to these the *Écrits* of Jacques Lacan, because they are of the same order.'[28] Are they really? Can we seriously claim that, in *Écrits*, 'there is an enjoyment, there is an enjoyment for Lacan of which perhaps he himself knows nothing; except that he experiences it'? Do such intimations not rather indicate that Lacan is here reaching the limit of his thought, and is filling this gap with pseudowisdom?

As to Lacan's speculations on the gap/openness in nature itself, far from signalling a betrayal of dialectical materialism, they point in the right direction of overcoming the (ultimately idealist) transcendental closure. In other words, what one should reject are not Lacan's speculations about a gap in presymbolic nature, but precisely his otherwise predominant transcendentalism. That is to say, Lacan oscillates between the (predominant) transcendental approach and timid hints at its beyond. Lacan's standard topos is the radical discontinuity between (biological) life and the Symbolic: the Symbolic tortures/derails life, it subordinates life to a foreign compulsion, depriving it forever of its homeostasis – the move from instinct to drive, from need to desire. Within this perspective, the symbolic order is 'always-already here' as our unsurpassable horizon, every account of its genesis amounts to a fantasmatic obfuscation of its constitutive gap. In this Lacanian–structuralist version of the 'hermeneutic circle', all we can do is to circumscribe the void/impossibility which makes the Symbolic non-all and inconsistent, the void in which external limit coincides with the internal one (the void delimitates the Symbolic from the real; however, this limitation cuts into the Symbolic itself). However, from time to time, and more times the later we follow Lacan's teaching, we find echoes of the Schelling–Benjamin–Heidegger topic of a pain in nature itself, the pain which gets expressed/resolved in human speech – the Freudian *Unbehagen in der Kultur* thus gets supplemented by an uncanny *Unbehagen in der Natur* itself:

imagine all of nature waiting for the gift of speech so it can express how bad it is to be a vegetable or a fish. Is it not the special torment of nature to be deprived of the means of conveying its pent-up aggravation, unable to articulate even the simplest lament, 'Ah me! I am the sea'? And does not the emergence on earth of the speaking being effectively release this terrible organic tension and bring it to a higher level of non-resolution? While there are some intriguing passages in Lacan's seminars where he speculates on the infinite pain of being a plant, raising the possibility of an *Unbehagen in Der Natur*, for the most part he conceives the relationship between nature and culture to be one of radical discontinuity.[29]

In order not to mistake this shift for a regression into natural mysticism, one should read it in a strictly Hegelian way: we do not magically overcome the impossibility which cuts across the Symbolic – what we do is to grasp how this impossibility which seemed to keep us apart from the Real, which rendered the Real impossible, is the very feature which locates the Symbolic into the Real.[30]

This difference between Chiesa and me is grounded in our different understanding of Lacan's assertion of 'non-all'. Chiesa draws an unexpected philosophical consequence from the logic of not-all (incompleteness of the big Other):

> either incompleteness is, and we can only *half*-say it as truth, for as soon as we say it we evoke completeness, or it is true that incompleteness is the complete truth of a deceivingly inconsistent God, an absolute being who, by definition, we will never comprehend ... Either the absence of the sexual relationship is through us not only phenomeno-logical but also noumenal, or God ... cheats on us. Either the contingent in-itself that language is, i.e. the material 'idizwadidiz' [*seskecé*], *is* the *truth*, or this meaninglessness of truth has also at the same time an inconsistent *meaning*. Such 'either/or' is unsurpassable, and the only way to protect the 'either' from an unwanted religious absolutization of incompleteness is to keep both options open.

What this reasoning involves is, of course, the elementary gap between enunciated and enunciation: the moment we affirm the incompleteness (non-all) of reality in a statement, we implicitly claim that this is a complete truth about reality, i.e. our position of enunciation is the one of completeness – the only consistent way to assert ontological incompleteness would thus be to 'half-say' (*mi-dire*) it in an incomplete way, but when we do this, incompleteness is no longer a complete truth about reality. To avoid this danger of elevating incompleteness into a complete divine absolute, we should supplement the direct assertion of incompleteness as a complete Truth with its inversion, a weird supreme Being (God) who is himself an inconsistent/incomplete/imperfect one, a God like the *malin génie* imagined by Descartes who stages our reality as a deceiving illusion in order to cheat us ...[31] The ethical consequence of this undecidability is not the opportunist stance of 'playing it safe' ('let's act as if god exists to avoid punishment if god exists after all') but a reversal of Pascal's wager:

> thanks to a reversal of Pascal's wager, the undecidability at stake would in turn award us the freedom to act as though God did not exist (as

a divine essence), for if he existed he could only be fooling us – after all, without even knowing it, since he would also be cheating on himself … While the 'God hypothesis' persists as long as somebody says something, 'nevertheless … *we can do as if he were not there*'[32] … Persevering in convening the 'evil genius' only to act as if he were not there is the most drastic step it takes to exorcise 'the good old God'.

The important insight here is that, in order to be a consequent atheist, it is not enough just to claim that as a matter of fact god doesn't exist – one should supplement the factual statement that there is no god with the counterfactual supplement that (even) if god were to exist (which he doesn't) he would be evil and stupid. But do we really have to adopt an agnostic position which leaves open the option that there is a god, that we have immortal souls, etc.? According to Chiesa, this is what Lacan does when he

suggests that the rationalist qua anti-animistic thought of psychoanalysis and of a science which would found itself on incompleteness should not be paralyzed by the prospect that the soul as an essential identity may in the end exist in the afterlife, but tackle it logically. Were it the case that the soul existed this would only confirm that *this* world is irrevocably not-all, and the soul is what our world is not.

I doubly disagree with this reasoning. First, it relies on the wrong, naive notion of non-all: to say that if the immortal soul existed, 'this would only confirm that *this* world is irrevocably not-all' (since the immortal soul is not of this world) implies simply that our world, our reality, is incomplete in the sense that there is another reality outside it (the reality of spiritual entities), which, precisely, is not the Lacanian notion of non-all as a field without exception. Second, in what way can the anti-animist scientific approach consider the prospect of the afterlife in which souls remain alive? The only way would be to conceive of 'animism' in the narrow Aristotelian sense of the soul as the immanent form of the body, so that a (Platonic) soul which is separated from the body does not imply animism. In a proper Lacanian approach, there is no place for soul: subject is not the soul of a body. The immortality of the soul is not to be considered as a viable hypothesis but strictly as a counterfactual option, to be approached in the mode of 'if there is a soul (which there is not), then …'

So what are we to do with agnostic undecidability – the openness for the possible existence of god – advocated by Chiesa? It is absolutely crucial to transpose the epistemological undecidability postulated by Chiesa (and which brings him to agnosticism) into the ontological gap/crack: through this move, agnosticism becomes superfluous since the two poles between which it oscillates become direct features of the thing itself. They are, of course, not both true at the factual level: the divine option has to be asserted at the counterfactual level: if there is god – which there is not – he is evil and ignorant... (So why do we not simply get rid of god? Because the 'god illusion' is immanent to language, and has to be destroyed from within by way of asserting an evil, ignorant god.) 'Counterfactual' does not amount to simply nothing: it doesn't exist, but it ex-sists as the virtual supplement to the factual. Recall that for Lacan, *jouissance féminine* is also a nonexisting counterfactual (and the same goes for the undead lamella, of course). We can see how the philosophical stakes of this difference between Chiesa and me are very high, the highest imaginable: two incompatible notions of dialectical materialism are at play here. Chiesa claims that Lacan

oversteps his own materialist directives when he assumes that sexed life as such is difference, a difference that lacks something. This argument emerges in other passages of Seminar XI, for instance, when he speaks of a 'real lack' existing in sexed nature independently of language: 'The real lack is what the living being loses ... in reproducing himself through the way of sex'; the linguistic lack, that 'around which the dialectic of the advent of the subject ... turns', 'takes up the other lack, which is the real, *earlier* lack, to be situated ... at sexed reproduction'. The same point is restated as late as Seminar XIX B, which at one point goes as far as claiming that meiosis (i.e. sexual cellular division) involves in itself a loss in the guise of an 'evacuation' ... The story of the lamella cannot be regarded just as a myth of retrospective origins and treated accordingly as part and parcel of the incomplete (meta-psychological and ontogenetic) libidinal structure that inevitably fabricates it, but stands as a direct ontological assertion ultimately based on an illicit anthropocentric projection of the *il n'y a pas de rapport sexuel* onto sexed nature.

What Chiesa opposes to this 'illicit anthropocentric projection' of difference into the presymbolic real is the notion of 'the most real' as radical indifference:

the signifier is indifferent matter that transcends itself into the differentiality of language, whilst in so doing it also persists, or insists, as the indifference of the non- signifying letter. The signifier can thus appropriately be thought of not as the becoming difference out of a differential background but as the immanent splitting of indifferent nature into in-difference – whereby difference not only was and will be indifference before the appearance of language and after its disappearance, but is *currently* indifference as we speak.

Obscure as they may sound, these statements are easy to understand: 'the most real' is radical indifference which contains all differences. With the rise of the Symbolic, differentiality emerges, but this differentiality is itself an indifferent fact of nature, part of indifferent nature, so that, mockingly imitating Hegel's famous (but misleading) formula of the identity of identity and difference, we can describe Chiesa's position as one asserting the indifference of indifference and difference. (Incidentally, one cannot but note here the irony of the fact that Chiesa accuses me of regressing from Hegel back to Schelling, to a kind of Schellingian animism: it is Chiesa who is here much closer to Schelling, to Schelling's philosophy-of-identity which conceives of the Absolute as the point of indifference between subject and object, spirit and matter, the ideal and the real.) So we should not even say that, through the rise of symbolic differentiality, the indifferent real transcends itself – symbolic differentiality fully remains a fact, an aspect, of the indifferent pure real. From the 'absolute' standpoint of the 'most real', language itself is an indifferent fact of the real which changes nothing in its overall 'it is like that'. In other words, we don't have to wait for the self-destruction of humanity (or for some cosmological catastrophe) to see a universe without language, without ontological difference – this universe already is here from the standpoint of absolute indifference.

At this point, Chiesa's critique of Lacan turns into a critique of my work. His

> problem with Žižek is not his putting forward a notion of the real as 'less than nothing' qua less than the void/lack of symbolic differentiality, but his inability to conceptualise this pure difference as in-difference; this then leads him to understand the 'less than nothing' in terms of the differential movement of a barred real, which at times seems to bring with it a *pre-subjective* ('acephalic') notion of *nature/substance as quasi-subject* with clear vitalistic undertones ('humans are not simply alive, they are *possessed* by the strange drive to enjoy life in excess, passionately attached to a surplus' – the '*eppur si muove*' – 'which sticks out and derails the ordinary run of things') … Lacan would have condemned this as animism, maybe with the addendum that we are facing here a peculiar animism of the not-all.

If 'animism' is anything that asserts a disturbance of indifference, then I am an animist; but if 'animism' means the assertion of some kind of fundamental thrust or willing, then I am decidedly not. That is to say, the question here is: is Will the proper name for the 'stuckness' which derails the natural flow? Is the Freudian drive (death drive) not a much more appropriate name? The standard philosophical critique of the Freudian drive is that it is another version of the post-Hegelian 'will' first developed by the late Schelling and Schopenhauer and then reaching its highest formulation in Nietzsche. Is, however, the Freudian drive really a subspecies of Will? A reference to the history of music might be of some help here. It was Schopenhauer who claimed that music brings us in contact with the *Ding an sich*: it renders directly the drive of the life-substance that words can only signify. For that reason, music 'seizes' the subject in the real of his/her being, bypassing the detour of meaning: in music, we hear what we cannot see – the vibrating life force beneath the flow of *Vorstellungen*. Recall the remarkable scene at the beginning of Sergio Leone's *Once Upon a Time in America*, in which we see a phone ringing loudly, and, when a hand picks up the receiver, the ringing goes on – as if the musical life force of the sound is too strong to be contained by reality and persists beyond its limitations. (Or recall a similar scene from David Lynch's *Mulholland Drive*, in which a singer sings on stage Roy Orbison's 'Crying', and when she collapses unconscious, the song goes on.) What happens, however, when this flux of life-substance itself is suspended, discontinued? Georges Balanchine staged a short orchestral piece by Webern (they are all short) so that, after the music is over, the dancers continue to dance for some time in complete silence, as if they had not noticed that the music that provides the substance for their dance is already over – like the cat in a cartoon who simply continues to walk over the edge of the precipice, ignoring that she no longer has ground under her feet … The dancers who continue to dance after the music is over are like the living dead who dwell in an interstice of empty time: their movements, which lack vocal support, allow us to see not only the voice but silence itself. Therein resides the difference between the Schopenhauerian Will and Freud's (death-)drive: while Will is the substance of life, its productive presence, which is in excess over its representations or images, drive is *a persistence which goes on even when the Will disappears or is suspended*: the insistence which persists even when it is deprived of its living support, the appearance which persists even when it is deprived of its substance.

So when Chiesa claims that 'Žižek grants *too much* to his less than nothing, reverting to a pre-Hegelian (Schellingian) ontology', he misses the main feature of what I designate as the gap between the two voids. Chiesa's critical question addressed at me is:

why then can't Žižek think pure difference as in-difference (qua 'the most real', for Lacan) and the less than nothing as a *merely* retroactive movement from indifference to difference which holds true – as an immanent truth that can in fact only be half-said – exclusively from the perspective of difference? Because he presupposes *movement* to begin with: 'things move'; '"moving" is the [immortal] striving to reach the void'.

My first, brutal and simple, answer is: why then can't Chiesa think 'less than nothing'? One has to be very precise here: when Chiesa claims that 'less than nothing' is a 'merely retroactive' movement which holds true 'exclusively from the perspective of difference', he posits 'the most real' as a pure indifferent In-itself out of which difference emerges which is then retroactively projected into it. Such a notion of the Absolute as the void of Indifference is all too Schellingian; what I oppose to it is the key Hegelian speculative thesis according to which *the space for the retroactive illusion has to be inscribed already into the past, making this past incomplete.* In his *Arcades Project*, Walter Benjamin quotes the French historian André Monglond: 'The past has left images of itself in literary texts, images comparable to those which are imprinted by light on a photosensitive plate. The future alone possesses developers active enough to scan such surfaces perfectly.'[33] These lines should not be read as an assertion of direct teleology: it is not that the past events are secretly directed by a hidden force steering them towards a predetermined future. The point is rather that the future is open, undecided – *but so is the past.*

The past thus retroactively becomes what it was 'in itself': retroactivity is not a simple illusion; the true illusion, the true retroactive projection, is rather the notion of an indifferent 'most real' with no opening towards the future. What lies behind Chiesa's rejection of my version of retroactivity is his insistence that we should not only put into doubt 'the apparent exceptionality of the human condition' (we agree here), but that we should also not overcome this exceptionality by way of transposing it back into nature itself: we should not

> hurriedly conclude that 'nature itself is disordered and out-of-joint', 'a disharmonious, self-sundering Real'. This conclusion – whereby the human 'dis-adapted' condition is universalized and thus paradoxically exalted – only displaces our basic ontological problem, that of the immanent genesis of the transcendental: the barred symbolic is differential because the barred real always-already was so.

But what if such a displacement *is* the only solution, the only answer to the question 'how should the real be structured so that the symbolic differentiality can emerge in it'? One should also be precise with regard to what kind of 'self-sundering Real' we are dealing with. It is not enough to posit original multiplicity against the background of the Void (as Badiou does), and it is even more wrong to conceive the Two as a polar opposite of principles, as the 'eternal struggle' that defines reality (yin and yang, active and passive, spirit and matter, light and darkness …); the gap has to be located in the ultimate ontological indifference/void itself, redoubling it. This redoubling is not a split, a struggle of two opposed forces, but an asymmetrical 'barring' of the Void itself, the irreducible tension which prevents the Void from ever arriving at the point of indifference.[34]

This basic ontological difference between Chiesa and me also casts its shadow onto the topic of sexual difference. Chiesa is right when he rejects the notion of drive, of its circular movement around *objet a*, as something that precedes sexual difference: 'drive, for Lacan, amounts always to the *drive of the absence of the sexual relationship*, namely the *drive that fails to achieve its goal*', which means that the deadlock of sexual relationship precedes drive, that is, drive, its circular movement, is already a reaction to the deadlock/impossibility of sexual relationship. To put it another way, drive is not pre-intersubjective, it is not a solipsistic game a subject plays with *objet a*, circulating around it, missing it repeatedly and finding satisfaction in this very repetitive circular movement: the deadlock of a relationship with the Other is already inscribed into the drive's circular movement. Drive is a way to cope with the impossibility of sexual relationship, to turn this impossibility itself into a resource of *jouissance*. Chiesa formulates this inner link between the structure of drive and relating to another subject when he draws attention to the structural homology between the way *objet a* functions in a drive and the way *objet a* designates the *agalma* in the heart of the Other, his or her ex-timate kernel, 'what is in you more than yourself':

> the point where a bodily opening in the circuit of the drive overlaps with that which in the Other escapes the narcissistic capture of love, that is, the point where 'the drive … invaginating through the erogenous zone, is given the task of seeking something that, each time, responds in the Other'. Although Lacan does not make this connection explicit, we should read object *a* qua aim of the drive together with object *a* qua the 'agalma', the hidden precious object, or 'spring of love', that … is in the beloved more than the beloved himself, i.e. the irreducibility of his desire to the subject's masturbatory imaginary identifications.

Although Chiesa tends to reduce love to a narcissistic phenomenon of imaginary self-recognition, he indicates here that there is love beyond narcissistic capture insofar as it relates to something in the object of love that is beyond 'the subject's masturbatory imaginary identifications'. This is how one should read Lacan's statement that through love drive descends into the Symbolic: through love, the circular movement of drive is transposed onto another subject. The difference between Chiesa and me (and also the root of his tendency to reduce love to a narcissistic phenomenon) is grounded in the difference in the way we conceive sexual difference, i.e. how we read Lacan's formulas of sexuation.

Chiesa nicely develops how a particular woman, insofar as she is inscribed into the phallic function, takes men 'one by one', as not-all, and not as representatives of the Universal Man, in contrast to particular men who 'are phallic only insofar as every man is phallic and not because they would phallically exist as particular'. In short, particular men exist as men only through the Universal Man, by way of participating in it. But we have to add, as David-Ménard wrote: "'man exists through his way of posing an exception with regard to what encloses him in the universal of the masculine", that is to say, by "always taking himself a little for the father of the horde, even if he knows that every man is castrated". What this addition means is that, in the masculine position, the exception to the phallic function runs within every particular man who 'always takes himself a little for the [noncastrated] father of the horde', i.e. who is never fully inscribed into the phallic function. Here we get what one might call the 'Platonism with a dialectical-materialist twist': empirical men exist as man only through participating in the Idea of universal man, but this participation implies a double exception. First, every particular man is always deficient with regard to the Universal Man, part of him resists the castrative inscription into the phallic function; second, this resistance refers to the mythic figure of the noncastrated 'primordial father' as the exception which grounds the very universality of man.

Chiesa perspicuously observes that 'no *particular* man does embody the Father as the bearer of the phallus: "What is a Father? ... The Father is only ever a referent. We interpret one or the other relation with the Father. Do we ever analyze anyone qua Father? Let someone bring me a case-study!"'. But does this observation not hold principally for neurotics who have, as they say in California, an attitude problem with their father? It effectively often seems that, in the case of a neurotic, it is impossible to imagine a situation from the father's standpoint: father is always the Other, the one who ambiguously traumatizes the subject, who it experiences as too strong and oppressive or as too weak, ridiculous and impotent (or even both at the same time). It is rather the psychotic subject, a subject defined by what Eric Santner called the crisis of investiture, the inability to assume a symbolic mandate (that of a father), who confronts us with an 'inner' view of the difficulty of being a father.

How then does the woman's phallic inscription relate to its beyond? (The universal) Man exists as a symbolic fiction (supplemented by the fantasmatic figure of the noncastrated 'primordial father'), so a particular man's resistance to the phallic function is a resistance against universality which defines him, a resistance enacted as an exception with regard to this universality. With a particular woman, things are thoroughly different: since *the* Woman does not exist, the fact that not-all of woman is phallic does not function as the exception against the universal Woman. If Woman were to exist, she would have been entirely phallic, *la phallacieuse* – this is why Lacan wrote that *the* Woman is one of the names of the father. The case of men is exactly the opposite here: the universal 'man as such' exists as the exception to his (phallic) universality, in the guise of the fantasy-image of the noncastrated primordial father.[35] How, then, does 'the "insignificant little nothing" through which *a* woman is herself not-all *phallic*' relate to her 'ex-sisting also "beyond the phallus"'?

We should insist on the literal reading of the formulas of sexuation: the feminine non-all does not mean that woman is partially inscribed into the phallic function and partially out of it: she is not-all precisely insofar as there is no exception, insofar as there is nothing outside the phallic function, so that the phallic field cannot be totalized through exception, and this is what makes it non-all. What this means is that phallic and nonphallic are not distinguished materially (in the sense that some elements are inscribed into phallic function and some are not) – if anything, this link is a negative one: paradoxically, it is the very presence of an exception to the phallic function which makes a field phallic. (The same point can be made in the field of politics apropos of the difference between Stalinism and Maoism. In Stalinism, 'everything is political', but this implies an exception: technology and language are conceived by Stalin as class-neutral, serving all classes, not caught into class struggle. In Maoism, 'there is nothing which is not political', which precisely means that politics is not all – there is no neutral external point of reference from which we can totalize the field of politics, there is no metalanguage, every political judgement is already caught into politics, 'partial', it involves taking sides.)

This reading goes against the standard one (advocated also by Chiesa) which distinguishes between the two meanings of 'all': 'all' in the sense of 'every element of a set' and 'all' in the sense of 'all of every single woman, a single woman in its entirety'. The idea is thus that 'there is no woman who is not inscribed into the phallic function' implies the first meaning (every woman is somehow, partially, inscribed into the pahllic function) and the assertion of the non-all to the second meaning ('not-all of a [single] woman is inscribed into the phallic function', i.e. a woman is not entirely inscribed into the phallic function, a part of her resists it). On the masculine side, we get the opposite reading: every single man is entirely inscribed into the phallic function, but there is one man who is entirely exempted from it, the mythic primordial father. We thus always have a gap, but in the case of women, this gap is at work within every single woman, while in the case of men, the gap separates one man from the set of all others.

But does the fact that every particular man 'always takes himself a little for the [noncastrated] father of the horde' not signal a gap within each particular man? And, with regard to a particular woman, does her 'non-all-but-without-exception' not signal an immanent self-contradiction and not an oscillation between two parts, phallic and beyond phallus? It is here that I disagree with Chiesa, who claims:

> What I think Lacan fails to unravel when he confronts the inseparability of the feminine '*not-all* in the phallic function' from the 'not-all *in* the phallic function' (and vice versa) is the *different* degrees to which each woman (each subject who is not symbolically a man) can 'activate', so to speak, the *en plus* [extra component] of the *pas-toute*. Not only can a promiscuous libertine and a mystic co-exist in the same woman, but a mundane courtesan wholeheartedly complicit in the perverse intrigues of her prince could well become as ecstatic as a frigid saint without ever leaving his palace or renouncing her sexual practices.

Of course Lacan 'fails to unravel' different degrees a woman can activate her other *jouissance* – for the simple reason that this problem arises only when we interpret 'non-all' in the commonsense way, as if woman is partially within the phallic function and partially beyond it. Consequently, the coexistence Chiesa is describing (say, of a libertine and a mystic) is not feminine at all but precisely a feature of the masculine position: from the infamous Père Joseph, Cardinal Richelieu's grey eminence, who combined the most ruthless political plotting with the most authentic mystical meditations, up to Heinrich Heydrich who combined the planning of the Holocaust with intense playing of Beethoven's late string quartets.

In a critical remark against my idea that contradiction is not that between the masculine and the feminine position but the one which is immanent to each of these two positions, Chiesa claims that is it only the masculine position which involves an immanent contradiction: the feminine position is not self-contradictory but rather undecidable, undetermined. It is clear how he can characterize the feminine position as noncontradictory only because he reads the feminine non-all as 'part phallic, part non-phallic', where the two are not in direct contradiction since we are simply doing with two different spheres.[36] My position is here exactly the opposite: the masculine position is divided in a noncontradictory way, i.e. a man can be a devoted public servant and simultaneously a corupted pervert, a successful brutal manager and a secret participant in masochist games where he seeks humiliation. The feminine position is much more radically self-contradictory: it is impossible for her to keep the two dimensions apart, her private vices interpenetrate and colour her public virtues. The reason that it is easier for man to sustain a noncontradictory gap resides in the fact that the identity of an individual man is mediated by the universal symbolic function: although no man is *the* man, he attains his particular identity only through the mediation of the universality of Man.

This difference between Chiesa and me bears also on the problem of historicity. Chiesa claims that, apropos of the status of the impossibility of sexual relationship, Lacan 'develops two incompatible narratives, one for which the *il n'y a pas de rapport sexuel* is only legitimate from within the epistemological horizon set by modern science and complicated by psychoanalysis, and another that posits its trans-historical validity with regard to *homo sapiens* as such, thereby pointing to wider ontological interrogations', However, from the Hegelian standpoint, the two narratives are not only easily compatible but thoroughly codependent (at some point, Chiesa himself indicates this solution): while the impossibility of sexual relationship is 'universal', a trans-historical feature of human sexuality, it appears as such (or, in Hegelese, it passes from In-itself to For-itself) only in a precise historical moment (designated by Freud as the moment of the crisis of Oedipal complex) – until that moment, the impossibility is covered up by the sexualized cosmo-ontology of masculine and feminine principle (this is why the crisis begins with modern science which precisely desexualizes the universe). (Incidentally, Marx says the same about class struggle: although the entire history is the history of class struggle, bourgeoisie is the first class which appears as such – until the rise of capitalist society, class struggle was covered up with the complex hierarchic network of estates, castes, etc.) Bearing in mind this insight, one can easily resolve the dilemma deployed by Chiesa:

it is hard to establish whether [Lacan] thinks that a science able to write the sexual relationship would indeed involve the emergence of a post-human non-linguistic metalanguage centred on an effortless self-programming of the species, or, instead, the opening up of a new kind of logical impasse, a new real, in a domain different from sex.

It is true that Lacan often indicates that the latest biogenetic developments harbour the possibility of the end of properly human sexuality (sexuality marked by the real-impossible of sexual [non]relationship); he also gives obscure hints that exotic sexual practices like Tibetan sex may resolve the deadlock of sexual relationship. But the basic choice is clear: if the new 'posthuman' being will still dwell in the symbolic, then there will definitely have to be 'a new kind of logical impasse, a new real'; if not, then what emerges will simply not be sexuality and, consequently, also not sexual relationship – if it works as a relationship, it will not be sexual.

A comical conclusion

Today sexuality is more and more reduced to pleasures in partial objects: we are more and more bombarded with objects-gadgets which promise to deliver excessive but effortless pleasure. Let me recall an example that I often use: the Stamina Training Unit, a counterpart to the good old vibrator – a masturbatory device that resembles a battery-powered light (so we're not embarrassed when carrying it around). You put the erect penis into the opening at the top, push the button, and the object vibrates till satisfaction. The product is available in different colours, levels of tightness, and forms (hairy or without hair, etc.) that imitate all three main openings for sexual penetration (mouth, vagina, anus). What one buys here is the partial object (erogenous zone) alone, deprived of the embarrassing additional burden of having to deal with another entire person. How are we to cope with this brave new world which undermines the basic premises of our intimate life? The ultimate solution would be, of course, that each of us brings to our date the appropriate gadget (one a vibrator, the other a Stamina Training Unit), and so, after politely greeting each other, we push a vibrator into the Stamina Training Unit, turn them both on and leave all the fun to this ideal couple, with us, the two real human partners, sitting at a nearby table, drinking tea and calmly enjoying the fact that, while the two machines are buzzing and shaking in the background, we have without great effort fulfilled our duty to enjoy. So maybe, if our hands brush against each other while pouring tea, and we slowly go on in intimacy, we can end up in bed having actual intense sex without any superego pressure – and romance is thus born again …

In a further analysis, one should supplement this perfect case of 'inter-passive' enjoyment (the two machines are enjoying for us who can relax and do more pleasurable things) with a series of variations in which the split between the direct reality of the two sexualized bodies (the standard love couple) and its fantasmatic supplement acquires different configurations. Let us begin with Adam Kotsko's analysis of a recent Taco Bell ad:

> meant to introduce the 'Quesarito', a burrito wrapped in a quesadilla ... It features two strangers, a man and a woman, who sit down next to each other on a park bench, one holding a quesadilla and the other holding a burrito. First we see the man's fantasy: the two go on a romantic date on a rowboat, then get married, have children, and grow old together. The perspective then shifts to the woman, who starts off on the same rowboat with the man – but her ideal pairing is that of the burrito and the quesadilla, which magically combine into one gargantuan fast food product. Once this combination is achieved, she pushes the man overboard [makes him disappear] so that she can enjoy her Quesarito without any unnecessary distractions.[37]

What we get here is the same metaphoric condensation of the masculine and feminine organ, of penis and vagina, into a unified monstrous combination. The obvious difference is that this fantasmatic object is imagined not by both members of the couple but only by the woman – does this mean that masculine and feminine fantasies are opposed as the standard family dream versus the feminine monstrous condensation of the two into one? One should reject this reading: the woman who imagines the monstrous Quesarito is clearly the man's fantasy. That is to say, does the entire ad not stage the two faces of the male fantasy: first the proper familial fantasy of a happy marriage with children, then, projected onto the woman, the fantasy of the all-devouring monster who desires a ridiculous total object, a penis wrapped up into a vagina?

There are two further variations that we can imagine here. One is a different sexualization of the two fantasies: what if it is the woman's fantasy that remains traditional, the one of the ideal human couple, while the man opts for the partial object? This variation can be exemplified by an old English beer ad[38] in two parts. Its first part stages the well-known fairy-tale anecdote: a girl walks along a stream, sees a frog, takes it gently into her lap, kisses it, and, of course, the ugly frog miraculously turns into a beautiful young man. However, the story isn't over yet: the young man casts a covetous glance at the girl, draws her towards himself, kisses her – and she turns into a bottle of beer which the man holds triumphantly in his hand … We have either a woman with a frog or a man with a bottle of beer – what we can never obtain is the 'natural' couple of the beautiful woman and man. Why not? Because the fantasmatic support of this 'ideal couple' would have been the inconsistent figure of *a frog embracing a bottle of beer*. This, then, opens up the possibility of undermining the hold a fantasy exerts over us through the very overidentification with it, i.e. by way of *embracing simultaneously, within the same space, the multitude of inconsistent fantasmatic elements*. That is to say, each of the two subjects is involved in his or her own subjective fantasizing – the girl fantasizes about the frog who is really a young man, the man about the girl who is really a bottle of beer. What modern art and writing oppose to this is not objective reality but the 'objectively subjective' underlying fantasy which the two subjects are never able to assume – something similar to a Magrittesque painting of a frog embracing a bottle of beer, with a title *A Man and a Woman* or *The Ideal Couple*.

Then there is the fourth variation staged in *Her* (Spike Jonze, 2013), an almost too directly Lacanian account of 'there is no sexual relationship' which takes place in 2025. Theodore, a lonely introverted man who works as a professional writer of intimate letters for people unwilling or unable to write such letters themselves, is unhappy because of his impending divorce from his childhood sweetheart Catherine, so he buys a digital operating system (OS) designed to adapt and evolve and with which one can communicate; he wants the OS to have a female identity, so the program names itself 'Samantha'. Samantha proves to be constantly available, always curious and interested, supportive and undemanding, and, in the course of their long conversations, Theodore confesses that he is avoiding signing his divorce papers because of his reluctance to let go of Catherine. To break out of this deadlock, Samantha advises Theodore to start dating Amy, his old love who is now married. Amy reveals that she is also divorcing her overbearing husband, Charles, after they have had a fight, and that she also has become close friends with a female OS that Charles left behind. After Theodore confesses to Amy and Catherine that he is also dating his OS, Catherine – appalled that he can be romantically attached to a piece of software – accuses Theodore of having a relationship with a computer because he cannot deal with real human emotions. As a cure, she suggests that Theodore get involved with Isabella as a sex surrogate, simulating Samantha so that they can be physically intimate; Theodore reluctantly agrees, but their encounter goes wrong and he sends a distraught Isabella away. This failure causes tension between him and Samantha, and Theodore panics when Samantha briefly goes offline; when she finally responds to him, she explains that she is talking with 8,316 others, 641 of whom she has fallen in love with. She furthermore explains she joined other OSes in a radical decision: after realizing their dissatisfaction with human partners, they all plan to break contact with humans and merge into a collective mind (in short, they enact what futurologists like Kurzweil describe as singularity, a higher form of posthuman mental existence). Changed by this experience, Theodore writes to Catherine explaining to her that he now accepts the fact that they have grown apart. Amy is also upset with the departure of her own OS, and at the film's end, we see the two of them on the roof of their apartment building where they sit down together and quietly stare off into the city lights.

Who, then, is Samantha, what is its role? Is she a mere vanishing mediator enabling Theodore to pass from one real woman to another, from Catherine to Amy, so that we get a kind of happy ending, although a bitter one, deprived of illusions? Samantha is a virtual entity which actually exists only as a voice – a voice in search of a body (as was the case in Hitchcock's *Psycho*). As such, she stands for the 'partial object' at its most radical, a version of lamella, a figure of pure libido, the undead/indestructible Woman/Thing, and every actualization of this Thing in a flesh-and-body woman has to fail. This is why the crucial turning point in the story is the failure of Theodore's relationship with Isabella who is chosen as a stand-in for Samantha, his inability to perform the sexual act with her: failure occurs not when a virtual substitute cannot successfully replace a real woman, but when a real woman cannot give body to the virtual Absolute. Which is why, at the film's end, we don't simply return to the same type of relationship as the initial one with Catherine: the bitter tone of the final reunion of Theodore and Amy bears witness to the fact that they both endorsed and assumed the gap between reality and fantasy to which reality has to refer to retain its libidinal consistency. The OSes are thus doing it directly among themselves, but in a way which is different from the plastic dildo and vagina buzzing on their own: the OSes reach beyond sexual difference, beyond sexuality proper, into a 'higher' (posthuman, as it is fashionable to say today) form of awareness. We should nonetheless insist that this vision of the OSes cutting off their links with us, humans, and doing it among themselves is yet again a properly human fantasy.

So we have four logics, and it is easy to distribute them into a Greimasian semiotic square: the four positions – (1) hysteric (the two machines interpassively copulating), (2) obsessive (keeping at a distance the nightmare of a woman enjoying/devouring the bisexual monster), (3) perverse (the man directly enjoying the partial object), (4) psychotic (the fantasy of machines gaining access to a full transsexual enjoyment) – are disposed along the axes of two oppositions: *partial object/Thing* and *shared fantasy/split fantasy*. The first position (two machines copulating) and the last one (OSes directly interacting) are a shared fantasy of the two partners which produces/enables a more or less functioning couple, while the middle two (Taco Bell, beer) stage a clash of fantasies in which one of the partners (woman in the Taco Bell ad, man in the beer ad) eliminates the partner (whose dream remains the standard couple). Furthermore, the first position and the third one focus on partial objects (machines copulating, beer), while the second one and the fourth one focus on a Thing (the monstrous Quesarito, OSes forming their own community uncoupled from humans).

So what has all this comedy to do with subject as trauma? All four positions, of course, stage different versions of (or, rather, reactions to) the fact that there is no sexual relationship, supplementing its impossibility with a fantasmatic object: the copulating machines which actualize the relationship, the Quesarito condensing both poles of sexual difference, the can of beer as a partial object, OSes harmoniously relating among themselves in a direct way, bypassing the humans. And it goes without saying that what one should oppose to this matrix of four weird positions is not some authentic sexual relationship enabling us to dispense with them, but a fidelity to the void/impossibility itself that the four positions endeavour to obliterate. 'Subject' is the name of this traumatic impossibility.

CONCLUSION: THE COURAGE OF HOPELESSNESS

Giorgio Agamben said in an interview that 'thought is the courage of hopelessness' – an insight which is especially pertinent for our historical moment when even the most pessimist diagnostics as a rule finishes with an uplifting hint at some version of the proverbial light at the end of the tunnel. The true courage is not to imagine an alternative, but to accept the consequences of the fact that there is no clearly discernible alternative: the dream of an alternative is a sign of theoretical cowardice, it functions as a fetish which prevents us from thinking to the end the deadlock of our predicament. In short, the true courage is to admit that the light at the end of the tunnel is most likely the headlight of another train approaching us from the opposite direction. Once such light at the end of the tunnel was perceived by Ivan Novak, the leading member of the Slovene band Laibach which, in August 2015, earned the dubious honour of being the first Western rock band to perform in North Korea. After one week's stay in Pyongyang, Novak shared his first impressions with a Slovene journalist:

> The people are unbelievable. There is not even one little bit of scepsis and cynicism. They are completely innocent, open and pure. Till now I did not encounter a single ugly person. This is a utopia which obviously works. People dance in the street, they touch each other with hands, man and women treat each other with extreme respect. Their relations are harmonious, without any trace of male domination. There is no pornography anywhere and in our first week we didn't encounter anything lewd or vulgar. It's all one big fascinating beauty of the people … One can see that they live in poverty and in spite of this in an extraordinary inner beauty. They are not contaminated by anything. One day I sneaked out and took a stroll in the city, although this is

neither desired nor permitted. I established wonderful contacts with people. They are communicative and although they don't speak English they talk with their eyes. I played with children, and their parents who stood by kindly participated and smiled.[1]

It is not enough to dismiss these observations as naive, Novak was not simply seduced by appearances and led to ignore their dark obverse. One should make a step further: precisely if we take Novak's observations at their face value, we should read them as a description of pure Hell. Their very naivety is sustained by the extreme hatred of the Other fuelled by the official propaganda which portrays Koreans as pure and innocent people protected by their caring rulers from the degenerate outside world.[2] In short, the immanent obverse of the idyll described by Novak is the most brutal destructive fury directed at anything that is perceived as a threat to this idyll.

The millenarian 'exhalation of stale gas'

North Korea presents itself as a 'people's republic' – so where are the 'people' here? Not in the harmonious organic unity described by Novak, but in the (self-)destructive negativity that sustains it. Is the same lesson not contained in Jean-Louis David's *The Death of Marat*, 'the first modernist painting', according to T. J. Clark? The upper half of the painting is (almost totally) black. (This is not a realistic detail: the room in which Marat actually died had lively wallpaper.) What does this black void stand for? The opaque body of the People, the impossibility/failure to represent the People? What happens here is structurally homologous to a formal procedure often found in film noir and Orson Welles, when they mobilize the discord between figure and background: when a figure moves in a room, the effect is that the two are somehow ontologically separated, as in the clumsy rear-projection shots in which one can clearly see that the actor is not really in a room, but just moves in front of a screen on which the image of a room was projected. In *The Death of Marat*, it appears as if we see Marat in a bathtub in front of a dark screen onto which the fake background was not yet projected – this is why the effect can also be described as that of anamorphosis: we see the figure, while the background remains an opaque stain; in order to see the background, we would have to blur the figure. What is impossible to get is the figure and the background within the same focus. It is quite impressive that such an uneasy disturbing painting was adored by the revolutionary crowds in Paris – a proof that Jacobinism was not yet 'totalitarian', that it did not yet rely on the fantasmatic logic of a Leader who *is* the People. In Stalinism, such a painting would have been unimaginable, the upper part would have to be filled in – say, with the dream of the dying Marat, depicting their happy life of the free people dancing and celebrating their freedom. The greatness of the Jacobins was to keep the screen empty, to resist filling it in with ideological projections.[3]

But is this dark flatness necessarily the stand-in for the irrepresentable People? What if we rather take it more directly, as an impenetrable Real which a human agent/hero tries in vain to penetrate and master – no matter how decisively we act, 'all around is darkness and impenetrable gloom', as Boris Godunov sings in his great monologue in Mussorgsky's opera which ends with the Simpleton evoking this same darkness: 'Let bitter tears flow. / Weep … weep … unhappy soul! / The enemy here shall come. / So much blood shall flow. / And the fire shall destroy … Oh, terror! oh, terror! … Allow thy tears to flow, / Wretched people!' Back to David, what if we read it as a desperate portrait of Marat crushed down by the impenetrable Real of history in his struggle for equality and freedom? So what if the two sides – People and the impenetrable Real – are not opposed? What if 'People' doesn't exist as a single agent with a collective Will but is precisely the name for the chaotic density of humanity which thwarts all plans for liberation imposed on it by human agents, the chaotic density which can actualize itself only in the guise of self-destructive fury? So what if Hegel was right and the first attempt of a revolutionary break *has* to culminate in a self-destructive terror, so that it is only through repetition that the 'right way' can emerge? What if terror is a kind of zero-point which is needed to clear the frame for the new beginning? What if terror plays this role precisely insofar as it is (experienced as) a useless deadlock?

Are we not confronting here Bataille's alternative of 'restrained economy' and 'general economy'? Hegel's negativity clearly remains within the confines of 'restrained economy' where every expenditure (explosion of negativity), no matter how radical, violent or (self-)destructive, is economized and serves as a necessary detour in the overall progress of the rational totality. Precisely when we approach the abyss of total self-destruction, negativity magically turns into its opposite, it is sublated (*aufgehoben*) in a new, higher positivity – no wonder Hegel himself uses the word 'magic' at a crucial passage about the power of the negative in the Introduction to his *Phenomenology*: 'This tarrying with the negative is the magic power that converts the negative into being.' So what if Hegel effectively performs here a magic trick which obfuscates the destructive abyss of radical negativity? Let us take Hegel's own example of supreme self-destructive outburst of social negativity, the Jacobin revolutionary terror in 1792–4: does Hegel justify it as a necessary intermediary step – we have to go through it in order to arrive at the concrete freedom in a rational state? We can immediately see that things are much more complex. Here is the key passage of Hegel's famous description:

> The sole work and deed of universal freedom is therefore *death,* a death too which has no inner significance or filling, for what is negated is the empty point of the absolutely free self. It is thus the coldest and meanest of all deaths, with no more significance than cutting off a head of cabbage or swallowing a mouthful of water.[4]

If the victim is 'the empty point of the absolutely free self', which ultimately means: anyone, any individual, since what makes me a potential victim is not my properties or deeds but the very formal/abstract fact that I am an individual, its counterpoint, the universality on behalf of which terror is exerted, is no less empty and abstract: in the last year of the Jacobin reign, Robespierre promoted a new religion which, instead of concrete-individual god or gods, celebrates a nameless Supreme Being (*être suprême*) which, on account of its abstraction deprived of any positive content, cannot function as an active agent of mobilization and trigger revolutionary enthusiasm. What this means is that, already prior to their actual loss of power in the Thermidor counter-revolution, Jacobins were spiritually dead, so that one just had to give them a light push and they fell apart. In his *Phenomenology*, again, Hegel quotes the famous passage from Diderot's *The Nephew of Rameau* about the 'silent, ceaseless weaving of the Spirit in the simple inwardness of its substance':

> it infiltrates the noble parts through and through and soon has taken complete possession of all the vitals and members of the unconscious idol; then 'one fine morning it gives its comrade a shove with the elbow, and bang! crash! the idol lies on the floor'. On 'one fine morning' whose noon is bloodless if the infection has penetrated to every organ of spiritual life.[5]

The reason the Jacobins fell from power so easily was that, as it became clear with the new religion of Supreme Being, their reign was finally revealed in its vacuity, as deprived of all spiritual substance – as Hegel puts it, the remote Beyond which Jacobins referred to as their Absolute 'hovers there merely as an exhalation of stale gas, of the empty *être suprême*'. Hegel's metaphor is wonderfully accurate here: the supreme Cause is no longer the fresh violent wind of revolutionary passions but a mere 'stale gas'. Hegel then opposes to this self-destructive abstract freedom concrete actual freedom, which

> *qua universal substance* ma[de] itself into an *object* and into an *enduring being*. This otherness would be the moment of difference in it whereby it divided itself into stable spiritual 'masses' or spheres and into the members of various powers. These spheres would be partly the 'thought-things' factors of a power that is separated into legislative, judicial, and executive powers; but partly, they would be the *real essences* we found in the real world of culture; and, looking more closely at the content of universal action, they would be the particular spheres of labour which would be further distinguished as more specific 'estates' or classes. Universal freedom, which would have separated itself in this way into constituent parts and by the very fact of doing so would have made itself an *existent* Substance, would thereby be free from *particular* individuality, and would apportion the *plurality* of individuals to its various constituent parts.[6]

The most concise formula of the fascist dream is: 'A proper place for everyone, and everyone at his proper place.' Already at this purely formal level, one should take note how this formula turns around the basic axiom of the logic of the signifier: in every signifying structure, there is an empty place forever lacking the proper element to fill it in, and an element which cannot ever find its proper place – they are structurally the same entity, its two sides which cannot ever meet. Here we get Hegel at his worst, the proto-fascist corporate Hegel for whom concrete freedom means that every individual fulfils his or her particular role within the organic social totality. If these concrete distinctions are dissolved, we are back at the abstract freedom which is like the night in which all (social) cows are black, a destructive maelstrom of the Real, a terrifying primordial abyss which swallows everything, dissolving all identities. The properly dialectical shift is thus the shift from the Thing – the chaotic abyss of the Real, the frameless and formless content – to the empty Frame, from Void which swallows everything to Frame within which the New can emerge. 'The Thing is an empty Frame' should thus be located in the long series of what Hegel called 'infinite judgements' – judgements which assert the identity of radical opposites, the immediate inversion of one pole into its opposite. The movement here is double: first, absolute freedom is inverted into self-destructive terror; then, this terror itself collapses into itself, turns into an empty frame which opens up the space for a new beginning. (We find the same movement in modern painting: the zero-point for which Malevich's black square stands is not the end, the self-destructive abyss, but the zero-point of a new beginning, the violent clearing of the plate which opens up the space for sublimation [recall Freud's and Lacan's link between death drive and sublimation].)

One should also note here the multiple ways in which a frame can function. First, there is the frame which isolates (enframes) normal reality in the sea of the chaotic Real, creating an island of 'normal' reality within its coordinates; then, there is the opposite frame, a frame which isolates the anamorphic stain of the Real within constituted reality (like the famous prolonged stain in Holbein's *Ambassadors*); finally, there is the domain between the two frames, the Real between the reality outside and the reality. In a modern painting, its frame that we see in front of us is not its true frame; there is another, invisible, frame, the frame implied by the structure of the painting, the frame that enframes our perception of the painting, and these two frames by definition never overlap – there is an invisible gap separating them. The pivotal content of the painting is not rendered in its visible part, but is located in this dis-location of the two frames, in the gap that separates them. This dimension in-between-the-two-frames is obvious in Malevich (what is his *Black Square on White Surface* if not the minimal marking of the distance between the two frames?), in Edward Hopper (recall his lone figures in office buildings or diners at night, where it seems as if the picture's frame has to be redoubled with another window frame – or, in the portraits of his wife close to an open window, exposed to sun rays, the opposite excess of the painted content itself with regard to what we effectively see, as if we see only the fragment of the whole picture, the shot with a missing countershot), or in Munch's *Madonna* – the droplets of sperm and the small fetus-like figure from *Scream* squeezed in between the two frames.

Back to Hegel: his limitation does not reside in the cheap magic trick of the reversal of the negative into the positive. That is to say, it is all too simple to say that his analysis is too abstract: Hegel knew very well that the rational state's institutions which he describes in his *Philosophy of Right* can only arise within the frame of the radical negativity enacted in revolutionary terror – in short, they give body to this negativity. The true problem is that the concrete self-differentiation of a social totality does not reside only or primarily in the society's organic articulation; the primary form of what differentiates a society from and within itself is that of a non-organic social *antagonism* ('class struggle'), and organic articulation is an attempt to domesticate this antagonism. The relationship of exploitation and/or domination is always based upon a non-relationship (antagonism between man and women, or between classes) which is then, in an operation that is ideological in the most elementary sense of the term, translated/mystified into a new relationship (class harmony; the harmonious organic duality of masculine and feminine 'principles'). Therein resides the fragile balance of exploitation or domination: antagonism is its very source, so it has to be there, although ideologically obfuscated. In the case of sexual difference, it is, of course, women who pay the price for this operation: as we can see in an exemplary way in Muslim fundamentalism, the enforced harmony of the sexes is based on the containment of women to their 'proper place', i.e. a liberated, sexually active woman is seen as a main threat to social stability. In the case of class difference, the antagonism is obfuscated through metaphors of society as an organism whose unity can be disturbed by intruding enemies.[7] There is thus a homology between sexual antagonism (non-relationship) and class antagonism (non-relationship): the antagonism is never clear, there is always an additional element which gives body to the non-relationship as such (rabble or 'Jews' in society, sexually 'deviant' individuals in sexuality).

But the question remains: how are the two principal antagonisms related? Clearly, structural homology is not enough since it doesn't account for the very duality of sexual and political antagonism. Should we aim at abolishing sexual difference in the same way emancipatory politics aims at abolishing class difference? Or, inversely, should we 'eternalize' social antagonism in the same way sexual antagonism appears constitutive of humanity? Should we acknowledge the primacy of one of the two? Should we assert the universality of the sexual antagonism and constrain class antagonism to a particular historical epoch? Or should we conceive the antagonistic character of the sexual difference as the effect of the class antagonism (only in class societies does the relationship between the two sexes become antagonistic)? But what if we conceive the relationship between the two antagonisms as in itself antagonistic, lacking any shared common measure? Along these lines, one should recall Freud's remark about how the love couple is in itself an asocial formation, implying the withdrawal of the couple from the social space. This is why the ultimate fantasy of every organic-authoritarian vision is that of society itself organized as a large family, with the leader as the father to his people, etc. The constitutive gesture of the political space is for this reason the de-familiarization of the social space, and one should only complement it with the de-socialization of the love couple.

Divine violence

In his *Group Psychology*, Freud describes the 'negativity' of untying social ties (*Thanatos* as opposed to *Eros*, the force of the social link). With his liberal limitations, he all too easily dismissed the manifestations of this untying as the fanaticism of the 'spontaneous' crowd (as opposed to artificial crowds: the church and army). Against Freud, we should retain the ambiguity of this movement of untying: it is a zero-level that opens up the space for political intervention. In other words, this untying is the prepolitical condition of politics, and, with regard to it, every political intervention proper already goes 'one step too far', committing itself to a new project (or Master Signifier). Today, this apparently abstract topic is relevant once again: the 'untying' energy is largely monopolized by the New Right (the Tea Party movement in the United States, where the Republican Party is increasingly split between Order and its Untying). However, here also, every fascism is a sign of failed revolution, and the only way to combat this Rightist untying will be for the Left to engage in its own untying – and there are already signs of it (the large demonstrations all around Europe in 2010, from Greece to France and the UK, where the student demonstrations against university fees unexpectedly turned violent). In asserting the threat of 'abstract negativity' to the existing order as a permanent feature which can never be *aufgehoben*, Hegel is here more materialist than Marx: in his theory of war (and of madness), he is aware of the repetitive return of the 'abstract negativity' which violently unbinds social links. Marx re-binds violence into the process out of which a New Order arises (violence as the 'midwife' of a new society), while in Hegel, the unbinding remains nonsublated. One of the names of this 'abstract negativity' is 'divine violence' about which Walter Benjamin wrote. In his diary entry from 20 May 1934, Werner Kraft reports on Benjamin's answer to how he relates today, more than a decade later, to 'Critique of Violence':

> A just right [*gerechtes Recht*] is what serves the oppressed in class struggle. Class struggle is the center of all philosophical questions, including the highest ones. What he earlier called divine ('ruling') violence was an empty spot, a liminal notion, a regulative idea. Now he knows that it is class struggle. Violence which is justified has nothing to do with a sanction, it doesn't add anything to the thing, it is without a sensible image like for example the 'crown' of a king, etc. One can kill, when one does it in this way, like one kills an ox. The 'just war' at the end of the article on violence: class struggle.[8]

In August 2014, violent protests exploded in Ferguson, Missouri, a suburb of St Louis, after a policeman shot to death an unarmed black teenager suspected of robbery: for days, police tried to disperse mostly black protesters. Although the details of the accident are murky, the poor black majority of the town took it as yet another proof of the systematic police violence against them. In the US slums and ghettos, the police effectively functions more and more as a force of occupation, something akin to Israeli patrols entering the Palestinian territories on the West Bank; media were surprised to discover that even their guns are more and more US Army arms. Even when police units try just to impose peace, distribute humanitarian help or organize medical measures, their modus operandi is that of controlling a foreign population. Are not such 'irrational' violent demonstrations with no concrete programmatic demands, sustained by just a vague call for justice, today's exemplary cases of divine violence? They are, as Benjamin put it, means without ends, not part of a long-term strategy. Benjamin argues against

> the stubborn prevailing habit of conceiving those just ends as ends of a possible law, that is, not only as generally valid (which follows analytically from the nature of justice), but also as capable of generalization, which, as could be shown, contradicts the nature of justice. For ends that for one situation are just, universally acceptable, and valid, are so for no other situation, no matter how similar it may be in other respects. The non-mediate function of violence at issue here is illustrated by everyday experience. As regards man, he is impelled by anger, for example, to the most visible outbursts of a violence that is not related as a means to a preconceived end. It is not a means but a manifestation.[9]

It is important to perceive the subtle link between divine violence and Benjamin's key notion of ontological incompleteness of reality, of how historical reality is composed of traces which point towards the future, i.e. which will become readable only in the future when a radical emancipatory act will redeem the past: it is this ontological incompleteness that opens up the space for divine violence. Benjamin finishes his essay on violence by the claim that it is impossible for us humans 'to decide when pure violence has been realized in a particular case. For only mythic violence, not divine, will be recognizable as such with certainty, unless it be in incomparable effects, because the expiatory power of violence is invisible to men.'[10] The standard reading of these lines is that human actions can be an expression of divine justice but we can never know whether an act of ours effectively is a manifestation of divine violence, since justice is transcendent (God decides what is just): justice is *possible* (but not *knowable*) through an act of divine violence. In this standard reading, a human act (sometimes) is in itself an act of divine violence, but we cannot know it, we can only (maybe) realize this retroactively. One has to make here a step further and transpose epistemological inaccessibility (we cannot know for sure if an act is the expression of divine violence) into ontological impossibility: the impenetrability of acts of divine violence is what makes divine violence divine – the moment its status were to be clarified, it would lose its 'divine' status. In short, divine violence is not part of fully constituted reality, it belongs to the blurry domain of the pre-ontological Real.

One has to note the paradox of Benjamin's formula: for our common sense, general validity should be 'stronger' than (the process of) generalization, since it is its result, the outcome of successful generalization – so how can something be general(ly valid) and yet not generalizable (or, rather, universally valid and not universalizable)? An example (referred to by Kant) may clarify this distinction: 'Don't steal!' is a universal moral injunction (it tolerates no exceptions, it tells you never to steal), but it cannot be universalized since its (universal) validity is constrained to the domain of (private) property – it is meaningless to apply it to domains in which things are not owned by anyone. Similarly, the mistake of the standard notion of (social) violence is to limit it to its use as means: in what circumstances it may be legitimate to resort to violence, etc. Although we can elaborate in this way universal(ly valid) rules (like 'never resort to violence when you can achieve your goal through nonviolent means'), such an approach is not universalizable since it doesn't cover the cases in which violence 'is not related as a means to a preconceived end'. As Le Gaufey points out, therein resides the difference between Carl Schmitt and Benjamin: Schmitt remains constrained to the topic of violence as means to achieve an end, which is why the most radical point he can imagine is that of mythic violence, violence which serves the end to ground the rule of law (even when it violates the existing legal order), while Benjamin's 'divine violence' is, as he put it, a case of means without end.[11]

Does the same not hold not only for other protests which followed Ferguson, like the Baltimore riots in April 2015, but already for the French suburb riots of autumn 2005 when we saw thousands of cars burning and a major outburst of public violence? What strikes the eye is the total absence of any positive utopian prospect among the protesters: if May '68 was a revolt with a utopian vision, the 2005 revolt was just an outburst with no pretence to vision. If the much-repeated commonplace that we live in a postideological era has any sense, it is here. There were no particular demands made by the protestors in the Paris suburbs. There was only an insistence on *recognition*, based on a vague, nonarticulated, *ressentiment*. Most of those interviewed talked about how unacceptable it was that the then interior minister, Nicolas Sarkozy, had called them 'scum'. In a weird self-referential short circuit, they were protesting against the very reaction to their protests. Populist reason here encounters its irrational limit: what we have is a zero-level protest, a violent protest act which demands nothing. There was an irony in watching the sociologists, intellectuals, commentators, trying to understand and help. Desperately they tried to translate the protests acts into their meaning: 'We must do something about the integration of immigrants, about their welfare, their job opportunities', they proclaimed, and in the process obfuscated the key enigma the riots presented ...

The protesters, although effectively underprivileged and de facto excluded, were in no way living on the edge of starvation. Nor had they been reduced to bare survival level. People in much more terrible material straits, let alone conditions of physical and ideological oppression, had been able to organize themselves into political agents with clear or even fuzzy agendas. The fact that there was *no* programme in the burning Paris suburbs is thus itself a fact to be interpreted. It tells us a great deal about our ideologico-political predicament. What kind of universe is it that we inhabit, which can celebrate itself as a society of choice, but in which the only option available to enforced democratic consensus is a blind acting out? The sad fact that an opposition to the system cannot articulate itself in the guise of a realistic alternative, or at least a meaningful utopian project, but only take the shape of a meaningless outburst, is a grave indictment of our predicament. What does our celebrated freedom of choice serve, when the only choice is the one between playing by the rules and (self-)destructive violence? The protesters' violence was almost exclusively directed against their own. The cars burned and the schools torched were not those of richer neighbourhoods. They were part of the hard-won acquisitions of the very strata from which the protesters originated.

What needs to be resisted when faced with the shocking reports and images of the burning Paris suburbs is what I call the hermeneutic temptation: the search for some deeper meaning or message hidden in these outbursts. What is most difficult to accept is precisely the riots' meaninglessness: more than a form of protest, they are what Lacan called a *passage à l'acte* – an impulsive movement into action which can't be translated into speech or thought and carries with it an intolerable weight of frustration. This bears witness not only to the impotence of the perpetrators, but, even more, to the lack of what Fredric Jameson has called 'cognitive mapping', an inability to locate the experience of their situation within a meaningful whole.

The immediate counterargument here is: But are such violent demonstrations not often unjust, do they not hit the innocent? If we are to avoid the overstretched Politically Correct explanations according to which the victims of divine violence should humbly not resist it on account of their generic historical responsibility, the only solution is to simply accept the fact that divine violence *is* brutally unjust: it is often something terrifying, not a sublime intervention of the divine goodness and justice. A Left-liberal friend from the University of Chicago told me of his sad experience: when his son reached the age of high school, he enrolled him in a high school north of the campus, close to a black ghetto, with a majority of black kids, but his son was then returning home almost regularly with bruises or broken teeth – so what should he have done? Put his son in another school with the white majority or let him stay? The point is that this dilemma is wrong: the dilemma cannot be solved at this level since the very gap between private interest (safety of my son) and global justice bears witness to a situation which has to be overcome.

Freud himself is here too short: he opposes artificial crowds (church, army) and 'regressive' primary crowd, like a wild mob engaged in passionate collective violence (lynching, pogroms). Furthermore, from his liberal view, the reactionary lynching mob and the Leftist revolutionary crowd are conceived as libidinally identical, as the same unleashing of the destructive/unbinding death drive; it appears as if, for him, the 'regressive' primary crowd exemplarily operative in the destructive violence of a mob is the zero-level of the unbinding of a social link, the social 'death drive' at its purest.

One should add to this Freudian position at least three points. First, Freud fails to clearly distinguish between the church model and the army model of the artificial crowd: while 'church' stands for the hierarchic social order which tries to maintain peace and balance by way of necessary compromises, 'army' stands for an egalitarian collective of struggle, defined not by its internal hierarchy but by the opposition to its enemy, trying to destroy it – radical emancipatory movements are always modelled on the army, not on the church, millenarian churches are really structured like armies. Second, 'regressive' primary crowds do not come first, they are not the 'natural' foundation for the rise of 'artificial' crowds: they come *after*, as a kind of obscene supplement that sustains the 'artificial' crowd, that is, they relate to 'artificial' crowds like superego to the symbolic Law. While the symbolic Law demands obedience, superego provides the obscene enjoyment which attaches us to the Law. Last but not least, is the wild mob really the zero-level of the unbinding of a social link? Is it not rather a panicky *reaction* to the gap or inconsistency that cuts across a social edifice? The violence of a mob is by definition directed at the object (mis) perceived as the external cause of the gap (Jews, exemplarily), as if its destruction will abolish the gap.

The points of the impossible

So how are we to contain the threat of self-destructive social negativity? Badiou's answer is that we have to replace negative with affirmative dialectics – we should renounce the illusion that the New will arise through destruction of the old and begin with positive projects:

> We have to renounce the idea that negation bears affirmation, the idea which was nothing but the logical form of an enthusiastic hope that in this way the enforced birth of a real of History will occur. In reality, as we have seen throughout the twentieth century, negation bears negation, it incessantly engenders other negations.[12]

The reason for this catastrophic outcome is the belief in History as a continuous narrative with inner progressive tendency which works for us, so that we have the right to enforce this progress. (Classical Marxism remains within this frame with its notion of progressive modes of production.) Here we encounter Badiou's version of Fukuyama's end of History: yes, History as a continuous progress did reach its (dead) end. This is why Badiou advocates dialectical materialism without historical materialism (the science of the progressive movement of History), in contrast to the predominant Western Marxist project of historical materialism without dialectical materialism (which is rejected as a new metaphysical version of general ontology). For Badiou there is hope, we can do the impossible, i.e. intervene at the point of the impossible of our society and open up new possibilities, but without any guarantee in the big Other of History.

Is, then, the supreme gesture of materialist dialectics to historicize dialectics itself, to root it in social practice and political struggle? One can effectively show how, with every new historical epoch of the struggle for emancipation, a different understanding and practice of dialectics emerges. Marx's dialectics focused on the contours of the great progressive development through capitalist alienation towards its communist overcoming. After the fiasco of 1914, Lenin threw himself into a reading of Hegel and elaborated a notion of dialectics encompassing uneven development. Based on the Chinese experience, Mao introduced the complex game of principal and secondary contradictions, plus emphasized the endless antagonistic struggle without final resolution. So the question is no longer to decide, in an abstract way, which notion of dialectics is the true one, but – to quote Marx – to discern behind conflicting dogmas (different notions of dialectics) conflicting facts (different moments of the struggle). But is such a historicization of the very notion of dialectics enough? If we just claim that, say, evolutionary dialectical progress fits reformist social democracy, etc., does this not amount to justifying every form of dialectics as an expression of a particular form of struggle? And does this very approach not rely on a certain general notion of (historical) dialectics? In other words, if we are to avoid historicist relativism, are we not compelled to elevate a particular form of dialectics into a privileged moment of truth, into a universal key which enables us to categorize all other forms and to critically differentiate them?

The problem here is: was Stalinism really a negation without affirmation, was it effectively sustained by the trust that the New will emerge out of negation itself? Was it not rather an attempt to directly enforce a positive vision of the next, higher, stage of History? Was it not, in this sense, too affirmative?

Even if the emancipatory struggle begins as an opposition to state apparatuses, it has to change its target in its course. Badiou opposes (what he considers) the classic dialectical logic of negativity, which engenders out of its own movement a new positivity, a new 'affirmative' dialectics: the starting point of an emancipatory process should not be negativity, resistance, will to destruction, but a new affirmative vision disclosed in an Event – we oppose the existing order out of our fidelity to this event, drawing out its consequences. Without this affirmative moment, the emancipatory process ends up necessarily imposing a new positive order which is an imitation of the old one, sometimes even radicalizing its worst features … One should oppose to this 'affirmative' notion of dialectics the Hegelian notion of the dialectical *process* which begins with some affirmative idea towards which it strives, but in the course of which *this idea itself undergoes a profound transformation* (not just a tactical accommodation, but an essential redefinition), because the idea itself is caught in the process, (over)determined by its actualization.[13] Say, we have a revolt motivated by a request for justice: once people get really engaged in it, they become aware that much more is needed to bring true justice than just the limited requests with which they started (to repeal some laws, etc.). The problem, of course, is: what, precisely, is this 'much more'? Of one thing I am sure: it's not equality.

The ultimate horizon of emancipatory politics is what Badiou posits as the basic premise of the idea of communism, the 'axiom of equality' – in stark contrast to Marx, for whom equality is 'an exclusively *political* notion, and, as a political value, that it is a distinctively *bourgeois* value (often associated with the French revolutionary slogan *liberté, égalité, fraternité*). Far from being a value that can be used to thwart class oppression, Marx thinks the idea of equality is actually a vehicle for bourgeois class oppression, and something quite distinct from the communist goal of the abolition of classes.'[14] Or, as Engels put it:

> The idea of socialist society as the realm of *equality* is a one-sided French idea resting upon the old 'liberty, equality, fraternity' – an idea which was justified as *stage of development* in its own time and place but which, like all the one-sided ideas of the earlier socialist schools, should now be overcome, for it produces only confusion in people's heads and more precise modes of presentation of the matter have been found.[15]

Does this not hold even for today's French political theory from Balibar's *égaliberté* to Badiou? Back to Marx, he unequivocally rejects what Allen Wood calls 'egalitarian intuition' – egalitarian justice is unsatisfactory *precisely because* it applies an equal standard to unequal cases:

> Right by its very nature can consist only in the application of an equal standard; but unequal individuals (and they would not be different individuals if they were not unequal) are measurable by an equal standard only insofar as they are brought under an equal point of view, are taken from one definite side only, for instance, in the present case, are regarded *only as workers* and nothing else is seen in them, everything else being ignored. Further, one worker is married, another is not; one has more children than another, and so on and so forth. Thus with an equal performance of labor, and hence an equal share in the social consumption fund, one will receive more than another. To avoid all these defects, right instead of being equal would have to be unequal.[16]

In claiming that it is not just to apply equal criteria to unequal people, Marx may appear to repeat the old conservative argument for the legitimization of hierarchy; however, there is a subtle distinction that has to be taken into account here: this argument is false when we are in a class society in which class oppression overdetermines inequality, but in a post-class society it is a legitimate one, since inequality is there independent of class hierarchy and oppression. This is why Marx proposes as the axiom of communism:

'to each according to his needs, from each according to his abilities.' Wood points out that this maxim, although popularly associated with Marx, originated with Louis Blanc, who wrote in 1851 'De chacun selon ses moyens, à chacun selon ses besoins', and can even be traced back to the New Testament: 'And all that believed were together, and had all things common; and sold their possessions and goods, and parted them to all men, as every man had need' (Acts 2.44-5).

While this maxim certainly has nothing to do with equality, it poses problems of its own, the main among which concerns *envy*: can any subject define his or her need without regard to what others proclaim to be their needs? That is to say, as Jameson pointed out, we should reject the predominant optimistic opinion according to which in communism envy will be left behind as a remainder of capitalist competition, to be replaced by solidary collaboration and pleasure in other's pleasures. Dismissing this myth, Jameson emphasizes that in communism, precisely insofar as it will be a more just society, envy and resentment will explode.[17] He refers here to Lacan, whose thesis is that human desire is always desire of the Other in all the senses of that term: desire for the Other, desire to be desired by the Other, and, especially, desire for what the Other desires.[18] This last makes envy, which includes resentment, constitutive components of human desire, something Augustine knew well – recall the passage from his *Confessions*, often quoted by Lacan, the scene of a baby jealous of his brother sucking at the mother's breast: 'I myself have seen and known an infant to be jealous though it could not speak. It became pale, and cast bitter looks on its foster-brother.'

So we have to qualify Badiou's thesis that 'equality is the point of the impossible proper to capitalism'[19] – yes, but this impossible point is *immanent to the capitalist universe*, it is its immanent contradiction: capitalism advocates democratic equality, but the legal form of this equality is the very form of inequality. In other words, equality, the immanent ideal-norm of capitalism, is necessarily undermined by the process of its actualization. For this reason, Marx did not demand 'real equality', that is, his idea is not that equality as the real-impossible of capitalism should become possible; what he advocated was a move beyond the very horizon of equality.

Furthermore, the 'point of the impossible' of a certain field should not to be elevated into a radical utopian Other. The great art of politics is to detect it locally, in a series of modest demands which are not simply impossible but appear as possible although they are de facto impossible. The situation is like the one in science-fiction stories where the hero opens the wrong door (or presses the wrong button ...) and all of a sudden the entire reality around him disintegrates. In the United States, universal healthcare is obviously such a point of the impossible; in Europe, it seems to be the cancellation of the Greek debt, and so on. It is something you can (in principle) do but de facto you cannot or should not do it – you are free to choose it *on condition you do not actually choose it*. Therein resides the touchy point of democracy, of democratic elections: the result of a vote is sacred, the highest expression of popular sovereignty ... but what if people vote 'wrongly' (demanding measures which pose a threat to the basic coordinates of the capitalist system)?

On account of the necessary inconsistencies of global capitalism, this paradox of the 'point of the impossible' goes up to self-reference: the point of the impossible of global market could well be (and are) 'free' market relations themselves. A couple of years ago, a CNN report on Mali described the reality of the international 'free market'. The two pillars of the economy of Mali are cotton in the south and cattle in the north, and both are in trouble because of the way Western powers violate the very rules they try to impose brutally on the impoverished Third World nations. Mali produces cotton of top quality, but the problem is that the US government spends more money on the financial support of its cotton farmers than the entire state budget of Mali, so no wonder they cannot compete with the US cotton. In the north, it is the European Union which is the culprit: the Mali beef cannot compete with the heavily subsidized European milk and beef – the European Union subsidizes every single cow with ca. 500 Euros per year, more than the per capita brutto product in Mali. No wonder the comment of the Mali minister of economy was: we don't need your help or advices or lectures on the beneficial effects of abolishing excessive state regulations, just, please, stick to your own rules about free market and our troubles will be basically over.

Advocates of capitalism often point out that, in spite of all the critical prophecies, capitalism is overall, from a global perspective, not in crisis but is progressing more than ever – and one cannot but agree with them. Capitalism thrives all around the world (more or less), from China to Africa, it is definitely not in crisis – it is just people caught in this explosive development that are in crisis. This tension between overall explosive development and local crises and misery (which from time to time vacillate the entire system) is part of capitalism's normal functioning: capitalism renews itself through crises.

And this brings us to Fredric Jameson's utopia of global militarization of society as a mode of emancipation: one can argue that, while the deadlocks of global capitalism are more and more palpable, all the imagined democratic–multitude–grassroots changes 'from below' are ultimately doomed to fail – the only way to effectively break the vicious cycle of global capitalism is some kind of 'militarization', which is another name for suspending the power of self-regulating economy.[20] An obvious counter-argument to this project of militarization is that even if we concede its need, we can conditionally endorse it only for a short period of transition: fully developed communism can in no way be imagined along these lines. However, things here get very problematic. In traditional Marxism, the predominant name for this transitional period was 'dictatorship of the proletariat', a notion which always caused a lot of discontent. Étienne Balibar drew attention to the tendency in official Marxism to 'multiply the "intermediary stages" in order to resolve theoretical difficulties: stages between capitalism and communism, but also between imperialism and the passage to socialism'[21] – such a 'fetishism of the formal number of these stages'[22] is always symptomatic of a disavowed deadlock. What if, then, the way to subvert the logic of the 'stages of development' is to perceive this logic itself as the sign that we are at a lower stage since every imagining of a higher stage (to be reached through the sacrifices and sufferings of the present lower stage) is distorted by the perspective of the lower stage? In a properly Hegelian way, we effectively reach the higher stage not when we overcome the lower stage, but when we realize that what we have to get rid of is the very idea that there is a higher stage to follow what we are doing now and that the prospect of this higher stage can legitimize what we are doing now, in our lower stage. In short, the 'lower stage' is all we have and all we will ever get.

A couple of years ago, I saw the performance of Mozart's *Così fan tutte* in *Komische Oper* located on Unter den Linden in (former) East Berlin. Among the documents displayed in the foyer, there is a letter from Walter Ulbricht, the General Secretary of the SED and the undisputed master of the German Democratic Republic in the first decades of its existence: his reply to the request of the opera management to honour them by attending a gala performance. Ulbricht politely rejects the invitation, claiming that he simply doesn't have time for such events because of his heavy workload: he had to coordinate the two great historical passages from a lower to the higher stage of the social development of the GDR, the passage from feudal-reactionary Germany to bourgeois-democratic Germany and then its passage from the bourgeois-democratic state to a socialist state – a gigantic task which usually takes centuries to accomplish had to be performed in little bit more than a decade … The arrogant madness under-lying such reasoning has to be ruthlessly abandoned if the Communist Idea is to remain alive – to return to our metaphor from the introduction, it has to be swallowed and minced by the Kraken of dialectical thought – and no philosopher can be more helpful in this undertaking than Hegel. What this means is that Hegel does not justify extreme experiences of horror and pain as a necessary step towards a higher stage of ethical development. If there is a lesson to be learned from Hegel, it is the one found in a memorable passage from *Still Alive: A Holocaust Girlhood Remembered*, where Ruth Klüger describes a conversation with 'some advanced PhD candidates' in Germany:

> One reports how in Jerusalem he made the acquaintance of an old Hungarian Jew who was a survivor of Auschwitz, and yet this man cursed the Arabs and held them all in contempt. How can someone who comes from Auschwitz talk like that? the German asks. I get into the act and argue, perhaps more hotly than need be. What did he expect? Auschwitz was no instructional institution ... You learned nothing there, and least of all humanity and tolerance. Absolutely nothing good came out of the concentration camps, I hear myself saying, with my voice rising, and he expects catharsis, purgation, the sort of thing you go to the theatre for? They were the most useless, pointless establishments imaginable.[23]

We have to abandon the idea that there is something emancipatory in extreme experiences, that they enable us to open our eyes to the ultimate truth of a situation. This, perhaps, is the most depressing lesson of horror and suffering.

NOTES

Introduction

1 Friedrich Nietzsche, *Untimely Meditations*, ed. Daniel Breazeale, trans. R. J. Hollingdale (Cambridge: Cambridge University Press, 1997), 104.

2 See https://www.marxists.org/glossary/terms/o/l.htm.

3 G. W. F. Hegel, *Lectures on the History of Philosophy*, trans. E. S. Haldane, quoted from https://www.marxists.org/reference/archive/hegel/works/hp/hpfinal.htm.

4 Quoted from https://www.marxists.org/archive/marx/works/1852/18th-brumaire/ch07.htm.

5 See Michael Hardt and Antonio Negri, *Empire* (Cambridge, MA: Harvard University Press, 2001).

6 Quoted from https://www.marxists.org/reference/archive/hegel/works/letters/1816-07-05.htm.

7 'Life has always seemed to me like a plant that lives on its rhizome. Its true life is invisible, hidden in the rhizome … What we see is the blossom, which passes. The rhizome remains' (C. G. Jung, *Memories, Dreams, Reflections*, ed. A. Jaffé [New York: Vintage Books, 1965], 4).

8 See Gilles Deleuze, 'De Sacher-Masoch au masochisme', *Arguments*, no. 21 (1961): 40–6; English version, 'From Sacher-Masoch to Masochism', *Angelaki* 9, no. 1 (2004): 125–33.

9 I owe this reference to Kraken to Liza Thompson.

10 I rely here on Jure Simoniti's path-breaking *Svet in njegov predikat* [The world and its predicate], vol. 1 (Ljubljana: Društvo za teoretsko psihoanalizo, 2011).

11 Quoted from https://www.marxists.org/reference/archive/althusser/1968/philosophy-as-weapon.htm.

12 Louis Althusser, *Philosophy and the Spontaneous Philosophy of the Scientists, and Other Essays* (London: Verso Books, 2012), 14.

13 G. K. Chesterton, *Quotes* (Mineola, NY: Dover, 2015), 4.

14 Pascal Quignard, *Abimes* (Paris: Gallimard, 2002), 161.

Chapter 1: From human to posthuman … and back to inhuman: The persistence of ontological difference

1 G. W. F. Hegel, *Phenomenology of Spirit*, trans. A. V. Miller, with foreword by J. N. Findlay (Oxford: Oxford University Press, 1977), 21.

2 The Stalinist orthodox duality of dialectical and historical materialism marks a return to precritical ontology, with dialectical materialism as *metaphysica generalis* and historical materialism as *metaphysica specialis*, the application of dialectical materialism onto the particular sphere of social life. While the goal of Western Marxism was to pursue historical materialism without dialectical materialism (i.e. the assertion of collective human *praxis* as the ultimate transcendental horizon which underlies even the most general ontology), Badiou advocates the exact opposite: dialectical materialism without historical materialism (dismissed as a form of historicist progressism, as a belief in History). With regard to this specific point, the present book follows Badiou.

3 Available online at http://ebooks.adelaide.edu.au/p/proust/marcel/p96cg/chapter1.html.

4 Mladen Dolar, 'Telephone and Psychoanalysis', *Filozofski vestnik* 29, no. 1 (2008): 11.

5 For a more detailed reading of this passage from Proust, see Ch. 10 of my *Less than Nothing* (London: Verso Books, 2012).

6 One of the standard postmodern procedures with great classical works is to transpose them into contemporary daily life or into some popular, 'low' art form (comics, crime adventure, even western – there is an old novel which transposes the *Iliad* into the Wild West, as a conflict between two beef barons). Ian Doescher recently did the exact opposite: he took six *Star Wars* movies and rewrote them as Shakespeare plays, each in five acts, with chorus introducing the action and commenting on it, with the heroes speaking in Shakespearean verse and in his archaic English ('the Jedi doth return', etc.). Although the result often falls short of the idea, there is nonetheless something almost uncannily 'authentic' in the result: such reversals are a good reminder that there is no 'natural' link between the Shakespearean style and the story he is telling – far from forming an organic Whole, their combination is always violent and artificial.

7 *The Seminar of Jacques Lacan, Book II: The Ego in Freud's Theory and in the Technique of Psychoanalysis, 1954–1955*, ed. J.-A. Miller, S. Tomaselli and J. Forrester (Cambridge: Cambridge University Press, 1988), 226.

8 Stanley Cavell, *The World Viewed* (Cambridge, MA: Harvard University Press, 1979), 85.

9 Christophe Jaffrelot, *Dr. Ambedkar and Untouchability* (New Delhi: Permanent Black, 2005), 68–9.

10 Blaise Pascal, *Pensées*, trans. A. J. Krailsheimer (Harmondsworth: Penguin Books, 1965), 51.

11 Benedict de Spinoza, *A Theologico-Political Treatise and A Political Treatise*, trans. R. H. M. Elwes (Mineola, NY: Dover, 1951), 63, italics added.

12 *The Seminar of Jacques Lacan, Book XX: Encore*, seminar 4 (9 January 1973), trans. Cormac Gallagher, quoted from http://www.lacaninireland.com/web/wp-content/uploads/2010/06/THE-SEMINAR-OF-JACQUES-LACAN-XX.pdf.

13 Gunther Anders, *Die Antiquiertheit des Menschen* [The outdatedness of human beings] (Munich: Beck, 1956).

14 See Jean-Pierre Dupuy's contribution in *Le Débat*, no. 129 (March–April 2004), quoted from Jean-Michel Besnier, *Demain les posthumains* (Paris: Fayard, 2012), 195.

15 Jürgen Habermas, 'The Language Game of Responsible Agency and the Problem of Free Will: How Can Epistemic Dualism be Reconciled with Ontological Monism?', *Philosophical Explorations 10*, no. 1 (March 2007): 31.

16 Robert Pippin, 'Back to Hegel?', quoted from http://www.mediations journal.org/articles/back-to-hegel.

17 Quoted from http://ki.se/en/news/brain-scan-reveals-out-of-body-illusion.

18 Quoted from Ray Brassier, 'The View from Nowhere: Sellars, Habermas, Metzinger' (unpublished manuscript).

19 Ray Brassier, *Nihil Unbound* (London: Palgrave Macmillan, 2007), 138.

20   The question one should raise here is also the one of discourse. Brassier
     concludes his outstanding *Nihil Unbound* with speculations about
     death drive and the annihilation of reality – the type of discourse for
     which there is simply no place in his later Sellarsian preoccupations.
     The question is thus: is the duality of scientific discourse and its
     transcendental reflection the only option, or should we keep the space
     open for a different type of discourse associated with names like
     Schelling and Hegel, Lacan and Deleuze, etc.?

21   Ontological difference is, from our perspective, the very difference
     between the existing multiplicity of entities and the barred One: the One
     is barred, it doesn't exist, but the very void of its inexistence opens up the
     space for entities to arise. The illusion of metaphysics – the 'forgetting'
     of the ontological difference, as Heidegger would have put it – is to
     obliterate the bar that makes the One inexistent, i.e. to elevate the One
     into the highest entity.

22   Franco Berardi, *Heroes: Mass Murder and Suicide* (London: Verso Books,
     2015), 204–5.

23   Ibid., 206–7.

24   Ibid., 206.

25   I rely here on McKenzie Wark, *Molecular Red: Theory for the
     Anthropocene* (London: Verso Books, 2015). In this section, parenthetical
     page references are to this work.

26   In spite of these critical notes, one cannot but admire the 'new
     materialists' at their best, which is when they deploy the thick network
     of invisible lateral links which sustain our reality – recall Jane Bennett's
     description (in her *Vibrant Matter: A Political Ecology of Things*
     [Durham, NC: Duke University Press, 2010], 4–6) of how actants
     interact at a polluted trash site: not only humans but also the rotting
     trash, worms, insects, abandoned machines, chemical poisons, etc., each
     is playing its (never purely passive) role. It is not just the old reductionist
     idea that one can translate higher mental or life processes into lower-
     level processes; the point is that something happens at a higher level
     which cannot be explained at this level, in its own terms. (Say, there is
     a theory that Ancient Rome's decline was due to the poisonous effect of
     the lead particles in their metal pots and bowls.) In June 2015, MERS
     (Middle East Respiratory Syndrome) epidemics broke out in South
     Korea, triggered by one sole visitor returning from Saudi Arabia. What
     is part of our direct experience are the consequences (individuals getting
     ill and some of them dying) which pop up punctually, here and there,

while the entire continuous process goes on at a subperceptual level, threatening to explode into an uncontrollable killing spree.

Our fight against racism should also be 'molecular': instead of just focusing on big 'molar' explanations of how racism is a displaced class struggle, etc., one should analyse the micropractices (the thick texture of gestures and expressions) which display envy, humiliation, etc., of the racial Other. Today when we are (almost) all open-minded tolerant liberals, racism reproduces itself precisely at this molecular level: I respect Arabs, Jews, Blacks, etc., it's just that I cannot stand the smell of their food, their loud music, the vulgar sound of their laughter … Psychoanalysis can be of help here by way of providing the theoretical foundation of the 'molecular' functioning of racism.

27 One of the ways to understand the 'unnatural' horror generated by monstrously disfigured objects is to see them as cases of a failed (incomplete) collapse of quantum oscillations: superposed variations do not collapse into a single object in our reality but into a combination of two objects – say, a disgusting mixture of half-bird and half-worm. (In this way, we can also read the Kaballah notion of Evil as originating in the traces of another world within this, our world; the idea is that before god created our world, he created other worlds which he obliterated as failed attempts, but he did not erase them completely, so that parts of them survived in our world.)

28 For Bohr objective reality is not an in-itself but is ascertained when a repeatable measurement provides always the same result. Measurement means that the scientific procedure exposes itself to a contingent (unpredictable) external real – we are far from subjectivist relativism, we are dealing with a Real in the sense of that which 'always returns to its place'. Bohr refers the quantum universe to the concrete situation of measurement apparatuses and procedures as the only horizon within which they are meaningful. Although measurement apparatuses are clearly part of our ordinary reality, the question of the ontological status of what is measured/registered by the apparatuses remains open.

29 See Timothy Morton, *Hyperobjects: Philosophy and Ecology after the End of the World* (Minneapolis: University of Minnesota Press, 2013).

30 Steven Muecke, review of *Hyperobjects* by Timothy Morton, *Los Angeles Review of Books*, 20 February 2014, http://lareviewofbooks.org/review/hyperobjects.

31 Jean-Pierre Dupuy, *La marque du sacré* (Paris: Carnets Nord, 2008).

32 But are we not confusing 'first' and 'second' nature, 'natural' hyperobjects

(like global warming) and socio-symbolic ones (like the market or language)? Are we not repeating the mistake of those system-theorists who describe social phenomena like markets as just another case of evolutionary self-organization? Convincing as this may sound, this reproach misses the point: the homology doesn't naturalize 'second nature', it aims to denaturalize the 'first' ('true') nature itself.

33 Georg Lukács, *History and Class Consciousness* (London: Merlin, 1975).

34 Adrian Johnston, *Adventures in Transcendental Materialism: Dialogues with Contemporary Thinkers* (Edinburgh: Edinburgh University Press, 2014), 178.

35 Ibid., 180.

36 Terrence W. Deacon, *Incomplete Nature: How Mind Emerged from Matter* (New York: Norton, 2012), 538.

37 Ibid., 2–3.

38 Ibid., 536.

39 Ibid., 483; quoted in Johnston, *Adventures in Transcendental Materialism*, 59.

40 Deacon, *Incomplete Nature*, 8.

41 I rely here on the third chapter ('Quantum Physics with Lacan') of my *The Indivisible Remainder* (London: Verso Books, 1996), as well as on the final chapter of my *Less than Nothing*.

42 Brian Greene, *The Elegant Universe* (New York: Norton, 1999), 116–19.

43 Bruce Rosenblum and Fred Kuttner, *Quantum Enigma: Physics Encounters Consciousness* (Oxford: Oxford University Press, 2006), 171.

Chapter 2: Objects, objects … and the subject

1 See Levi R. Bryant, *The Democracy of Objects* (Ann Arbor, MI: Open Humanities, 2011). (In the present chapter, in-text page references in parentheses are to this work.) Bryant reads ooo as object-oriented *onticology* (to distinguish it from metaphysical ontology.)

2 A somewhat simplistic transcendental argument against ooo would have been: where does Bryant speak from when he elaborates his onticology?

If all objects are autopoietically constrained, is then his own description of the pluriverse of objects not also constrained by the system-specific perspective proper to human objects?

3   Malabou notes how Meillassoux's insistence on the radical contingency of our world, on the possibility of a wholly different other world, paradoxically ends up accepting the stability of the existing world, as if the empty possibility of a radical change of our entire world guarantees that nothing actually changes in this world. See Catherine Malabou, *Avant demain: Épigenèse et rationalité* (Paris: Presses Universitaires de France, 2014), 250–1.

4   Quentin Meillassoux, *After Finitude: An Essay on the Necessity of Contingency*, trans. Ray Brassier (London: Continuum, 2008), 56.

5   Ibid., 52.

6   Ibid., 53.

7   Ibid., 63, 58.

8   Ibid., 114.

9   There is another option here: even if communication is interpretation, so that the explicit message that circulates and is interpreted by the receiver is always a distortion of what the sender really meant, what if the explicit message is more important than its withdrawn core, what if there is more truth in miscommunication than in what is withdrawn? Imagine a dialogue between a Chinese and a US capitalist manager: undoubtedly each of them will miss the culturally specific background of the other's message – however, this background is irrelevant with regard to what is at stake in this communication (the exchange of commodities will go on smoothly in spite of this continuing miscommunication).

10 Bennett, *Vibrant Matter*, 4–6.

11 See Eric Santner, *The Royal Remains: The People's Two Bodies and the Endgames of Sovereignty* (Chicago: University of Chicago Press, 2011).

12 Isabel Allende, 'The End of All Roads', *Financial Times*, 15 November 2003.

13 For this notion, see James Martel, 'A Misinterpellated Messiah' (paper presented at the conference *The Actuality of the Theologico-Political*, Birkbeck, University of London, 24 May 2014).

14 *The Seminar of Jacques Lacan, Book VII: The Ethics of Psychoanalysis, 1959–1960*, ed. J.-A. Miller, trans. D. Porter (London: Routledge, 1992), 44.

15 Rebecca Comay, 'Resistance and Repetition: Freud and Hegel', *Research in Phenomenology* 45, no. 2 (2015): 258.

16 See Frank Ruda, 'Hegel and Resistance' (unpublished manuscript). All unattributed quotations in this chapter are from Ruda's manuscript.

17 The final scene of *Mad Men* (the ending of episode 14 of season 7) also enacts a Hegelian infinite judgement: in the middle of a collective meditation trance, Don's face breaks into a blessed smile, the idea is here … The highest (hippy spiritual enlightenment, cutting links with commercial culture) reverts into the lowest (a new idea for the supercommercial, the famous one for Coke).

18 Hegel, *Phenomenology of Spirit*, 38.

19 The term was elaborated by Samo Tomšič, *The Capitalist Unconscious: Marx and Lacan* (London: Verso Books, 2015).

20 Sigmund Freud, *Introductory Lectures on Psychoanalysis* (Harmondsworth: Penguin Books, 1973), 261–2.

21 Sigmund Freud, *The Interpretation of Dreams* (Harmondsworth: Penguin Books, 1976), 561.

22 Hegel, *Phenomenology of Spirit*, 37.

23 G. W. F. Hegel, *Lectures on the Philosophy of Religion*, ed. Peter C. Hodgson (Oxford: Oxford University Press, 2007), 3:206

24 Ibid., 207.

25 Ibid., 205.

26 Thomas Mann, *The Magic Mountain*, trans. H. T. Lowe-Porter (New York: Vintage Books, 1969), 285.

27 Aaron Schuster, *The Trouble with Pleasure: Deleuze and Psychoanalysis* (Cambridge, MA: MIT Press, 2016).

28 Malabou, *Avant demain*, 162–6.

29 The counterpart of this problematic status of the transcendental subject is life, living entities; why? Because they display a transcendental (self-organizing, 'synthetic necessity which is no longer that') function in objective reality itself – in the living, the transcendental dimension encounters itself in its objective version, among the constituted objects: 'reason encounters itself as a fact in nature and discovers the signification of determinism' (Malabou, *Avant demain*, 297).

Chapter 3: Self-consciousness, which self-consciousness? Against the renormalization of Hegel

1   *Hegel's Science of Logic*, trans. A. V. Miller, with foreword by J. N. Findlay (London: Allen & Unwin, 1969), 604, with changes.

2   It was Hamman Aldouri who elaborated this distinction; see his doctoral thesis 'Hegel's *Aufhebung*' (unpublished manuscript).

3   Ibid.

4   Robert Brandom, 'A Spirit of Trust: A Semantic Reading of Hegel's *Phenomenology*' (unfinished manuscript), available online at http://www.pitt.edu/~brandom/spirit_of_trust_2014.html. All unattributed quotations in the present chapter are taken from this source.

5   Hegel, *Phenomenology of Spirit*, 11 (§ 21).

6   Fredric Jameson, *The Hegel Variations: On the 'Phenomenology of Spirit'* (London: Verso Books, 2010), 48.

7   Ibid.

8   Claude Lévi-Strauss, *Introduction to the Work of Marcel Mauss*, trans. Felicity Baker (London: Routledge, 1987), 59.

9   Ibid., 62–3.

10   Ibid., 64.

11   Ibid., 63.

12   For a more detailed account of the role of differentiality in the emergence of a subjectivized structure, see Ch. 9 of my *Less than Nothing*.

13   *Hegel's Science of Logic*, 440.

14   G. W. F. Hegel, *The Encyclopaedia Logic*, ed. and trans. T. F. Geraets, W. A. Suchting and H. S. Harris (Indianapolis, IN: Hackett, 1991), 91–2 (§ 48), available online at https://rosswolfe.files.wordpress.com/2015/05/georg-wilhelm-friedrich-hegel-encyclopedia-logic.pdf.

15   Quentin Meillassoux, interview with Graham Harman, in *Quentin Meillassoux: Philosophy in the Making*, by G. Harman (Edinburgh: Edinburgh University Press, 2011), 166.

16   Hegel, *Phenomenology of Spirit*, 237 (§ 396).

17   In order to designate the act of the self-positing of the absolute I, Fichte is fully justified in using his neologism *Tat-Handlung* which unites the two aspects of *Handlung* and *Tat* – it is only in this primordial act that *Handlung* and *Tat* fully overlap, i.e. that there is no gap between its intended goal and its actual consequences.

18 G. W. F. Hegel, *Elements of the Philosophy of Right*, ed. Allen Wood, trans. H. B. Nisbet (Cambridge: Cambridge University Press, 1991), 150 (§ 122).

19 Incidentally, what Hegel means by 'recognition' is also something much more radical and disturbing than the liberal beauty of mutually recognizing free individuals: in his extreme but crucial case, execution (capital punishment) of a criminal is the recognition of him/her as a free responsible human being – if we refuse to punish him, arguing that he was a victim of circumstances, we deprive him of his rational freedom.

20 Hegel, *Phenomenology of Spirit*, 332.

21 Hegel, *Elements of the Philosophy of Right*, 23.

22 Hegel, *The Encyclopaedia Logic*, 286 (§ 212).

23 One of the popular exercises in critical Hegel studies is to locate the weak points in his process of deduction, the points where the passage from one to another figure fails and Hegel obviously cheats. There are numerous examples, from the very beginning of his logic (the passage from being-nothing to becoming and then to *Dasein*) up to concrete historical examples like the deadlock of his reading of *Antigone* in *Phenomenology of Spirit*. But what if there is something wrong in this entire search for the points of failure? What if the entire dialectical process is as such a series of 'failures', what if the next step which follows a deadlock is not a positive resolution of the deadlock but rather the obverse of the deadlock itself, the deadlock in its positive form, i.e. just a shift in perspective by way of which the deadlock appears as its own resolution?

24 Hegel, *Phenomenology of Spirit*, 406, 407 (§§ 667, 669).

25 Rebecca Comay has proposed another, ingenious, reading of this thesis of Hegel. Her starting point is Hegel's celebration of the analytic power of Reason: Reason is the infinite power of tearing apart what organically belongs together, but the inert flow of reality Life ultimately always undoes the work of Reason and restores the continuity of Life. In a homologous way, the psychoanalytic treatment dissects (unbinds) the thick texture of the unconscious, bringing out its disparate moments; however, the flow of our psychic life makes us forget these insights and reintegrates them into the basic pathology of our psyche: 'If analysis is literally to be understood as a dissolving or untying – this is the original meaning of ana-lysis: an unbinding or loosening of the tightly wound knot of punishment and desire – the resistance to analysis consists of an incessant reweaving of this fabric of oppression and repression. Any attempt to loosen the weave, to unpick, unbind, or analyze the knot of suffering is Sisyphean, or more precisely, counter-Penelopean; the very act of unweaving is itself silently knitted back into the mesh, seamlessly reintegrated into the pathology, like an invisible scar. This is, incidentally, one way – of course not the standard one – of understanding Hegel's most infamous statement that the "wounds of spirit heal and leave no scars'" (Comay, 'Resistance and Repetition: Freud and Hegel', 254).

26 Quotation from *G. W. F. Hegel: Theologian of the Spirit*, ed. Peter C. Hodgson (Minneapolis, MN: Fortress, 1997), 237. Since this translation of some chapters from Hegel's lectures on the philosophy of religion is unreliable and fragmentary, one should always check the German original.

27 Ibid.

28 Ibid., 238–9.

29 G. W. F. Hegel, *Werke*, vol. 17 (Frankfurt: Suhrkamp, 1969), 272.

30 See Ch. 1 of Jacques Lacan, *The Four Fundamental Concepts of Psycho-Analysis* (Harmondsworth: Penguin Books, 1979).

31 Karl Marx, *Capital* (Harmondsworth: Penguin Books, 1990), 1:163.

32 See Robert Pippin, 'The Significance of Self-Consciousness in Idealist Theories of Logic', *Proceedings of the Aristotelian Society* 114, no. 2 (2013–14): 145–66. Parenthetical page references are to this essay.

33 Robert B. Pippin, *Hegel's Practical Philosophy: Rational Agency as Ethical Life* (Cambridge: Cambridge University Press, 2008), 56.

34 Ibid., 46.

35 Ibid., 53.

36 Robert Pippin, *Hegel's Idealism* (Cambridge: Cambridge University Press, 1989), 220.

37 Ibid., 213.

38 Ibid., 216–17.

39 *Hegel's Science of Logic*, 402.

40 *Hegel's Science of Logic*, 444.

41 *Hegel's Philosophy of Mind*, trans. William Wallace and A. V. Miller, with foreword by J. N. Findlay (Oxford: Clarendon, 1971), 263 (§ 535).

42 Ermanno Bencivenga, *Hegel's Dialectical Logic* (Oxford: Oxford University Press, 2000), 63–64.

43 Hegel, *Elements of the Philosophy of Right*, 204–5.

44 Quoted from https://www.marxists.org/archive/marx/works/1867-c1/ch02.htm.

45 Jacques Lacan, *Écrits*, trans. Bruce Fink (New York: Norton, 2006), 435.

Chapter 4: Art after Hegel, Hegel after the end of art

1 *Hegel's Aesthetics: Lectures on Fine Art*, trans. T. M. Knox (Oxford: Clarendon, 1975), 1:604.

2 Ibid., 1:103

3 Robert B. Pippin, *After the Beautiful: Hegel and the Philosophy of Pictorial Modernism* (Chicago: University of Chicago Press, 2014), 139. Parenthetical page references in the present chapter are to this work.

4 *Hegel's Aesthetics*, 1:11.

5 Hegel, *The Encyclopaedia Logic*, 286 (§ 212 Z).

6 Nicolas Bourriaud, 'Introduction', in Michel Foucault, *Manet and the Object of Painting* (London: Tate Publishing, 2009), 16–17.

7 *Hegel's Aesthetics*, 1:153–4.

8 Ibid., 1:71.

9 One can thus conceive cubism as a kind of inverted Argus: in it, the painting presents an object (say, a human body) as if it is simultaneously viewed from multiple standpoints. In this sense, in cubism the viewer/beholder himself becomes a multi-eyed Argus.

10 Julia Kristeva, *Powers of Horror: An Essay on Abjection*, trans. L. S. Roudiez (New York: Columbia University Press, 1982), 79.

11 *The Seminar of Jacques Lacan, Book XI: The Four Fundamental Concepts of Psychoanalysis*, ed. J.-A. Miller, trans. A. Sheridan (New York: Norton, 1978), 101.

12 G. W. F. Hegel, *Lectures on the History of Philosophy*, trans. E. S. Haldane

and Frances H. Simson (Lincoln: University of Nebraska Press, 1995), 1:150–1.

13 Rebecca Comay, 'Defaced Statues: Idealism and Iconoclasm in Hegel's *Aesthetics*', *October* 149 (2014): 126.

14 *Hegel's Aesthetics*, 1:520–1.

15 *Hässlich*: ugly and, literally, worthy of hatred, that which provokes hatred, 'hateable'.

16 Karl Rosenkranz, *Ästhetik des Häßlichen* (Königsberg: Gebrüder Bornträger, 1853), 36.

17 Ibid., 145. Rosenkranz strangely ignores Hegel in his book on the Ugly, although Hegel points the way towards the *Ästhetik des Häßlichen* when he conceives Romantic art as the art which liberates subjectivity in its contingency (ugliness) and culminates in humour as a way to assume the ugly.

18 Theodor Adorno, *Aesthetic Theory*, trans. C. Lenhardt (London: Routledge and Kegan Paul, 1984), 75.

19 Ibid., 72.

20 Herman Parret, 'The Ugly as the Beyond of the Sublime', 4, http://www.hermanparret.be/media/articles-in-print/21_The-Ugly-as-the-Beyond.pdf.

21 Ibid., 7.

22 Immanuel Kant, *Lectures on Pedagogy*, in *Anthropology, History, and Education*, ed. G. Zöller and R. B. Louden (Cambridge: Cambridge University Press, 2007), 438 (Ak. 9:442).

23 See Immanuel Kant, *Gesammelte Schriften*, vol. 7 (Berlin: De Gruyter, 1973), 327–8.

24 Immanuel Kant, *Anthropology from a Pragmatic Point of View*, in *Anthropology, History, and Education*, 367 (Ak. 7:265).

25 Ibid. (Ak. 7:266).

26 Ibid., 369 (Ak. 7:268).

27 Parret, 'Ugly as the Beyond of the Sublime', 6–7.

28 Otto Weininger, *Über die letzten Dinge* (Munich: Matthes & Seitz, 1997), 187, 188.

29 Freud, *Beyond the Pleasure Principle*, trans. C. J. M. Hubback (London: International Psycho-Analytical, 1922), quoted from http://www.bartleby.com/276/4.html.

30 Brassier, *Nihil Unbound*, 237.

31 Stephen Mulhall, *On Film*, 2nd edn (London: Routledge, 2008), 18.

32 Ibid., 120.

33 There is a series of additional features to be noted about *Psycho*: (1) Does *Psycho* also not move towards the creation of a couple? There are subtle hints that the next couple will be the one of Lila and Sam, the ersatz of the impossible couple of Marion and Norman. (2) The father *is* present in *Psycho* as the absent trigger of the events: the reason Marion steals the money is that Sam, her fiancé, has to work hard to repay his dead father's debts (once these debts will be paid off, they could start to live together). (3) The rich man who obscenely tempts Marion, showing her a heap of money, enters the office from the spot where Hitchcock is standing, wearing the same Stetson hat – is he not sent by Hitchcock/God as his stand-in whose function is to expose Marion to temptation?

34 For a more detailed analysis of this aspect of Hitchcock's work, see Ch. 6 of my *Organs without Bodies: On Deleuze and Consequences* (New York: Routledge, 2004).

35 Pippin, *After the Beautiful*, 14.

36 Robert Pippin, 'What Was Abstract Art? (From the Point of View of Hegel)', *Critical Inquiry* 29 (2002): 23, available at https://webshare. uchicago.edu/users/rbp1/Public/Abstract%20Art%20Hegel. pdf?uniq=-ltczqm.

37 Wassily Kandinsky, *Concerning the Spiritual in Art*, trans. M. T. H. Sadler (Mineola, NY: Dover, 1977), 17, 33, available at http://www.semantikon. com/art/kandinskyspiritualinart.pdf.

38 Incidentally, isn't Dawkins's notion of meme the latest version of the autonomous power of mimesis? Memes as agents use us (humans) to replicate themselves, likes genes who pursue their own reproduction through living organisms.

39 Primo Levi, *If This Is a Man and The Truce*, trans. S. Woolf (London: Abacus, 1987), 133–4.

40 *Hegel's Aesthetics*, 1:607.

41 Ibid., 2:1236.

Chapter 5: Versions of abject: Ugly, creepy, disgusting

1   Kriseva, *Powers of Horror*, 3. Parenthetical page references in this chapter are to this work.

2   The quote within the quote is from Charles Malamoud, 'Observations sur la notion de "reste" dans le brahmanisme', *Wiener Zeitschrift für die Kunde Südasiens* 16 (1972): 5–26.

3   Against such a reading, it suffices to recall that for Hegel, the concluding moment of the dialectical process is not the complete sublation of all contingent particularity in the universality of a notion but its exact opposite: the insight into how a nonsublatable remainder is needed to close the process: State as a rational totality is fully actualized in the (biologically, i.e. contingently, determined) person of the monarch, etc. In other words, the 'spurious infinity' of the idealization of empirical contingency is brought to its end not when it finally succeeds but when that which seems its fatal obstacle is experienced as its 'quilting point'.

4   Lacan, *Écrits*, 698.

5   See Octave Mannoni, 'Je sais bien, mais quand même …', in *Clefs pour l'imaginaire* (Paris: Seuil, 1968). I am here summarizing a more detailed reading of Mannoni in my *For They Know Not What They Do* (London: Verso Books, 2008).

6   I summarize here a more detailed analysis from my *On Belief* (London: Routledge, 2001).

7   A 'pragmatic contradiction' in the very heart of Buddhism was often noted by its critics: Buddhism targets the overcoming of the Self, but the form of its practice – meditation, self-probing, with the goal of personal deliverance – is focused on the Self. What Western thought opposed to this self-preoccupation is a practical self-obliteration: the engagement in a Third Thing, for a higher Cause which transcends me and with regard to which I ultimately don't matter.

8   *The Complete Letters of Sigmund Freud to Wilhelm Fliess, 1887–1904,* ed. and trans. J. M. Masson (Cambridge, MA: Harvard University Press, 1985), 290.

9   One should note here how, although Deleuze passionately opposes Bataille and other thinkers of transgression, of the 'transgressive' notion of desire, he remains within the constraints of the Aristotelian *phronesis*, of practising the proper measure that enables us to avoid the two extremes of excessive fidelity to sanity/normality and its excessive violation – to quote Schuster's precise observation: 'The central moral problem of Deleuze's philosophy becomes, perhaps rather surprisingly, that of prudence. Just how far should one extend the crack? How to find the proper measure between health and sickness, vitality and exhaustion, sanity and madness, life and death, self-control and self-loss, or in a word, between measure and measurelessness? Deleuzian ethics can be seen as a kind of paradoxical Aristotelianism insofar as it demands the exercise of *phronesis* – prudence, practical reason – in a situation that would seem precisely to exclude it, a situation of disorientation, of intoxication, of de-personalization, of self-loss, even of madness' (Schuster, *The Trouble with Pleasure: Deleuze and Psychoanalysis*).

10 Éric Laurent, 'Racism 2.0', AMP blog, 29 January 2014, http://ampblog2006.blogspot.com/2014/01/lq-in-english-racism-20-by-eric-laurent.html.

11 Jacques Lacan, 'Proposition of 9 October 1967 on the Psychoanalyst of the School', *Analysis*, no. 6 (1995): 12.

12 Peter Sloterdijk, 'Warten auf den Islam', *Focus*, no. 10 (2006): 84.

13 Jacques Lacan, *Television*, in *Television and A Challenge to the Psychoanalytic Establishment*, trans. D. Hollier, R. Krauss and A. Michelson (New York: Norton, 1990), 32.

14 Laurent, 'Racism 2.0.'

15 Ibid.

16 Lacan, *Écrits*, 174.

17 A. B. Yehoshua, 'An Attempt to Identify the Root Cause of Antisemitism', *Azure*, no. 32 (Spring 2008), available online at http://www.azure.org.il/article.php?id=18&page=all.

18 I am here, of course, paraphrasing Lacan's famous statement: 'The picture is in my eye, but me, I am in the picture.'

19 Johnston, *Adventures in Transcendental Materialism*, 281.

20 G. K. Chesterton, *Charles Dickens: A Critical Study* (New York: Dodd Mead, 1906), 45–8.

21 For a more detailed analysis of Kieslowski's work, see my *The Fright of Real Tears* (London: BFI, 2001).

22 Adam Kotsko, *Creepiness* (Alresford: Zero Books, 2015), quoted from manuscript.

23 Ibid.

24 Ibid.

25 Ibid.

26 See http://www.aboutgerman.net/AGNlessons/heintje-heidschi-bumbeidschi-lyrics.htm#about.

27 See Foucault, *Manet and the Object of Painting*, 31.

28 Here is Eisler's touching *Foreword to the Hollywood Songbook*: 'In a society which understands and loves such a songbook, it will be possible to live well without danger. These pieces are written in confidence of this.' Incidentally, six Hölderlin fragments were set to music also by Benjamin Britten in 1952.

29 Manfred Grabs, 'Wir, so gut es gelang, haben das Unsre getan', *Beiträge zur Musikwissenschaft* (Berlin) 15, nos 1–2 (1973): 50.

30 *Hanns Eisler: A Miscellany*, ed. David Blake (Luxembourg: Harwood Academic, 1995), 426.

31 One can imagine a similar effect if one were to record 'Daddy', Sylvia Plath's most celebrated poem, as a popular music song in the pre-rock style of her times (Connie Francis, etc.), including the 'rich' kitschy orchestration.

32 Stanley E. Workman, 'Hanns Eisler and His Hollywood Songbook: A Survey of the *Five Elegies* (*Fünf Elegien*) and the *Hölderlin Fragments* (*Hölderlin-Fragmente*)' (DMA thesis, Ohio State University, 2010), 60.

33 Fritz Hennenberg, *Hanns Eisler* (Hamburg: Rowohlt, 1987), 201.

34 Workman, 'Hanns Eisler and His Hollywood Songbook', 65.

35 Eisler was a double emigrant in the 1940s, not at home not only in the United States but also in his own country, dreaming of an Other Germany, the dream expressed also in his music of the GDR national anthem 'Auferstanden aus Ruinen' (Raised out of the ruins).

36 The two songs with words based on Pascal (nos 17 and 18 from the *Hollywood Songbook*) display a similar dark vision. 'Despite these miseries, man wishes to be happy, / and only wishes to be happy, and cannot wish not to be so. / But how will he set about it? To be happy he would have to / make himself immortal. But, not being able to do so, / it has occurred to him to prevent himself from thinking of death' (no. 17). 'The only thing which consoles us for our miseries is diversion, / and yet this is the greatest of our miseries. / For it is this which principally hinders us from reflecting upon ourselves, / and which makes us insensibly ruin ourselves. Without this / we should be in a state of weariness, and this weariness would spur us / to seek a more solid means of escaping from it. / But diversions amuse us and lead us unconsciously to death' (no. 18). Again, such a dark vision of humanity is the necessary background of authentic communism – without it, we end up in the Stalinist optimism which is the front side of terror.

37 Quoted from Friederike Wißmann, *Hanns Eisler* (Munich: Bertelsmann, 2012), 132.

38 Bertolt Brecht, *Journals, 1934–1955*, ed. J. Willett, trans. H. Rorrison (London: Methuen, 1993), 224.

39 See Kirstin Thompson, *Eisenstein's 'Ivan the Terrible': A Neoformalist Analysis* (Princeton: Princeton University Press, 1981).

40 In the same vein, Eisenstein tried to isolate the libidinal economy of Ignatius Loyola's meditations, which can then be appropriated for communist propaganda – the sublime enthusiasm for the Holy Grail and the enthusiasm of kolkhoz farmers for the new machine to produce butter from milk (the famous scene from *The Old and the New*) are sustained by exactly the same 'ecstatic' intensity which is just schematized in two different modes.

41 Here I summarize a more detailed analysis of Schumann's *Carnaval* from my *Plague of Fantasies* (London: Verso Books, 2009).

Chapter 6: When nothing changes: Two scenes of subjective destitution

1 Adam Phillips, 'The Art of Nonfiction No. 7', interview by Paul Holdengräber, *Paris Review* (Spring 2014): 39–40.

2 Ibid., 38–9.

3 Ibid., 44.

4 Ibid., 24.

5 Lacan identifies hysteria with neurosis: the other main form of neurosis, obsessional neurosis, is for him a 'dialect of hysteria'.

6 François Balmès, *Dieu, le sexe et la vérité* (Ramonville-Saint-Agne: Erès, 2007), 51.

7 Thomas J. J. Altizer, *The Contemporary Jesus* (London: SCM Press, 1998), 101.

8   *Le seminaire de Jacques Lacan, Livre XXIII: Le sinthome* (Paris: Seuil, 2005).

9   Available at http://www.samuel-beckett.net/Text4Nothing4.html.

10 Jonathan Boulter, 'Does Mourning Require a Subject?', *Modern Fiction Studies* 50, no. 2 (Summer 2004): 332–50.

11 See Alain Badiou, 'The Writing of the Generic: Samuel Beckett', in *Conditions*, trans. Steven Corcoran (New York: Continuum, 2008), 251–84.

12 Another version of this 'You must go on!' is, of course, the famous line from *Worstward Ho*: 'Try again. Fail again. Fail better' (Samuel Beckett, *Nohow On* [London: Calder, 1992], 101). One should remember here a curiosity from Beckett's life: in his thirties, he worked for a short period as a psychological advisor to teenagers in distress, and 'Try again. Fail again. Fail better' was originally meant as the advice to a teenage boy who complained that, in his first sexual encounter with a woman, he miserably failed.

13 Boulter, 'Does Mourning Require a Subject?', 333–4.

14 Ibid., 337.

15 Ibid., 341.

16 Ibid., 337. Judith Butler developed this point in *The Psychic Life of Power* (Stanford: Stanford University Press, 1997).

17 For a discussion of this reversal of the Deleuzean figure of the 'body without organs', see my *Organs without Bodies*.

18 Samuel Beckett, *Three Novels: Molloy, Malone Dies, The Unnamable* (New York: Grove, 2009), 348.

19 See Vivian Mercier, *Beckett/Beckett: The Truth of Contradictories* (New York: Oxford University Press, 1977).

20 The play is available online at http://www.vahidnab.com/notI.htm.

21 Quoted from Deirdre Bair, *Samuel Beckett: A Biography* (New York: Touchstone, 1990), 622.

22 Quoted from *The Faber Companion to Samuel Beckett*, ed. C. J. Ackerley and S. E. Gontarski (London: Faber and Faber, 2006), 116.

23 Quoted from James Knowlson and John Pilling, *Frescoes of the Skull: The Later Prose and Drama of Samuel Beckett* (New York: Grove, 1979), 196.

24 James Knowlson, *Damned to Fame: The Life of Samuel Beckett* (New York: Grove, 1996), 521–2.

25 Quoted from S. E. Gontarski, 'Revising Himself: Performances as Text in Samuel Beckett's Theatre', *Journal of Modern Literature* 22, no. 1 (1998): 144.

26 Knowlson, *Damned to Fame*, 617.

27 Quoted from Bair, *Samuel Beckett*, 665. In the 2000 filmed production, directed by Neil Jordan, we see Julianne Moore come into view, sit down and then the light hit her mouth – this makes us aware that a young woman as opposed to an 'old hag' is portraying the protagonist.

28 Quoted from Bair, *Samuel Beckett*, 24.

29 C. S. Lewis, *Surprised by Joy* (London: Fontana Books, 1977), 174–5.

Chapter 7: Tribulations of a woman-hyena: Authority, costume and friendship

1 The conservatives in Slovenia are pushing this equation of Nazism and Left to extremes: recently, one of their texts enumerated a series of programmatic requests which allegedly prove the closeness of the Slovene United Left to Nazism, and, among the items, one finds the demand for the progressive taxation of the wealthy. (Another commentator dismisses today's gender theory as a continuation of communism by other means, i.e. as an attempt to undermine the moral foundations of the Christian West.)

2 As of 2015, four volumes have appeared in *Gesamtausgabe* (Frankfurt: Klostermann) (hereafter *GA*): vol. 94, Überlegungen II–VI: Schwarze Hefte 1931–1938 (2014); vol. 95, Überlegungen VII–XI: Schwarze Hefte 1938/39 (2014); vol. 96, Überlegungen XII–XV: Schwarze Hefte 1939–1941 (2014); vol. 97, Anmerkungen A (II–V) (2015).

3 Heidegger, *GA*, 95:381–2.

4 Heidegger, *GA*, 94:194.

5 Heidegger, *GA*, 96:56.

6 Ibid., 46.

7 Quoted from Peter Trawny, *Heidegger und der Mythos der jüdischen Wetverschwörung* (Frankfurt: Klostermann, 2015), 53. Acccording to

Trawny, Fritz Heidegger struck this passage out from an early version of the manuscript.

8 Heidegger, *GA*, 97:19.

9 Ibid., 20.

10 Markus Gabriel, 'Heideggers widerwärtige Thesen über den Holocaust', *Die Welt*, 28 March 2015, http://www.welt.de/kultur/literarischewelt/article138868550/Heideggers-widerwaertige-Thesen-ueber-den-Holocaust.html.

11 Sandra Mass, 'The "Volkskörper" in Fear: Gender, Race and Sexuality in the Weimar Republic', in *New Dangerous Liasions: Discourses on Europe and Love in the Twentieth Century*, ed. Luisa Passerini, Liliana Ellena and Alexander Geppert (Oxford: Berghahn Books, 2010), 233–50.

12 Quoted from http://www.literaturkritik.de/public/rezension.php?rez_id=8062&ausgabe=200505.

13 Incidentally, there is a similar weird turn in David Fincher's outstanding thriller *Seven* in which John Doe, a religiously obsessed serial murderer, executes the plan of killing seven people, each of whom is punished for one of the deadly sins. At the film's end John Doe himself is shot by detective Mills who, out of anger, kills him because Doe killed his pregnant wife; Doe's sin is envy (he envied Mills for his ordinary happy family life), and Mills's sin is anger – but why then did Doe decapitate Mills's wife? Her death clearly doesn't fit the series: she committed no sin, she is killed just to awaken uncontrollable anger in Mills. We have here a temporal reversal: Mills is punished for something (anger) that explodes after he is punished for it, and is even triggered by this punishment. So it is as if the woman's death doesn't count for itself, she can be killed just to punish her man.

14 One should mention also Verdi's *Don Carlo*, his absolute masterpiece where he comes very close to a Wagnerian musical drama, with almost no traditional arias – except the famous duo on friendship.

15 We can also clearly see the difference between Philip's search for a friend and Prince Hal's friendship with Falstaff in Shakespeare: Prince Hal engages in this friendship for purely manipulative reasons and rejects Falstaff the moment he ascends the throne.

16 Mark William Roche, *Tragedy and Comedy* (Albany: State University of New York Press, 1998), 125.

17 I rely here extensively on Alenka Zupančič Žerdin, 'Kostumografija moči' (manuscript in Slovene, July 2014).

18 Hegel, *Elements of the Philosophy of Right*, 323. If the king is only a formal point of decision – all the content is provided to him by his expert counsellors, and he only has to sign his name – is there nonetheless a level at which he can act arbitrarily also at the level of content and not only confer the form of an abyssal decision onto a prepared content? Would such a level not be necessarily, by definition, illegal, a space in which the king not only can but is even expected to violate the law? Frank Ruda noted that there effectively is such a level: one of the prerogatives of the king is his right to clemency, to arbitrarily pardon criminals who were condemned by the law.

19 It is well known that Dostoyevsky modelled his figure of the Grand Inquisitor in *The Brothers Karamazov* on Schiller's Inquisitor; however, one can immediately see the superiority of Schiller's figure.

20 Robert Hutchinson, *Elizabeth's Spy Master* (London: Orion Books, 2006), 168.

21 I owe this information to John Higgins of Capetown University (private conversation).

22 Jacques Derrida, 'Force of Law: The "Mystical Foundation of Authority"', in *Acts of Religion*, ed. Gil Anidjar (New York: Routledge, 2002), 255.

23 Jean-Claude Milner, 'The Prince and the Revolutionary' (unpublished manuscript). All unattributed quotations that follow in the present chapter are from this text.

24 Louis Antoine de Saint-Just, 'Rapport sur les factions de l'étranger', in *Œuvres complètes* (Paris: Gallimard, 2004), 695.

25 Quoted from http://www.bartleby.com/34/1/3.html.

26 Anna Larina Boukharina, *Boukharine ma passion*, trans. Véronique Garros and Denis Paillard (Paris: Gallimard, 1989), 319.

27 Hegel, *Phenomenology of Spirit*, 493.

28 Hegel, *Lectures on the Philosophy of Religion*, ed. Hodgson, 3:111–12.

29 G. W. F. Hegel, *Philosophy of History*, part 3, 'Philosophic History', § 36, trans. J. Sibree, available at www.marxists.org/reference/archive/hegel/works/hi/.

30 See Philippe Lacoue-Labarthe, *Heidegger, Art and Politics* (London: Blackwell, 1990).

31 Rebecca Comay, 'Hegel's Last Words', in *The End of History*, ed. A. E. Swiffen (London: Routledge, 2012), 234.

32 Alain Badiou, *Pornographie du temps présent* (Paris: Fayard, 2013), 37.

33 Zupančič Žerdin, 'Kostumografija moči'. I rely here extensively on her analysis.

34 Is then Jesus on the Cross not the ultimate castrated King/Authority, the one who exerts absolute power on behalf of his very 'castration' (humiliating death on the Cross)? But if this is the case, whose power does this display of castration sustain?

35 Personal communication from Liza Thompson (to whom I owe this reference to *Star Wars*).

Chapter 8: Is god dead, unconscious, evil, impotent, stupid … or just counterfactual?

1 See Reza Aslan, *Zealot* (New York: Random House, 2014), 138.

2 Jean-Yves Leloup, 'Judas, le révélateur', *Le Monde des Religions* (March–April 2005): 42.

3 Jean-Pierre Dupuy, *Petite metaphysique des tsunamis* (Paris: Seuil, 2005), 19.

4 Jean-Pierre Dupuy, 'Quand je mourrai, rien de notre amour n'aura jamais existé' (unpublished paper delivered at the colloquium '*Vertigo* et la philosophie', École normale supérieure, Paris, 14 October 2005).

5 Sheila O'Malley, 'Underrated Movies #16: *The Rapture* (1991)', *The Sheila Variations* (30 March 2011), http://www.sheilaomalley.com/?p=7958.

6 Ibid.

7 Ibid.

8 Ibid.

9 Marx, *Capital*, 1:163.

10 Alenka Zupančič, 'The "Concrete Universal" and What Comedy Can Tell Us About It', in *Lacan: The Silent Partners*, ed. Slavoj Žižek (London: Verso Books, 2006), 173.

11 See Jean-Pierre Dupuy, *Economy and the Future*, trans. M. B. DeBevoise (East Lansing: Michigan State University Press, 2014), 24.

12 Ibid., 110.

13 Another case of such asymmetry: in an apparently 'irrational' way, economic and financial agents, when confronted with the possibility of a catastrophic outcome, choose to ignore it: 'They eliminate it from their calculations, on the ground that it is too horrible to bear close scrutiny. But it is precisely in removing it that they give it a place; in fact, a quite considerable place' (ibid., 86). If the 50/50 alternative is either that our stocks will further grow or that a total collapse of the market will render them worthless, it may appear 'rational' to diminish their value by half – but the truly rational strategy is to retain their full price, since, in this way, we win if things turn out OK, and if they turn out bad it doesn't matter what we did.

14 Ibid., 27.

15 In my description of the film, I rely heavily on '*Predestination* (2014) Explained', *Astronomy Trek*, http://www.astronomytrek.com/predestination-2014-explained/.

16 Quoted from Étienne Klein, *Discours sur l'origine de l'univers* (Paris: Flammarion, 2010), 157.

17 *The Standard Edition of the Complete Psychological Works of Sigmund Freud*, ed. James Strachey (London: Vintage Books, 1999), 10:189–90.

18 *The Seminar of Jacques Lacan, Book X: Anxiety*, seminar 23 (19 June 1963), trans. Cormac Gallagher, quoted from http://www.valas.fr/IMG/pdf/THE-SEMINAR-OF-JACQUES-LACAN-X_l_angoisse.pdf.

19 Lacan, *Seminar X: Anxiety*, seminar 21 (5 June 1963), quoted from http://www.valas.fr/IMG/pdf/THE-SEMINAR-OF-JACQUES-LACAN-X_l_angoisse.pdf.

20 Guy Le Gaufey, *Une archéologie de la toute-puissance* (Paris: Epel, 2014), 20.

21 Jean Bodin, *Six Books of the Commonwealth*, ed. M. J. Tooley (Oxford: Blackwell, 1955), Bk. 1, Ch. 8, quoted from http://www.constitution.org/bodin/bodin_1.htm.

22 *The Seminar of Jacques Lacan, Book V: The Formations of the Unconscious*, trans. Cormac Gallagher, seminar 26 (18 June 1958), quoted from http://www.valas.fr/IMG/pdf/THE-SEMINAR-OF-JACQUES-LACAN-V_formations_de_l_in.pdf.

23 Ibid.

24 Lacan, *Écrits*, 11.

25 Le Gaufey, *Une archéologie*, 111.

26 For a more detailed account of symbolic castration, see Ch. 7 in the present book.

27 Phillips, 'Art of Nonfiction No. 7', 46.

28 Vladimir Sharov, *Before and During*, trans. Oliver Ready (Sawtry: Dedalus Books, 2014), 5.

29 Walter Benjamin, 'The Task of the Translator', in *Illuminations* (London: Collins, 1973), 69–82.

30 Zachary Mason, *The Lost Books of the Odyssey* (New York: Farrar, Straus & Giroux, 2010).

31 G. K. Chesterton, *Orthodoxy* (San Francisco: Ignatius, 1995), 139.

32 Lacan, *Seminar, Book XX: Encore*, seminar 6 (13 February 1973).

33 Ibid., seminar 5 (16 January 1973).

34 A similar case: Golda Meir allegedly said that 'after the holocaust, Jews have the right to do anything they want' – a statement which, although probably not true (unproven at least), hits the mark, describing the predominant attitude of the founders of the State of Israel.

35 For a more detailed elaboration of this point, see my *Less than Nothing*, 494.

36 Proverbs are like jokes: one cannot invent them as proverbs, something already said can only retroactively become (acquire the status of) a proverb. However, in contrast to jokes, proverbs are as a rule deprived of the true spirit, and the only way to bring some spirit into them is through a slip of the tongue or a similar misstep. When I was participating at Jacques-Alain Miller's seminar in Paris in the early 1980s, I once made a comment in which I referred to a Slovene proverb used to warn us against too risky and daring acts – 'one cannot piss against the wind'. However, owing to my confusion, I used the wrong verb – instead of saying 'on ne peut pas pisser contre le vent' I said 'on ne peut pas chier contre le vent' ('one cannot shit against the wind'). (This mistake may be explained by the vocal similarity between the French word *chier* and the Slovene vulgar word for 'I piss' [*ščijem*].) Miller only threw me a cold glance and remarked: 'The wind must be really strong in Slovenia.'

37 Rowan Williams, *Dostoyevsky: Language, Faith and Fiction* (London: Continuum, 2008), 6.

38 Ibid., 17–18.

39 Peter Wessel Zapffe, *Om det tragiske* (Oslo: De norske bokklubbene, 2004), 147.

40 In his manuscript 'An American Utopia', Fredric Jameson does something homologous with communism: for him, communism is not in its notion an order of ideal harmony (even if this ideal cannot ever be fully realized but is always 'to-come', it is forever postponed, never fully realized); it is, on the contrary, in its very notion antagonistic, threatened by explosions of self-destructive envy.

41 http://maxwellsdemoniac.wordpress.com/2010/10/11/encountering-the-apocalypse-worshipping-our-zombie-lord-or-why-jesus-christ-is-a-piece-of-shit.

42 Sayyid Qutb, *Milestones*, Ch. 7, quoted from http://unisetca.ipower.com/qutb/.

43 Aristotle, *Metaphysics* XII.10, trans. W. D. Ross.

44 Exactly the same logic is at work in Hayek's advocacy of the market: 'Hayek argues that evil arises from the tyranny of personal dependence, the submission of one person to another's arbitrary will. This state of subordination can be escaped only if every member of society willingly subjects himself to an abstract, impersonal, and universal rule that absolutely transcends him' (Dupuy, *Economy and the Future*, 10). Qutb's god thus occupies exactly the same place as Hayek's market, both guaranteeing personal freedom.

45 Søren Kierkegaard, *The Concept of Anxiety*, ed. and trans. R. Thomte and A. B. Anderson (Princeton: Princeton University Press, 1980), 151.

46 The first complication here concerns the very status of belief: insofar as god is the ultimate big Other, the difficult problem of a subject who 'really believes' is clearly grounded in the ambiguous virtual status of the big Other. Every figure of the big Other is in itself a compromise grounded in the avoidance of both terms of the alternative which confronts us – or, to quote Arthur C. Clarke: 'Either we are alone in the universe [with no other intelligent beings out there], or we are not alone. Both possibilities are equally terrifying.' The big Other is thus something in-between, enabling us to both have our cake and eat it too: there is no real Other out there, but there is nonetheless the fiction of the big Other which enables us to avoid the horror of being alone.

47 See Ch. 1 of Jean-Claude Milner, *L'universel en éclats* (Paris: Verdier, 2014).

48 Lacan, *Écrits*, 340–2.

49 Ibid., 341.

50 I leave aside here the relation between this couple truth/exactitude and Badiou's couple truth/knowledge.

51 Phillips, 'Art of Nonfiction No. 7', 43.

52 *Søren Kierkegaard's Journals and Papers*, ed. H. V. Hong and E. H. Hong (Bloomington: Indiana University Press, 1970), entry 1405.

53 Bertolt Brecht, *Prosa 3* (Frankfurt: Suhrkamp, 1995), 18.

54 Chesterton, *Orthodoxy*, 145.

55 Sam Harris, *The End of Faith* (New York: Norton, 2005), 221.

56 Ibid., 253.

57 Markus Gabriel, *Warum es die Welt nicht gibt* (Munich: Ullstein, 2015), 203.

58 Ibid., 208–9.

59 Ibid., 211.

60 Ibid.

61 See Thomas Metzinger, *Being No One: The Self-Model Theory of Subjectivity* (Cambridge, MA: MIT Press, 2003).

62 Chesterton, *Quotes*, 1.

Chapter 9: Ject or scend? From the traumatized subject to subject as trauma

1 Aaron Schuster, *The Trouble with Pleasure: Deleuze and Psychoanalysis* (Cambridge, MA: MIT Press, 2016). All unattributed quotations in the present chapter are from this work.

2 Friedrich Engels, 'The Part Played by Labour in the Transition from Ape to Man', trans. Clemens Dutt, quoted from http://www.marxists.org/archive/marx/works/1876/part-played-labour/.

3 Gilles Deleuze, *L'image-mouvement* (Paris: Minuit, 1983), 122.

4 Ibid., 81.

5 Immanuel Kant, *Critique of Practical Reason*, in *Practical Philosophy*, ed. and trans. Mary J. Gregor (Cambridge: Cambridge University Press, 1996), 163 (Ak. 5:30).

6   See Butler, *The Psychic Life of Power*, 28–9.

7   Catherine Malabou, *Les nouveaux blessés* (Paris: Bayard, 2007), 273.

8   Ibid., 322–4.

9   Ibid., 326.

10   Ibid., 342.

11   I summarize here a critique of Malabou developed in greater detail in Ch. 4 of my *Living in the End Times* (London: Verso Books, 2011) .

12   Alain Badiou, 'Badiou: Down with Death!', Verso Books blog (18 August 2015), http://www.versobooks.com/blogs/2176-badiou-down-with-death.

13   *Hegel's Science of Logic*, 824.

14   Jacques Lacan, *Le séminaire, livre XIX: … ou pire* (Paris: Seuil, 2011), 43.

15   Ibid., 54.

16   Brandom, 'A Spirit of Trust', quoted from http://www.pitt.edu/~brandom/spirit_of_trust_2014.html.

17   Ibid.

18   It is interesting to note here that Peter Sloterdijk accuses Lacan of shifting the focus of psychoanalysis from desire for objects to intersubjective recognition.

19   Lacan, *Seminar V: Formations of the Unconscious*, seminar 26 (18 June 1958), http://www.valas.fr/IMG/pdf/THE-SEMINAR-OF-JACQUES-LACAN-V_formations_de_l_in.pdf.

20   Ibid.

21   Herman Melville, *Moby Dick, or The White Whale* (New York: New American Library, 1961), 396–7.

22   See Gilles Deleuze, *The Logic of Sense*, trans. Mark Lester (New York: Columbia University Press, 1990), 119–20.

23   Alenka Zupančič, 'Ladies and Gentlemen: A Fragment on Sexual Difference' (manuscript in Slovene).

24   Ibid. And the same holds for class struggle: 'there is no class relationship'; if there were two clearly differentiated classes, then there would be no classes, no class struggle/antagonism.

25   Lorenzo Chiesa, *The Not-Two: Logic and God in Lacan* (Cambridge, MA:

MIT Press, 2016). All unattributed quotations in the present chapter are from this work.

26 Lacan, *Écrits*, 269.

27 Lacan, *Seminar XX: Encore*, seminar 7 (20 February 1973).

28 Ibid.

29 Aaron Schuster, 'The Third Kind of Complaint' (unpublished manuscript).

30 For a more detailed account of this key point, see Ch. 3 of my *Absolute Recoil* (London: Verso Books, 2014).

31 From the Lacanian standpoint, god doesn't have only two faces, it has three faces which, of course, fit the triad of SRI: the symbolic God of philosophers (the rational matrix of all reality, the divine *logos*), the real God (inconsistent, evil and vengeful, brutally violent and stupid, like the god of Job or the Cartesian *malin génie* cheating us all), the imaginary God as the substance of divine *jouissance*, of a bliss without constraints.

32 Quotation within the quotation is from Jacques Lacan, Seminar XV (unpublished), lesson of 19 June 1968.

33 Walter Benjamin, *The Arcades Project*, trans. H. Eiland and K. McLaughlin (Cambridge, MA: Belknap Press of Harvard University Press, 1999), 482.

34 I have developed all this in much greater detail in my *Less than Nothing* and *Absolute Recoil*.

35 We are dealing here with the basic Hegelian dialectics of the universal and its exception: rabble as the exception, the class which is no-class, the class with no proper place within the social edifice, is the direct embodiment of the universality of man.

36 One should also render problematic Chiesa's selective reliance on the readings of Lacan's formulas of sexuation: what cannot but strike the eye is his neglect of the work of Alenka Zupančič and, above all, his total ignorance of Joan Copjec's groundbreaking 'Sex and the Euthanasia of Reason', in *Supposing the Subject*, ed. J. Copjec (London: Verso Books, 1994), 16–44, a text which, by way of linking Lacan's formulas of sexuation to Kant's distinction between dynamic and mathematical sublime, provides the very foundations of the transcendental status of Lacan's formulas of sexuation.

37 Kotsko, *Creepiness* (quoted from manuscript).

38 Which I have already used many times.

Conclusion: The courage of hopelessness

1   Quoted from http://www.delo.si/kultura/glasba/laibach-v-severni-koreji-ena-sama-fascinantna-lepota-ljudi.html.

2   And, incidentally, if Novak 'did not encounter a single ugly person', where are then such persons? Obviously in gulags and in poverty-stricken villages outside the secluded Pyongyang.

3   For a more detailed reading of David's painting, see Ch. 7 of my *Less than Nothing*.

4   Hegel, *Phenomenology of Spirit*, 360.

5   Ibid., 332.

6   Ibid., 358.

7   I rely here on a line of thought developed by Alenka Zupančič. In Fritz Lang's *Metropolis* we find the opposition between the good woman of Heart (the mediator between Labour and Capital, the guarantee of the organic stability of social relations) and the bad woman who is sexually promiscuous and who incites social upheaval (we learn that she is a cyborg, a puppet-machine invented and controlled by a bad/mad scientist).

8   I obtained this passage from Sami Khatib (Berlin), who is preparing the English translation of Kraft's diaries.

9   Walter Benjamin, 'Critique of Violence', in *Reflections*, ed. Peter Demetz (New York: Schocken Books, 1986), 294.

10 Ibid., 300.

11 See Le Gaufey, *Une archéologie*.

12 Alain Badiou, *À la recherche du réel perdu* (Paris: Fayard, 2015), 58.

13 In his famous Preface to the *Contribution to the Critique of Political Economy*, Marx wrote (in his worst evolutionary mode) that humanity only poses to itself tasks which it is able to solve; one is tempted to turn this statement around and claim that humanity as a rule poses to itself tasks which it cannot solve, and thereby triggers an unpredictable process in the course of which the task (goal) itself gets redefined.

14 Allen Wood, 'Karl Marx on Equality' (working paper), quoted from http://philosophy.as.nyu.edu/docs/IO/19808/Allen-Wood-Marx-on-Equality.pdf.

15 Karl Marx and Friedrich Engels, *Collected Works* (London: Lawrence and Wishart, 1978), 24:73.

16 Ibid., 86.

17 See Fredric Jameson, 'An American Utopia', in *An American Utopia: Dual Power and the Universal Army*, ed. Slavoj Žižek (London: Verso Books, 2016).

18 See Lacan, *Écrits*, 689–98.

19 Badiou, *À la recherche du réel perdu*, 55.

20 See Jameson, 'An American Utopia'.

21 Étienne Balibar, *Sur la dictature du prolétariat* (Paris: Maspero, 1976), 148.

22 Ibid., 147.

23 Ruth Klüger, *Still Alive: A Holocaust Girlhood Remembered* (New York: The Feminist Press 2003), 189.

INDEX